CIMA

Paper C03

Fundamentals of Business Mathematics

Study Text

CIMA Certificate in Business Accounting

Published by: Kaplan Publishing UK

Unit 2 The Business Centre, Molly Millars Lane, Wokingham, Berkshire RG41 2QZ

Acknowledgements

The CIMA Publishing trade mark is reproduced with kind permission of CIMA.

Notice

The text in this material and any others made available by any Kaplan Group company does not amount to advice on a particular matter and should not be taken as such. No reliance should be placed on the content as the basis for any investment or other decision or in connection with any advice given to third parties. Please consult your appropriate professional adviser as necessary. Kaplan Publishing Limited and all other Kaplan group companies expressly disclaim all liability to any person in respect of any losses or other claims, whether direct, indirect, incidental, consequential or otherwise arising in relation to the use of such materials.

British Library Cataloguing in Publication Data
A catalogue record for this book is available from the British Library

ISBN: 978-1-78415-110-2

Printed and bound in Great Britain

Contents

		Page
Chapter 1	Basic Mathematics	1
Chapter 2	Summarising and analysing data – I	49
Chapter 3	Summarising and analysing data – II	97
Chapter 4	Index Numbers	141
Chapter 5	Inter-relationships between variables	183
Chapter 6	Forecasting	231
Chapter 7	Financial Mathematics	279
Chapter 8	Probability	351
Chapter 9	Spreadsheet Skills using Excel	427
Chapter 10	Preparing for the Assessment	459
Chapter 11	Mock Assessment 1	533
Chapter 12	Mock Assessment 2	563

chapter
Intro

Paper Introduction

How to Use the Materials

These Official CIMA learning materials brought to you by CIMA Publishing and Kaplan Publishing have been carefully designed to make your learning experience as easy as possible and to give you the best chances of success in your *Fundamentals of Business Mathematics* computer based assessments.

The product range contains a number of features to help you in the study process. They include:

- a detailed explanation of all syllabus areas
- extensive 'practical' materials
- generous question practice, together with full solutions
- a computer based assessments preparation section, complete with computer based assessments standard questions and solutions.

This Study Text has been designed with the needs of home-study and distance-learning candidates in mind. Such students require very full coverage of the syllabus topics, and also the facility to undertake extensive question practice. However, the Study Text is also ideal for fully taught courses.

This main body of the text is divided into a number of chapters, each of which is organised on the following pattern:

- *Detailed learning outcomes* expected after your studies of the chapter are complete. You should assimilate these before beginning detailed work on the chapter, so that you can appreciate where your studies are leading.
- *Step-by-step topic coverage*. This is the heart of each chapter, containing detailed explanatory text supported where appropriate by worked examples and exercises. You should work carefully through this section, ensuring that you understand the material being explained and can tackle the examples and exercises successfully. Remember that in many cases knowledge is cumulative: if you fail to digest earlier material thoroughly, you may struggle to understand later chapters.
- *Activities*. Some chapters are illustrated by more practical elements, such as comments and questions designed to stimulate discussion.

- *Question practice*. The test of how well you have learned the material is your ability to tackle exam-standard questions. Make a serious attempt at producing your own answers, but at this stage do not be too concerned about attempting the questions in computer based assessments conditions. In particular, it is more important to absorb the material thoroughly by completing a full solution than to observe the time limits that would apply in the actual computer based assessments.
- *Solutions*. Avoid the temptation merely to 'audit' the solutions provided. It is an illusion to think that this provides the same benefits as you would gain from a serious attempt of your own. However, if you are struggling to get started on a question you should read the introductory guidance provided at the beginning of the solution, where provided, and then make your own attempt before referring back to the full solution.

Having worked through the chapters you are ready to begin your final preparations for the computer based assessments. The final section of the Study Text provides you with the guidance you need. It includes the following features:

- A brief guide to revision technique.
- A note on the format of the computer based assessments. You should know what to expect when you tackle the real computer based assessments, and in particular the number of questions to attempt.
- Guidance on how to tackle the computer based assessments itself.
- A table mapping revision questions to the syllabus learning outcomes allowing you to quickly identify questions by subject area.
- Revision questions. These are of computer based assessments standard and should be tackled in computer based assessments conditions, especially as regards the time allocation.
- Solutions to the revision questions.
- Two mock computer based assessments.

You should plan to attempt the mock tests just before the date of the real computer based assessments. By this stage your revision should be complete and you should be able to attempt the mock computer based assessments within the time constraints of the real computer based assessments.

If you work conscientiously through the official CIMA Study Text according to the guidelines above you will be giving yourself an excellent chance of success in your computer based assessments. Good luck with your studies!

Quality and accuracy are of the utmost importance to us so if you spot an error in any of our products, please send an email to mykaplanreporting@kaplan.com with full details.

Our Quality Coordinator will work with our technical team to verify the error and take action to ensure it is corrected in future editions.

Icon Explanations

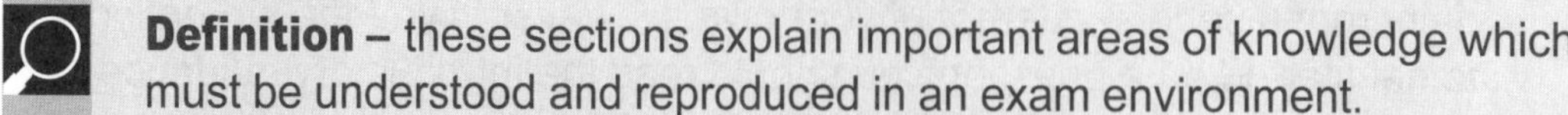

Definition – these sections explain important areas of knowledge which must be understood and reproduced in an exam environment.

Key Point – identifies topics which are key to success and are often examined.

Supplementary reading – indentifies a more detailed explanation of key terms, these sections will help to provide a deeper understanding of core areas. Reference to this text is vital when self studying.

Test Your Understanding – following key points and definitions are exercises which give the opportunity to assess the understanding of these core areas.

Illustration – to help develop an understanding of particular topics. The illustrative exercises are useful in preparing for the Test your understanding exercises.

Exclamation Mark – this symbol signifies a topic which can be more difficult to understand, when reviewing these areas care should be taken.

Study technique

Passing exams is partly a matter of intellectual ability, but however accomplished you are in that respect you can improve your chances significantly by the use of appropriate study and revision techniques. In this section we briefly outline some tips for effective study during the earlier stages of your approach to the computer based assessments. Later in the text we mention some techniques that you will find useful at the revision stage.

Planning

To begin with, formal planning is essential to get the best return from the time you spend studying. Estimate how much time in total you are going to need for each subject you are studying for the Certificate in Business Accounting. Remember that you need to allow time for revision as well as for initial study of the material. You may find it helpful to read "Pass First Time!" second edition by David R. Harris ISBN 978-1-85617-798-6. This book will provide you with proven study techniques. Chapter by chapter it covers the building blocks of successful learning and examination techniques. This is the ultimate guide to passing your CIMA exams, written by a past CIMA examiner and shows you how to earn all the marks you deserve, and explains how to avoid the most common pitfalls. You may also find "The E Word: Kaplan's Guide to Passing Exams" by Stuart Pedley-Smith ISBN: 978-0-85732-205-0 helpful. Stuart Pedley-Smith is a senior lecturer at Kaplan Financial and a qualified accountant specialising in financial management. His natural curiosity and wider interests have led him to look beyond the technical content of financial management to the processes and journey that we call education. He has become fascinated by the whole process of learning and the exam skills and techniques that contribute towards success in the classroom. This book is for anyone who has to sit an exam and wants to give themselves a better chance of passing. It is easy to read, written in a common sense style and full of anecdotes, facts, and practical tips. It also contains synopses of interviews with people involved in the learning and examining process.

With your study material before you, decide which chapters you are going to study in each week, and which weeks you will devote to revision and final question practice.

Prepare a written schedule summarising the above and stick to it!

It is essential to know your syllabus. As your studies progress you will become more familiar with how long it takes to cover topics in sufficient depth. Your timetable may need to be adapted to allocate enough time for the whole syllabus.

Students are advised to refer to the notice of examinable legislation published regularly in CIMA's magazine (Financial Management), the students e-newsletter (Velocity) and on the CIMA website, to ensure they are up-to-date.

The amount of space allocated to a topic in the Study Text is not a very good guide as to how long it will take you. For example, the material relating to Section A 'Basic Mathematics' and Section C 'Summarising and Analysing Data' each account for 15% of the syllabus, but the latter has more pages because there are more illustrations, which take up more space. The syllabus weighting is the better guide as to how long you should spend on a syllabus topic.

Tips for effective studying

(1) Aim to find a quiet and undisturbed location for your study, and plan as far as possible to use the same period of time each day. Getting into a routine helps to avoid wasting time. Make sure that you have all the materials you need before you begin so as to minimise interruptions.

(2) Store all your materials in one place, so that you do not waste time searching for items around your accommodation. If you have to pack everything away after each study period, keep them in a box, or even a suitcase, which will not be disturbed until the next time.

(3) Limit distractions. To make the most effective use of your study periods you should be able to apply total concentration, so turn off all entertainment equipment, set your phones to message mode, and put up your 'do not disturb' sign.

(4) Your timetable will tell you which topic to study. However, before diving in and becoming engrossed in the finer points, make sure you have an overall picture of all the areas that need to be covered by the end of that session. After an hour, allow yourself a short break and move away from your Study Text. With experience, you will learn to assess the pace you need to work at.

(5) Work carefully through a chapter, making notes as you go. When you have covered a suitable amount of material, vary the pattern by attempting a practice question. When you have finished your attempt, make notes of any mistakes you made, or any areas that you failed to cover or covered more briefly.

(6) Make notes as you study, and discover the techniques that work best for you. Your notes may be in the form of lists, bullet points, diagrams, summaries, 'mind maps', or the written word, but remember that you will need to refer back to them at a later date, so they must be intelligible. If you are on a taught course, make sure you highlight any issues you would like to follow up with your lecturer.

(7) Organise your notes. Make sure that all your notes, calculations etc can be effectively filed and easily retrieved later.

Computer based assessment (CBA)

CIMA uses objective test questions in the computer based assessment. The most common types are:

- Multiple choice, where you have to choose the correct answer from a list of four possible answers. This could either be numbers or text.
- Multiple choice with more choices and answers, for example, choosing two correct answers from a list of eight possible answers. This could either be numbers or text.
- Single numeric entry, where you give your numeric answer, for example, profit is $10,000.
- True/false questions, where you state whether a statement is true or false.
- Matching pairs of text, for example, matching a technical term with the correct definition.
- Other types could be matching text with graphs and labelling graphs/diagrams.

All questions are now worth 2 marks, and there are no multi-part questions, i.e. questions which have sub-questions using the same stem.

It is also recommended that you look at the Certificate exam information webpage on the CIMA website www.cimaglobal.com/Students/Certificate-exams/ with particular emphasis on the guidance notes given.

For any papers that have a formulae sheet, this is now provided within the assessment as a 'drop down.' rather than a separate paper copy being provided.

Additional CBA resources, including sample assessment questions are available online at www.cimaglobal.com/cba2011

Guidance re CIMA online calculator

As part of the CIMA Certificate level computer based assessment software, candidates are now provided with a calculator. This calculator is on-screen and is available for the duration of the assessment. The calculator is available in each of the five Certificate level assessments and is accessed by clicking the calculator button in the top left hand corner of the screen at any time during the assessment.

All candidates must complete a 15 minute tutorial before the assessment begins and will have the opportunity to familiarise themselves with the calculator and practice using it.

Candidates may practise using the calculator beforehand by either of two routes:

(1) From the CIMA certifcate webpage cited above, www.cimaglobal.com/Students/Certificate-exams/, students may view a guidance document pertaining to the on screen calculator, and may practice using the calculator, using a demo via the links given in the document.

(2) By downloading and installing the practice exam at http://www.vue.com/athena/ . The calculator can be accessed from the fourth sample question (of 12). Please note that the practice exam and tutorial provided by Pearson VUE at http://www.vue.com/athena/ is not specific to CIMA and includes the full range of question types the Pearson VUE software supports, some of which CIMA does not currently use.

Fundamentals of Business Mathematics Syllabus

The computer based assessments for Fundamentals of Business Mathematics are 2 hour assessments comprising 45 compulsory questions. There will be no choice and all questions should be attempted.

In every chapter of this StudyText we have exam style questions, but obviously we have had to label answers A, B, C etc rather than using click boxes. For learning purposes we have also included other styles of questions such as ones where an initial scenario leads to a number of sub-questions.

Structure of subjects and learning outcomes

Each subject within the syllabus is divided into a number of broad syllabus topics. The topics contain one or more lead learning outcomes, related component learning outcomes and indicative knowledge content.

A learning outcome has two main purposes:

(a) To define the skill or ability that a well prepared candidate should be able to exhibit in the examination

(b) To demonstrate the approach likely to be taken in examination questions

The learning outcomes are part of a hierarchy of learning objectives. The verbs used at the beginning of each learning outcome relate to a specific learning objective e.g.

Calculate the break-even point, profit target, margin of safety and profit/volume ratio for a single product or service

The verb **'calculate'** indicates a level three learning objective. The following table lists the learning objectives and the verbs that appear in the syllabus learning outcomes and examination questions.

Certificate level verbs

CIMA VERB HIERARCHY

CIMA place great importance on the choice of verbs in exam question requirements. It is thus critical that you answer the question according to the definition of the verb used.

In Certificate level exams you will meet verbs from levels 1, 2, and 3. These are as follows:

Level 1: KNOWLEDGE

What you are expected to know

VERBS USED	DEFINITION
List	Make a list of.
State	Express, fully or clearly, the details of/facts of.
Define	Give the exact meaning of.

Level 2: COMPREHENSION

What you are expected to understand

VERBS USED	DEFINITION
Describe	Communicate the key features of.
Distinguish	Highlight the differences between.
Explain	Make clear or intelligible/state the meaning or purpose of.
Identify	Recognise, establish or select after consideration.
Illustrate	Use an example to describe or explain something.

Level 3: APPLICATION

How you are expected to apply your knowledge

VERBS USED	DEFINITION
Apply	Put to practical use.
Calculate	Ascertain or reckon mathematically.
Demonstrate	Prove with certainty or exhibit by practical means.
Prepare	Make or get ready for use.
Reconcile	Make or prove consistent/compatible.
Solve	Find an answer to.
Tabulate	Arrange in a table.

PAPER C03
FUNDAMENTALS OF BUSINESS MATHEMATICS

Syllabus overview

This paper primarily deals with the tools and techniques to understand the mathematics associated with managing business operations. Probability and risk play an important role in developing business strategy. Preparing forecasts and establishing the relationships between variables are an integral part of budgeting and planning.

Financial mathematics provides an introduction to interest rates and annuities and to investment appraisal for projects. Preparing graphs and tables in summarised formats and using spreadsheets are important in both the calculation of data and the presentation of information to users.

Syllabus structure

The syllabus comprises the following topics and study weightings:

A	Basic mathematics	15%
B	Probability	15%
C	Summarising and analysing data	15%
D	Relationships between variables	15%
E	Forecasting	15%
F	Financial mathematics	15%
G	Spreadsheets	10%

Assessment strategy

There will be a two hour computer based assessment, comprising 45 compulsory questions, each with one or more parts.

A variety of objective test question styles and types will be used within the assessment.

C03 – A. BASIC MATHEMATICS (15%)

Learning outcomes **On completion of their studies students should be able to:**			**Indicative syllabus content**
Lead	**Component**	**Level**	
1. demonstrate the use of basic mathematics.	(a) calculate answers using formulae; (b) calculate percentages and proportions; (c) calculate answers to appropriate decimal places or significant figures.	3 3 3	• Use of formulae, including negative powers as in the formula for the learning curve. [1] • Order of operations in formulae, including brackets, powers and roots. [1] • Percentages and ratios. [1] • Rounding of numbers. [1]
2. solve equations and inequalities.	(a) solve simple equations, including two variable simultaneous equations and quadratic equations; (b) prepare graphs of linear and quadratic equations; (c) solve simple inequalities.	3 3 3	• Basic algebraic techniques and solution of equations, including simultaneous equations and quadratic equations. [1] • Graphs of linear and quadratic equations. • Manipulation of inequalities. [1]

C03 – B. PROBABILITY (15%)

Learning outcomes **On completion of their studies students should be able to:**			**Indicative syllabus content**
Lead	**Component**	**Level**	
1. calculate probability.	(a) calculate simple probability; (b) demonstrate the addition and multiplication rules of probability; (c) calculate a simple conditional probability.	3 3 3	• Probability and its relationship with proportion and percent. [8] • Addition and multiplication rules of probability theory. [8] • Venn diagrams. [8]
2. demonstrate the use of probability where risk and uncertainty exists.	(a) calculate an expected value; (b) demonstrate the use of expected value tables in decision making; (c) explain the limitations of expected values; (d) explain the concepts of risk and uncertainty.	3 3 2 2	• Expected values and expected value tables. [8] • Risk and uncertainty. [8]

C03 – C. SUMMARISING AND ANALYSING DATA (15%)

Learning outcomes On completion of their studies students should be able to:			Indicative syllabus content
Lead	**Component**	**Level**	
1. apply techniques for summarising data.	(a) explain the difference between data and information; [2] (b) identify the characteristics of good information; [2] (c) tabulate data; [2] (d) prepare graphs, charts and diagrams; [2] (e) calculate for both ungrouped and grouped data: arithmetic mean, median, mode, range, variance, standard deviation and coefficient of variation; [3] (f) explain the concept of frequency distribution; [2] (g) prepare graphs/diagrams of normal distribution; [3] (h) explain the properties of normal distribution; [8] (i) demonstrate the use of normal distribution tables. [8]	2 2 3 3 3 2 3 2 3	• Data and information. [2] • Tabulation of data. [2] • Graphs, charts and diagrams: scatter diagrams, histograms, bar charts and ogives. [2] • Summary measures of central tendency and dispersion for both grouped and ungrouped data. [3] • Frequency distributions. [3] • Normal distribution. [8]
2. apply techniques for analysing data.	(a) apply the Pareto distribution and the '80:20' rule; [3] (b) explain how and why indices are used; [4] (c) calculate indices using either base or current weights; [4] (d) apply indices to deflate a series. [4]	3 2 3 3	• Pareto distribution and the '80:20 rule'. [3] • Index numbers. [4]

C03 – D. RELATIONSHIPS BETWEEN VARIABLES (15%)

Learning outcomes On completion of their studies students should be able to:			Indicative syllabus content
Lead	**Component**	**Level**	
1. calculate correlation coefficient for bivariate data.	(a) prepare a scatter diagram; (b) calculate the correlation coefficient and the coefficient of determination between two variables.	3 3	• Scatter diagrams. [5] • Correlation coefficient: Spearman's rank correlation coefficient and Pearson's correlation coefficient. [5]
2. apply techniques of simple regression.	(e) calculate the regression equation between two variables; (f) apply the regression equation to predict the dependent variable, given a value of the independent variable.	3 3	• Simple linear regression. [5]

C03 – E. FORECASTING (15%)

Learning outcomes **On completion of their studies students should be able to:**			**Indicative syllabus content**
Lead	**Component**	**Level**	
1. demonstrate techniques used for forecasting.	(a) prepare a time series graph; (b) identify trends and patterns using an appropriate moving average; (c) identify the components of a time series model; (d) prepare a trend equation using either graphical means or regression analysis.	3 2 2 3	• Time series analysis – graphical analysis. [6] • Trends in time series – graphs, moving averages and linear regressions. [6]
2. prepare forecasts.	(a) calculate seasonal factors for both additive and multiplicative models; (b) explain when each of the additive or multiplicative models is appropriate; (c) calculate predicted values given a time series model; (d) identify the limitations of forecasting models.	3 2 3 2	• Seasonal variations using both additive and multiplicative models. [6] • Forecasting and its limitations. [6]

C03 – F. FINANCIAL MATHEMATICS (15%)

Learning outcomes **On completion of their studies students should be able to:**			**Indicative syllabus content**
Lead	**Component**	**Level**	
1. calculate present and future values of cash flows.	(a) calculate future values of an investment using both simple and compound interest; (b) calculate an annual percentage rate of interest given a monthly or quarterly rate; (c) calculate the present value of a future cash sum; (d) calculate the present value of an annuity and a perpetuity.	3 3 3 3	• Simple and compound interest. [7] • Present value (including using formulae and CIMA tables). [7] • Annuities and perpetuities. [7]
2. apply financial mathematical techniques.	(a) calculate loan/mortgage repayments and the value of the loan/mortgage outstanding; (b) calculate the future value of regular savings and/or the regular investment needed to generate a required future sum; (c) calculate the net present value (NPV) and the internal rate of return (IRR) of a project; (d) explain whether and why a project should be accepted or rejected.	3 3 3 2	• Loans and mortgages. [7] • Sinking funds and savings funds (including using formulae for the sum of a geometric progression). [7] • Discounting to find net present value (NPV) and internal rate of return (IRR). [7] • The concept of shareholder value. [7] • Interpretation of NPV and IRR. [7]

C03 – G. SPREADSHEETS (10%)

Learning outcomes **On completion of their studies students should be able to:**			**Indicative syllabus content**
Lead	**Component**	**Level**	
1. apply spreadsheets to calculate and present data.	(a) explain the features and functions of spreadsheet software;	2	• Features and functions of commonly used spreadsheet software: workbook, worksheet, rows, columns, cells, data, text, formulae, formatting, printing, graphics and macros. [9] • ***Note:*** knowledge of Microsoft Excel type spreadsheet vocabulary/formulae syntax is required. Formulae tested will be that which is constructed by users rather than pre-programmed formulae. [9] • Advantages and disadvantages of spreadsheet software, when compared to manual analysis and other types of software application packages. [9] • Use of spreadsheet software in the day-to-day work of the Chartered Management Accountant: budgeting, forecasting, reporting performance, variance analysis, what-if analysis, discounted cash flow calculations. [9]
	(b) explain the use and limitations of spreadsheet software in business;	2	
	(c) apply spreadsheet software to the normal work of a Chartered Management Accountant.	3	

Tables and Formulae

Note: Candidates should check the cimaglobal.com website for up to date information about the tables and formulae provided in the assessment.

LOGARITHMS

	0	1	2	3	4	5	6	7	8	9	1	2	3	4	5	6	7	8	9
10	0000	0043	0086	0128	0170						4	9	13	17	21	26	30	34	38
						0212	0253	0294	0334	0374	4	8	12	16	20	24	28	32	37
11	0414	0453	0492	0531	0569						4	8	12	15	19	23	27	31	35
						0607	0645	0682	0719	0755	4	7	11	15	19	22	26	30	33
12	0792	0828	0864	0899	0934	0969					3	7	11	14	18	21	25	28	32
							1004	1038	1072	1106	3	7	10	14	17	20	24	27	31
13	1139	1173	1206	1239	1271						3	7	10	13	16	20	23	26	30
						1303	1335	1367	1399	1430	3	7	10	12	16	19	22	25	29
14	1461	1492	1523	1553							3	6	9	12	15	18	21	24	28
					1584	1614	1644	1673	1703	1732	3	6	9	12	15	17	20	23	26
15	1761	1790	1818	1847	1875	1903					3	6	9	11	14	17	20	23	26
							1931	1959	1987	2014	3	5	8	11	14	16	19	22	25
16	2041	2068	2095	2122	2148						3	5	8	11	14	16	19	22	24
						2175	2201	2227	2253	2279	3	5	8	10	13	15	18	21	23
17	2304	2330	2355	2380	2405	2430					3	5	8	10	13	15	18	20	23
							2455	2480	2504	2529	2	5	7	10	12	15	17	19	22
18	2553	2577	2601	2625	2648						2	5	7	9	12	14	16	19	21
						2672	2695	2718	2742	2765	2	5	7	9	11	14	16	18	21
19	2788	2810	2833	2856	2878						2	4	7	9	11	13	16	18	20
						2900	2923	2945	2967	2989	2	4	6	8	11	13	15	17	19
20	3010	3032	3054	3075	3096	3118	3139	3160	3181	3201	2	4	6	8	11	13	15	17	19
21	3222	3243	3263	3284	3304	3324	3345	3365	3385	3404	2	4	6	8	10	12	14	16	18
22	3424	3444	3464	3483	3502	3522	3541	3560	3579	3598	2	4	6	8	10	12	14	15	17
23	3617	3636	3655	3674	3692	3711	3729	3747	3766	3784	2	4	6	7	9	11	13	15	17
24	3802	3820	3838	3856	3874	3892	3909	3927	3945	3962	2	4	5	7	9	11	12	14	16
25	3979	3997	4014	4031	4048	4065	4082	4099	4116	4133	2	3	5	7	9	10	12	14	15
26	4150	4166	4183	4200	4216	4232	4249	4265	4281	4298	2	3	5	7	8	10	11	13	15
27	4314	4330	4346	4362	4378	4393	4409	4425	4440	4456	2	3	5	6	8	9	11	13	14
28	4472	4487	4502	4518	4533	4548	4564	4579	4594	4609	2	3	5	6	8	9	11	12	14
29	4624	4639	4654	4669	4683	4698	4713	4728	4742	4757	1	3	4	6	7	9	10	12	13
30	4771	4786	4800	4814	4829	4843	4857	4871	4886	4900	1	3	4	6	7	9	10	11	13
31	4914	4928	4942	4955	4969	4983	4997	5011	5024	5038	1	3	4	6	7	8	10	11	12
32	5051	5065	5079	5092	5105	5119	5132	5145	5159	5172	1	3	4	5	7	8	9	11	12
33	5185	5198	5211	5224	5237	5250	5263	5276	5289	5302	1	3	4	5	6	8	9	10	12
34	5315	5328	5340	5353	5366	5378	5391	5403	5416	5428	1	3	4	5	6	8	9	10	11
35	5441	5453	5465	5478	5490	5502	5514	5527	5539	5551	1	2	4	5	6	7	9	10	11
36	5563	5575	5587	5599	5611	5623	5635	5647	5658	5670	1	2	4	5	6	7	8	10	11
37	5682	5694	5705	5717	5729	5740	5752	5763	5775	5786	1	2	3	5	6	7	8	9	10
38	5798	5809	5821	5832	5843	5855	5866	5877	5888	5899	1	2	3	5	6	7	8	9	10
39	5911	5922	5933	5944	5955	5966	5977	5988	5999	6010	1	2	3	4	5	7	8	9	10
40	6021	6031	6042	6053	6064	6075	6085	6096	6107	6117	1	2	3	4	5	6	8	9	10
41	6128	6138	6149	6160	6170	6180	6191	6201	6212	6222	1	2	3	4	5	6	7	8	9
42	6232	6243	6253	6263	6274	6284	6294	6304	6314	6325	1	2	3	4	5	6	7	8	9
43	6335	6345	6355	6365	6375	6385	6395	6405	6415	6425	1	2	3	4	5	6	7	8	9
44	6435	6444	6454	6464	6474	6484	6493	6503	6513	6522	1	2	3	4	5	6	7	8	9
45	6532	6542	6551	6561	6571	6580	6590	6599	6609	6618	1	2	3	4	5	6	7	8	9
46	6628	6637	6646	6656	6665	6675	6684	6693	6702	6712	1	2	3	4	5	6	7	7	8
47	6721	6730	6739	6749	6758	6767	6776	6785	6794	6803	1	2	3	4	5	5	6	7	8
48	6812	6821	6830	6839	6848	6857	6866	6875	6884	6893	1	2	3	4	4	5	6	7	8
49	6902	6911	6920	6928	6937	6946	6955	6964	6972	6981	1	2	3	4	4	5	6	7	8

LOGARITHMS

	0	1	2	3	4	5	6	7	8	9	1	2	3	4	5	6	7	8	9
50	6990	6998	7007	7016	7024	7033	7042	7050	7059	7067	1	2	3	3	4	5	6	7	8
51	7076	7084	7093	7101	7110	7118	7126	7135	7143	7152	1	2	3	3	4	5	6	7	8
52	7160	7168	7177	7185	7193	7202	7210	7218	7226	7235	1	2	2	3	4	5	6	7	7
53	7243	7251	7259	7267	7275	7284	7292	7300	7308	7316	1	2	2	3	4	5	6	6	7
54	7324	7332	7340	7348	7356	7364	7372	7380	7388	7396	1	2	2	3	4	5	6	6	7
55	7404	7412	7419	7427	7435	7443	7451	7459	7466	7474	1	2	2	3	4	5	5	6	7
56	7482	7490	7497	7505	7513	7520	7528	7536	7543	7551	1	2	2	3	4	5	5	6	7
57	7559	7566	7574	7582	7589	7597	7604	7612	7619	7627	1	2	2	3	4	5	5	6	7
58	7634	7642	7649	7657	7664	7672	7679	7686	7694	7701	1	1	2	3	4	4	5	6	7
59	7709	7716	7723	7731	7738	7745	7752	7760	7767	7774	1	1	2	3	4	4	5	6	7
60	7782	7789	7796	7803	7810	7818	7825	7832	7839	7846	1	1	2	3	4	4	5	6	6
61	7853	7860	7868	7875	7882	7889	7896	7903	7910	7917	1	1	2	3	4	4	5	6	6
62	7924	7931	7938	7945	7952	7959	7966	7973	7980	7987	1	1	2	3	3	4	5	6	6
63	7993	8000	8007	8014	8021	8028	8035	8041	8048	8055	1	1	2	3	3	4	5	5	6
64	8062	8069	8075	8082	8089	8096	8102	8109	8116	8122	1	1	2	3	3	4	5	5	6
65	8129	8136	8142	8149	8156	8162	8169	8176	8182	8189	1	1	2	3	3	4	5	5	6
66	8195	8202	8209	8215	8222	8228	8235	8241	8248	8254	1	1	2	3	3	4	5	5	6
67	8261	8267	8274	8280	8287	8293	8299	8306	8312	8319	1	1	2	3	3	4	5	5	6
68	8325	8331	8338	8344	8351	8357	8363	8370	8376	8382	1	1	2	3	3	4	4	5	6
69	8388	8395	8401	8407	8414	8420	8426	8432	8439	8445	1	1	2	2	3	4	4	5	6
70	8451	8457	8463	8470	8476	8482	8488	8494	8500	8506	1	1	2	2	3	4	4	5	6
71	8513	8519	8525	8531	8537	8543	8549	8555	8561	8567	1	1	2	2	3	4	4	5	5
72	8573	8579	8585	8591	8597	8603	8609	8615	8621	8627	1	1	2	2	3	4	4	5	5
73	8633	8639	8645	8651	8657	8663	8669	8675	8681	8686	1	1	2	2	3	4	4	5	5
74	8692	8698	8704	8710	8716	8722	8727	8733	8739	8745	1	1	2	2	3	4	4	5	5
75	8751	8756	8762	8768	8774	8779	8785	8791	8797	8802	1	1	2	2	3	3	4	5	5
76	8808	8814	8820	8825	8831	8837	8842	8848	8854	8859	1	1	2	2	3	3	4	5	5
77	8865	8871	8876	8882	8887	8893	8899	8904	8910	8915	1	1	2	2	3	3	4	4	5
78	8921	8927	8932	8938	8943	8949	8954	8960	8965	8971	1	1	2	2	3	3	4	4	5
79	8976	8982	8987	8993	8998	9004	9009	9015	9020	9025	1	1	2	2	3	3	4	4	5
80	9031	9036	9042	9047	9053	9058	9063	9069	9074	9079	1	1	2	2	3	3	4	4	5
81	9085	9090	9096	9101	9106	9112	9117	9122	9128	9133	1	1	2	2	3	3	4	4	5
82	9138	9143	9149	9154	9159	9165	9170	9175	9180	9186	1	1	2	2	3	3	4	4	5
83	9191	9196	9201	9206	9212	9217	9222	9227	9232	9238	1	1	2	2	3	3	4	4	5
84	9243	9248	9253	9258	9263	9269	9274	9279	9284	9289	1	1	2	2	3	3	4	4	5
85	9294	9299	9304	9309	9315	9320	9325	9330	9335	9340	1	1	2	2	3	3	4	4	5
86	9345	9350	9355	9360	9365	9370	9375	9380	9385	9390	1	1	2	2	3	3	4	4	5
87	9395	9400	9405	9410	9415	9420	9425	9430	9435	9440	0	1	1	2	2	3	3	4	4
88	9445	9450	9455	9460	9465	9469	9474	9479	9484	9489	0	1	1	2	2	3	3	4	4
89	9494	9499	9504	9509	9513	9518	9523	9528	9533	9538	0	1	1	2	2	3	3	4	4
90	9542	9547	9552	9557	9562	9566	9571	9576	9581	9586	0	1	1	2	2	3	3	4	4
91	9590	9595	9600	9605	9609	9614	9619	9624	9628	9633	0	1	1	2	2	3	3	4	4
92	9638	9643	9647	9652	9657	9661	9666	9671	9675	9680	0	1	1	2	2	3	3	4	4
93	9685	9689	9694	9699	9703	9708	9713	9717	9722	9727	0	1	1	2	2	3	3	4	4
94	9731	9736	9741	9745	9750	9754	9759	9763	9768	9773	0	1	1	2	2	3	3	4	4
95	9777	9782	9786	9791	9795	9800	9805	9809	9814	9818	0	1	1	2	2	3	3	4	4
96	9823	0827	9832	0836	9841	9845	9850	9854	9859	9863	0	1	1	2	2	3	3	4	4
97	9868	9872	9877	9881	9886	9890	9894	9899	9903	9908	0	1	1	2	2	3	3	4	4
98	9912	9917	9921	9926	9930	9934	9939	9943	9948	9952	0	1	1	2	2	3	3	4	4
99	9956	9961	9965	9969	9974	9978	9983	9987	9991	9996	0	1	1	2	2	3	3	3	4

AREA UNDER THE NORMAL CURVE

This table gives the area under the normal curve between the mean and a point Z standard deviations above the mean. The corresponding area for deviations below the mean can be found by symmetry.

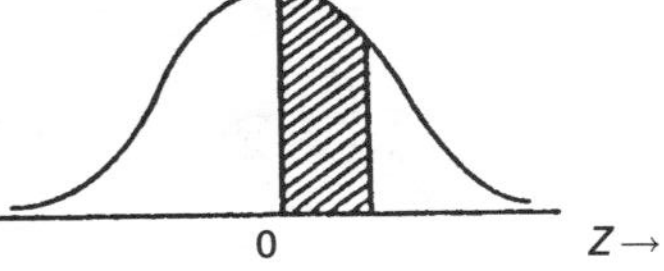

$Z = \frac{(x-\mu)}{\sigma}$	0.00	0.01	0.02	0.03	0.04	0.05	0.06	0.07	0.08	0.09
0.0	.0000	.0040	.0080	.0120	.0159	.0199	.0239	.0279	.0319	.0359
0.1	.0398	.0438	.0478	.0517	.0557	.0596	.0636	.0675	.0714	.0753
0.2	.0793	.0832	.0871	.0910	.0948	.0987	.1026	.1064	.1103	.1141
0.3	.1179	.1217	.1255	.1293	.1331	.1368	.1406	.1443	.1480	.1517
0.4	.1554	.1591	.1628	.1664	.1700	.1736	.1772	.1808	.1844	.1879
0.5	.1915	.1950	.1985	.2019	.2054	.2088	.2123	.2157	.2190	.2224
0.6	.2257	.2291	.2324	.2357	.2389	.2422	.2454	.2486	.2518	.2549
0.7	.2580	.2611	.2642	.2673	.2704	.2734	.2764	.2794	.2823	.2852
0.8	.2881	.2910	.2939	.2967	.2995	.3023	.3051	.3078	.3106	.3133
0.9	.3159	.3186	.3212	.3238	.3264	.3289	.3315	.3340	.3365	.3389
1.0	.3413	.3438	.3461	.3485	.3508	.3531	.3554	.3577	.3599	.3621
1.1	.3643	.3665	.3686	.3708	.3729	.3749	.3770	.3790	.3810	.3830
1.2	.3849	.3869	.3888	.3907	.3925	.3944	.3962	.3980	.3997	.4015
1.3	.4032	.4049	.4066	.4082	.4099	.4115	.4131	.4147	.4162	.4177
1.4	.4192	.4207	.4222	.4236	.4251	.4265	.4279	.4292	.4306	.4319
1.5	.4332	.4345	.4357	.4370	.4382	.4394	.4406	.4418	.4430	.4441
1.6	.4452	.4463	.4474	.4485	.4495	.4505	.4515	.4525	.4535	.4545
1.7	.4554	.4564	.4573	.4582	.4591	.4599	.4608	.4616	.4625	.4633
1.8	.4641	.4649	.4656	.4664	.4671	.4678	.4686	.4693	.4699	.4706
1.9	.4713	.4719	.4726	.4732	.4738	.4744	.4750	.4756	.4762	.4767
2.0	.4772	.4778	.4783	.4788	.4793	.4798	.4803	.4808	.4812	.4817
2.1	.4821	.4826	.4830	.4834	.4838	.4842	.4846	.4850	.4854	.4857
2.2	.4861	.4865	.4868	.4871	.4875	.4878	.4881	.4884	.4887	.4890
2.3	.4893	.4896	.4898	.4901	.4904	.4906	.4909	.4911	.4913	.4916
2.4	.4918	.4920	.4922	.4925	.4927	.4929	.4931	.4932	.4934	.4936
2.5	.4938	.4940	.4941	.4943	.4945	.4946	.4948	.4949	.4951	.4952
2.6	.4953	.4955	.4956	.4957	.4959	.4960	.4961	.4962	.4963	.4964
2.7	.4965	.4966	.4967	.4968	.4969	.4970	.4971	.4972	.4973	.4974
2.8	.4974	.4975	.4976	.4977	.4977	.4978	.4979	.4980	.4980	.4981
2.9	.4981	.4982	.4983	.4983	.4984	.4984	.4985	.4985	.4986	.4986
3.0	**.49865**	.4987	.4987	.4988	.4988	.4989	.4989	.4989	.4990	.4990
3.1	**.49903**	.4991	.4991	.4991	.4992	.4992	.4992	.4992	.4993	.4993
3.2	**.49931**	.4993	.4994	.4994	.4994	.4994	.4994	.4995	.4995	.4995
3.3	**.49952**	.4995	.4995	.4996	.4996	.4996	.4996	.4996	.4996	.4997
3.4	**.49966**	.4997	.4997	.4997	.4997	.4997	.4997	.4997	.4997	.4998
3.5	**.49977**									

PRESENT VALUE TABLE

Present value of £1 ie $(1+r)^{-n}$ where r = interest rate; n = number of periods until payment or receipt.

Periods (n)	Interest rates (r)																			
	1%	2%	3%	4%	5%	6%	7%	8%	9%	10%	11%	12%	13%	14%	15%	16%	17%	18%	19%	20%
1	.990	.980	.971	.962	.952	.943	.935	.926	.917	.909	.901	.893	.885	.877	.870	.862	.855	.847	.840	.833
2	.980	.961	.943	.925	.907	.890	.873	.857	.842	.826	.812	.797	.783	.769	.756	.743	.731	.718	.706	.694
3	.971	.942	.915	.889	.864	.840	.816	.794	.772	.751	.731	.712	.693	.675	.658	.641	.624	.609	.593	.579
4	.961	.924	.888	.855	.823	.792	.763	.735	.708	.683	.659	.636	.613	.592	.572	.552	.534	.516	.499	.482
5	.951	.906	.863	.822	.784	.747	.713	.681	.650	.621	.593	.567	.543	.519	.497	.476	.456	.437	.419	.402
6	.942	.888	.837	.790	.746	.705	.666	.630	.596	.564	.535	.507	.480	.456	.432	.410	.390	.370	.352	.335
7	.933	.871	.813	.760	.711	.665	.623	.583	.547	.513	.482	.452	.425	.400	.376	.354	.333	.314	.296	.279
8	.923	.853	.789	.731	.677	.627	.582	.540	.502	.467	.434	.404	.376	.351	.327	.305	.285	.266	.249	.233
9	.914	.837	.766	.703	.645	.592	.544	.500	.460	.424	.391	.361	.333	.308	.284	.263	.243	.225	.209	.194
10	.905	.820	.744	.676	.614	.558	.508	.463	.422	.386	.352	.322	.295	.270	.247	.227	.208	.191	.176	.162
11	.896	.804	.722	.650	.585	.527	.475	.429	.388	.350	.317	.287	.261	.237	.215	.195	.178	.162	.148	.135
12	.887	.788	.701	.625	.557	.497	.444	.397	.356	.319	.286	.257	.231	.208	.187	.168	.152	.137	.124	.112
13	.879	.773	.681	.601	.530	.469	.415	.368	.326	.290	.258	.229	.204	.182	.163	.145	.130	.116	.104	.093
14	.870	.758	.661	.577	.505	.442	.388	.340	.299	.263	.232	.205	.181	.160	.141	.125	.111	.099	.088	.078
15	.861	.743	.642	.555	.481	.417	.362	.315	.275	.239	.209	.183	.160	.140	.123	.108	.095	.084	.074	.065
16	.853	.728	.623	.534	.458	.394	.339	.292	.252	.218	.188	.163	.141	.123	.107	.093	.081	.071	.062	.054
17	.844	.714	.605	.513	.436	.371	.317	.270	.231	.198	.170	.146	.125	.108	.093	.080	.069	.060	.052	.045
18	.836	.700	.587	.494	.416	.350	.296	.250	.212	.180	.153	.130	.111	.095	.081	.069	.059	.051	.044	.038
19	.828	.686	.570	.475	.396	.331	.277	.232	.194	.164	.138	.116	.098	.083	.070	.060	.051	.043	.037	.031
20	.820	.673	.554	.456	.377	.312	.258	.215	.178	.149	.124	.104	.087	.073	.061	.051	.043	.037	.031	.026

CUMULATIVE PRESENT VALUE OF £1

This table shows the Present Value of £1 per annum, Receivable or Payable at the end of each year for n years $\frac{1-(1+r)^{-n}}{r}$.

Periods (n)	Interest rates (r)																			
	1%	2%	3%	4%	5%	6%	7%	8%	9%	10%	11%	12%	13%	14%	15%	16%	17%	18%	19%	20%
1	.990	.980	.971	.962	.952	.943	.935	.926	.917	.909	.901	.893	.885	.877	.870	.862	.855	.847	.840	.833
2	1.970	1.942	1.913	1.886	1.859	1.833	1.808	1.783	1.759	1.736	1.713	1.690	1.668	1.647	1.626	1.605	1.585	1.566	1.547	1.528
3	2.941	2.884	2.829	2.775	2.723	2.673	2.624	2.577	2.531	2.487	2.444	2.402	2.361	2.322	2.283	2.246	2.210	2.174	2.140	2.106
4	3.902	3.808	3.717	3.630	3.546	3.465	3.387	3.312	3.240	3.170	3.102	3.037	2.974	2.914	2.855	2.798	2.743	2.690	2.639	2.589
5	4.853	4.713	4.580	4.452	4.329	4.212	4.100	3.993	3.890	3.791	3.696	3.605	3.517	3.433	3.352	3.274	3.199	3.127	3.058	2.991
6	5.795	5.601	5.417	5.242	5.076	4.917	4.767	4.623	4.486	4.355	4.231	4.111	3.998	3.889	3.784	3.685	3.589	3.498	3.410	3.326
7	6.728	6.472	6.230	6.002	5.786	5.582	5.389	5.206	5.033	4.868	4.712	4.564	4.423	4.288	4.160	4.039	3.922	3.812	3.706	3.605
8	7.652	7.325	7.020	6.733	6.463	6.210	5.971	5.747	5.535	5.335	5.146	4.968	4.799	4.639	4.487	4.344	4.207	4.078	3.954	3.837
9	8.566	8.162	7.786	7.435	7.108	6.802	6.515	6.247	5.995	5.759	5.537	5.328	5.132	4.946	4.772	4.607	4.451	4.303	4.163	4.031
10	9.471	8.983	8.530	8.111	7.722	7.360	7.024	6.710	6.418	6.145	5.889	5.650	5.426	5.216	5.019	4.833	4.659	4.494	4.339	4.192
11	10.368	9.787	9.253	8.760	8.306	7.887	7.499	7.139	6.805	6.495	6.207	5.938	5.687	5.453	5.234	5.029	4.836	4.656	4.486	4.327
12	11.255	10.575	9.954	9.385	8.863	8.384	7.943	7.536	7.161	6.814	6.492	6.194	5.918	5.660	5.421	5.197	4.988	4.793	4.611	4.439
13	12.134	11.348	10.635	9.986	9.394	8.853	8.358	7.904	7.487	7.103	6.750	6.424	6.122	5.842	5.583	5.342	5.118	4.910	4.715	4.533
14	13.004	12.106	11.296	10.563	9.899	9.295	8.745	8.244	7.786	7.367	6.982	6.628	6.302	6.002	5.724	5.468	5.229	5.008	4.802	4.611
15	13.865	12.849	11.938	11.118	10.380	9.712	9.108	8.559	8.061	7.606	7.191	6.811	6.462	6.142	5.847	5.575	5.324	5.092	4.876	4.675
16	14.718	13.578	12.561	11.652	10.838	10.106	9.447	8.851	8.313	7.824	7.379	6.974	6.604	6.265	5.954	5.668	5.405	5.162	4.938	4.730
17	15.562	14.292	13.166	12.166	11.274	10.477	9.763	9.122	8.544	8.022	7.549	7.120	6.729	6.373	6.047	5.749	5.475	5.222	4.990	4.775
18	16.398	14.992	13.754	12.659	11.690	10.828	10.059	9.372	8.756	8.201	7.702	7.250	6.840	6.467	6.128	5.818	5.534	5.273	5.033	4.812
19	17.226	15.679	14.324	13.134	12.085	11.158	10.336	9.604	8.950	8.365	7.839	7.366	6.938	6.550	6.198	5.877	5.584	5.316	5.070	4.843
20	18.046	16.351	14.878	13.590	12.462	11.470	10.594	9.818	9.129	8.514	7.963	7.469	7.025	6.623	6.259	5.929	5.628	5.353	5.101	4.870

Formulae — Sheet 1

PROBABILITY

$A \cup B = A$ **or** B. $A \cap B = A$ **and** B (overlap).
$P(B \mid A)$ = probability of B, **given** A.

Rules of Addition

If A and B are *mutually exclusive*: $P(A \cup B) = P(A) + P(B)$
If A and B are **not** mutually exclusive: $P(A \cup B) = P(A) + P(B) - P(A \cap B)$

Rules of Multiplication

If A and B are *independent*: $P(A \cap B) = P(A) * P(B)$
If A and B are **not** independent: $P(A \cap B) = P(A) * P(B \mid A)$

$E(X)$ = expected value = probability * payoff

Quadratic Equations

If $aX^2 + bX + c = 0$ is the general quadratic equation, then the two solutions (roots) are given by:

$$X = \frac{-b \pm \sqrt{b^2 - 4ac}}{2a}$$

Formulae (continued) — Sheet 2

DESCRIPTIVE STATISTICS

Arithmetic Mean

$$\bar{x} = \frac{\sum x}{n} \qquad \bar{x} = \frac{\sum fx}{\sum f} \quad \text{(frequency distribution)}$$

Standard Deviation

$$SD = \sqrt{\frac{\sum (x - \bar{x})^2}{n}} \qquad SD = \sqrt{\frac{\sum fx^2}{\sum f} - \bar{x}^2} \quad \text{(frequency distribution)}$$

INDEX NUMBERS

Price relative = 100 * P_1/P_0 Quantity relative = 100 * Q_1/Q_0

Price: $\sum W * P_1/P_0 \Big/ \sum W$ * 100, where W denotes weights

Quantity: $\sum W * Q_1/Q_0 \Big/ \sum W$ * 100, where W denotes weights

TIME SERIES

Additive Model

Series = Trend + Seasonal + Random

Multiplicative Model

Series = Trend * Seasonal * Random

LINEAR REGRESSION AND CORRELATION

The linear regression equation of y on x is given by:

$$Y = a + bX \quad \text{or} \quad Y - \bar{Y} = b(X - \bar{X})$$

where

$$b = \frac{\text{Covariance}\,(XY)}{\text{Variance}\,(X)} = \frac{n\sum XY - (\sum X)(\sum Y)}{n\sum X^2 - (\sum X)^2}$$

and

$$a = \bar{Y} - b\bar{X}$$

or solve

$$\sum Y = na + b\sum X$$

$$\sum XY = a\sum X + b\sum X^2$$

Coefficient of correlation

$$r = \frac{\text{Covariance}\,(XY)}{\sqrt{\text{Var}\,(X).\,\text{Var}\,(Y)}} = \frac{n\sum XY - (\sum X)(\sum Y)}{\sqrt{(n\sum X^2 - (\sum X)^2)(n\sum Y^2 - (\sum Y)^2)}}$$

$$R(\text{rank}) = 1 - \frac{6\sum d^2}{n(n^2 - 1)}$$

FINANCIAL MATHEMATICS

Compound Interest (Values and Sums)

Future Value of S, of a sum X, invested for n periods, compounded at r% interest

$$S = X[1 + r]^n$$

Annuity

Present value of an annuity of £1 per annum receivable or payable for n years, commencing in one year, discounted at r% per annum:

$$\text{PV} = \frac{1}{r}\left[1 - \frac{1}{[1 + r]^n}\right]$$

Perpetuity

Present value of £1 per annum, payable or receivable in perpetuity, commencing in one year, discounted at r% per annum

$$\text{PV} = \frac{1}{r}$$

chapter

1

Basic Mathematics

Chapter learning objectives

On completion of their studies students should be able to:

- calculate answers using formulae
- calculate percentages and proportions
- calculate answers to appropriate number of decimal places or significant figures
- solve simple equations, including two variable simultaneous equations and quadratic equations
- prepare graphs of linear and quadratic equations
- solve simple inequalities.

1 Introduction

Many students feel intimidated by mathematics when they encounter it. Often this is because they do not 'speak the language' of mathematics and understand all the various symbols used. Learning a new language does not require great intellect and depth of thought. Rather practice is needed to become familiar with what first appears to be foreign. Many aspects of mathematics are similar.

In this first chapter, a number of basic concepts are introduced that are fundamental to many areas of business mathematics.

2 The order of mathematical operations and the use of brackets

The basic mathematical operations are addition, subtraction, multiplication and division; and there is a very important convention about how we write down exactly what operations are to be carried out and in what order.

Consider how you would calculate 2 + 3 × 4.

(a) Would you do the 2 + 3 first to get 5 and then do 5 × 4 to get 20?

(b) Would you do the 3 × 4 first to get 12 and then add it to the 2 to get 14?

(c) Do you think the expression is ambiguous and could mean either?

The correct answer is (b) 14 – the multiplication must be done before the addition.

Why? Because that is one of the rules of the language of mathematics. You could have a parallel universe where the rules are different but here 2 + 3 × 4 = 14 is the only correct answer.

Note: It would be useful at this point to briefly digress and check your calculator. Type '2 + 3 × 4 =' into it. If the answer is 14, you have a scientific calculator that obeys mathematical priorities. If the answer is 20, your calculator is non-scientific and perhaps will not be suitable for your CIMA studies.

Brackets are used to clarify the order of operations and are essential when the normal priority of operations is to be broken. The order is:

(1) work out the values inside **b**rackets first;

(2) powers and roots (also known as **e**xponents - see later in this chapter);

(3) **d**ivision and **m**ultiplication are next in priority;

(4) finally, **a**ddition and **s**ubtraction.

This order can be remembered by taking the leading letter of each highlighted word: BEDMAS.

For example, suppose you want to add 2 and 3 and then multiply the answer by 4. You cannot write this as

$$2 + 3 \times 4$$

The above rule means that the multiplication will take priority over the addition. What you have written will be interpreted as an instruction to multiply 3 by 4 and then add 2.

Returning to the main problem, if you want to add 2 to 3 first and then multiply by 4, you must use brackets to give priority to the addition – to ensure that it takes place first. You should write

$$(2 + 3) \times 4.$$

The contents of the bracket total 5, and this is then multiplied by 4 to give 20.

Test Your Understanding 1

Evaluate the following:

A $5 + 6 \times 8$

B $(3 + 1) \times 2$

C $9 - 7 \div 2$

D $(4 + 5) /10$

E $5 + 7 \times 8 - 2$

F $(9 - 1) \times (6 + 4)$

Giving answers in the exam

Many of the questions in the C03 assessment require final answers to be given to a specified degree of accuracy, such as to 2 decimal places.

It is vital to be aware of how to round using decimal places and significant figures, in particular, otherwise you may carry out the correct method to arrive at an answer, but lose the credit for the question because of inaccurate rounding.

Supplementary reading – Different types of numbers

A whole number such as –5, 0 or 5 is called an *integer*, whereas numbers that contain parts of a whole number are either *fractions* (such as $^3/_4$) or *decimals* (such as 0.75).

Any type of number can be *positive* or *negative*. If you add a positive number to something, the effect is to increase it whereas, adding a negative number has the effect of reducing the value. If you add $-B$ to any number A, the effect is to subtract B from A. The rules for arithmetic with negative numbers are as follows:

- adding a negative is the same as subtracting, that is $A + (-B) = A - B$;
- subtracting a negative is the same as adding, that is $A - (-B) = A + B$
- if you multiply or divide a positive and a negative, the result is negative, that is
  (+) × (–) and (–) × (+) and (+) ÷ (–) and (–) ÷ (+) are all negative
- if you multiply or divide two negatives, the result is positive, that is (–) × (–) and (–) ÷ (–) are both positive.

Notice that brackets are often used for clarity when a negative number follows one of the mathematical operators like + or ×, but they are not strictly necessary.

Illustration

Evaluate the following:

(a) $9 - 7 \times (-2)$

(b) $(5 - 8) \times (-6)$

(c) $12 - 8 \div (-4)$

(d) $(4 - 16)/(-2)$

(e) $(17 - 6) \times (8 - 3)$

(f) $7 - (2 - 20)/(6 - 4)$

Solution

(a) Multiplication takes priority; $7 \times (-2) = -14$, so $9 - 7 \times (-2) = 9 - (-14) = 9 + 14 = 23$

(b) Work out the bracket first; $(5 - 8) \times (-6) = -3 \times (-6) = +18$

(c) Division takes priority; $12 - 8 \div (-4) = 12 - (-2) = 12 + 2 = 14$

(d) Work out the bracket first; $(4 - 16)/(-2) = (-12)/(-2) = +6$

(e) $(17 - 6) \times (8 - 3) = 11 \times 5 = 55$

(f) Brackets first, then the division, and only then subtract the result from 7; $7 - (2 - 20) \div (6 - 4) = 7 - (-18) \div 2 = 7 - (-9) = 7 + 9 = 16$

Supplementary reading – Rounding

Quite often, numbers have so many digits that they become impractical to work with and hard to grasp. This problem can be dealt with by converting some of the digits to zero in a variety of ways.

Rounding to the nearest whole number

For example, 78.187 = 78 to the nearest whole number. The only other nearby whole number is 79 and 78.187 is nearer to 78 than to 79. Any number from 78.0 to 78.49 will round down to 78 and any number from 78.5 to 78.99 will round up to 79.
The basic rules of rounding are that:

(1) digits are discarded (i.e. turned into zero) from right to left;

(2) reading from left to right, if the first digit to be discarded is in the range 0 – 4, then the previous retained digit is unchanged; if the first digit is in the range 5 – 9 then the previous digit goes up by one.

Depending on their size, numbers can be rounded to the nearest whole number, or 10 or 100 or 1,000,000, and so on. For example, 5,738 = 5,740 to the nearest 10; 5,700 to the nearest 100; and 6,000 to the nearest 1,000.

Significant figures

For example, 86,531 has five digits but we might want a number with only three. The '31' will be discarded. Reading from the left the first of these is 3, which is in the 0 – 4 range, so the previous retained digit (i.e. the '5') is unchanged. So 86,531 = 86,500 to three significant figures (s.f.).

Suppose we want 86,531 to have only two significant figures. The '531' will be discarded and the first of these, '5', is in the 5 – 9 range, so the previous digit ('6') is increased by 1. So 86,531 = 87,000 to two s.f.

Zeros sometimes count as significant figures; sometimes they do not. Reading a number from the right, any zeros encountered before you meet a non-zero number do not count as significant figures. However, zeros sandwiched *between* non-zeros are significant. Hence, 87,000 has two s.f., while 80,700 has three.

Decimal places

The other widely used rounding technique is to discard digits so that the remaining number only has a specified number of decimal places (d.p.).

For example, round 25.7842 to two d.p. The digits to be discarded are '42', the first ('4') is in the 0–4 range and so the next digit ('8') remains unchanged. So 25.7842 = 25.78 to two d.p.

Strings of '9' can be confusing. For example, if we want to round 10.99 to one d.p., the first digit to be discarded is '9' and so the next digit, also '9', goes up to '10'. In consequence, the rounded number is written as 11.0 to one d.p.

Rounding up or rounding down

A number to be rounded up will be changed into the next higher whole number so, for example, 16.12 rounds up to 17.

A number to be rounded down will simply have its decimal element discarded (or truncated).

Numbers can also be rounded up or down to, say, the next 100. Rounding up, 7,645 becomes 7,700 since 645 is increased to the next hundred which is 700. Rounding down, 7,645 becomes 7,600.

Illustration

This exercise covers all the topics of this chapter so far. Evaluate the following to the accuracy specified.

(a) 89.56 – 56.4/4.3 to two d.p.

(b) (5.9 – 8.2) ÷ (3.6 – 7.1) to one d.p.

(c) 8,539 – 349.1 ÷ (32.548 – 1) to three s.f.

(d) 56/5 – 28 to the nearest whole number.

Solution

In what follows, before rounding, we have not written out the full calculator display if it was plainly not going to be needed. However, note that it is good practice to retain full calculator accuracy throughout your calculation, only rounding at the final answer stage. Doing so avoids errors due to premature rounding at intermediate stages.

(a) 89.56 – 56.4/4.3 = 89.56 – 13.11627 = 89.56 – 13.12 = 76.44 to two d.p.

(b) (5.9 – 8.2) ÷ (3.6 – 7.1) = (–2.3) ÷ (–3.5) = 0.65714 = 0.7 to one d.p.

(c) 8,539 – 349.1 ÷ (32.548 – 1) = 8,539 – 349.1 ÷ 31.548 = 8,539 – 11.066 = 8527.934 = 8,530 to three s.f.

(d) 56/5 – 28 = 11.2 – 28 = –16.8 = –17 to the nearest whole number.

Correct rounding is essential in computer-based assessments. Don't move on to the next topic until you are quite sure about this.

Supplementary reading – Accuracy and approximation

All business data are subject to errors or variations. Simple human error, the rounding of a figure to the nearest hundred or thousand (or whatever), and the inevitable inaccuracies that arise when forecasting the future value of some factor, are examples of why business data may not be precise.

In certain circumstances, errors can accumulate, especially when two or more variables, each subject to error, are combined. The simplest such forms of combination are addition and subtraction.

Suppose an actual value is 826 and you round it to 830 (two s.f.). Your rounded value contains an error of 4. Someone else using the rounded figure does not know the true original value but must be aware that any rounded figure is likely to be erroneous.

The rounded value 830 could represent a true value as low as 825, or one as high as 835 (or, strictly speaking, 834.9999). There is a possible error of plus or minus 5.

In general, rounded values have a possible error given by substituting ± 5 in the position of the first discarded digit.

For example, with a value of 830, the first discarded digit is in the position of the ' 0 ', which is the units position. This gives a possible error of ±5 units.

If the rounded figure were 82.391 (to three d.p.), the first discarded digit is immediately to the right of the ' 1 ' and the possible error is ±0.0005.

3 Powers and roots

Consider the expression

$$5\times5\times5\times5\times5\times5\times5\times5\times5\times5.$$

We have multiplied 10 fives together. This looks untidy and is tedious to work out on a calculator. A much neater way of writing such an expression down is to use powers:

$$5\times5\times5\times5\times5\times5\times5\times5\times5\times5 = 5^{10}$$

This is read as '5 to the power 10'. In spreadsheet packages this is often shown as "5^10".

More generally, the nth power of a number, a, is the number multiplied by itself n times in total, and is denoted by a^n or a^n.

General rules for powers and roots

(1) Any number to the power of zero is **defined** to be 1.

For example, $7^0 = 1$

(2) Any number to the power of 1 is equal to itself.

For example, $5^1 = 5$

(3) Any number to the power of -1 is equal to 1 divided by the number.

For example, $10^{-1} = 1/10 = 0.1$

(4) More generally a^{-n} is the reciprocal of a^n, that is $a^{-n} = 1 \div a^n = 1 / a^n$

For example, $10^{-2} = 1/10^2 = 1/100 = 0.01$

(5) The nth root of a number, a, is denoted by $a^{1/n}$ and it is the number that, when multiplied by itself n times in total, results in a.

For example, the square root, $a^{1/2}$, is generally written as $\sqrt{a}$ without the number 2.

For example, the square root of 9 = $9^{1/2} = \sqrt{9} = 3$ (or –3)

(6) Powers of powers. $(a^m)^n = a^{mn}$.

For example, $(a^3)^4 = a^{3\times4} = a^{12}$

(7) Multiplication of powers. $a^m \times a^n = a^{m+n}$

For example, $3^4 \times 3^5 = 3^9$

(8) Division of powers: $a^m \div a^n = a^m / a^n = a^{m-n}$

For example, $2^7 \div 2^5 = 2^2 = 4$

(9) Quotients: $a^{n/m}$ can be interpreted as the mth root of a^n or as the mth root of a multiplied by itself n times.

$$a^{n/m} = (\sqrt[m]{a})^n = \sqrt[m]{(a^n)}$$

$$a^{3/2} = (\sqrt{a})^3 = \sqrt{(a^3)}$$

For example. $25^{3/2} = (\sqrt{25})^3 = 5^3 = 125$

Test Your Understanding 2

The expression $(x^2)^3/x^5$ equals:

A 0

B 1

C x

D x^2.

Test Your Understanding 3

Each of the following has been algebraically simplified. Which of the answers given are correct, and which incorrect?

A $((a^6)^2)/a^8$ Answer: a^4

B $(a^6)/a^{-5}$ Answer: a

C $(a^8)^{1/4}$ Answer: a^2

D $1/a^{-7}$ Answer: a^{-6}

Test Your Understanding 4

Calculate the value of $64^{2/3}$.

4 Percentages

Percentages are a useful way of discussing relative values, rather than using fractions.

For example, which of the following two (equivalent) statements is easier to understand?

(1) Prices are expected to rise by one twenty-fifth next year due to inflation.

(2) Prices are expected to rise by 4% next year due to inflation.

'Per cent' means 'out of 100'. The rule is: to convert a fraction or decimal into a percentage, multiply by 100; to convert a percentage into a fraction or decimal, divide by 100.

Using the example above;

- 4% = 4/100 = 1/25 or 0.04
- Or alternatively, 1/25 = 100% × 1/25 = (100/25)% = 4%

The key thing in exam questions is to recognise what represents 100%.

Illustration 1 – Percentages

Expressing profits as percentages

For example, suppose I buy something for $8 and sell it for $10, making $2 profit.

As a percentage I could compare the profit with the cost of $8 or the selling price of $10:

- As a % of cost, profit = (2/8) × 100% = 25% (this is known as the 'mark-up' on cost)
- As a % of selling price, profit = (2/10) × 100% = 20% (this is known as the 'gross margin')

Sales tax and Value Added Tax (VAT)

VAT is usually expressed as a percentage, for example 20%, and works like a mark-up. The price paid by a customer includes the VAT (i.e. is "gross") and that the percentage applies to the "net" figure.

For example, suppose I buy something for $60, inclusive of VAT at 20%. How much is the VAT?

- The *gross* price I pay will be 120% of the *net* price for the retailer;
- The net price will be 60 × (100/120) = $50, giving VAT of $10 (the difference);
- Alternatively, the VAT = 60 ×(20/120) = $10.

Test Your Understanding 5

A During a certain year, a company declares a profit of $15.8 m, whereas, in the previous year, the profit had been $14.1 m. What percentage increase in profit does this represent?

B A consultant has forecast that the above company's profit figure will fall by 5 per cent next year. What profit figure is the consultant forecasting for the next year?

C If this year's profit is $6.2 m, and if the increase from last year is known to have been 7.5 per cent, what was last year's profit?

Test Your Understanding 6

A price of $2,500 includes VAT at 17.5%. Find the price *exclusive* of VAT correct to the nearest $.

Test Your Understanding 7

At a value added tax (VAT) rate of 12.5%, an article sells for 84c, including VAT. If the VAT rate increases to 17.5%, the new selling price, to the nearest cent, will be:

A 87c

B 88c

C 94c

D 99c.

5 Ratios

A ratio shows how something should be divided up.

The relative shares are usually (but not necessarily) expressed as whole numbers and they are separated by a colon, e.g. 2:3:5.

A proportion describes the relationship of some part of a whole to the whole itself and is usually given as a fraction.

- For example, in a class there are 30 girls and 15 boys;
- The ratio of girls to boys is 2:1, but
- The proportion of girls in the class is 30 out of 45, or 30/45, or (less usefully in this case) 2/3.

To apply a ratio to a set of figures, it is usually easier to convert to the related proportions.

Illustration 2 – Ratios

Example: profit sharing

Split $60 between A, B and C in the ratio 2:3:5

Step 1: add up the different figures in the ratio: 2 + 3 + 5 = 10

Step 2: express the ratio in proportions: 2/10 : 3/10 : 5/10

Step 3: apply to the figure concerned:

- A gets 60 × 2/10 = 12
- B gets 60 × 3/10 = 18
- C gets 60 × 5/10 = 30

Test Your Understanding 8

James, Justin and Roger are in business together and one year make a profit of $88,000.

They had previously agreed to share profits in the ratio 5:2:4 respectively.

How much does each partner receive in money terms?

6 Formulae and equations

A *formula* is a statement that is given in terms of mathematical symbols: it is a mathematical expression that enables you to calculate the value of one variable from the value(s) of one or more others.

Many formulae arise in financial and business calculations, and we shall encounter several during the course of this text.

Inserting figures into formulae

The key thing when putting values into formulae is to follow the BEDMAS rules we looked at earlier.

Supplementary reading – Variables and functions

A variable is something which can take different values. Variables are often denoted by letters.

Thus, the set of positive whole numbers can be considered as a variable. If we denote it by x, then this variable can have many values.

$x = 1$ or $x = 2$ or $x = 3$ and so on

Another example is the set of the major points of a compass. If this variable is denoted by c, then it can have more than one value, but only a limited number.

c = north or c = south, and so on

These examples show that variables can take on non-numerical values as well as numerical ones. In this text we shall concentrate on numerical variables, that is, those whose values are numbers, like the first case above, although we will rarely limit ourselves just to whole numbers.

A mathematical function is a rule or method of determining the value of one numerical variable from the values of other numerical variables. We shall concentrate on the case where one variable is determined by or depends on just one other variable.

The first variable is called the dependent variable, and is usually denoted by y, while the second is called the independent variable, denoted by x.

The relationship between them is a function of one variable, often referred to as a function, for brevity. Note that whilst functions are similar to formulae there are specific conditions relating to the definition of a function, but these are outside the scope of this book.

A very useful way of stating a function is in terms of an equation, which is an expression containing an 'equals' sign.

The equation of a function will thus take the typical form:

y = a mathematical expression containing x

If we know the value of the independent variable x, then the expression will completely determine the corresponding value of the dependent variable, y.

Test Your Understanding 9

The following equations represent functions with one independent variable (x). Evaluate the dependent variable (y) when the independent variable (x) has the value 2.

A $y = 3 + 2x$

B $y = x$

C $y = 1 + x + 3x^2$

Test Your Understanding 10

In the theory of learning curves you will come across the following formula:

$$y = ax^b$$

Calculate y when a = 10, x = 4 and b = –0.152

Rearranging equations

You may be asked to rearrange an equation either to change its subject or to help you solve it.

The key to doing this successfully is to ensure that you do the same thing to both sides of the equation. That way the equality is preserved.

Illustration 3 – Rearranging equations

Example: to change the subject

Suppose we want to rearrange the expression '$y = 3x^2 – 7$' to make x the subject.

This could be done in the following steps:

(1) Add 7 to both sides:

$$y+7 = 3x^2$$

(2) Divide both sides by 3:

$$(y+7)/3 = x^2$$

(3) Square root both sides:

$$x = +\sqrt{(y+7)/3} \text{ or } -\sqrt{(y+7)/3}$$

Example: to solve an equation

Suppose we want to solve the following:

$$\frac{50}{x} = \frac{24}{x-3}$$

(1) Cross-multiply up by the two denominators – i.e. multiply both sides by x and (x–3), giving

$$50(x - 3) = 24x$$

(2) Multiply out the bracket on the left:

$$50x - 150 = 24x$$

(3) Add 150 to both sides:

$$50x = 150 + 24x$$

(4) Deduct 24x from both sides

$$50x - 24x = 150$$

$$26x = 150$$

(5) Divide both sides by 26

$$x = 150 \div 26 = 5.77 \text{ to two d.p.}$$

Test Your Understanding 11

In the following formula substitute Q = 100, C = 10, P = 6 and R = 0.2

$$Q^2 = \frac{2DC}{PR}$$

D, to the nearest unit, is:

A 598

B 599

C 600

D 601.

Test Your Understanding 12

The formula $V = P \times (1 + r)^n$ occurs in compound interest calculations Rearrange the formula to make *r* the subject. Which one of the following answers is correct?

A $r = (V/P - 1)^{1/n}$

B $r = (V/P)^{1/n} - 1$

C $r = (V - P)/n - 1$

If $P = 250$, $r = 0.04$ and $n = 6$, calculate *V* to the nearest whole number.

Test Your Understanding 13

A Solve $6 - 3X = 0$

B Solve $200 = 5(X - 2) + 80$

C Solve $\frac{60}{X} = \frac{48}{X - 2}$

7 Linear equations

Linear equations are so named because a graph of them would show a straight line.

You can tell if an equation is linear if it has no term with powers greater than 1, that is, no squared or cubed terms, etc.

All linear equations can be rearranged to conform to the same general format:

$y = a + bx$ LEARN

Where: x and y are variables.

- "a" represents the point where the line cuts the y-axis (the intercept)
- "b" represents the gradient or slope of the line.

Graph of linear function y = a +bx

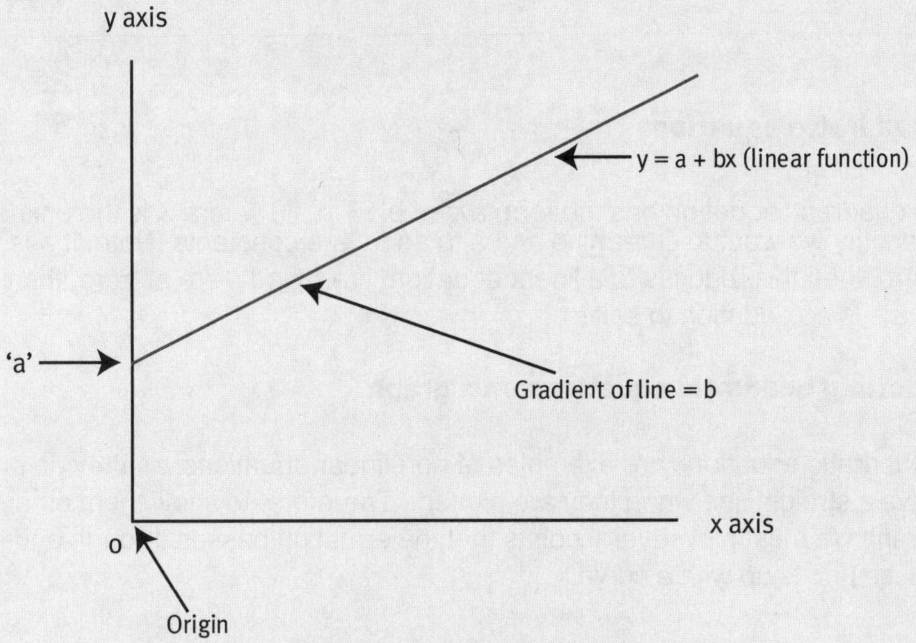

Test Your Understanding 14

Calculate the values of y in the function

$$y = 3 + 2x$$

corresponding to the values: × = 2; × = 1; × = 3; × = 4; × = –1.
Plot the five corresponding pairs of values on a graph and hence draw the graph of the function.

Test Your Understanding 15

Which of the following equations does not have a straight line graph?

A $y = 10x + 3$

B $y = (15x - 7)/6$

C $y = 4x^2 + 2x - 7$

D $y = 23$

Quadratic equations

A quadratic equation has the form $aX^2 + bX + c = 0$ where X is the unknown quantity we want to determine and *a*, *b* and *c* are constants (Note: if *a* is zero, then this reduces to a linear equation. If *a*,*b* and *c* are all zero, then there is no equation to solve).

Plotting quadratic equations on a graph

Quadratic equations are examples of non-linear equations, as they do not give a straight line when they are plotted. Therefore, to show them on a graph we must plot several points that the equation passes through and join these points up with a curve.

A quadratic has one of two basic graph shapes:

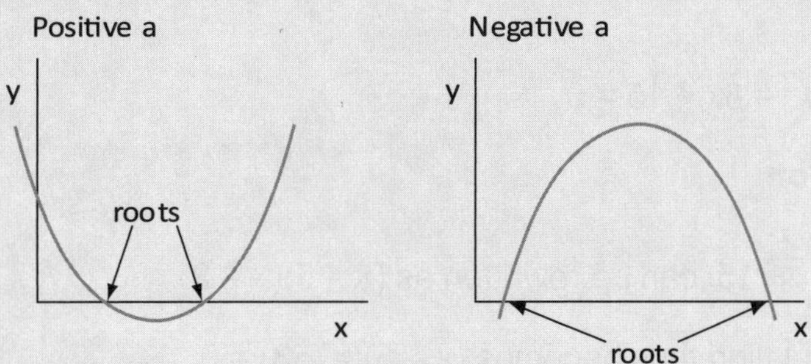

Quadratic functions

It is a symmetrical parabola, depending on the sign of a.

Another way of saying the same thing is that the y-values drop to a minimum and then rise again if a is positive, whereas they rise to a maximum and then fall if a is negative. This is of some importance in your later studies, when you may need to investigate the maximum or minimum values of functions for profits or costs, etc.

The "roots" or "solutions" of the equation are given by the intercepts on the x-axis, and by symmetry the maximum or minimum is always halfway between them.

Some quadratic equations do not have real roots, and in these cases the graph simply does not cut the x-axis at all:

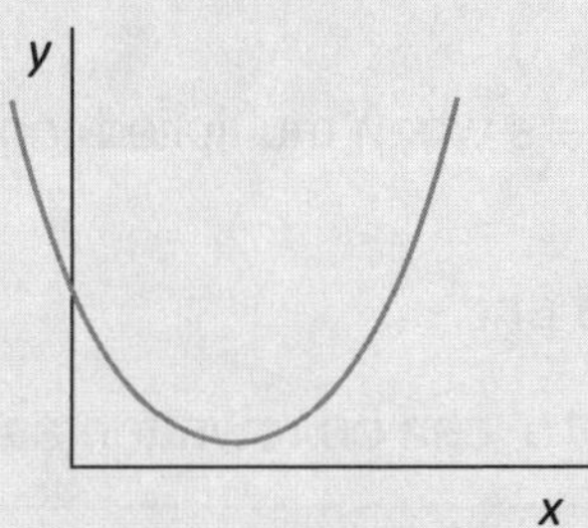

Quadratic equation with no roots

There are four methods for finding the roots:

(1) Take a reading from a graph – only if given a graph in the exam.

(2) Trial and error – can be useful in the exam if the question lists four possible solutions.

(3) Try to factorise the equation – can be very quick for some students.

Illustration 4 – Solving quadratics by factorising the equation

Example

Solve $x^2 - 8x + 15 = 0$

Solution

$x^2 - 8x + 15$ can be rewritten as $(x - 5)(x - 3)$

Our equation thus becomes $(x - 5)(x - 3) = 0$

Now if two things multiplied together equal zero, then one or other of the terms must be zero

- i.e. either $(x - 5) = 0$, giving $x = 5$
- or $(x - 3) = 0$, giving $x = 3$

The issue is spotting that $x^2 - 8x + 15$ can be rewritten as $(x - 5)(x - 3)$ in the first place.

More generally, if we expand $(x + m)(x + n)$ we get $x^2 + (m+n)x + mn$

i.e. the x coefficient is the sum of the two numbers in the brackets (m+n) and the constant at the end is the product of them (mn).

Effectively what we have to do to factorise the quadratic is work backwards:

- Which two numbers when multiplied together give 15 but when added give –8?
- The answer is ×5 and –3
- Hence $x^2 - 8x + 15$ can be rewritten as $(x - 5)(x - 3)$

(4) Use a formula to calculate the roots – usually the best approach unless you can factorise the equation.

For quadratic equations all of whose coefficients are non-zero, the easiest method of solution is the formula. If the equation is $aX^2 + bX + c = 0$, then the roots are given by:

$$x = \frac{- b \pm \sqrt{b^2 - 4ac}}{2a}$$

The "plus or minus" symbol means that there are 2 solutions (or roots). To get one you add (+) and to get the other you subtract (–).

Note: for some quadratics the two roots are the same (effectively giving one root). If you think you have to calculate the square root of a negative number in the exam, then rework your numbers as you will not be expected to do this.

Illustration 5 – Solving quadratics using the formula

Example

Find the roots of the quadratic equation $y = x^2 - 8x + 15$ using the formula.

Solution

$$x = \frac{-b \pm \sqrt{b^2 - 4ac}}{2a} = \frac{-(-8) \pm \sqrt{(-8)^2 - 4(1)(15)}}{2(1)}$$

$$x = \frac{8 \pm \sqrt{64 - 60}}{2} = \frac{8 \pm \sqrt{4}}{2} = \frac{8 \pm 2}{2}$$

$$x = \frac{8+2}{2} = 5 \quad \text{or } x = \frac{8-2}{2} = 3$$

Test Your Understanding 16

Solve the equation $X^2 - 50X + 600 = 0$

Test Your Understanding 17

Solve the following equations:

A $Y^2 - 16 = 0$

B $2Y^2 - 5Y = 0$

C $Y^2 - 20Y - 800 = 0$

8 Simultaneous equations

Simultaneous equations are where you have two equations that must both be satisfied at the same time.

In C03 the ones you will meet will be of the type:

$3X + 4Y = 18$ (i)
$5X + 2Y = 16$ (ii)

which must both be satisfied by the solutions X and Y.

Provided you multiply both sides of an equation by the same amount, it continues to be true. In the solution of these equations, one or both of the equations are multiplied by numbers chosen so that either the *X* or the *Y* terms in the two equations become numerically identical.

We have labelled the equations (i) and (ii) for clarity. Suppose we were to multiply (i) by 5 and (ii) by 3. Both equations would contain a 15*X*-term that we could eliminate by subtraction, it being the case that you can add or subtract two equations and the result remains true.

In this case, however, the simplest method is to multiply equation (ii) by 2, so that both equations will contain 4*Y* and we can subtract to eliminate *Y*. The full solution is shown below.

$3X + 4Y = 18$ (i)
$5X + 2Y = 16$ (ii)

Multiply (ii) by 2:

$10X + 4Y = 32$ (iii)

Subtract (iii) – (i):

$7X + 0 = 14$
$X = 14 \div 7 = 2$

Substitute X = 2 into (i)

$6 + 4Y = 18$
$4Y = 18 - 6 = 12$
$Y = 12 \div 4 = 3$

Check the results in (ii):

$5 \times 2 + 2 \times 3 = 16$

The solution is X = 2, Y = 3.

Had we chose to substitute X = 2 into equation (ii), it would not have affected the result but we would then have checked in the other equation (i).

Test Your Understanding 18

Solve the equations:

$2X - 3Y = 23$ (i)
$7X + 4Y = 8$ (ii)

Solving simultaneous linear equations using graphs

Each equation represents a straight line and solving simultaneous equations is the same as identifying the point at which the two lines cross.

This is the graphical interpretation of the solution of simultaneous linear equations, and a graphical method could be used instead of an algebraic method (provided that the scale was big enough to give the required accuracy).

Test Your Understanding 19

Solve the simultaneous equations

$2x + 3y = 8$ (i)
$5x - 2y = 1$ (ii)

by first graphing the lines using the values x = 0 and x = 5 and then by solving algebraically .

9 Manipulating inequalities

Inequalities are treated in almost exactly the same way as equations. In fact an inequality says much the same thing as an equation, except that one side will be

- less than the other (<)
- greater than the other (>),
- less than or equal to the other (≤), or
- greater than or equal to the other (≥).

Inequalities can be manipulated in the same way as equations, except that when multiplying or dividing by a negative number it is necessary to **reverse** the inequality sign.

For example,

$5 - 2x < 25$

$-2x < 20$ (deduct 5 from each side)

$-x < 10$ (divide each side by 2)

$x > -10$ (divide each side by -1, so reverse direction of inequality)

Test Your Understanding 20

Solve for x in each of the following:

A $3x + 10 > 40$

B $5x + 20 < 60$

C $10 - 3x > 40$

Chapter Summary

Basic mathematics covers a wide range of topics and underlies virtually all the elements of business mathematics. The key contents of the chapter are:

- the rules for the order of mathematical operations and the use of brackets
- rounding
- dealing with powers and roots
- manipulating formulae
- solving equations
- manipulating inequalities
- dealing with percentages and ratios.

10 Further practice questions

Test Your Understanding 21

Evaluate the following *without* rounding.

A 7 + 2 × 5

B (5 + 2) × 8

C 28 – 48/4

D (7 + 3)/5

E 8 + 4 × 5 – 2

F (8 – 4) × (3 + 7).

Test Your Understanding 22

The number 268.984 is to be rounded. In each case write the correct answer, to the accuracy specified.

A to two decimal places.

B to one decimal place.

C to the nearest whole number.

D to the nearest 100.

E to three significant figures

F to four significant figures.

Test Your Understanding 23

The term x^{-1} equals:

A $2x$

B $1/x$

C x^2

D $x-1$.

Test Your Understanding 24

A person pays no tax on the first $3,500 of earnings and then 23 per cent tax on the remainder of earnings. If he/she wishes to have $15,000 net of tax earnings, what gross earnings (to the nearest $) does he/she need?

A $15,000

B $18,435

C $18,500

D $19,481.

Test Your Understanding 25

An item priced at $90.68, including local sales tax at 19 per cent, is reduced in a sale by 20 per cent. The new price before sales tax is added is:

A $60.96

B $72.54

C $75.57

D $76.20.

Test Your Understanding 26

A Express 4.6 as:

(i) a ratio compared to 23.0;

(ii) a percentage of 23.0.

B Evaluate 30 per cent of 450.

C For a particular company's shares, the ratio of the price to its earnings (known as a P/E ratio) is 18.5. If the earnings per share figure is $1.50, what is the price per share?

D If a variable, A, increases by 8 per cent, what does it become?

E If a variable, B, changes to 0.945B, what percentage change has occurred?

Test Your Understanding 27

Solve the following simple quadratic equations (note that the variable used is Y, but as there is only one variable used, this is fine.):

A $4Y^2 = 100$

B $Y^2 - 9 = 0$

C $Y^2 + 2Y = 0$

D $(Y - 5)^2 = 0$

Test Your Understanding 28

Solve the following equations:

A $10 + 3Y = 8Y - 7$

B $\dfrac{6.1}{Y} = \dfrac{4.9}{10 - Y}$

Test Your Understanding 29

Calculate the value of A from the formula

$$A = \frac{B(C + 1)(3 - D)}{(2E - 3F)}$$

when B = 2, C = 3, D = –1.6, E = –1 and F = –2.5

Test Your Understanding 30

If a number P is increased by 5 per cent, what will its new value be? Which of the following answers is/are correct?

A $P + 5P/100$

B $1.05P$

C $0.95P$

D $0.05P$.

Test Your Understanding 31

The equation $60/Y = 25/(20 - Y)$ is to be solved to find Y correct to one decimal place. A solution comprises the following five lines, (A) – (E). Which of the lines (A) – (E) follows correctly from the line immediately prior to them (regardless of whether or not you believe the prior line to be correct)?

A $60(20 - Y) = 25Y$

B $1{,}200 - Y = 25Y$

C $1{,}200 = 26Y$

D $Y = 1{,}200/26$

E $Y = 46.15$ to two d.p.

Test Your Understanding 32

Each of the following solutions of quadratic equations contains one line that does not follow correctly from that immediately prior to it. In each case identify the incorrect line.

A $Y^2 - 36 = 0$

$Y^2 = 36$

$Y = +6$

B $Y^2 - 5Y = 0$

$Y(2Y - 5) = 0$

$Y = 0$ or $5/2$

C $(Y + 6)^2 = 0$

$Y + 6 = \pm 0$

$Y = \pm 6$

D $Y^2 + Y - 12 = 0$

Using the formula with $a = 2$, $b = 1$, $c = -12$ gives

$Y = (-1 \pm (1 + 4 \times 2 \times 12)^{0.5})/(2 \times 2)$

$Y = 2.2$ or -2.7 to one d.p.

Test Your Understanding 33

For each of the following solve for x in the inequality

A $5x + 10 > 20$

B $2x - 5 < 15$

C $x/2 - 10 > 30$

D $-5x + 20 < 120$

Test Your Understanding 34

A buyer has spent $30,151 on 550 units of a particular item. The first 100 units cost $50 each, the next 150 units cost $8,250 in total, the next batch cost $11,200 in total and the final 100 cost $x each. The value of x is:

A $55

B $56

C $57.01

D $60.30.

Test Your Understanding 35

A buyer purchases twenty cases of Product A at $7.84 per case, ten cases of Product B at $8.20 per case, twelve cases of Product C at $8.50 per case and a number of cases of Product D at $8.60 per case. He spends $469.80 in total. If there are twelve items in each case of Product D, how many items of Product D does he buy?

A 120

B 144

C 150

D 180.

Test Your Understanding 36

A square-ended rectangular box has a volume of 1,458 cm^3. The length of the box is twice that of one side of the square end.

One side of the square end therefore measures:

A 6 cm

B 9 cm

C 18 cm

D 24 cm.

Test Your Understanding 37

Geoff, a farmer, is trying to measure the area of a field to help determine how much fertilizer to buy. One of his farm workers has come up with the following measurements:

- Length = 200m
- Width = 100m
- Area = 200 × 100 = 20,000m^2

Both the length and width measurements were rounded to the nearest 10m. In order to ensure he has sufficient fertlizer to cover the field, what additional percentage should Geoff buy, compared to the amount needed for 20,000m^2?

A 20%

B 15.25%

C 15%

D 7.6%

Test your understanding answers

Test Your Understanding 1

A **53**

6 × 8 takes priority, then add 5, so 5 + 6 × 8 = 5 + 48 = 53

B **8**

Work out the bracket first, then multiply by 2; 3 + 1 = 4, so (3 + 1) × 2 = 4 × 2 = 8

C **5.5**

7 ÷ 2 takes priority, and is then subtracted from 9; 9 – 3.5 = 5.5

D **0.9**

Work out the bracket first, then divide by 10; 4 + 5 = 9, and 9/10 = 0.9

E **59**

The multiplication of 7 × 8 takes priority, giving 5 + 56 – 2 = 59

F **80**

Work out the brackets first – the order is unimportant but it is usual to work from left to right; 9 – 1 = 8, and 6 + 4 = 10, giving 8 × 10 = 80

Test Your Understanding 2

C

$$\frac{(X^2)^3}{X^5} = \frac{X^6}{X^5} = X$$

based on the rules $(X^m)^n = X^{m \times n}$ and $X^m \div X^n = X^{(m-n)}$

Test Your Understanding 3

The correct responses are shown with some of the workings:

A Correct	$a^{12}/a^{8} = a^{4}$
B Incorrect	$a^{(6-(-5))} = a^{11}$
C Correct	$a^{(8/4)} = a^{2}$
D Incorrect	$1/a^{n} = a^{-n}$, so $1/a^{-7} = a^{7}$.

Test Your Understanding 4

Two approaches:

(1) $64^{2/3} = (64^{1/3})^{2} = 4^{2} = 16$.

(2) $64^{2/3} = (64^{2})^{1/3} = 4{,}096^{1/3} = 16$.

Test Your Understanding 5

A The increase in profit is \$1.7 m, which as a percentage of the previous year's profit is:

$$\frac{1.7\text{ m}}{14.1\text{ m}} \times 100\% = 12.1\% \text{ to one d.p.}$$

B The forecast decrease in profit is 5 per cent of \$15.8 m

$$\frac{5}{100} \times 15.8 = \$0.79\text{ m}$$

Hence, the forecast profit for the following year is \$15.01 m.

C This year's profit is 107.5 per cent of last year's

$$\frac{\text{This year's profit}}{107.5} \times 100 = \text{Last year's profit}$$

Last year's profit = \$6.2m ÷ 107.5 × 100 = \$5.77 m to three s.f.

Test Your Understanding 6

The price exclusive of VAT is \$2,500/1.175 = \$2,128

Test Your Understanding 7

B

Our approach is to remove the VAT at 12.5% to get the net value and then add VAT at 17.5%.

$$84c \times \frac{100}{112.5} = 74.6c = \text{price without VAT (net)}$$

$$74.67c \times \frac{117.5}{100} = 87.73 = 88c \text{ to nearest cent}$$

Test Your Understanding 8

5 + 2 + 4 = 11

James receives = 88 × 5/11 = $40,000
Justin receives = 88 × 2/11 = $16,000
Roger receives = 88 × 4/11 = $32,000

Test Your Understanding 9

To find the value of y, we write the known value of x (2 in this case) in place of x in the mathematical expression and perform the necessary arithmetical calculations. This is known as the substitution of the x-value into the equation.

A Substituting x = 2 gives:
$y = 3 + 2 \times 2 = 3 + 4 = 7$

B Clearly, this dependent variable has the value 2, the same as x.

C Substituting x = 2:
$y = 1 + 2 + 3 \times 2^2 = 1 + 2 + 12 = 15.$

Test Your Understanding 10

$y = ax^b = 10 \times 4^{-0.152} = 10 \times 0.81 = 8.10$

Note: make sure you work out how to enter the terms into your calculator to get $4^{-0.152} = 0.81$. This will probably involve a button that looks like x^y but different calculators expect you to enter the information in different orders – either the 4 first or the –0.152 first.

Test Your Understanding 11

C

Rearranging:

$$Q^2PR = 2DC$$

$$D = \frac{Q^2PR}{2C} = \frac{100^2 \times 6 \times 0.2}{2 \times 10}$$

D = 600

Test Your Understanding 12

A **B**

The steps are:

$V/P = (1 + r)^n$

$(V/P)^{1/n} = 1 + r$

$(V/P)^{1/n} - 1 = r.$

B $V = 250 \times 1.04^6$, so the answer is 316

Test Your Understanding 13

A Add $3X$ to both sides to give
$6 = 3X$
Then divide both sides by 3 to give
$X = 6 \div 3 = 2$

B Expand the brackets
$200 = 5X - 10 + 80$
$200 = 5X + 70$
$130 = 5X$
$X = 130 \div 5 = 26$

C $60(X - 2) = 48X$
$60X - 120 = 48X$
$12X = 120$
$X = 120/12 = 10$

Test Your Understanding 14

x	2	1	3	4	–1
y	7	5	9	11	1

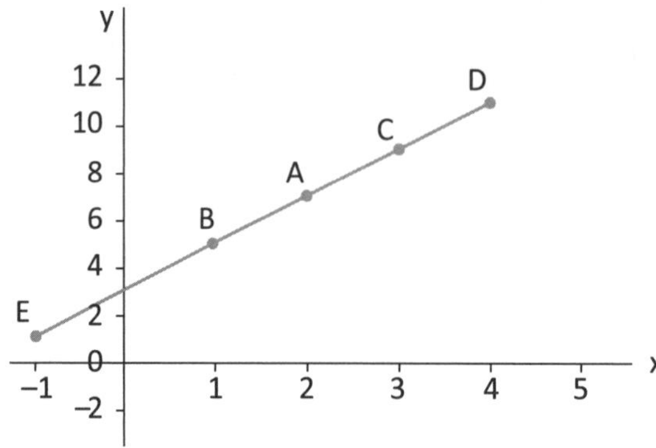

Plot of points and line

Test Your Understanding 15

C

This is the only equation with powers of x other than 0 or 1.

Test Your Understanding 16

$x^2 - 50x + 600 = 0$

a = 1 b = –50 c = 600

$$x = \frac{50 \pm \sqrt{(-50)^2 - 4 \times 1 \times 600}}{2 \times 1}$$

$$= \frac{50 \pm \sqrt{2500 - 2400}}{2}$$

$$= \frac{50 \pm \sqrt{100}}{2}$$

$$x = \frac{50 + 10}{2} \quad \text{or} \quad x = \frac{50 - 10}{2}$$

$x = 30$ $\qquad$ $x = 20$

Test Your Understanding 17

A $y^2 = 16$

$y = \pm\sqrt{16} = \pm 4$

B $2y^2 - 5y = 0$

$y(2y - 5) = 0$

either $y = 0$ or $2y - 5 = 0$, in which case $y = 2.5$

C $Y^2 - 20Y - 800 = 0$

$a = 1$ $b = -20$ $c = -800$ and use formula

$$Y = \frac{20 \pm \sqrt{(-20)^2 - 4 \times 1 \times -800}}{2 \times 1}$$

$$= \frac{20 \pm \sqrt{400 + 3200}}{2}$$

$$= \frac{20 \pm \sqrt{3600}}{2}$$

$$Y = \frac{20 + 60}{2} \quad \text{or } Y = \frac{20 - 60}{2}$$

$$Y = 40 \quad \text{or} \quad Y = -20$$

Test Your Understanding 18

Multiply (i) by 4 and (ii) by 3:

$8X - 12Y = 92$ (iii)
$21X + 12Y = 24$ (iv)

Add the equations:

$29X = 116$
$X = 116 \div 29 = 4$

Substitute $X = 4$ in (ii):

$28 + 4Y = 8$
$4Y = 8 - 28 = -20$
$Y = -20 \div 4 = -5$

Check in (i):

$2 \times 4 - 3 \times (-5) = 8 + 15 = 23$

The solution is $X = 4$, $Y = -5$

Test Your Understanding 19

To plot the lines we simply need two points they go through:

Equation (i),

- When $x = 0$, $3y = 8$, so $y = 8 \div 3 = 2.67$.
- When $x = 5$, $3y = 8 - 10 = -2$, so $y = -2/3$.

Equation (ii),

- When $x = 0$, $-2y = 1$, so $y = -1/2$.
- When $x = 5$, $-2y = 1 - 25 = -24$, so $y = -24 \div -2 = 12$.

These values are plotted below.

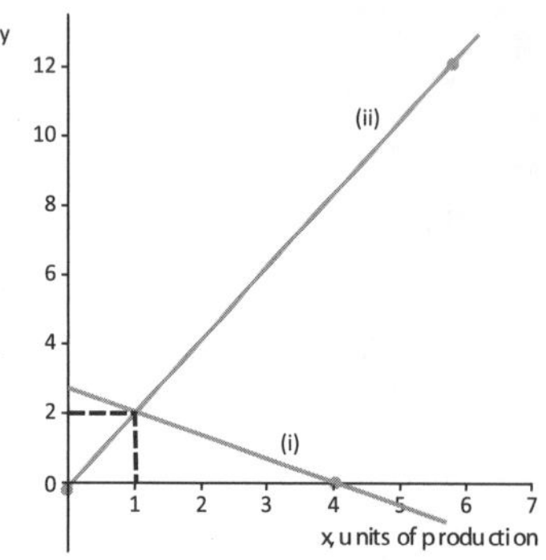

The lines meet when $x = 1$ and $y = 2$, which is the solution of the equations.

Algebraic Solution

$2x + 3y = 8$ (i)

$5x - 2y = 1$ (ii)

Equation (i) × 5 gives $10x + 15y = 40$ (iii)

Equation (ii) × 2 gives $10x - 4y = 2$ (iv)

(iii) – (iv) gives $19y = 38$

$y = 38/19 = 2$

Substitute $y = 2$ into (i) gives

$2x + 6 = 8$

$2x = 8 - 6 = 2$

$x = 1$

Check in (ii)

$(5 \times 1) - (2 \times 2) = 5 - 4 = 1$ OK

Test Your Understanding 20

A $3x > 40 - 10$
$3x > 30$
$x > 10$

B $5x < 60 - 20$
$5x < 40$
$x < 8$

C $-3x > 40 - 10$
$-3x > 30$
$x < -10$

Test Your Understanding 21

A 7 + 10 = 17

B 7 × 8 = 56

C 28 –12 = 16

D 10/5 = 2

E 8 + 20 – 2 = 26

F 4 × 10 = 40.

Test Your Understanding 22

The correct answers are:

A 268.98

B 269.0

C 269

D 300

E 269

F 269.0.

Test Your Understanding 23

B

$x^{-1} = 1/x$, by definition.

Test Your Understanding 24

B

\$15,000 – \$3,500 = \$11,500, which is the taxable part of earnings, after tax at 23 per cent. Hence, taxable earnings are (\$11,500 ÷ 0.77) = \$14,935 before tax, and gross earnings are \$14,935 + \$3,500 = \$18,435.

Test Your Understanding 25

A

Reduced price, including sales tax = \$90.68 × 80% = \$72.54. Without sales tax: \$72.54 × (100/119) = \$60.96.

Test Your Understanding 26

A (i) 4.6/23.0 = 0.2 or 1:5
(ii) (4.6/23.0) × 100% = 20%

B 450 × (30/100) = 135

C Earnings = 18.5 × price = 18.5 × 1.50 = \$27.75

D An increase of 8 per cent of A is

$$\frac{8}{100} \times A \text{ or } 0.08\,A$$

The variable therefore becomes

$$A + 0.08A = 1.08A$$

E If a variable has decreased by

$$B - 0.945B = 0.055B$$

As a percentage, this is

$$\frac{0.055B}{B} \times 100 = 5.5\%$$

Test Your Understanding 27

A $Y^2 = 100 \div 4 = 25$
$Y = +\sqrt{25}$ and $-\sqrt{25} = \pm 5$

B $Y^2 = 9$
$Y = \pm\sqrt{9} = \pm 3$

C $Y(Y + 2) = 2$
Either $Y = 0$; or $Y + 2 = 0$, so $Y = -2$

D The only solution is that $Y - 5 = 0$, so $Y = 5$ (effectively the answer is 5 twice)

Test Your Understanding 28

A $10 + 3Y = 8Y - 7$
$10 + 7 = 8Y - 3Y$
$17 = 5Y$
$Y = 17 \div 5 = 3.4$

B
$$\frac{6.1}{Y} = \frac{4.9}{10 - Y}$$

$6.1(10 - Y) = 4.9Y$

$61 - 6.1Y = 4.9Y$

$61 = 4.9Y + 6.1Y = 11Y$

$Y = 61 \div 11 = 5.55$ to two d.p.

Test Your Understanding 29

$(C + 1) = (3 + 1) = 4$

$(3 - D) = (3 - (-1.6)) = 3 + 1.6 = 4.6$

B $(C + 1)(3 - D) = 2 \times 4 \times 4.6 = 36.8$

$(2E - 3F) = (2 \times -1) - (3 \times -2.5) = -2 - (-7.5) = 5.5$

A $= 36.8 \div 5.5 = 6.690909$

Test Your Understanding 30

A and B

Five per cent of *P* is 5*P*/100, so the result will be *P* + 5*P*/100 = *P* + 0.05*P* = 1.05*P*.

In answer **C**, *P* has been reduced by 5 per cent. In **D**, the 5 per cent of *P* has been calculated but not added to the original amount.

Test Your Understanding 31

The correct answers are as follows:

A	$60(20 - Y) = 25Y$	Correct
B	$1{,}200 - Y = 25Y$	Incorrect: the Y should have been multiplied by the 60
C	$1{,}200 = 26Y$	Correct following last error
D	$Y = 1{,}200/26$	Correct
E	$Y = 46.15$ to two d.p.	Correct

Test Your Understanding 32

The incorrect lines were as follows:

A $Y = +6$ is incomplete as it only shows one possible solution. The corrected version should state $Y = \pm 6$

B $Y(2Y - 5) = 0$ is wrong: Y^2 is not $2 \times Y \times Y$.
The correct factorisation would be $Y(Y - 5) = 0$, giving $Y=0$ or $Y=5$

C $Y = +6$ part of the answer is wrong: $(Y + 6)(Y + 6) = 0$ so $Y + 6 = 0$ giving $Y = -6$ twice.

D The line "$a = 2$, $b = 1$, $c = -12$" is wrong: a = 1, not 2.

Test Your Understanding 33

A $5x + 10 > 20$
$5x > 20 - 10$
$5x > 10$
$x > 2$.

B $2x - 5 < 15$
$2x < 15 + 5$
$2x < 20$
$x < 10$.

C $x/2 - 10 > 30$
$x/2 > 30 + 10$
$x/2 > 40$
$x > 80$.

D $-5x + 20 < 120$
$-5x < 120 - 20$
$-5x < 100$
$x > 100 \div (-5)$
$x > -20$.

Test Your Understanding 34

C

Batch	*Cost \$*	*Cumulative cost \$*
100 at \$50	5,000	
Next batch of 100	8250	13,250
Next batch	11,200	24,450
Final 100 at \$*x*	100*x*	24,450 + 100*x*

Total = 30,151 = 24,450 + 100x
30,151 – 24,450 = 100x = 5,701
x = 5701/100 = 57.01.

Test Your Understanding 35

D

Let there be X cases of product D. Then:

$20 \times \$7.84 + 10 \times \$8.20 + 12 \times \$8.50 + X \times \$8.60 = \$469.80$
i.e. $340.8 + 8.6X = 469.8$
$8.6X = 469.8 - 340.8$
$8.6X = 129$
$X = 129 \div 8.6$
$X = 15$

Number of items = $12X = 12 \times 15 = 180$.

Test Your Understanding 36

B

Volume = $2x^3 = 1{,}458$

$x^3 = 1{,}458/2 = 729$

$x = (729)^{1/3} = 9$.

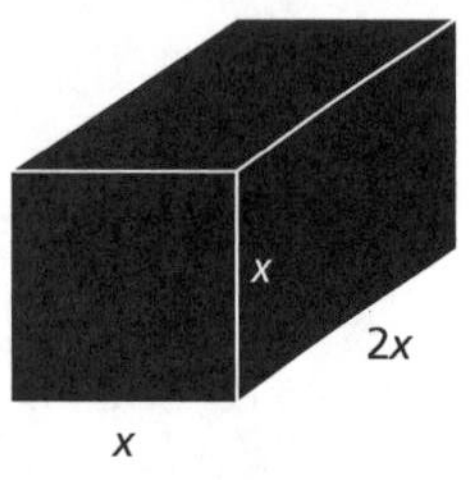

Test Your Understanding 37

D

If we are looking at how much extra Geoff needs, then we must look at the possibility that the measurements are too small.

Potentially the length could be as high as 204.9999

Similarly the width could be as high as 104.9999

This would give an area as high as 204.9999 × 104.9999 = 21,524.999...

This equates to an extra 7.6% compared to the original estimate of 20,000.

chapter

2

Summarising and analysing data – I

Chapter learning objectives

On completion of their studies students should be able to:

- explain the difference between data and information
- identify the characteristics of good information
- tabulate data
- prepare graphs, charts and diagrams
- explain the concept of a frequency distribution
- apply the Pareto distribution and the '80:20 rule'.

1 Introduction

Data, when first collected, are often not in a form that conveys much information. Such *raw* data, as they are called, may just consist of a list or table of individual data values: if the list or table is of any appreciable size then it may need some refinement before anyone can draw conclusions from it.

In this chapter we look at ways in which raw data can be collated into more meaningful formats, and then go on to see some pictorial representations of data that provides convenient ways of communicating them to others, having already looked at linear and quadratic graphs in chapter 1.

2 Data and information

Immediately after collection, in what is often termed its raw form, data is not very informative. We cannot learn about the situation from it or draw conclusions from it.

After it has been sorted and analysed, data becomes *information* that, it is to be hoped, is understandable and useful.

The word data means facts. Data consists of numbers, letters, symbols, raw facts, events and transactions which have been recorded but not yet processed into a form which is suitable for making decisions.

Information is data which has been processed in such a way that it has meaning to the person who receives it.

Illustration 1 – Data and information

In management accounting, the accounting system records a large number of facts (data) about materials, times, expenses and other transactions.

These facts are then classified and summarised to produce accounts, which are organised into reports designed to help management to plan and control the firm's activities.

Supplementary reading – Data and information

The difference between information and data

Sometimes the issue of the quality of data is raised and often there is not a clear understanding of this issue. Quality data has several characteristics including being:

- error free
- available at the right time
- available at the right place
- available to the appropriate individuals.

The arrival of the Internet has made it much easier for organisations and individuals to access data at the right time and the right place. However, at the same time the Internet have opened up questions about data being error free and about who can have access to it.

As well as the issue of data quality there is the question of how data, information and knowledge relate to one another. Russell Ackoff was one of the first people to speak of there being a hierarchy which he referred to as the Data Information Knowledge Wisdom (DIKW) Hierarchy. According to this model, data (which is by the way sometimes said to be a plural word as it is the actual plural for the word datum) are simple facts or figures or maybe even a photograph or an illustration. In this form data is unstructured and uninterrupted. Information comes from processing or structuring data in a meaningful way. Another way of looking at this is that information is interpreted data. An interesting story is told by Joan Magretta in her book *What Management is*? about Steve Jobs (the then CEO of Apple) which clearly illustrates the difference between data and information.

Despite its small share of the total market for personal computers, Apple has long been a leader in sales to schools and universities. When [the then] CEO Steve Jobs learned that Apple's share of computer sales to schools was 12.5 per cent in 1999, he was dismayed, but unless you're an industry analyst who knows the numbers cold, you won't appreciate just how dismayed he was. That's because, in 1998, Apple was the segment leader with a market share of 14.6 per cent. And, while Apple slipped to the number two spot in 1999, Dell grew and took the lead with 15.1 per cent. Alone each number is meaningless. Together they spell trouble, if you're Steve Jobs, you see a trend that you'd better figure out how to reverse. This isn't number crunching, it's sense making. (Magretta, 2003, p. 123)

In this example the 12.5 per cent was data and when it was seen in conjunction with the 15.1 per cent it became information.

Knowledge is again different to data and information. Knowledge is much more personal and the presence or absence of knowledge can normally only be seen through the actions of individuals. When knowledge is written down it effectively becomes information.

Finally with respect to wisdom it is difficult to define this concept. Wisdom has something to do with understanding or insight. It is to do with achieving a good long-term outcome in relation to the circumstances you are in.

The DIKW Hierarchy is often expressed graphically:

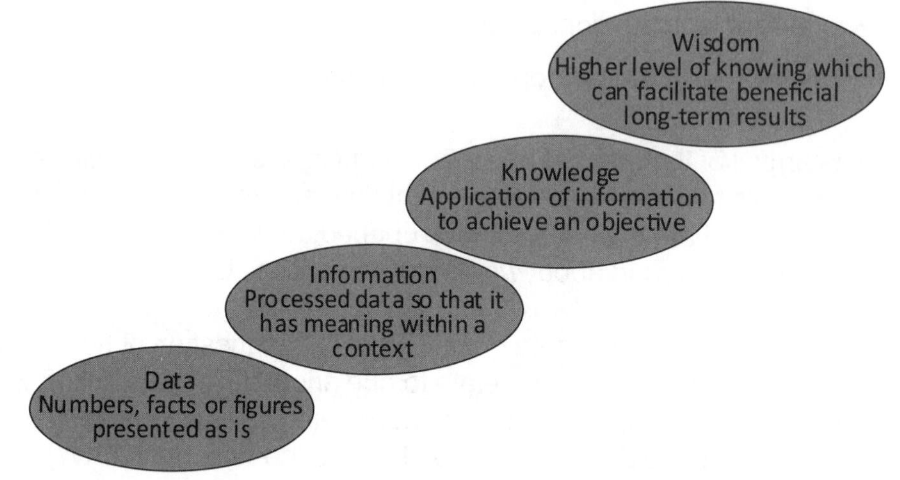

The Data Information Knowledge Wisdom (DIKW) Hierarchy

3 Characteristics of good information

Information is provided to management to assist them with planning, controlling operations and making decisions. Management decisions are likely to be better when they are provided with better quality information. The attributes of good information can be identified by the '**ACCURATE**' acronym as shown below:

A. Accurate

- The degree of accuracy depends on the reason why the information is needed.
- For example, reports may show figures to the nearest dollar, or nearest thousand dollars for a report on the performance of different divisions.
- Alternatively, when calculating the cost of a unit of output, managers may want the cost to be accurate to the nearest cent.

C. Complete

- Managers should be given all the information they need, but information should not be excessive.
- For example, a complete control report on cost variances should include all standard and actual costs necessary to understand the variance calculations.

C. Cost effective

- The value of information should exceed the cost of producing it.
- Management information is valuable, because it assists decision making.
- If a decision backed by information is different from what it would have been without the information, the value of information equates the amount of money saved as a result.

U. Understandable

- Use of technical language or jargon must be limited. For example, accountants must always be careful about the way in which they present financial information to non-financial managers.

R. Relevant

- The information contained within a report should be relevant to its purpose.
- Redundant parts should be removed.

A. Accessible

- Information should be accessible via the appropriate channels of communication (verbally, via a report, a memo, an email etc.).
- In the context if responsibility accounting, information about costs and revenues should be reported to the manager responsible, who is in a position to control them.

T. Timely

- Information should be provided to a manager in time for him/her to make decisions based on that information.

E. Easy to use!

4 Tabulating data

Tallying

Tallying is one way of converting raw data into a more concise format to make it easier to use.

Illustration 2 – Processing raw data

In order to monitor the efficiency of his department, the head of the finance section of a large company spot-checks the number of invoices left unprocessed at the end of each day. At the end of the first period of this check (26 working days), he has collected the following data:

1	5	3	3	2
3	0	4	1	4
3	3	2	1	2
1	1	0	3	6
5	0	3	4	2
3				

Collate this raw data into a more meaningful form.

Solution

By scanning the table we can see that all the values lie between 0 and 6 inclusive. It might be useful to find out how often each value in this range occurs in the table. This could be achieved simply by counting, but there are no safeguards against human error in doing this. Instead we use a tallying procedure, which is more accurate than counting, especially with large tables of figures. After going along the first row, the tally will look like:

Number of invoices left unprocessed	*Tally*
0	
1	I
2	I
3	II
4	
5	I
6	

As we go through the table, one 'notch' is put against the appropriate number each time it appears. For ease of counting, when each fifth notch is reached, it is separated out or crossed to make adding easier:

Number of invoices left unprocessed	*Tally*	*Total*
0	|||	3
1	|||||	5
2	||||	4
3	||||| |||	8
4	|||	3
5	||	2
6	|	1
		26

The 'totals' in the above table are called *frequencies* and the table is called the *frequency distribution* of the sample. Thus the frequency of 0 invoices is 3 and so on.

Test Your Understanding 1

The daily absentee rate at a small factory is recorded for one calendar month (22 working days):

Number of employees absent:

			6	8
7	3	5	5	6
8	2	4	5	7
6	2	3	3	4
8	3	5	4	7

Tally these data into a frequency distribution.

Grouped distributions

In some cases if we try to tally using each possible measurement taken, then we will still have too many values to be really useful.

A far more sensible approach is to tally the number of values in a certain range or *class*. The choice of classes is somewhat arbitrary, but should be such that they are neither too narrow, which would result in most of the frequencies being zero, as above, nor too wide, which would produce only a small number of classes and thereby tell us little.

As a rough guide, between four and twelve groups are often used.

Illustration 3 – Grouped distributions

In order to assist management negotiations with the trade unions over piecework rates, the management services department of a factory is asked to obtain information on how long it takes for a certain operation to be completed. Consequently, the members of the department measure the time it takes to complete 30 repetitions of the operation, at random occasions during a month. The times are recorded to the nearest tenth of a minute.

19.8	21.3	24.6	18.7	19.1	15.3
20.6	22.1	19.9	17.2	24.1	23.0
20.1	18.3	19.8	16.5	22.8	18.0
20.0	21.6	19.7	25.9	22.2	17.9
21.1	20.8	19.5	21.6	15.6	23.1

Form the frequency distribution of this sample.

Solution

A scan of the table shows that the smallest value is 15.3 minutes and the largest 25.9 minutes. If we tallied as in the previous illustration:

Time (minutes)	Tally
15.3	
15.4	
15.5	
...	
...	
25.9	

We should obtain a format of little more use than the original data, because most of the frequencies would be 0, interspersed by the occasional frequency of 1. Using ranges or classes we could tally as follows:

Time (minutes)	*Tally*	*Frequency*
15–under 17	III	3
17–under 19	IIIII	5
19–under 21	IIIII IIIII	10
21–under 23	IIIII II	7
23–under 25	IIII	4
25–under 27	I	1
		30

Even though some precision has been lost, this grouped frequency distribution is of considerably more use to the management services department than the raw data, because, for example, one can see at a glance where the bulk of the times lie, how often the time exceeds some target figure such as 23 minutes, say, and so on.

Test Your Understanding 2

At a factory the daily outputs, in units, of a certain product (A) are recorded during the same month as:

Daily output, units

			49	47
33	58	56	59	45
39	53	51	44	49
37	53	48	47	40
36	50	55	44	42

Tally these data into a frequency distribution using the intervals 30–under 35; 35–under 40; and so on.

Supplementary reading – Continuous and discrete data

Discrete variables

Discrete variables can consist of certain values. For example the number of invoices could be

0 or 1 or 2 or …
but never 1.6, 2.3 and so on.

Continuous variables

On the other hand, the time taken to undertake a certain operation can theoretically take a value to any level of precision:

20.2 minutes
20.19 minutes
20.186 minutes
20.1864 minutes and so on.

In practise the issue it is the degree of accuracy to which management want to measure. However, a number of invoices *cannot* be measured any more accurately than in whole numbers.

Tallying

This distinction has a number of consequences. Here, it can affect the way we tally. Continuous variables, such as the times to undertake a certain operation, can rarely be tallied as individual values, since few of them will coincide to give meaningfully large frequencies.

Classifying is therefore almost always necessary with continuous variables.

As Illustration 3 demonstrated. discrete variables can sometimes be tallied with single values.

However, with a wider range from (0 to 100, for example), the problem of having frequencies being mostly 0, interspersed with a few 1 s, could still arise: it is therefore sometimes necessary to use classes for discrete data too. When doing this try to define classes so it is clear where measurements go:

e.g. from 10 to below 20, from 20 to below 30, etc

Test Your Understanding 3

At the factory mentioned earlier the daily outputs of a different product (Q) are measured to the nearest kg and are recorded as:

Daily output, kg

			383	351
362	377	392	369	351
368	382	398	389	360
359	373	381	390	354
369	375	372	376	361

Tally these data into a frequency distribution using the intervals 350–under 360; 360–under 370 and so on.

5 Cumulative frequency distribution

It is sometimes helpful to develop the idea of frequency further and to look at *cumulative frequencies*. These are the number of data values up to – or up to and including – a certain point. They can easily be compiled as running totals from the corresponding frequency distribution, as the following will illustrate.

Illustration 4 – Cumulative frequency distributions

Form the cumulative frequency distributions from the data given in Illustrations 2 and 3.

Hence estimate:

(a) for illustration 2, how often there are more than four invoices left unprocessed at the end of the day;

(b) for illustration 3, how often the time taken beats the target of 23 minutes.

Solution

The frequency distribution of the number of unprocessed invoices can be used to obtain:

Number of invoices left unprocessed (less than or equal)	*Cumulative frequency*	
0	3	(simply the frequency of '0')
1	8	(i.e. 3 + 5)
2	12	(i.e. 8 + 4)
3	20	
4	23	
5	25	
6	26	

In the same way, for the distribution of times taken to undertake the operation:

Time (minutes) (less than)	Cumulative frequency	
15	0	(no values below 15 minutes)
17	3	(frequency of the first class)
19	8	(i.e. 3 + 5)
21	18	(8 + 10)
23	25	
25	29	
27	30	

In the latter example, we have to take the *upper* limit of each class to ensure that all the values in the class are definitely *less than* it. We must use 'less than' as opposed to 'less than or equal' here because it corresponds to the way the frequency table has been compiled.

It is now a simple matter to estimate:

(a) 26 – 23 = 3 occasions out of 26: that is, 11.5 per cent;

(b) 25 occasions out of 30: that is, 83.3 per cent.

How reliable these estimates are depends on how typical or representative is the period or month in which the samples are taken.

We shall see further applications of cumulative frequency in the following section.

Test Your Understanding 4

Form the **cumulative** frequency distribution for the data in TYU 2 where you obtained the following distribution:

Output of A units	No. of days (frequency)
30–under 35	1
35–under 40	3
40–under 45	4
45–under 50	6
50–under 55	4
55–under 60	4

6 Pie charts

Many people find it easier to understand numerical information if it is presented in a pictorial form, rather than as a table of figures.

There are a number of simple charts and graphs commonly used to represent business data. In this section we look at one of the most basic: pie charts.

Pie charts are a very easily understood way of depicting the percentage or proportional breakdown of a total into various categories. They are so called because the total is represented by a circle, with each component shown as a sector with area proportional to percentage. Overall, the chart looks rather like a 'pie' with 'slices' in it.

Sometimes two pie charts are used to compare two totals, along with the manner in which they are broken down. In such cases the areas of the pies, in other words the squares of their radii, are proportional to the total frequencies.

Illustration 5 – Pie charts

A company trades in five distinct geographical markets. In the last financial year, its turnover was:

	$m
UK	59.3
EU, outside UK	61.6
Europe, outside EU	10.3
North America	15.8
Australasia	9.9
Total	156.9

Display these turnover figures as a pie chart.

Solution

The first step is to calculate the percentage of the total turnover for each region:

	%
UK: (59.3/156.9) =	37.8
EU	39.3
Europe	6.6
North America	10.1
Australasia	6.3

Second, in order to make each 'slice' of the 'pie' proportional in area to these percentages, the whole circle (360°) has to be apportioned into five sections:

	Angle,°
UK: 37.8% of 360° =	136.1
EU	141.5
Europe	23.8
North America	36.4
Australasia	22.7

Alternatively, the angles can be calculated directly as proportions of 360°, for example,

360° × (59.3/156.9) = 136.1°
360° × (61.6/156.9) = 141.5°, etc

The resulting pie chart is then.

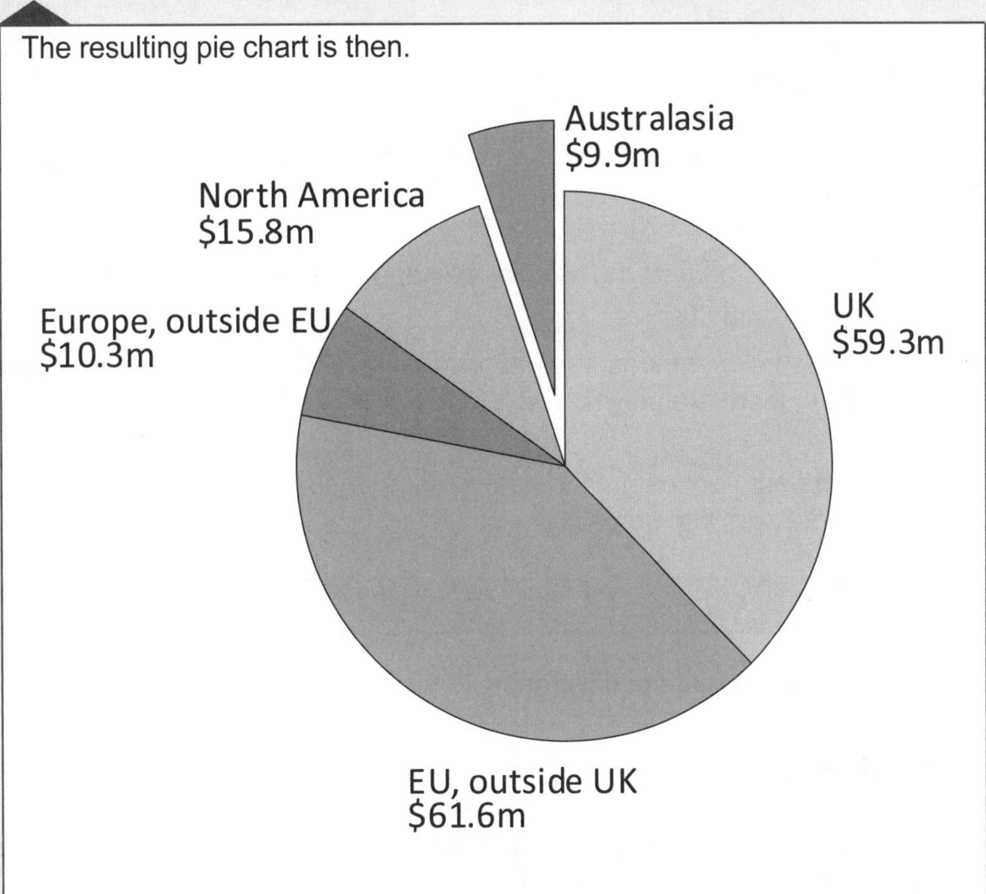

Note how the Australasia 'slice' is pulled out for emphasis. This is easy to do when using a computer.

Test Your Understanding 5

Display the following data using a pie chart:

Sales of furniture	*($000)*
Settees	34
Armchairs	27
Dining sets	38
Shelving	18
Others	12

7 Bar charts

Bar charts are a simple way of representing actual data pictorially, subject to the following rules:

- Distances against the vertical axis are measurements and represent numerical data.
- Horizontal *distances have no meaning. There is no horizontal axis or scale*, there are only labels.

Bar charts are very useful for making comparisons between different data items, data sets and so on.

Illustration 6 – Bar charts

Represent the data of Illustration 5 as a bar chart.

Solution

For this example we want to illustrate the difference in turnover between the various geographical markets.

To draw this chart, it is simply a matter of drawing five vertical 'bars', with heights to represent the various turnover figures, and just labels for regions in the horizontal direction.

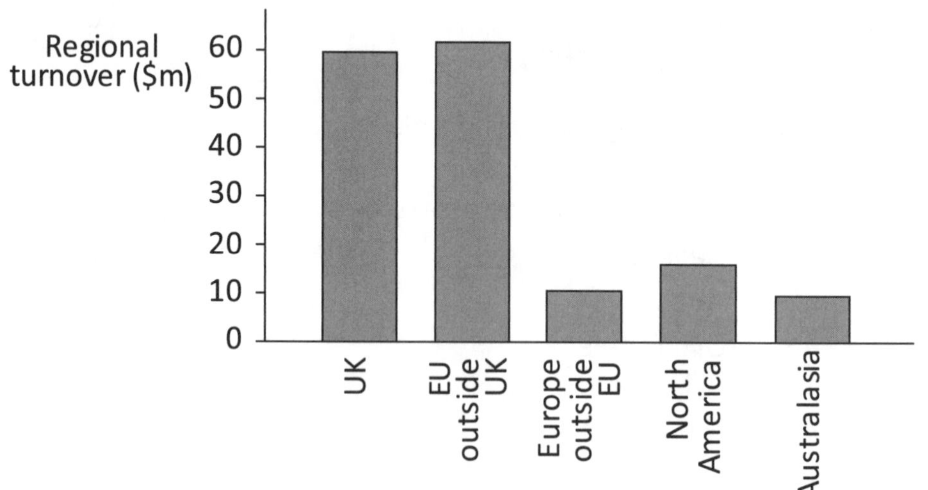

Using this chart it is easy to see, for example, that revenue is highest in the EU outside the UK.

There are a number of variations on such a basic bar chart, used to display more data or more complex data. An example will show just one.

Illustration 7 – Bar charts continued

A rival company to the one mentioned earlier trades in the same five geographical markets. Its turnover in the last financial year was:

	$m
UK	60.2
EU, outside UK	69.0
Europe, outside EU	11.1
North America	18.0
Australasia	8.8
Total	167.1

Display the turnover figures for both companies on a single chart.

There are at least two types of bar chart which can be used here: a *multiple bar chart* and a *compound* (or *component or stacked*) bar chart:

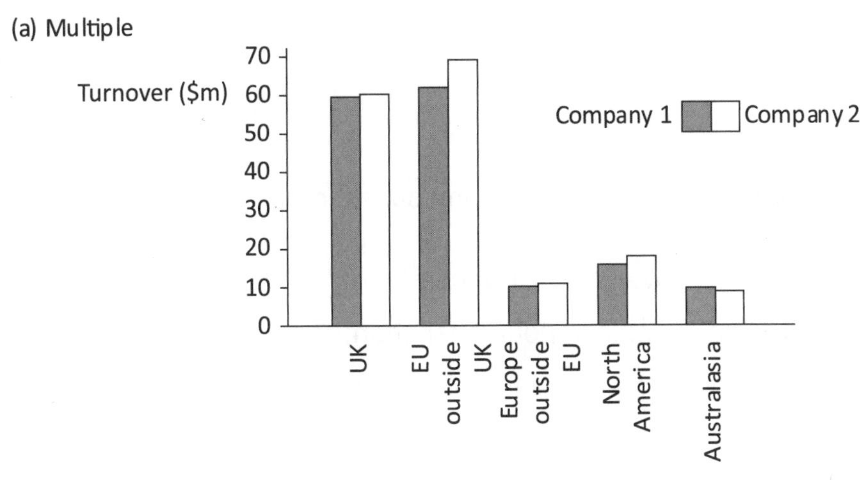

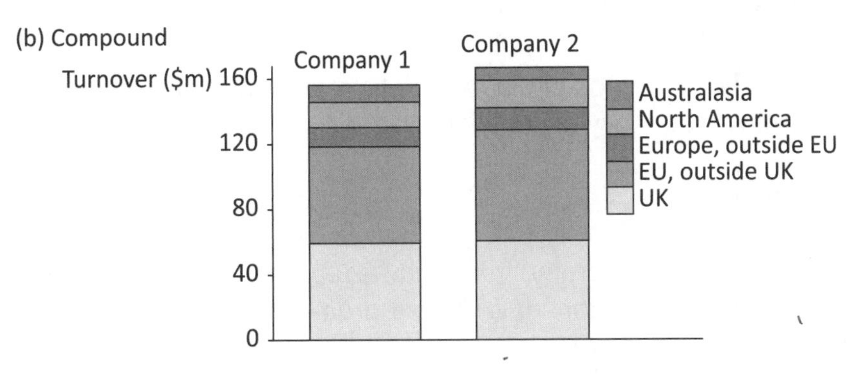

The multiple bar chart readily displays how well the two companies have performed in each market, but not so clearly in total. Conversely, the relative total performance of the two companies can be seen easily from the compound bar chart, but not so the breakdown by region.

At present you cannot be asked to actually draw charts during a computer-based assessment. Exam questions therefore take the form of labelling charts, calculating particular values, selecting a type of chart appropriate to particular data and drawing conclusions from charts.

Test Your Understanding 6

The following are percentage distributions of household income in two regions:

Income ($000)	*Region A*	*Region B*
0–10	25	15
10–20	30	29
20–30	32	38
30–40	10	9
40 or more	3	9
Total	100	100

Display the data by the following bar charts:

A region A by a simple bar chart;

B region A by a compound bar chart;

C both regions by a multiple bar chart.

8 Histograms and ogives

In this section we look at diagrammatic representations of frequency and cumulative frequency distributions.

Histograms

In the examples so far, the frequency is represented by the *height* of a block in a bar chart, for instance. With *histograms* the frequency is represented by the *area* of a block or rectangle.

More specifically, a histogram is a diagram consisting of rectangles whose *area* is proportional to the frequency of a variable and whose width is equal to the class interval. The *x*-axis is the variable being measured and the *y*-axis is the corresponding frequency.

Consider the following illustration.

Illustration 8 – Histograms

Draw a histogram for the data in Illustration 3

Solution

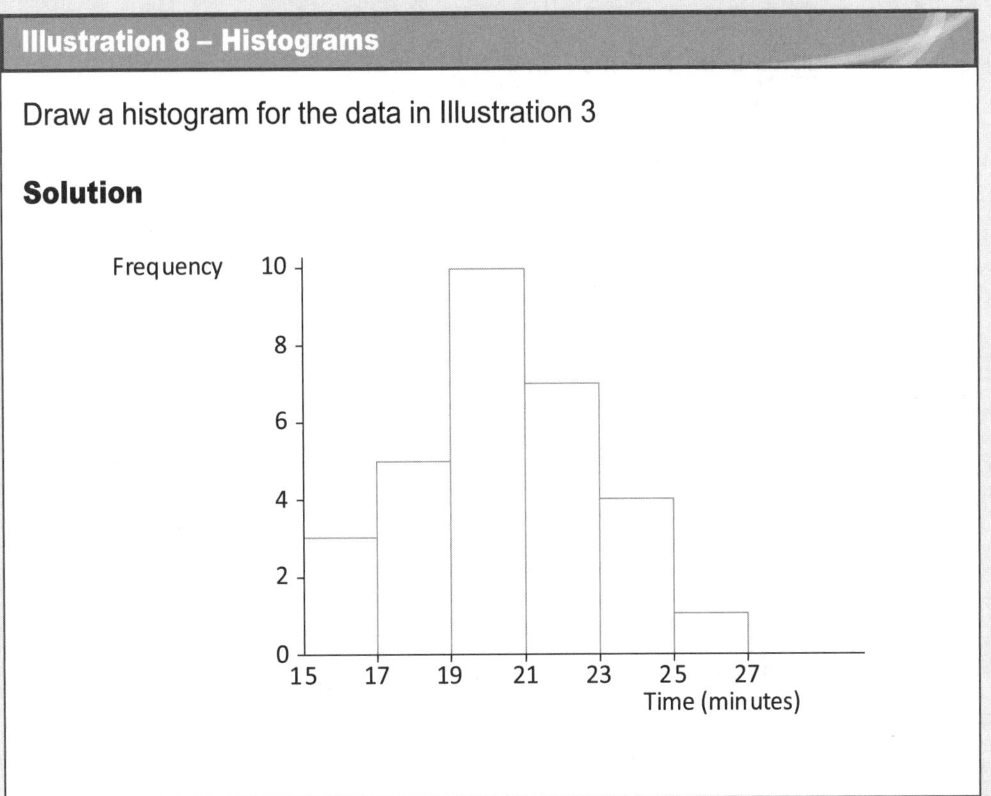

At first glance this looks no different from what we have seen before. However, when we look at examples with *uneven* class sizes, we will see that representing frequency by height alone can be misleading and a switch to areas (histograms) gives a fairer representation of the underlying data. This is discussed in more detail below.

Ogives

An *ogive* is a graph of the cumulative frequency distributions met earlier.

The *x*-axis is the variable being measured and the *y*-axis is the corresponding cumulative frequency, the x- and y-values being plotted in exactly the same way as we discussed earlier. With a discrete variable, intermediate x-values have no meaning in reality (recall 1.6 invoices) and so the ogive would consist of a series of discrete points. It is usual therefore not to draw it. With a continuous variable, the intermediate values do have a meaning, and so it makes sense to join the plotted points.

This can be done with a series of straight lines, which is tantamount to assuming that the values are evenly spread throughout their classes.

Illustration 9 – Ogives

(a) Draw an ogive for the data in Illustration 3

Solution

The cumulative frequency distribution was

Time (minutes) (less than)	Cumulative frequency
15	0
17	3
19	8
21	18
23	25
25	29
27	30

This gives the following ogive

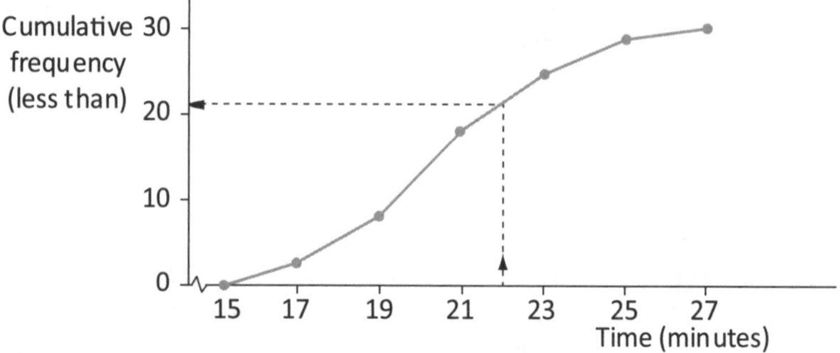

Note:

The horizontal axis has been started at 15 rather than 0 to make it easier to read. Having part of the of axis missing like this is known as a broken scale.

Once we have an ogive we can use it to estimate probabilities.

(b) For example, suppose the management wishes to reduce the target time for the operation to 22 minutes. Assuming the distribution of times remains unaltered, how often will this target be met?

Solution

First of all, it is not possible to answer this as a straight reading from the cumulative frequency distribution, as 22 minutes does not correspond to a value in the table. If we look at the ogive, however, we can estimate how many of the 30 occasions took less than 22 minutes, by reading off the graph, as shown.

Thus, we estimate that the target will be met on 21.5 out of every 30 occasions: that is, 72 per cent of the time.

Unequal class sizes

In some questions the class sizes are not constant. If we draw block heights equal to frequencies, we exaggerate those with larger class widths. Thus, in a case like this, where there are *unequal* class widths, one must compensate by adjusting the heights of some of the blocks.

Instead of the height it is now the **area** of each block that reflect the frequency.

e.g

Illustration 10 – Unequal class sizes

The compiler of a careers guide is given the following information on the initial salaries of graduates entering a certain profession during the year prior to the guide's publication.

Annual salary ($)	*Number of graduate entrants*
9,000–under 11,000	108
11,000–under 13,000	156
13,000–under 14,000	94
14,000–under 14,500	80
14,500–under 15,000	25

In order to convey the information in a quickly assimilated form, the compiler decides to represent it as a histogram. Draw this histogram and frequency polygon.

Solution

Before referring to the histogram, we point out that, strictly speaking, the data here are discrete. The 'gaps', however, are only of width equal to one cent, which is very small compared with thousands of dollars. We therefore effectively treat this as a continuous case.

If we now draw the histogram as usual, we obtain the following:

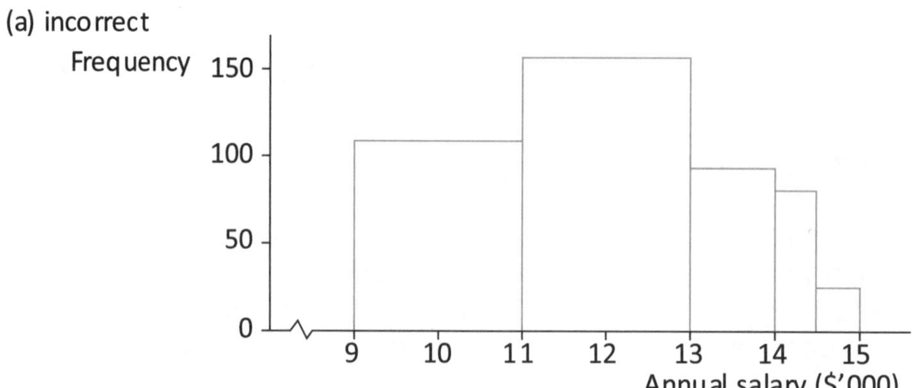

Close inspection of this will show that some discrepancies have arisen.

For example, the left-hand block is supposed to represent approximately four times more graduates than the right-hand block, and yet the ratio of the size of these two blocks is nearer to 16. There are other examples of disproportion in the size of the blocks, the underlying reason being that, by drawing block heights equal to frequencies, we exaggerate those with larger class widths.

Thus, in a case like this, where there are *unequal* class widths, one must compensate by adjusting the heights of some of the blocks:

13,000-under 14,000 is half the width of the first two, so	Height = 94 × 2 = 188
14,000-under 14,500 is quarter the width,	Height = 80 × 4 = 320
14,500-under 15,000	Height = 25 × 4 = 100

(Alternatively, we could leave the frequencies of the last two classes unaltered, and divide the frequency of the first class by four and so on.)

This would leave the shape of the histogram as:

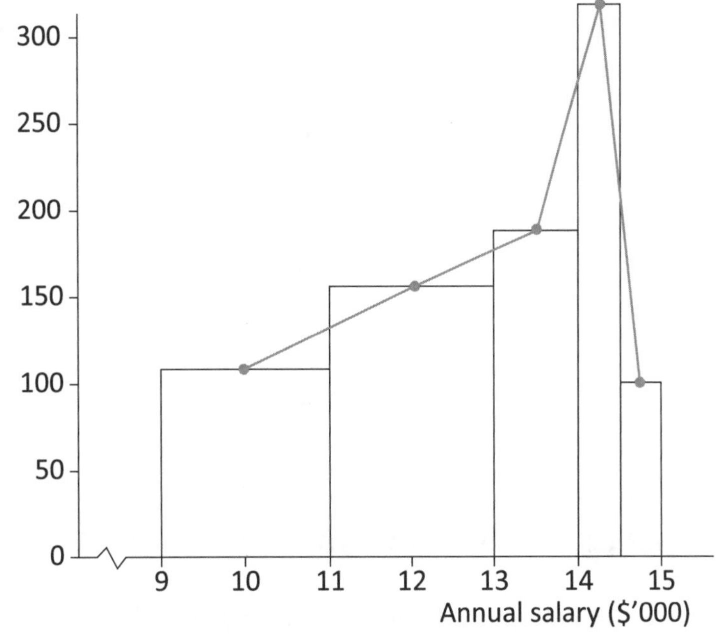

Formally, it is the area of the block that is proportional to the frequency. It will be noted that the areas of the blocks are now in the correct proportion and that the vertical axis of the graph can no longer be labelled 'frequency', but is now 'frequency density'.

Before leaving this example, it is worth pointing out that the ogive of this distribution would present no extra problems. As this consists only of plotting the upper limit of each class against cumulative frequency, the unequal class intervals do not affect matters.

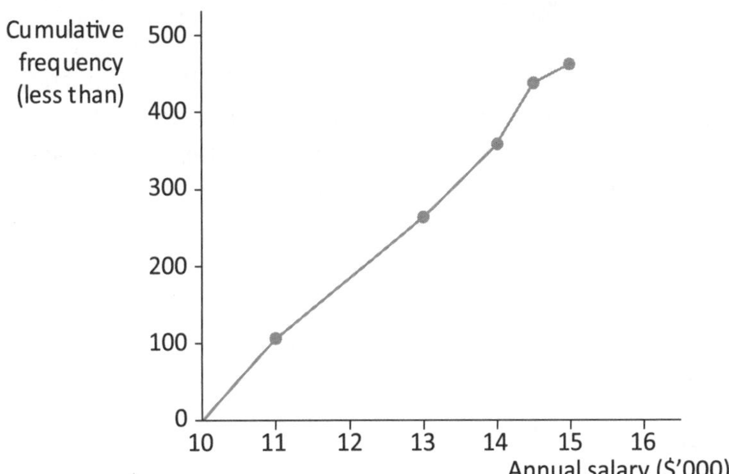

Test Your Understanding 7

Plot the histogram for the following distribution:

Time taken to complete repeated task (minutes)	*Frequency*
10–under 20	63
20–under 30	52
30–under 40	46
40–under 60	60
60–under 80	48
80–under 120	40

Test Your Understanding 8

Plot the histogram for the following distribution:

Weekly sales ($000)	*Frequency*
Under 5	8
5–under 10	23
10–under 20	98
20–under 30	80
30 and over	22

Test Your Understanding 9

In a histogram, the common class width is $10.00. For analysis purposes, the analyst has set one class width at $12.50 and the frequency recorded is 80 respondents. To maintain the accuracy of the histogram, the score that must be plotted is:

A 48

B 64

C 80

D 100

It is quite a frequent exam question to work out the heights of bars where there are unequal intervals.

9 Pareto analysis – The 80-20 rule

Pareto analysis was proposed by an Italian economist Vilfredo Pareto to describe how a relatively small part of a population may be so important. Pareto initially referred to wealth among individuals. He pointed out that a small number of individuals own a large portion of the wealth of any society. This idea is sometimes expressed more simply as the Pareto principle or the 80-20 rule.

In a business context the 80-20 rule states that a small number of clients will be responsible for a large proportion of the turnover, or a small number of inventory items will be responsible for a large amount of sales, or a small number of staff will present a disproportionate level of challenges to the management. When the term '80-20 rule' is used in this it does not always mean that it will actually be 20 per cent of the clients that produce 80 per cent of the profit as sometime it may be a smaller percentage like 10 which will produce the over whelming share of the profit.

In business the 80-20 rule essentially says that one should identify the really important elements of the business and focus the majority of one's time and effort on these elements.

For example, suppose we have a business with 21 different product lines. The first thing we need to do is order them by sales. Suppose this gives the following table:

Product Line	No of Items	Unit Sales
F	3	1720
U	20	1513
L	6	1234
T	17	1011
I	4	891
D	2	656
A	1	598
R	12	521
G	3	484
J	4	309
B	1	267
O	9	102
Q	11	70
N	7	55
K	5	32
S	13	18
P	9	10
H	3	5
M	6	4
E	2	2
C	1	1
Total		**9502**

Data sorted by UNIT SALES

The second step is to calculate the percentage of the total that each product line represents. To do this the following formula is entered into cell F7.

= E7/$E$28 *100

This formula can be copied to the range F8:F27

Now the third step is to calculate the cumulative sales in column G. Into cell G7 enter:

= F7

And into cell G8 enter:

= G7 + F8

This formula can be copied into the range G9:G27.

The completed 80-20 rule table would then be as follows:

	A	B	C	D	E	F	G	H
3			**Application of Paretos Law to a range**					
4								
5								
6			**Product Line**	**No of Items**	**Unit Sales**	**% of total**	***Cum. Total***	
7			F	3	1720	18%	*18%*	
8			U	20	1513	16%	*34%*	
9			L	6	1234	13%	*47%*	
10			T	17	1011	11%	*58%*	
11			I	4	891	9%	*67%*	
12			D	2	656	7%	*74%*	
13			A	1	598	6%	***80%***	
14			R	12	521	5%	*86%*	
15			G	3	484	5%	*91%*	
16			J	4	309	3%	*94%*	
17			B	1	267	3%	*97%*	
18			O	9	102	1%	*98%*	
19			Q	11	70	1%	*99%*	
20			N	7	55	1%	*99%*	
21			K	5	32	0%	*99%*	
22			S	13	18	0%	*100%*	
23			P	9	10	0%	*100%*	
24			H	3	5	0%	*100%*	
25			M	6	4	0%	*100%*	
26			E	2	2	0%	*100%*	
27			C	1	1	0%	*100%*	
28			**Total**		**9503**			
29								

Completed table showing cumulative total and 80% marker

From this analysis it may be seen that Products F, U, L, T, I, D and A are the best performers and it is on these products that most effort should be expended.

Chapter Summary

Data, information and variables

- *Data* often needs converting into *information* to make it more useful.
- *Quality* information satisfies the *ACCURATE* acronym.
- *Tallying* is a more reliable method of compiling frequency distributions from raw data than is mere counting. Very often we have to tally into classes rather than individual values.
- *Continuous* variables can, in theory, be measured to any level of precision, while discrete variables can take only certain values, e.g. integers, or whole numbers.
- *The cumulative frequency* of a value is the number of readings up to (or up to and including) that value.

Representing data in charts and graphs

- *Pie charts* represent the breakdown of a total figure into percentage component parts. Each sector of the 'pie' has an area proportional to the percentage it is representing.
- *Bar charts, multiple-bar charts* and *compound-bar* (or *component-bar*) charts represent data through vertical 'bars' whose lengths are measured against a vertical scale, as with ordinary graphs.
- Sometimes a table is to be preferred to a chart, but tables need to be kept as simple as possible.
- The *histogram* and the *ogive* are graphical representations of a frequency distribution and a cumulative frequency distribution respectively. If intervals are unequal, calculate frequency density before drawing the histogram.
- *Pareto Analysis* – The 80-20 rule is discussed and an example provided.

10 Further Practice Questions

Test Your Understanding 10

An ogive is:

A another name for a histogram.

B a chart showing any linear relationship.

C a chart showing a non-linear relationship.

D a graph of a cumulative frequency distribution.

Test Your Understanding 11

In a histogram, one class is three-quarters of the width of the remaining classes. If the score in that class is 21, the correct height to plot on the histogram is:

A 15.75

B 21

C 28

D 42

Test Your Understanding 12

A pie chart shows total sales of $350,000 and a second pie chart shows total sales of $700,000. If drawn correctly to scale, the ratio of the radius of the second pie chart to the first pie chart, to two decimal places, should be:

A 1.41 times

B 2 times

C 2.82 times

D 3.14 times

Test Your Understanding 13

In the equation $y = 5 + 4x$, what does the '4' tell us?

A y increases by 4 whenever x increases by 1.

B $y = 4$ when $x = 0$.

C 4 is the intercept on the y-axis.

D The slope is 1/4.

Test Your Understanding 14

A pie chart is used to display the following data:

percentage voting for P 52
percentage voting for Q 32
percentage voting for R 11

What angle in degrees on the pie chart will represent R's share of the vote?

A 39.6

B 11.0

C 44.4

D 3.1

Test Your Understanding 15

Which of the following is not recommended in tabulation?

A Rounding.

B Amalgamating unimportant sections.

C Using percentages where necessary to make comparisons.

D Keeping maximum accuracy.

Test Your Understanding 16

Categorise each of the following variables as either discrete or continuous:

A Age of 5 years.

B Time of 2.5 hours.

C Output of 12,000 kg

D Output of 5,000 units.

Test Your Understanding 17

Convert the following distribution of the number of employees absent per day into a cumulative frequency distribution:

Number absent	*Frequency*
0	10
1	15
2	7
3	4
4	2

Test Your Understanding 18

A cumulative frequency distribution of weekly wages is as follows:

Weekly wage	*Cumulative frequency*
Less than $150	45
Less than $200	125
Less than $300	155
Less than $400	170
Less than $600	175

A How many were paid less than $300?

B How many were paid more than $200?

C How many were paid between $200 and $300?

Test Your Understanding 19

If the following data is to be illustrated by means of a histogram and if the standard interval is taken to be 10 kg, calculate the heights of the bars of the histogram (to the nearest whole number).

Weight	*Frequency*
0–10	65
10–20	89
20–40	140
40–60	76
60–100	64

Test Your Understanding 20

Which of the following correctly describe(s) a frequency polygon?

A A graph of frequency on values for ungrouped discrete data.

B A graph of frequency on interval mid-points for continuous data with equal width intervals.

C A graph of frequency on interval upper limits for continuous data with equal width intervals.

D A graph joining the mid-points of the top sides of the bars of a histogram.

Test Your Understanding 21

The following data are to be illustrated by means of a pie chart. Calculate the angles (in degrees) that correspond to each category (to the nearest whole number).

Categories	%
A	42
B	38
C	15
D	5

Test Your Understanding 22

Associate the following types of bar charts with the examples given:

Bar charts

A Simple

B Multiple

C Compound

Examples

P Two adjacent bars then a gap and two more and a further two after a final gap.

Q Eight separate bars.

R Three bars each of which is divided into four component parts.

Charts

The following information is relevant to the next 5 TYUs.

	Number of pies sold			
Pie flavourings	*1995*	*1996*	*1997*	*1998*
Chocolate	240	305	290	360
Toffee	120	135	145	210
Apple	70	105	125	190
Banana	30	35	40	35

Test Your Understanding 23

The following compound bar chart illustrates the 1995 section of the above data. What are the heights of the four horizontal lines in the bar?

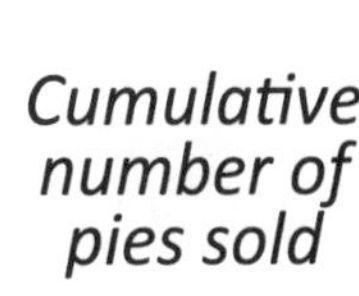

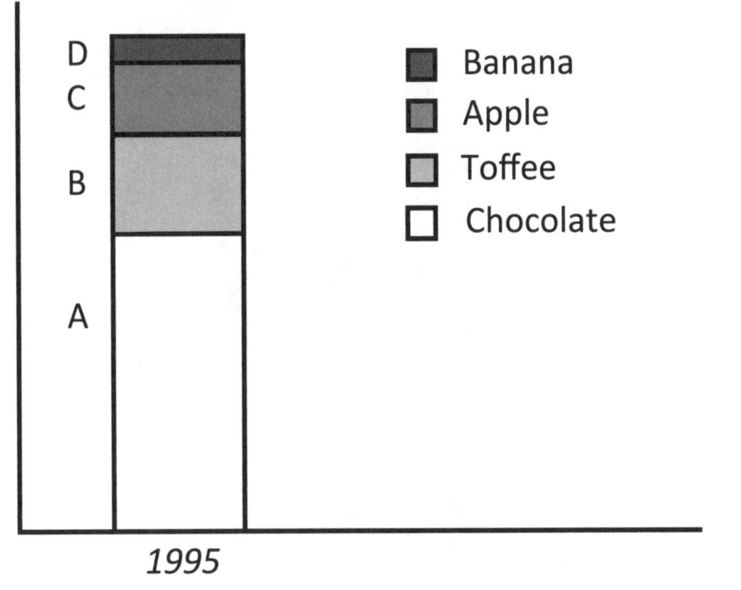

Test Your Understanding 24

Which of the following statements correctly describe aspects of the data which are illustrated by the 1995 bar?

A In 1995, chocolate sold more than all the other flavours put together.

B Sales rose from 1995 to 1996.

C In 1995, banana was the least popular flavour.

D The popularity of banana increased very little over the 4 years.

E In 1995, toffee was less popular than apple.

F In 1995, chocolate was the most popular flavour.

Test Your Understanding 25

The data may be illustrated by the following chart. What type of chart is it?

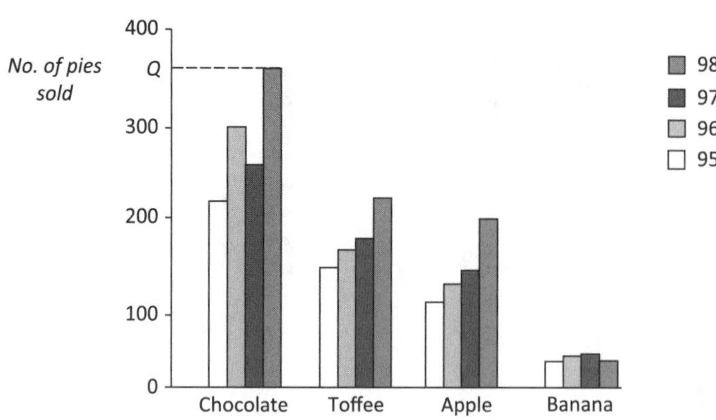

A Multiple bar chart.

B Simple bar chart.

C Histogram.

D Pictogram.

E Ogive.

F Component bar chart.

Test Your Understanding 26

Which of the following statements correctly describe aspects of the data which are illustrated by the chart in TYU25?

A Sales of chocolate rose steadily over the 4 years.

B Banana was the least popular over the entire period.

C There was a big increase in the sales of all flavours in 1998.

D After 1995 sales of apple began to catch up with those of toffee.

E Total sales have fallen over the four-year period.

Data classification/frequency diagram

The managers of a sales department have recorded the number of successful sales made by their 50 telesales persons for one week, and the raw scores are reproduced below:

20	10	17	22	35	43	29	34	12	24
24	32	34	13	40	22	34	21	39	12
10	49	32	33	29	26	33	34	34	22
24	17	18	34	37	32	17	36	32	43
12	27	43	32	35	26	38	32	20	21

Sales persons who achieve fewer than twenty sales are required to undertake further training.

Test Your Understanding 27

Complete the table displaying the data as a grouped frequency distribution.

Sales	*Frequency*
10–14	6
15–19	4
20–24	A
25–29	B
C	14
D	6
40–44	E
45–49	F

Test Your Understanding 28

Suppose the frequency distribution for the data was as follows:

Sales	*Frequency*	*Cumulative frequency*
10 and under 15	6	G
15 and under 20	12	H
20 and under 25	17	I
25 and under 30	7	J

Find the cumulative frequencies G, H, I and J.

Test Your Understanding 29

Suppose the frequency distribution and cumulative frequencies were as follows:

Sales	*Frequency*	*Cumulative frequency*
10 and under 15	7	7
15 and under 20	16	23
20 and under 25	13	36
25 and under 30	4	40

Based on this the following cumulative frequency graph has been drawn.

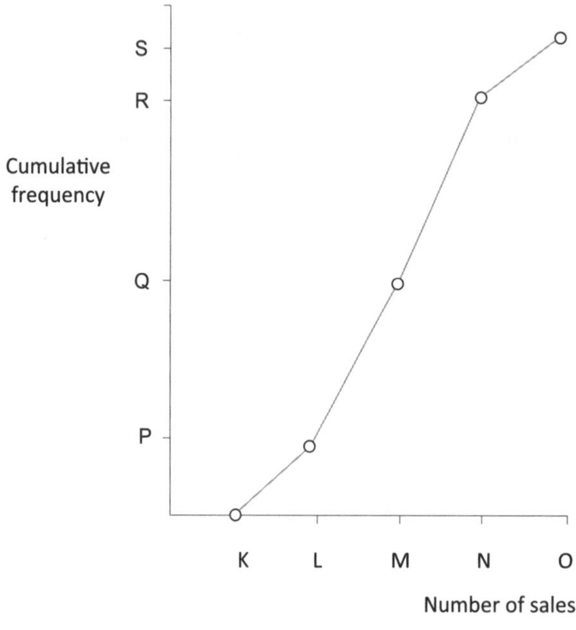

Find the values corresponding to the letters K–S.

Test Your Understanding 30

In the distribution given in TYU 29, what percentage of the sales force sold less than 20?

Test your understanding answers

Test Your Understanding 1

No. of employees absent	No. of days (frequency)
2	2
3	4
4	3
5	4
6	3
7	3
8	3

Test Your Understanding 2

Output of A units	No. of days (frequency)
30–under 35	1
35–under 40	3
40–under 45	4
45–under 50	6
50–under 55	4
55–under 60	4

Test Your Understanding 3

Output of Q kg	No. of days (frequency)
350–under 360	4
360–under 370	6
370–under 380	5
380–under 390	4
390–under 400	3

Test Your Understanding 4

Output of A units	*Cumulative frequency*
under 30	0
under 35	1
under 40	4
under 45	8
under 50	14
under 55	18
under 60	22

Test Your Understanding 5

Category	*Sales*	*Angle,°*
Settees	34	95
Armchairs	27	75
Dining sets	38	106
Shelving	18	50
Others	12	34
Total	129	360

The angle is given by 360° × (sales/total sales), for example 360° × 34/129 =95, rounded to the nearest degree. The resulting pie chart is shown on the following page.

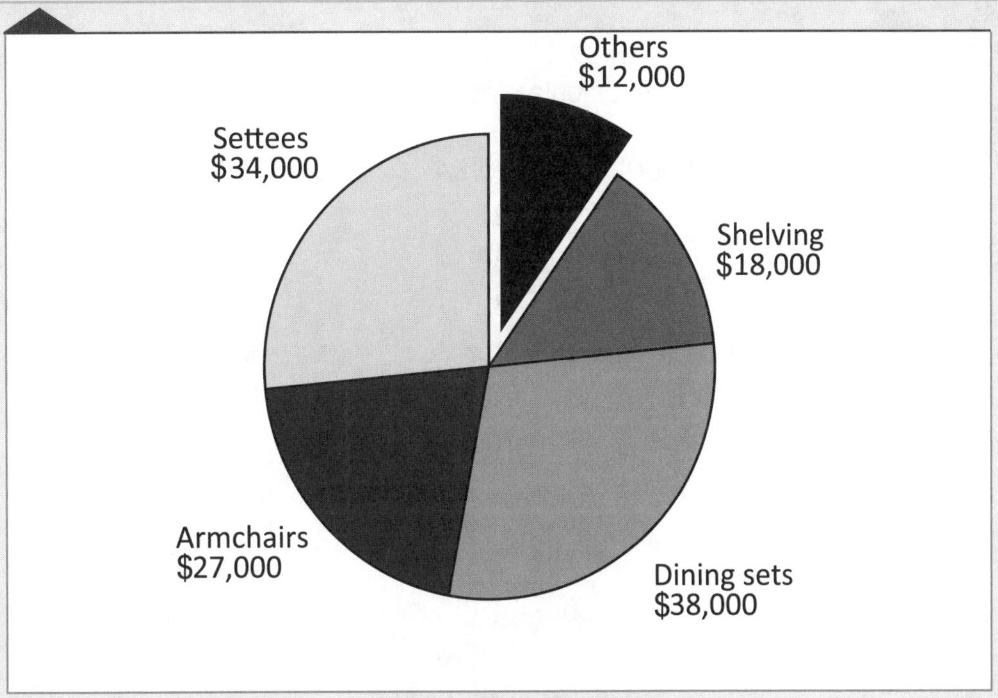

Test Your Understanding 6

(a)

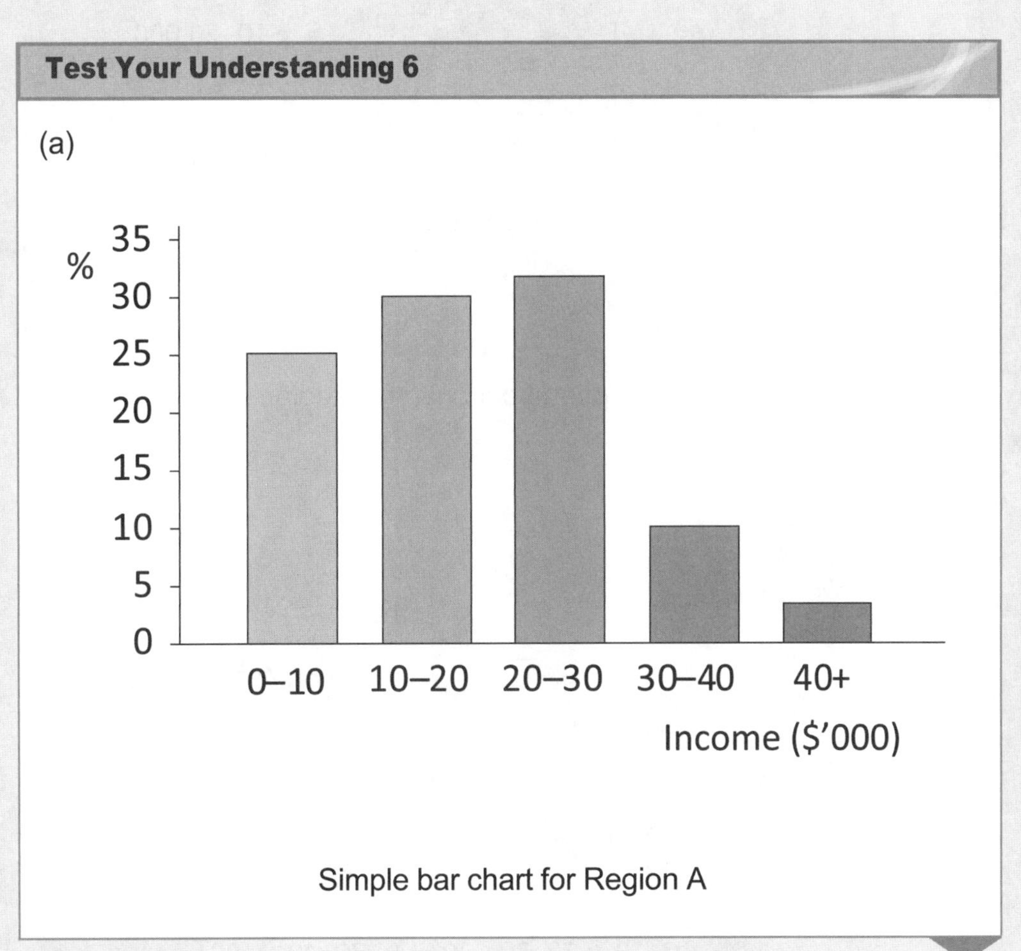

Simple bar chart for Region A

(b) It is easiest to first calculate cumulative frequencies:

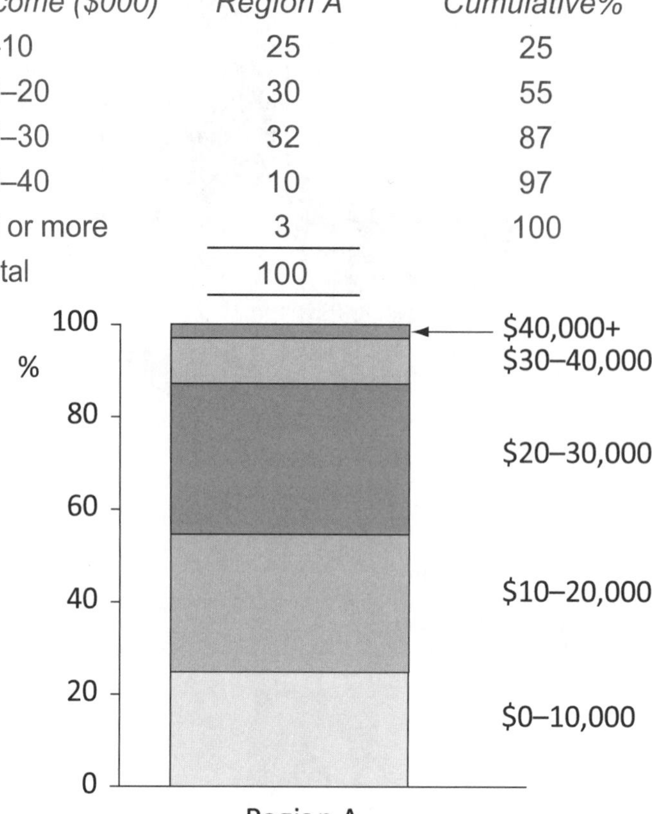

Income ($000)	*Region A*	*Cumulative%*
0–10	25	25
10–20	30	55
20–30	32	87
30–40	10	97
40 or more	3	100
Total	100	

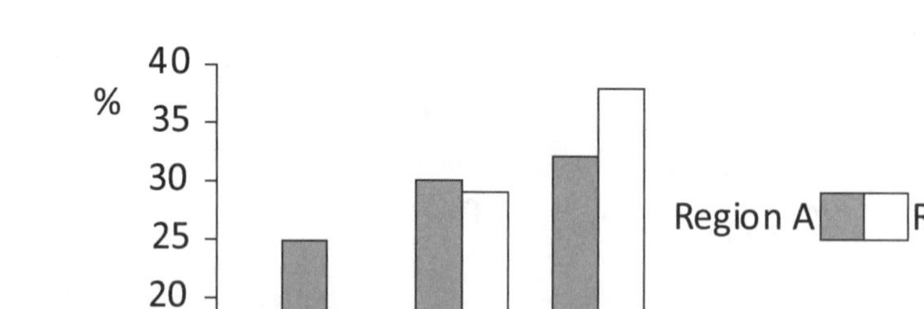

Compound bar chart for Region A

(c)

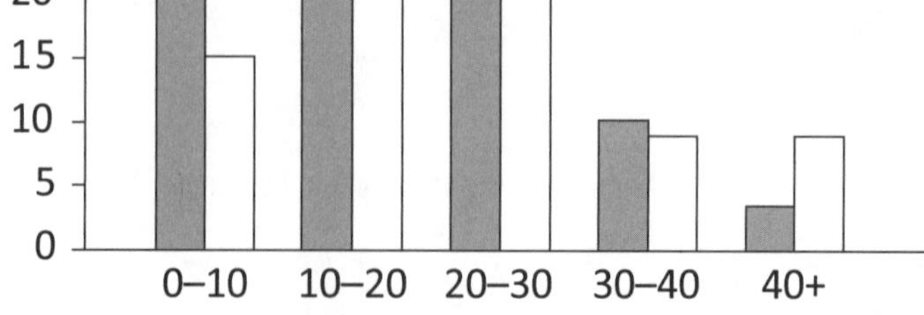

Multiple bar chart

Test Your Understanding 7

Time taken (minutes)	*Class width*	*Frequency*	*Frequency density*
10–20	10	63	63
20–30	10	52	52
30–40	10	46	46
40–60	20	60	60/2 = 30
60–80	20	48	48/2 = 24
80–120	40	40	40/4 = 10

We have taken the standard class width to be ten minutes. For the two classes whose widths are twice the standard, we have divided frequency by two to get the frequency density. We have divided by four for the final class, whose width is four times the standard. The figure below shows the histogram.

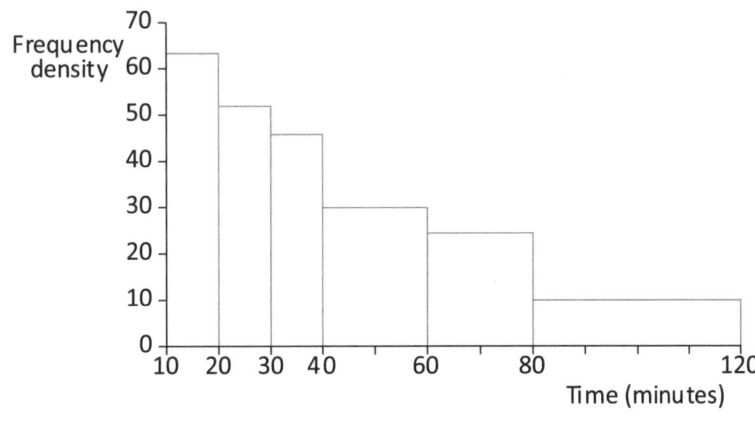

Test Your Understanding 8

We have closed the two open intervals, taking the widths of the adjacent intervals as our guide. We have then calculated frequency densities using a standard interval width of five units.

Weekly sales ($000)	*Frequency*	*Frequency density*
Under 5	8	8
5–under 10	23	23
10–under 20	98	98/2 = 49
20–under 30	80	40
30–under 40	22	11

The histogram is:

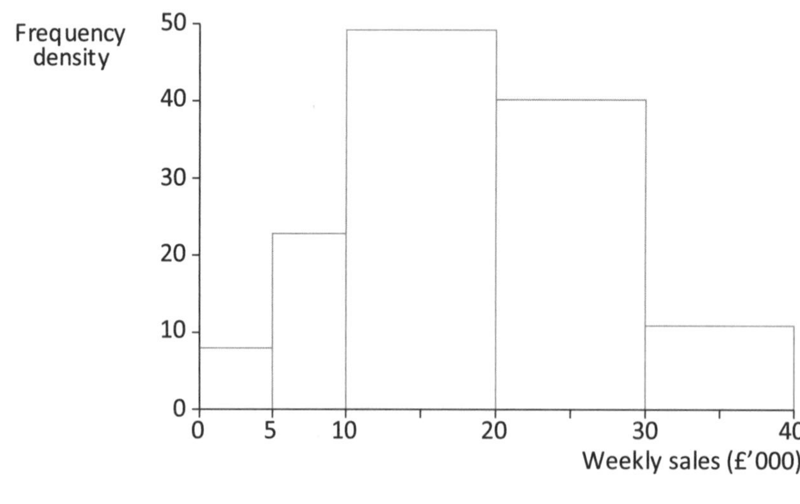

Test Your Understanding 9

B

The interval is 12.50/10.00 = 1.25 times the standard width, so the score to be plotted is 80/1.25 = 64.

Test Your Understanding 10

D

In an ogive, the cumulative frequency associated with each interval is graphed on the upper limit of the interval.

Test Your Understanding 11

C

The correct height is 21/0.75 = 28.

Test Your Understanding 12

A

Step 1: Find R for the first pie chart:

$R^2 = 350000/\pi$

$R^2 = 350{,}000/3.1415926$

$= 111{,}408.46$

$R = 333.779$

Step 2: Find R for the second pie chart:

$R^2 = 700000/\pi$

$R^2 = 700{,}000/3.1415926$

$= 222{,}816.92$

$R = 472.03$

The ratio is 472.03/333.779 = 1.41 times

Test Your Understanding 13

A

In this equation of a straight line, the '4' is the gradient so Y increases by 4 when X increases by 1. Answer D at least recognises it is something to do with the gradient but has the reciprocal of the slope. The '5' gives the intercept that is the value of Y when $X = 0$.

Test Your Understanding 14

A

R's angle is given by 11% × 360 = 39.6 °. Answer (B) is simply a repetition of the 11 per cent figure; (C) appears to replace the 11 per cent by the ratio 11/(52 + 32 + 5). In answer (D) it seems that 11 has been divided by 360 but then multiplied by 100 to give an answer that is hopelessly small.

Test Your Understanding 15

D

All the others are standard procedures in tabulation. While there may be rare occasions when maximum accuracy is retained, it is unusual because it makes the table very unapproachable and hard to grasp.

Test Your Understanding 16

A	Age of 5 years	Continuous
B	Time of 2.5 hours	Continuous
C	Output of 12,000 kg	Continuous
D	Output of 5,000 units	Discrete

Test Your Understanding 17

The cumulative frequency distribution is as follows:

Number absent	*Frequency*	*Cumulative frequency*
0	10	10
1	15	25
2	7	32
3	4	36
4	2	38

Test Your Understanding 18

A 155 were paid less than $300.

B 50 were paid more than $200.

C 30 were paid between $200 and $300.

Test Your Understanding 19

The correct heights are as follows:

Weight	*Frequency*	*Height of bar*
0–10	65	65
10–20	89	89
20–40	140	70
40–60	76	38
60–100	64	16

Test Your Understanding 20

All the answers are correct *except* for (*C*).

Test Your Understanding 21

The correct angles are given by 360° × the appropriate percentage:

Categories	*%*	*Angle*
A	42	151
B	38	137
C	15	54
D	5	18

Test Your Understanding 22

The correct associations are as follows:

Bar charts	*Examples*
A Simple	Q
B Multiple	P
C Compound	R

Test Your Understanding 23

Chocolate on its own gives a bar height of 240. Putting a bar for toffee on top of this raises the height by a further 120, to a total of 360. The 70 added by apple raises the height to 430 and finally banana takes it up a further 30 to give an overall bar height of 460.

Answers:

A 240

B 360

C 430

D 460.

Test Your Understanding 24

The bar clearly shows the total sale in 1995 and additionally enables us to see the relative importance of the various fillings. Without the bars for the other years we cannot make comparisons from one year to the next so, although statements (B) and (D) are correct they cannot be deduced from the chart. (E) is incorrect because toffee is more popular than apple. The correct answers are (A), (C) and (F).

Test Your Understanding 25

A

Multiple bar chart showing sales of pies

Test Your Understanding 26

Sales in chocolate dipped in 1997, sales of banana fell in 1998 and total sales rose quite markedly over the period so (A), (C) and (E) are all incorrect. (B) and (D) are the correct answers.

Test Your Understanding 27

Sales	*Frequency*
10–14	6
15–19	4
20–24	10
25–29	5
30–34	14
35–39	6
40–44	4
45–49	1

Test Your Understanding 28

Sales	*Frequency*	*Cumulative frequency*
10 and under 15	6	G = 6
15 and under 20	12	H = 18
20 and under 25	17	I = 35
25 and under 30	7	J = 42

Test Your Understanding 29

In a cumulative frequency diagram, cumulative frequencies are plotted (vertically) on the upper limits of the corresponding intervals (horizontally). The cumulative frequency of the very bottom limit (of 10 in this case) is always zero.

K 10

L 15

M 20

N 25

O 30

P 7

Q 23

R 36

S 40

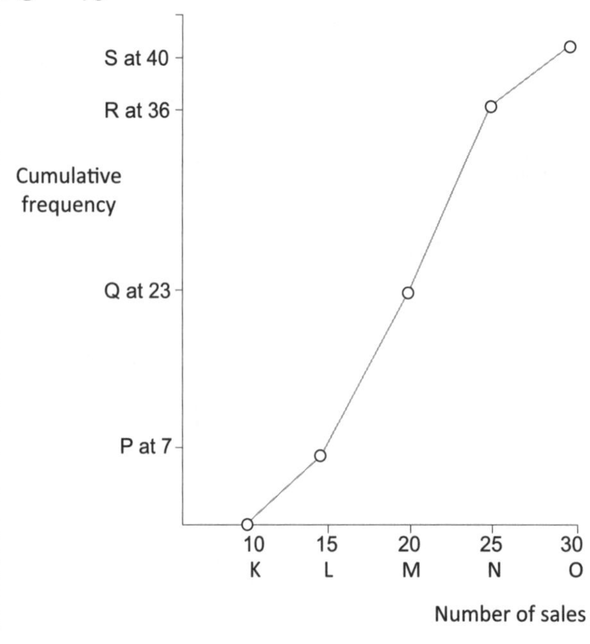

Test Your Understanding 30

Twenty-three people out of the sales force of 40 made less than 20 sales so the percentage is 100 × 23/40 = 57.5

chapter

3

Summarising and analysing data – II

Chapter learning objectives

On completion of their studies students should be able to:

- calculate for both ungrouped and grouped data: arithmetic mean, median, mode, range, variance, standard deviation and coefficient of variation.

1 Introduction

In Chapter 2 we saw how a set of raw data can be made more meaningful by forming it into a frequency distribution.

Often it is advantageous to go further and to calculate values that represent or describe the whole data set; such values are called descriptive statistics.

The most important are the various averages that aim to give a typical or representative value for the distribution. The other major group of descriptive statistics are the measures of spread, which tell us how variable the data are.

Even simplifying a complex set of data into two figures can still give valuable information upon which to make decisions.

2 The arithmetic mean

Most people would understand an 'average' to be the value obtained by dividing the sum of the values in question by the number of values.

This measure is the *arithmetic mean*, or, where there is no possibility of confusion, simply the mean.

To understand the notation, consider the following example.

Supplementary reading – Sample means

Suppose you wanted to determine the mean weight of 5 year old children as part of an investigation into childhood obesity. It would be impractical to measure every child, so you would most likely pick a sample of 5 year olds and measure them instead.

Having calculated a "sample mean", you could use this to comment on the likely mean of the whole population of 5 year olds. For such statements to retain credibility it is vital that the sample is considered to be representative – e.g. did it contain the same proportions of boys to girls present in the population as a whole? One way of trying to make the sample representative is to use a large sample, say, over a 1,000 children.

Illustration 1

A shopkeeper is about to put his shop up for sale. As part of the details of the business, he wishes to quote the average weekly takings. The takings in each of the last 6 weeks are:

$1,120 $990 $1,040 $1,030 $1,105 $1,015

Determine the mean weekly takings that the shopkeeper could quote.

Solution

If the weekly takings are denoted by the variable x, then the sample mean value of x, pronounced 'x-bar', is given by:

$$\bar{x} = \frac{\text{Sum of the values of x}}{\text{Number of values of x}}$$

$$\text{or } \bar{x} = \frac{\Sigma x}{n}$$

where Σ, a Greek capital letter 'sigma', is the mathematical symbol for 'add up', and n is the number of values of x. In this example:

$$\bar{x} = \frac{1{,}120 + 990 + 1{,}040 + 1{,}030 + 1{,}105 + 1{,}015}{6} = \frac{6{,}300}{6} = 1050$$

The shopkeeper could therefore quote a sample mean weekly takings figure of $1,050.

As we can see, this formula is very easy to apply and, as indicated above, merely reflects the arithmetical procedures most people would recognise as the determination of an average. It will, however, need some modification before it can be used to determine the mean from a frequency distribution, a form in which many data sets appear.

Illustration 2

A company is implementing an efficiency drive and, as part of a leaflet it is to distribute to its employees, it wishes to point out the average daily absenteeism rate. The following data is collated from the records of a sample of 200 working days: compute the sample mean number of absentees per day.

Number of absentees per day (x)	*Number of days*
0	9
1	28
2	51
3	43
4	29
5	18
6	10
7	7
8	5

It should be noted that the 'number of days' column simply gives the frequency of the corresponding x values, and so we shall denote this quantity by *f*. Now, to find the sample mean, the above formula can be applied in a straightforward manner:

Solution

$$\overline{x} = \frac{\Sigma x}{n}$$

$$= \frac{\overbrace{(0+0+0+0+0+0+0+0+0)}^{\text{9 values of 0}} + \overbrace{(1+1+1+\cdots+1)}^{\text{28 values of 1}} + \overbrace{(2+2+2+\cdots+2)}^{\text{51 values of 2}} + \cdots + \overbrace{(8+8+8+8+8)}^{\text{5 values of 8}}}{200}$$

Thus

$$= \frac{(9 \times 0) + (28 \times 1) + (51 \times 2) + (43 \times 3) + (29 \times 4) + (18 \times 5) + (10 \times 6) + (7 \times 7) + (5 \times 8)}{200}$$

$$= \frac{614}{200} = 3.07$$

The mean number of absentees in the sample is 3.07 per day.

Note how, in general, each x-value is multiplied by its corresponding frequency, *f*, and the products are then summed. That is, we evaluate the product fx for each x-value and then add all the values of *fx*. As we are denoting addition by 'Σ" this sum can be written of Σ*fx*. The formula for the sample mean from a frequency distribution is thus:

$$= \overline{x} = \frac{\Sigma fx}{\Sigma f}$$

$$= \frac{614}{200} = 3.07$$

The denominator of this expression, Σf, is simply the sum of the frequencies, which is, of course, the same as n in the earlier expression for x.

Test Your Understanding 1

Find the arithmetic mean for the following distribution, which shows the number of employees absent per day

No. of employees absent	*No. of days (frequency)*
2	2
3	4
4	3
5	4
6	3
7	3
8	3

This formula, which is given in the exam, will now prove adequate for all our purposes. In order to illustrate how to deal with a minor problem that can, however, arise and to demonstrate a systematic way of performing and setting out the calculations involved, we give a further illustration.

Illustration 3

As part of its preparation for a wage negotiation, the personnel manager of a company has collated the following data from a sample of payslips. She wishes to be able to use the average weekly wage figure in the negotiations. Evaluate the mean of the sample.

Weekly wage ($)	*Number of employees (f)*
180–under 185	41
185–under 190	57
190–under 195	27
195–under 200	23
200–under 205	15
205–under 210	7

Solution

The extra difficulty in this problem is clear: as the data has been collated into classes, a certain amount of detail has been lost and hence the values of the variable x to be used in the calculation of the mean are not clearly specified. Short of actually having the raw data, the actual wages of the employees in the sample, we can only approximate the value of the mean. To do this, we adopt the obvious approach of taking x to be a representative value of each class, the most plausible being the mid-point.

Doing this, we have:

x	f	fx
182.50	41	7,482.5
187.50	57	10,687.5
192.50	27	5,197.5
197.50	23	4,542.5
202.50	15	3,037.5
207.50	7	1,452.5
	170	32,400.0

It is advisable to set out such statistical calculations in the way shown: very often figures have to be summed, and so they are best arranged in columns. Further, if you are using a calculator with a memory key, each 'fx' figure can be added into the memory as it is calculated, so that the total 'Σfx' is ready for use when the memory total is recalled.

Now we have:

$$\bar{x} = \frac{\Sigma fx}{\Sigma f} = \frac{32{,}400}{170} = 190.60\text{, approx}$$

Hence, the manager can use an average weekly wage of $190.60 in the negotiations.

Before moving on, it is worth recalling that there are a number of ways of classifying data into grouped frequency distributions. Hence, a set of weekly wages expressed in whole numbers of $ could be grouped:

180–under 185, 185-under 190 and so on
or 180–184, 185–189 and so on
or 179.5–184.5, 184.5–189.5 and so on

Although it has been stated earlier that the first method is recommended, other types may be encountered, and so we shall look briefly at how to deal with them when calculating means, etc.

Where there is an apparent 'gap', it can be 'closed'. Thus, with salaries, which could in fact be measured to the nearest $0.01, a class of 180–184 is actually the same as:

- either 180–under 185 (if any amounts over the $ figure have been ignored);
- or 179.5–under 184.5 (if arithmetical rounding has been used).

Where there is an overlap, such as with 184.50, 189.50, etc. in the third case, the equivalent form is:

- 179.5–under 184.5

and so on, provided that 184.5, 189.5, etc. are counted in the higher class each time.

Test Your Understanding 2

Find the arithmetic mean for the following distribution of output levels of product Q:

Output of Q (kg)	*No. of days (frequency)*
350–under 360	4
360–370	6
370–380	5
380–390	4
390–400	3

The formula for the arithmetic mean will be given in your exam.

3 The median

So far we have dealt with the most commonly used average, the mean. We now consider another widely used average, the median.

In Illustration 3, we computed a mean weekly wage of $190.60 which the personnel manager could quote in the wage negotiations. An impartial commentator could argue (and the manager might agree) that this is a rather high figure for a supposedly representative average. As 98 out of the sampled 170 people (i.e. 58 per cent) actually earn less than $190 per week, it may well be that in excess of 60 per cent of the workforce earn less than the 'average' of $190.60 per week.

If we look at this wage distribution, shown below, it is easy to see the cause of this phenomenon. The two highest frequencies occur at the lowest wage classes and then the frequencies decrease slowly as the wages increase. The relatively small number of large wages has caused the mean value to be so large.

Distributions of this type are said to be *skewed* – i.e. the frequency distribution does not look (even roughly) symmetric. It is a criticism of the mean as an average that very skewed distributions can have mean values that appear unrepresentative, in that they are higher or lower than a great deal of the distribution.

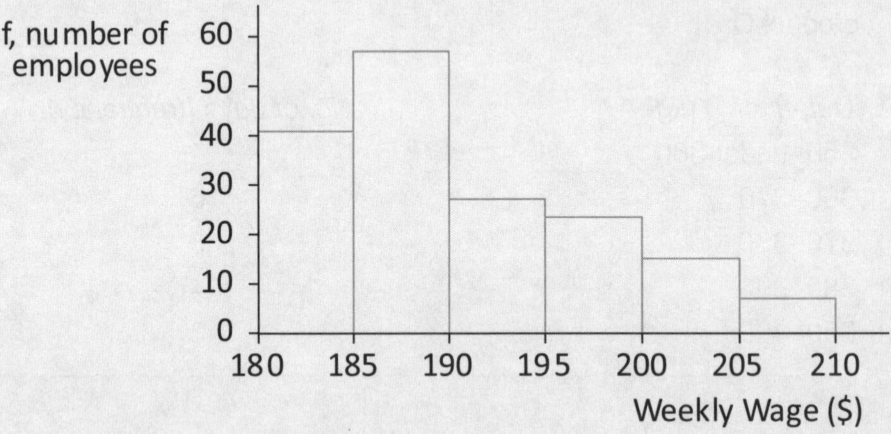

To address this problem, we introduce another measure of average, the *median*. This is defined as the middle of a set of values, when arranged in ascending (or descending) order. This overcomes the above problem, since the median has half the distribution above it, and half below.

Similarly the median is unaffected by any particularly large or unusual individual measurements whereas the mean would be.

We leave the wage distribution for now, and look at a simpler exercise.

Illustration 4

Shop A's weekly takings are given by the following sample over six weeks. The sample has an arithmetic mean of $1,050.

$1,120	$990	$1,040	$1,030	$1,105	$1,015

A prospective purchaser of the business notices that the mean is higher than the takings in four of the 6 weeks. Calculate the median for him.

Solution

First of all, we arrange the takings figures in ascending order:

$990	$1,015	$1,030	$1,040	$1,105	$1,120

The question now is: what is the middle number of a list of six? With a little thought, you can see that there are two 'middle' values, the third and fourth. The median is thus taken to be the mean of these two values.

$$\text{Median} = \frac{(1{,}030 + 1{,}040)}{2} = 1{,}035$$

Hence, the median weekly takings figure that the prospective purchaser could quote is $1,035.

After this example, it is clear that, in the case of an odd number of values, the determination of the median is even easier, as there is a clear *single* middle item in an odd number of values. In general, if there are *n* observations, the position of the median is given by $(n + 1)/2$. With six observations, this gives 7/2 = 3.5, which is the position halfway between the third and fourth observations. In the case of frequency distributions, the determination of the median is not as straightforward, but can be illustrated by returning to the earlier wage distribution.

Test Your Understanding 3

A Calculate the median of the following data:

25 52 18 43 27

B Calculate the median of the data on staff absences (hint: use cumulative frequencies).

No. of employees absent	*No. of days (f)*
2	2
3	4
4	3
5	4
6	3
7	3
8	3

Illustration 5

Using the data of Illustration 3, find the more representative median weekly wage figure that the personnel manager could argue in the wage negotiations.

Solution

It is clear that the middle wage figure in a set of 170 is halfway between the 85th and 86th. Unfortunately, we do not have the raw data from which the frequency distribution was compiled, and so cannot tell what these two wage figures are. It is therefore necessary to make an assumption about the wage distribution and to deduce an approximate value from the assumption.

If we consider the wage values to be evenly spread throughout their classes, then we can draw the ogive as in Chapter 3 and then estimate the median from a construction based on this ogive. First of all, we need the cumulative frequency distribution.

Weekly wage ($): (less than)	*Cumulative frequency*
185	41
190	98
195	125
200	148
205	163
210	170

The ogive of this cumulative frequency distribution is shown as follows:

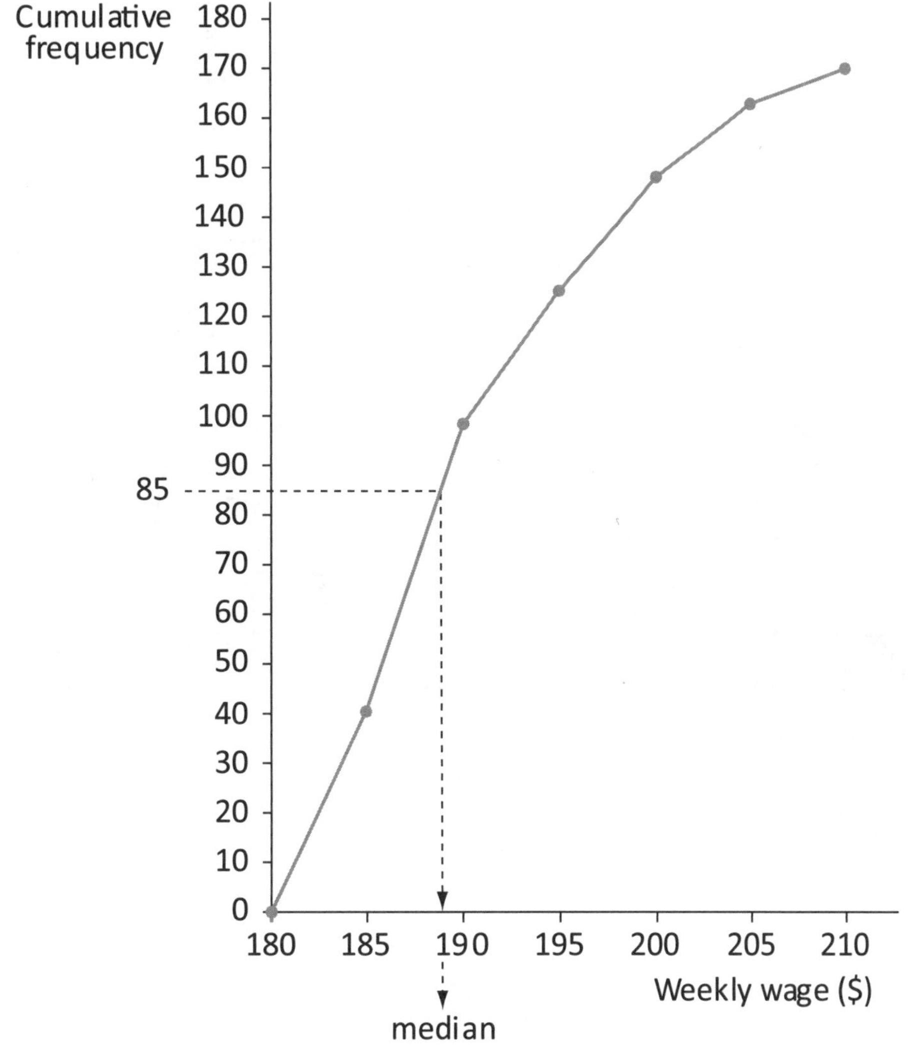

Now, as the median has the property that half of the wage figures lie below it, and half above it, the construction shown on the ogive, drawn at a cumulative frequency of 85 (half of 170), gives the approximate median weekly wage as $188.80. This value is arguably more representative of the sample than the earlier mean value, precisely because half the wages lie below and half above it.

Test Your Understanding 4

Draw the ogive for the following data on the output of product Q and find the median from the ogive.

Output of Q (kg)	*No. of days (frequency)*
350–under 360	4
360–370	6
370–380	5
380–390	4
390–400	3

In your exam you cannot be asked to draw the histogram so you just have to know how to obtain the mode from it. It is possible to calculate the mode using formulae but this is not required in your syllabus and the formula is not given.

4 The mode

The *mode* or *modal value* of a data set is that value that occurs most often, and it is the remaining most widely used average. The determination of this value, when you have raw data to deal with, consists simply of a counting process to find the most frequently occurring value, and so we do not dwell on this case here, but move on to look at frequency distributions.

Illustration 6

Find the mode for the following distributions:

(a)

Complaints per week	*No of weeks*
0	5
1	12
2	7
3	2
4	1

(b)

Weekly wage ($)	*No of weeks*
180–under 185	41
185–190	57
190–195	27
195–200	23
200–205	15
205–210	7

Solution

(a) The mode is the value with the highest frequency, so here the mode is one complaint per week.

(b) The frequency distribution in the second case shows that the *modal class* (that one with the highest frequency) is $185 to under $190.

The graph shows a way of finding a single value to represent the mode: basically, the construction shown weights the mode towards the second most frequent class neighbouring the modal class, the one to the left in this case.

The figure shows that the *modal weekly wage* is approximately $*186.60*.

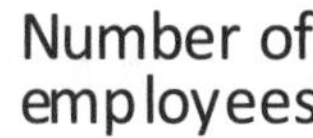

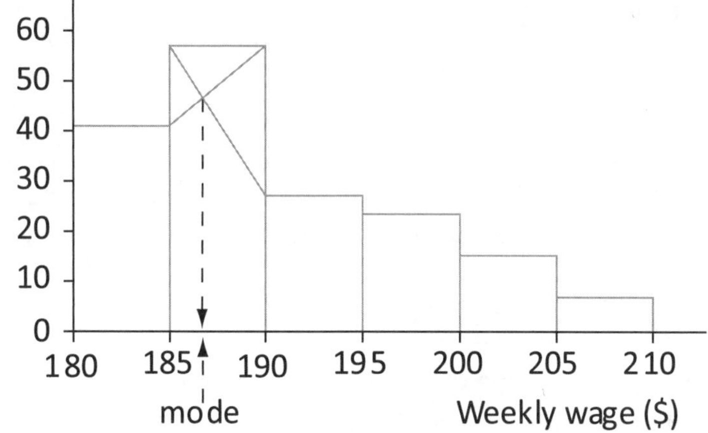

This construction can still be used when there are unequal class intervals.

Test Your Understanding 5

Find the mode of the following data on the output of product Q.

Output of Q (kg)	*No. of days (frequency)*
350–under 360	4
360–370	6
370–380	5
380–390	4
390–400	3

5 A comparison of the three averages

As our earlier discussion of the weekly wage distribution indicates, it is often just as important to use a measure of average appropriate to the situation as it is to evaluate the measure accurately. In this section we further discuss the relative merits and demerits of the three averages encountered in this chapter.

Mode

It is arguable that the mode is the least useful and important of the three. There are many distributions that have no definite single 'peak' in their probability distributions, and so it is difficult to attribute any sensible meaning to a modal value in such cases.

Further, the mode is often unrepresentative of the whole data set: it may occur at one extremity of a skewed distribution or, at the very least, it takes no account of a high proportion of the data, only representing the most common value.

All in all, it is fair to say that, in the vast majority of cases, the mode renders only a general description of one feature of a distribution, and is a relatively unimportant average when compared with the median or the mean.

Mean

The mean, on the other hand, has a number of features that usually make it the most appropriate and representative measure.

First of all, it has the great advantage of being what most people recognise as 'the average'. It is therefore most easily communicated to non-specialists.

Second, the mean is the only one of the three that takes account of all the data. Like the mode, the median is unaffected by extreme values or "outliers". The mean is thus arguably the most representative of *all* of a distribution. (Note: you could argue that it is precisely because the mean *is* affected by extreme values , that it is less useful than the median)

Finally, the mean is the measure that is most useful for further statistical analysis and this explains why the mean is often preferred to the median.

Median

Having said that, there are some circumstances in which one might consider the median to be more appropriate than the mean. We have already encountered one important such occasion in the skewed wage distribution of Illustration 3.

6 Measures of spread

Having obtained an average value to represent a set of data, it is natural to question the extent to which the single value is representative of the whole set. Through a simple example we shall see that part of the answer to this lies in how 'spread out' the individual values are around the average. In particular, we shall study four measures of *spread*, or *dispersion*, as it is sometimes called:

- the range
- the standard deviation
- the variance
- the coefficient of variation.

7 The range

The range is defined as the highest value minus the lowest value. For example, if measuring heights then the range is the difference in height between the tallest and shortest persons measured.

However, this definition this can be misleading. Where the data is arranged in classes:

Range = Upper most interval limit – Lowest interval limit

Where the data is not grouped, the range is best viewed as the number of values from the very bottom to the very top and is given by:

Range = Highest value – Lowest value + 1

These apparently different definitions amount in practice to the same thing. If we regard the highest value as being at the centre of an interval of unit width, then the uppermost interval limit is given by the highest value plus 0.5. Similarly, the lowest interval limit will be given by the lowest value minus 0.5. Consequently, the value of the range is the same whichever method is used.

The following example will illustrate the calculation of the range, and will demonstrate why such a measure may be needed.

Illustration 7

A recently retired couple are considering investing their pension lump sums in the purchase of a small shop. Two suitably sited premises, A and B, are discovered. The average weekly takings of the two shops are quoted as $1,050 and $1,080 for A and B, respectively. Upon further investigation, the investors discover that the averages quoted come from the following recent weekly takings figures:

Shop A:	$1,120	$990	$1,040	$1,030	$1,105	$1,015
Shop B:	$1,090	$505	$915	$1,005	$2,115	$850

Advise the couple.

Solution

You can easily check that the 'averages' quoted are, in fact, the means of the two samples. Based on these two figures alone, it might seem sensible for the couple to prefer shop B to shop A, but a glance at the actual data casts doubt on this conclusion. It is clear that the values for shop B are far more spread out than those for shop A, thereby making the mean for shop B arguably less representative. This difference is illustrated well by the ranges of the two sets:

Range of A = Highest – Lowest + 1 = 1,120 – 990 + 1 = $131
Range of B = 2,115 – 505 + 1 = $1,611

It can be seen that the much larger range in the latter case is almost entirely due to the single value '$2,115'. The retired couple would therefore be well advised to look at larger samples of weekly takings figures to see if this value is some sort of freak and whether shop B does indeed generate higher weekly takings on average.

8 The standard deviation and variance

The standard deviation is a way of measuring how far away on average the data points are from the mean. In other words, they measure average variability about the mean. As such standard deviation is often used with the mean when describing a data set.

For example, suppose a data set has just two observations: 10 and 30. The mean here is 20 and the standard deviation will be 10 as both observations are 10 units away from the mean.

For more complex examples, calculating the standard deviation involves the following steps:

(1) Look at the difference between each data value and the mean

(2) To get rid of the problem of negative differences cancelling out positive ones, square the results

(3) Work out the average squared difference (this gives the *variance*)

(4) Square root to get the standard deviation

The basic formula for calculating standard deviation is thus

$$s = \sqrt{\frac{\Sigma(x - \bar{x})^2}{n}}$$

(Note: the variance is simply the standard deviation squared. For most calculations and discussions the standard deviation is perfectly adequate but the variance is used in more advanced statistics and probability theory)

In practice, this formula can turn out to be very tedious to apply. It can be shown that the following, more easily applicable, formula is the same:

$$s = \sqrt{\frac{\Sigma fx^2}{\Sigma f} - \left(\frac{\Sigma fx}{\Sigma f}\right)^2}$$

Illustration 8

An analyst is considering two categories of company, X and Y, for possible investment. One of her assistants has compiled the following information on the price-earnings ratios of the shares of companies in the two categories over the past year.

Price-earnings ratios	*Number of category X companies*	*Number of category Y companies*
4.95–under 8.95	3	4
8.95–under 12.95	5	8
12.95–under 16.95	7	8
16.95–under 20.95	6	3
20.95–under 24.95	3	3
24.95–under 28.95	1	4

Compute the standard deviations of these two distributions and comment. (You are given that the means of the two distributions are 15.59 and 15.62, respectively.)

Solution

Concentrating first of all on category X, we see that we face the same problem as when we calculated the mean of such a distribution, namely that we have classified data, instead of individual values of *x*. Adopting a similar approach as before, we take the mid-point of each class:

x (mid-point)	x^2	*f*	*fx*	fx^2
6.95	48.3025	3	20.85	144.9075
10.95	119.9025	5	54.75	599.5125
14.95	223.5025	7	104.65	1,564.5175
18.95	359.1025	6	113.70	2,154.6150
22.95	526.7025	3	68.85	1,580.1075
26.95	726.3025	1	26.95	726.3025
		25	389.75	6,769.9625

Thus the standard deviation is:

$$s = \sqrt{\frac{\Sigma fx^2}{\Sigma f} - \left(\frac{\Sigma fx}{\Sigma f}\right)^2}$$

$$s = \sqrt{\frac{6{,}769.9625}{25} - \left(\frac{389.75}{25}\right)^2}$$

$$= \sqrt{270.7985 - 243.0481} = \sqrt{27.7504} = 5.27$$

The standard deviation of the price-earnings ratios for category X is therefore 5.27. In the same way, you can verify that the standard deviation in the case of category Y is 6.29. These statistics again emphasise the wider spread in the category Y data than in the category X data. Note how a full degree of accuracy (four decimal places) is retained throughout the calculation in order to ensure an accurate final result.

The calculation for Y should be as for X above. In outline:

x (mid-point)	x^2	*f*	*fx*	fx^2
6.95	48.3025	4	27.80	193.210
26.95	726.3025	4	107.80	2,905.210
		30	468.50	8,503.075

s = √(283.4358 – 243.8803) = 6.289

Test Your Understanding 6

Using the data relating to absences from work, find the standard deviation.

No. of employees absent	*No. of days (frequency)*
2	2
3	4
4	3
5	4
6	3
7	3
8	3

It is probably easiest to calculate fx^2 by multiplying *fx* by *x*, for example, 2 × 4, 3 × 12, etc.

Test Your Understanding 7

Using the data relating to output of product Q, find the standard deviation.

Output of Q (kg)	*No. of days (frequency)*
350–under 360	4
360–370	6
370–380	5
380–390	4
390–400	3

9 The coefficient of variation

The coefficient of variation is a statistical measure of the dispersion of data points in a data series around the mean. It is calculated as follows:

$$\text{Coefficient of variation} = \frac{\text{Standard deviation}}{\text{Mean}}$$

The coefficient of variation is the ratio of the standard deviation to the mean, and is useful when comparing the degree of variation from one data series to another, even if the means are quite different from each other. Dividing by the mean gives a sense of scale to the standard deviation, so the coefficient of variation is often given as a percentage to aid comparison.

In a financial setting, the coefficient of variation allows you to determine how much risk you are assuming in comparison to the amount of return you can expect from an investment. The lower the ratio of standard deviation to mean return, the better your risk-return tradeoff.

Note that if the mean in the denominator of the calculation is negative or zero, the ratio will not make sense.

If the means of two sets of data are similar, then it is relatively easy to compare the spreads by looking at the standard deviation figures alone. Another example will show that it is not always so straightforward.

Test Your Understanding 8

Government statistics on the basic weekly wages of workers in two countries show the following. (All figures converted to dollar equivalent.)

Country V:	mean = 120	standard deviation = 55
Country W:	mean = 90	standard deviation = 50

Can we conclude that country V has a wider spread of basic weekly wages?

10 A comparison of the measures of spread

Like the mode, the range is little used except as a very quick initial view of the overall spread of the data. The problem is that it is totally dependent on the most extreme values in the distribution, which are the ones that are particularly liable to reflect errors or one-off situations. Furthermore, the range tells us nothing at all about how the data is spread between the extremes.

The standard deviation is undoubtedly the most important measure of spread. It has a formula that lends itself to algebraic manipulation and so, along with the mean, it is the basis of almost all advanced statistical theory. This is a pity because it does have some quite serious disadvantages. However, if data is not symmetric about the mean (i.e. it is *skewed*), the standard deviation will exaggerate the degree of spread because of the large squared deviations associated with extreme values. Similarly, if a distribution has open intervals at the ends, the choice of limits and hence of mid-points will have a marked effect on the standard deviation.

Finally, it is often the case that data is intended to be compared with other data, perhaps nationwide figures or previous year's figures, etc. In such circumstances, unless you have access to *all* the raw data, you are obliged to compare like with like, regardless perhaps of your own better judgement.

Chapter Summary

All the averages give a typical or expected value for the distribution. The mean is the total shared out equally, the median is the halfway value and the mode is the most common value.

Measures of spread tell you how variable the data is. If the measures are relatively large, it means that the data is very variable. The standard deviation finds the average distance of the observations from the mean. In other words, it measures average variability about the mean. The range measures the spread of the data from the very bottom to the very top.

Aside from understanding and being able to explain what the various statistics mean, there are other points of relevance to interpretation:

(1) Can you rely on the data – was the sample large, representative and randomly taken?

(2) Are you comparing like with like?

(3) If you have to compare variability in two samples that have markedly different means, use the coefficient of variation rather than the standard deviation.

(4) Finally, always remember to interpret statistics in their proper context. Give them units and do not simply interpret them in an abstract manner.

(5) Think about which averages (measures of location) are used with which measures of spread, for example, the mean is used with the standard deviation (or variance).

Formulae definitions

- The mean, or $x = \Sigma fx/\Sigma f$ for frequency distributions.
- The median is the middle value when the data is arranged in ascending or descending order. It can be evaluated directly except in grouped frequency distributions, when it can be estimated from an ogive as the x-value corresponding to half the total frequency.
- The mode is the most commonly occurring value.
- The standard deviation,

$$s = \sqrt{\frac{\Sigma(x - \bar{x})^2}{n}}$$

or

$$s = \sqrt{\frac{\Sigma f x^2}{\Sigma f} - \left(\frac{\Sigma f x}{\Sigma f}\right)^2}$$

for frequency distributions.

- Coefficient of variation = Standard deviation/mean
- Range = Highest interval limit – Lowest interval limit.

11 Further Practice Questions

Test Your Understanding 9

A driver makes a number of deliveries in a week. In a week where his average journey was 267 miles, his individual journey distances, in miles, were 286, 192, x, 307, 185, y, 94.
When $y = 4x$, the value of x is:

A 161

B 167

C 267

D 644.

Test Your Understanding 10

Sales for the first 5 months of the year averaged $8,200 per month. For the last 4 months of the year sales averaged $8,500 per month. If sales for the year totalled $102,000, the average for the sixth, seventh and eighth months must be:

A $8,500

B $9,000

C $9,500

D $10,200.

Test Your Understanding 11

A group of people have the following ages in years: 21, 32, 19, 24, 31, 27, 17, 21, 26, 42. The median age of the group is:

A 21 years

B 25 years

C 26 years

D 31 years.

Test Your Understanding 12

The following set of data

13, 42, x, 7, 51, 69, 28, 33, 14, 8

has a median of 29. What is the value of x?

A 25

B 29

C 30

D 32.

Test Your Understanding 13

If the standard deviation of a sample of 100 people is 49, what is the value of the variance?

A 7

B 0.7

C 2,401

D 24.01.

Test Your Understanding 14

All the following except one are advantages of using the standard deviation to measure spread. Which is incorrect?

A It is not distorted by skewed data.

B It is well known and widely used.

C It uses all the data.

D Its formula lends itself to mathematical manipulation.

Test Your Understanding 15

Complete the missing entries in the following table and calculate the arithmetic mean (to two decimal places).

x	f	fx
0	10	?
1	15	?
2	25	?
3	5	?
Totals	?	?

Test Your Understanding 16

State whether the following statements about the arithmetic mean are true or false.

A It measures the variability of the data.

B It is a measure of central tendency.

C It gives an average level for the data.

D It gives the value of the total shared out equally.

Test Your Understanding 17

The arithmetic mean is given by the formula $\Sigma fx/\Sigma f$. For grouped data, which one or more of the following can constitute the x in the formula?

A Interval mid-points.

B Interval upper limits.

C Interval lower limits.

D The sum of the interval upper and lower limits divided by two.

Test Your Understanding 18

State whether the following statements about the mode are true or false.

A It is the most widely used average.

B It is a measure of dispersion.

C It gives the most common value.

D Some distributions have several modes.

Test Your Understanding 19

In country P, the coefficient of variation for the salaries of trainee accountants is 40 per cent, while in country Q it is 60 per cent. Which of the following statements can be made on the basis of this information?

A In P, 40 per cent of trainee accountants have a below-average salary.

B In Q, the lowest salary of trainee accountants is 60 per cent of the average.

C Salaries of trainee accountants are more variable in Q than in P.

D Salaries of trainee accountants are higher on average in Q than in P.

Test Your Understanding 20

Which one or more of the following are advantages of using the standard deviation?

A It has an exact algebraic formula.

B It is not distorted by data being skewed.

C It is the most widely used measure of spread.

D It is not affected by open-ended intervals.

Test Your Understanding 21

Match the following statistics to the charts that may be used to directly estimate them. Note that the same charts may be used for several statistics, some charts may be of no such use, and it may not be possible to estimate some statistics from charts.

Statistics

A The mean.

B The median.

C The mode.

Chart

Q The histogram.

R The ogive.

S Cannot be estimated from a chart.

Test Your Understanding 22

Mean/SD/histogram

The managers of an import agency are investigating the length of time that customers take to pay their invoices, the normal terms for which are 30 days net.

They have checked the payment record of 100 customers chosen at random and have compiled the following table:

Payment in (days)	*Interval*	Mid-point *(x)*	frequency *(f)*	*fx*	fx^2
5–9	5 and less than 10	7.5	4	30.0	225.00
10–14	A	12.5	10	125	1562.5
15–19	15 and less than 20	17.5	17	B	5,206.25
20–24	20 and less than 25	C	20	450.0	10,125.00
25–29	25 and less than 30	27.5	22	605.0	D
30–34	30 and less than 35	32.5	16	520.0	16,900.00
35–39	35 and less than 40	37.5	8	300.0	11,250.00
40–44	40 and less than 45	42.5	3	127.5	5,418.75
			100		

Fill in the gaps in the table, working with two decimal places (2 d.p.) where appropriate.

Test Your Understanding 23

If in the above table $\Sigma fx = 2{,}500$. Calculate the arithmetic mean.

Test Your Understanding 24

If in the above table $\Sigma fx = 2{,}400$ and $\Sigma fx^2 = 67{,}000$. Calculate the standard deviation, giving your answer to two d.p.

Test Your Understanding 25

A company is investigating the cost of absenteeism within its production department. Computer records revealed the following data:

Days absent last year	*Number of people*
0	94
1–5	203
6–10	105
11–20	68
21–30	15
31–40	10
41+	5
Total	500

[Source: Internal company records]

Complete the following cumulative frequency distribution table:

No. of days absent	*Cumulative number of people*
0	94
1 and < 6	297
6 and <11	402
A	470
21 and < 31	B
31 and < 41	495
41 and < 51	C

Test Your Understanding 26

Descriptive statistics/charts

A firm is comparing the age structure of its workforce in the current year with that of 5 years ago, as shown in the table below:

Age group (years)	*Five years ago Number in group*	*Current year Number in group*
25 – 30	2	5
30 – 35	6	10
35 – 40	8	13
40 – 45	13	28
45 – 50	15	21
50 – 55	35	12
55 – 60	12	8
60 – 65	9	3

The mean age and standard deviation of ages 5 years ago were:

Mean age	49.05 years
Standard deviation	8.45 years

Complete the following table, working with two d.p. where appropriate:

Mid-point x	x^2	*Score* f	fx	fx^2
27.5	756.25	5	137.5	3,781.25
32.5	1,056.25	10	325.0	10,562.50
37.5	1,406.25	13	487.5	18,281.25
42.5	1,806.25	28	1190.0	50,575.00
47.5	2,256.25	21	997.5	47,381.25
52.5	2,756.25	12	630.0	33,075.00
57.5	3,306.25	8	460.0	26,450.00
62.5	3,906.25	3	187.5	11,718.75
		100	A	B

Test Your Understanding 27

If the current mean were 40 years and the standard deviation were 8 years, which of the following comments would be correct?

A Over the last 5 years there has been little change in age variability from one employee to the next.

B The most common age group has dropped from 50 to 55 years to 40 to 45 years.

C Variability of ages around the mean has increased greatly since 5 years ago.

D A quarter of employees are now less than 32 years old.

E The average recruit is now 8 years younger than 40 years.

F Average age of employees has fallen.

G A half of employees are now less than 40 years old.

Test Your Understanding 28

The chart illustrates the changes in the age structure of a workforce over the 5-year period.

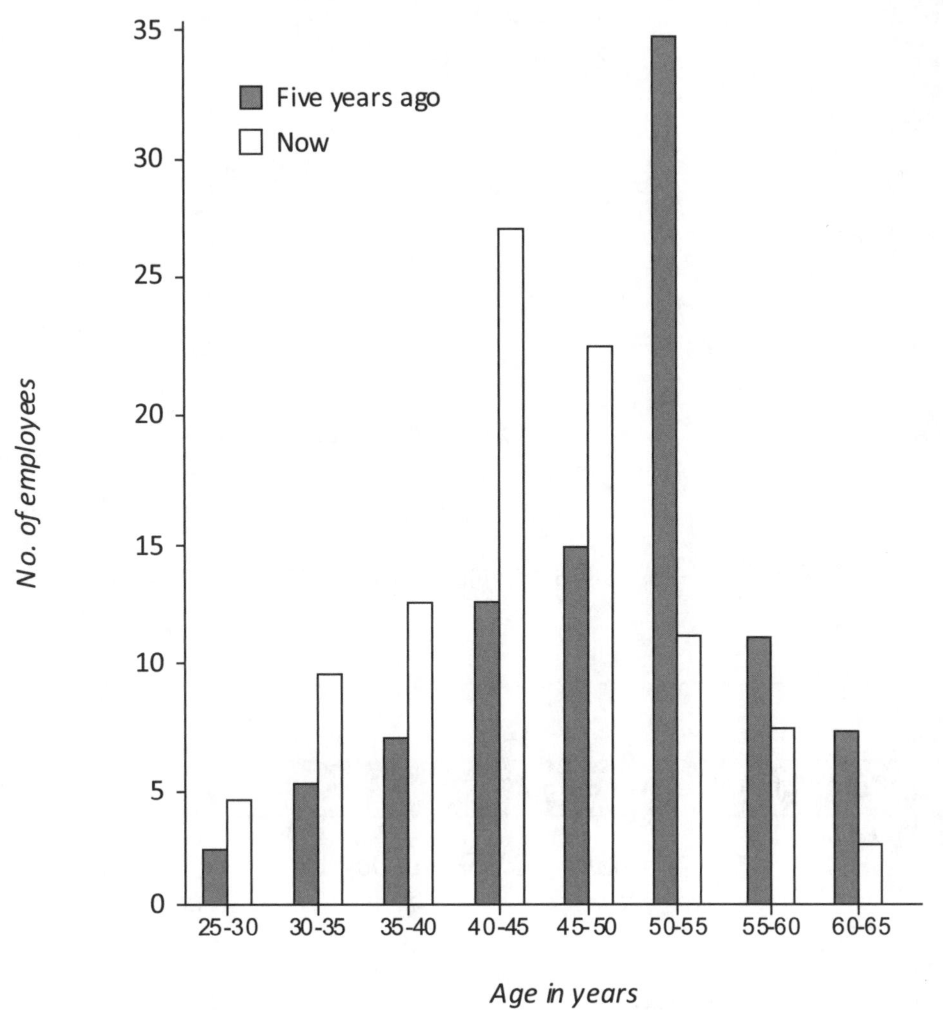

What type of chart is it?

Bar chart/pie chart/histogram/ogive/multiple bar chart/component bar chart.

Test your understanding answers

Test Your Understanding 1

x	f	fx
2	2	4
3	4	12
4	3	12
5	4	20
6	3	18
7	3	21
8	3	24
	$\Sigma f=$ 22	$\Sigma fx=$ 111

Mean, $\bar{x} = \frac{\Sigma fx}{\Sigma f} = \frac{111}{22} = 5.045 = 5$ employees, to nearest whole number.

Test Your Understanding 2

Mid-point X	Frequency f	fx
355	4	1,420
365	6	2,190
375	5	1,875
385	4	1,540
395	3	1,185
	$\Sigma f=$ 22	$\Sigma fx=$ 8,210

Mean, $\bar{x} = \frac{\Sigma fx}{\Sigma f} = \frac{8,210}{22} = 373.18$kg (to two d.p.)

Test Your Understanding 3

(a) First write the data in order of magnitude:

18 25 27 43 52

The median is in the third position [check: (5 + 1)/2 = 3] and is therefore 27.

(b) Find cumulative frequencies:

No. of employees absent	*No. of days (f)*	*Cumulative frequency*
2	2	2
3	4	6
4	3	9
5	4	13
6	3	16
7	3	19
8	3	22

There are 22 observations, so the position of the median is given by (22 + 1)/2 = 11.5, that is, the median is midway between the eleventh and twelfth observations. From the cumulative frequencies it is clear that both the eleventh and twelfth observations have value 5, so the median is 5.

Test Your Understanding 4

Output of Q (kg)	*No. of days (frequency)*	*Cumulative frequency*
350–under 360	4	4
360–370	6	10
370–380	5	15
380–390	4	19
390–400	3	22

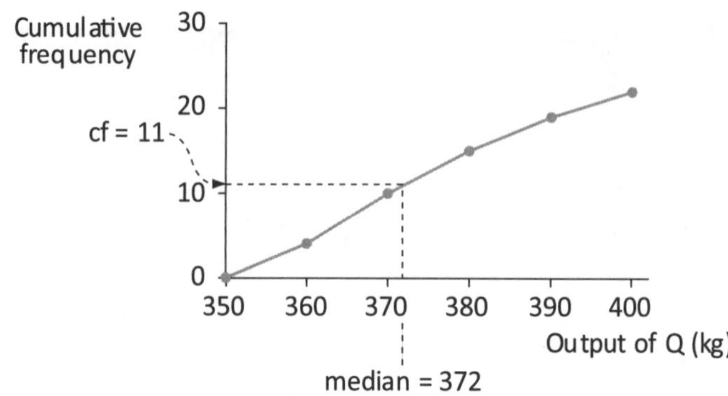

Total frequency is 22, so cumulative frequency of the median is 22/2 = 11. From the ogive, the median = 372 kg.

Test Your Understanding 5

From the histogram, the mode is 366.6 kg (approximately).

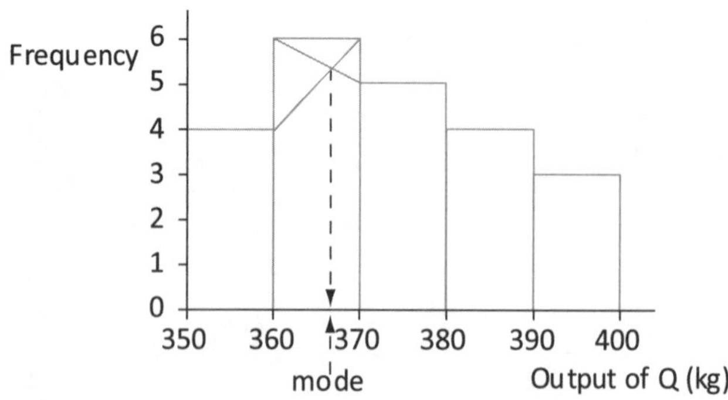

Test Your Understanding 6

x	f	fx	fx^2
2	2	4	8
3	4	12	36
4	3	12	48
5	4	20	100
6	3	18	108
7	3	21	147
8	3	24	192
	22	111	639

$$s = \sqrt{\frac{\sum fx}{\sum f} - \bar{x}^2} = \sqrt{\frac{639}{22} - \left(\frac{111}{22}\right)^2}$$

$$= \sqrt{(29.0455 - 25.4566)} = \sqrt{3.5889} = 1.89 \text{ (to two d.p)}$$

Test Your Understanding 7

Mid-point x	Frequency f	fx	fx^2
355	4	1,420	504,100
365	6	2,190	799,350
375	5	1,875	703,125
385	4	1,540	592,900
395	3	1,185	468,075
	22	8,210	3,067,550

$$s = \sqrt{\frac{\Sigma fx^2}{\Sigma f} - \bar{x}^2} = \sqrt{\frac{3,067,550}{22} - \left(\frac{8,210}{22}\right)^2}$$

$$= \sqrt{(139,434.0909 - 139,264.6694)} = \sqrt{169.4215} = 13.02 \text{ (to two d.p.)}$$

Test Your Understanding 8

By simply looking at the two standard deviation figures, we might be tempted to answer 'yes'. In doing so, however, we should be ignoring the fact that the two mean values indicate that wages in country V are inherently higher, and so the deviations from the mean and thus the standard deviation will tend to be higher. To make a comparison of like with like we must use the coefficient of variation:

$$\text{Coefficient of variation} = \frac{\text{Standard deviation}}{\text{Expected return}}$$

Thus

$$\text{Coefficient of variation of wages in country V} = \frac{55}{120} = 45.8\%$$

$$\text{Coefficient of variation of wages in country W} = \frac{50}{90} = 55.6\%$$

Hence we see that, in fact, it is country W that has the higher variability in basic weekly wages.

Test Your Understanding 9

A

The average is given by

$$\frac{286 + 192 + x + 307 + 185 + 4x + 94}{7} = 267$$

Thus 267 × 7 = 1,869 = 1,064 + 5x
Hence, 5*x* = 1,869 – 1,064
Hence, *x* = 805/5=161

Test Your Understanding 10

B

Let $X be the average sales for the sixth, seventh and eighth months.

(8,200 × 5) + (8,500 × 4) + (X × 3) = 102,000

3X = 27,000

X = 9,000

Test Your Understanding 11

B

Putting the ages in order gives 17, 19, 21, 21, 24, 26, 27, 31, 32, 42

Given we have an even number of observations, the median is 25.

Test Your Understanding 12

C

In order of magnitude, without x, the values are

7, 8, 13, 14, 28, 33, 42, 51, 69

Including x, there are ten values so the median of 29 is the average of the fifth and sixth. The only possible solution is that x lies between 28 and 33 and has a value such that $(28 + x)/2 = 29$. Hence, $x = 30$.

Test Your Understanding 13

C

The variance is the square of the standard deviation = 2,401. Answers (A) and (B) have both taken the square root of 49, dividing by the square root of sample size in the case of (B), and (D) has divided the variance by the sample size.

Test Your Understanding 14

A

The standard deviation is increased when data is skewed and this is a major disadvantage. All the others are correct.

Test Your Understanding 15

The answers are as follows:

x	f	fx
0	10	0
1	15	15
2	25	50
3	5	15
Totals	55	80

Arithmetic mean = 80/55 = 1.45

Test Your Understanding 16

All are correct with the exception of statement **A**

Test Your Understanding 17

The correct answers are (A) and (D) since the interval mid-point is calculated by adding the limits and dividing by two.

Test Your Understanding 18

C and D are true,

A and B are false

Test Your Understanding 19

Only statement (C) can be made on the basis of the information given.

Test Your Understanding 20

A and C

Test Your Understanding 21

The correct answers are as follows:

Statistics	*Chart*
A The mean	S
B The median	R
C The mode	Q

Test Your Understanding 22

The interval A follows the same pattern as all the others; mid-point (C) is given by adding 20 and 25 and dividing the result by 2; fx is given by multiplying f (i.e. 17) by x (i.e. 17.5) and fx^2 is given by multiplying 27.5 squared by 22.

Answers:

A 10 and under 15

B 297.5

C 22.5

D 16,637.5

Test Your Understanding 23

Arithmetic mean (x) $= \frac{\Sigma fx}{fx} = \frac{2500}{100} = 25$ days

Test Your Understanding 24

Standard deviation

$$= \sqrt{\frac{\Sigma fx^2}{\Sigma f} - \left(\frac{\Sigma fx}{\Sigma f}\right)^2}$$

$$= \sqrt{\frac{67000}{100} - \left(\frac{2400}{100}\right)^2}$$

$$= \sqrt{670 - 24^2}$$

$$= \sqrt{94}$$

= 9.70 (to2dp)

Test Your Understanding 25

The intervals follow the previous pattern so A is 11 and less than 21. The cumulative frequency B is 470 + 15 and C is the total frequency 500.

Answers:

A 11 and < 21

B 485

C 500.

Test Your Understanding 26

A 4,415

B 201,825

Test Your Understanding 27

A, B and F.

The average is given by the mean which has fallen from 49 to 40 years, so (F) is correct. Variability in age is given by the standard deviation which has changed very little so (A) is correct. It can also be seen that (B) is correct from the original data. All the other statements are incorrect. (C) needs to be checked given that the mean has decreased. In fact the coefficient of variation given by 100 × *s/m* has only increased a little from 17 to 20 per cent, so (G) is incorrect.

Test Your Understanding 28

Multiple bar chart

chapter

4

Index Numbers

Chapter learning objectives

On completion of their studies students should be able to:

- explain how and why indices are used
- calculate indices using either base or current weights
- apply indices to deflate a series.

1 Introduction

Index numbers measure how a group of related commercial quantities vary, usually over time.

For example, suppose you wanted to know how UK companies had fared during difficult economic circumstances in 2011. One way of answering this would be to look at the share prices of companies listed on the UK Stock Exchange and compare the prices at the start and end of the year.

However, this would very time consuming, particularly if a large number of companies were chosen. A simpler approach would be to look at one of many Stock Exchange indices.

For example the Financial Times 100 shares index (FTSE 100) incorporates the values of the shares of the 100 largest companies listed on the UK Stock Exchange. As such any movement in this figure shows us quickly how larger businesses performed.

- At 1st January 2011 FTSE 100 index was 5,900
- At 1st January 2012 FTSE 100 index was 5,572
- Overall the average change in value during 2011 of the UK's 100 largest companies was a decrease of 5.6%, bad news for UK pensions!

As we shall see, most well-known index numbers are averages, but they have the extra property that they relate the quantities being measured to a fixed point or base period.

2 Definitions

If a series of values relating to different times are all expressed as a percentage of the value for a particular time, they are called index numbers with that time as the base.

$$\text{Index number} = \frac{\text{Value in any given year}}{\text{Value in base year}} \times 100$$

We shall generally refer to years but monthly data might have a particular month as base and so forth, so strictly speaking we should say 'time point' rather than 'year'.

Illustration 1

Express the following data with 2005 as the base:

Year	*2005*	*2006*	*2007*	*2008*	*2009*
Value	46	52	62	69	74

Solution

We have to express each value as a percentage of the value for 2005. That means we must divide each by the 2005 value (i.e. by 46) and multiply by 100.

For example, the index for 2007 will be (62/46) × 100 = 135.

The full set of figures is as follows:

Year	*2005*	*2006*	*2007*	*2008*	*2009*
2005 = 100	100	113	135	150	161

A few points of note:

- The base year did not have to be the first of the series. We could have chosen any year.
- Expressions such as '2005 = 100' tell us that the associated values are index numbers with base 2005.
- The index number for the base year (2005 in this case) will always be 100.
- We have rounded to the nearest whole number simply to avoid cluttering the text, while you get used to the idea of index numbers. In fact, they could be expressed to any degree of accuracy.

3 Interpretation of index numbers

An index of 113 tells us that there has been a 13 per cent increase since the base year.

In Illustration 1 we can see that values increased by 13 per cent from 2005 to 2006, by 35 per cent over the 2 years from 2005 to 2007, by 50 per cent over 3 years and by 61 per cent over the 4 years 2005–2009.

It is essential to realise that the percentage changes always refer back to the base year. It is not possible to derive the percentage increase from one year to the next by subtracting index numbers.

Illustration 2

Find the percentage increase from 2008 to 2009 for the data in Illustration 1.

Solution

$$\frac{161}{150} \times 100 = 107.3$$

Therefore, the percentage increase is 7.3 per cent.

If we were to subtract the index numbers we would get 161 – 150 = 11 points, which is clearly not the same as 11%. Were the *Financial Times* 250 Share Index (which, at the time of writing, is at about 6,000) to rise by 50 points, that represents a rise of only 100 × 50/6000 = 0.8%. This 50 point rise must not be confused with a 50% rise!

To derive the percentage increase from year A to year B, the easiest method is to index the year B figure with base year A and then subtract 100.

If values have declined, the index number will be less than 100, and when you interpret them by subtracting 100 the resulting negative tells you there has been a decline. For example, an index of 94 means there has been a decline of 6% (94 – 100 = – 6) since the base year.

Finally, some index numbers become very large, like the FT100 index mentioned above. A 6,000 level means that there has been a 5,900% increase in share prices since the base year – not a very meaningful interpretation, even to those of us who are quite numerate. A much better interpretation is that share prices are now 60 times what they were in the base year.

Hence, there are two ways of interpreting an index number:

- subtracting 100 gives the percentage increase since the base year;
- dividing by 100 gives the ratio of current values to base-year values.

Test Your Understanding 1

Year	*2001*	*2002*	*2003*	*2004*	*2005*	*2006*	*2007*
Profits ($ m)	1.2	1.5	1.8	1.9	1.6	1.5	1.7

A Express the profits figures above as index numbers with:
(i) base *2001*
(ii) base *2004*

B Interpret both the index numbers for *2005*.

C Find the percentage increase from *2006* to *2007*.

D Interpret the index number 2,500 with *1999* = 100.

4 Choice of base year

Although a particular base may be satisfactory for several years, it becomes less meaningful as time passes and eventually it is necessary to shift to a new base this is called rebasing.

The only requirements of a suitable base year are, first, that it should be a fairly typical year. For example, if prices are being indexed then a year should be chosen in which prices were neither specially high nor specially low. Second, it should be sufficiently recent for comparisons with it to be meaningful. For example, it might be useful to know that production had changed by a certain percentage over the last year or two or perhaps over 10 years, but an index with base, say, 50 years ago would not be very relevant.

It is also the case, as we shall see shortly, that many index numbers span a wide range of popular goods and, reflecting what people actually buy, they are very different now from 20 or 30 years ago. The base year has to move in order to keep up with the composition of index numbers to some extent.

5 Change of base year

If at all possible you should return to the original data and recalculate the index numbers with the new base year. However, if only the index numbers are available, they can be indexed as if they were the original data. The only problem is that sometimes rounding errors will build up. As the following example shows, changing the base using index numbers instead of raw data can give very good results.

Illustration 3

Staffing levels in a particular business have been as follows:

Year	*2000*	*2001*	*2002*	*2003*	*2004*	*2005*	*2006*	*2007*	*2008*
Staff	8	9	9	12	20	22	24	25	27

(a) Express the data as index numbers with base *2000*.

(b) Using the original data, change the base to *2005*.

(c) Using the index with base *2000*, change the base to *2005* and compare your results with those in part (b).

Express your answers to one decimal place throughout.

Solution

	Year	*2000*	*2001*	*2002*	*2003*	*2004*	*2005*	*2006*	*2007*	*2008*
	Staff	8	9	9	12	20	22	24	25	27
(a)	2000 =100	100.0	112.5	112.5	150.0	250.0	275.0	300.0	312.5	337.5
(b)	2005 = 100	36.4	40.9	40.9	54.5	90.9	100.0	109.1	113.6	122.7
(c)	2005 = 100	36.4	40.9	40.9	54.5	90.9	100.0	109.1	113.6	122.7

The index labelled (b) has been obtained from the original data, by dividing by 22 and multiplying by 100. The index labelled (c) has been obtained from the 2000 = 100 index numbers by dividing by 275 and multiplying by 100. As you can see, the results are identical when rounded to one decimal place in this case.

Test Your Understanding 2

The following index numbers have base 1999. Recalculate them with base 2006.

Year	*2005*	*2006*	*2007*	*2008*	*2009*
1999 = 100	129.0	140.3	148.5	155.1	163.2

Interpret the two index numbers for 2009, with bases 1999 and 2006.

6 Combining series of index numbers

When a series of index numbers is subject to a change of base or perhaps a small change of composition, you will find in the series a year with two different index numbers, and the change of base will be shown in the series. The technique involved in combining two series into a single one is called *splicing the series together*.

e.g

Illustration 4

The price index below changed its base to 2003 after many years with base 1990. Recalculate it as a single series with base 2003. By how much have prices risen from 2001 to 2005?

Year	*Price index*
	(1990 = 100)
2000	263
2001	271
2002	277
2003	280
	(2003 = 100)
2004	104
2005	107

Solution

The index numbers from 2003 onwards already have 2003 = 100, so nothing need be done to them. What we have to do is to change the base of the original series, so it too is 2003. In this series the value for 2003 is 280, so we must divide the index numbers for 2000–02 by 280 and multiply by 100:

Year	*Price index*	*Price index*	
	(1990 = 100)	(2003 = 100)	
2000	263	94	= 100 × (263/280)
2001	271	97	= 100 × (271/280) etc.
2002	277	99	
2003	280	100	
	(2003 = 100)		
2004	104	104	
2005	107	107	

Now that we have a single series spanning both 2001 and 2005, we can compare the two.

$$100 \times \frac{107}{97} = 110$$

So prices have risen by 10 per cent from 2001 to 2005.

You may notice that we rounded to the nearest whole number in this example. This is because the original index numbers had plainly been rounded to the nearest whole number and at best we can hope that our results will be accurate to that same extent. You cannot acquire increased accuracy in the course of calculating.

Test Your Understanding 3

The following price index has undergone a change of base in 2005. Splice the two series together with base 2005.

Year	*Price index* (1995 = 100)
2002	141
2003	148
2004	155
2005	163

Year	*Price* index (2005 = 100)
2006	106
2007	110
2008	116

7 Chain-base index numbers

So far we have dealt with index numbers that have the same base for several years. These are called fixed-base index numbers and, unless you are informed to the contrary, it is reasonable to assume that index numbers are of this type. However, it is often of more interest to know the annual increase. A chain-base index number (or simply a chain index) expresses each year's value as a percentage of the value for the previous year.

$$\text{Chain-base Index} = \frac{\text{This year's value}}{\text{Last year's value}} \times 100$$

Illustration 5

Express the following series as a series of chain-base index numbers:

Year	*2005*	*2006*	*2007*	*2008*	*2009*
Value	46	52	62	69	74

Solution

Year	*2005*	*2006*	*2007*	*2008*	*2009*
Value	46	52	62	69	74
Chain index	n/a	113.0	119.2	111.3	107.2

We cannot calculate the chain index for 2005 because we do not have the 2004 figure ('n/a' means 'not available').

The interpretation is the same as for fixed-base index numbers, except that the percentage change is each time over the previous year. In this example, the results tell us that values rose by 13.0 per cent from 2005 to 2006, by 19.2 per cent from 2006 to 2007, by 11.3 per cent the next year and by 7.2 per cent from 2008 to 2009.

Fixed-base index numbers can easily be changed into chain-base indices by treating them as if they were the original data. The only problem is to not pick up spurious accuracy. Try the next example.

Test Your Understanding 4

Convert the following fixed-base index numbers into a chain-base index and interpret your results:

Year	*2005*	*2006*	*2007*	*2008*	*2009*
1999 =100	129.0	140.3	148.5	155.1	163.2

Test Your Understanding 5

Express the following chain index as a fixed-base index with 2000 = 100:

Year	*2000*	*2001*	*2002*	*2003*	*2004*
Chain index	105.4	105.0	104.5	104.1	103.9

Test Your Understanding 6

Convert the following chain index into a fixed-base index: (a) with base 2006; and (b) with base 2008:

Year	*2006*	*2007*	*2008*	*2009*	*2010*	*2011*
Chain index	106.1	103.7	103.6	104.2	105.7	108.1

8 Composite index numbers

In practice, most price indices cover a whole range of items and so there are two processes involved in the construction of the index number. One is indexing - comparing current values with those of the base year – and the other is averaging or somehow combining together the items under consideration.

We shall begin by using the method of combining individual price indices by means of a *weighted average*. In Chapter 4, we used the formula $\Sigma fx/\Sigma f$ for the average or arithmetic mean. The formula for a weighted average is the same as this but with weights, denoted by *w*, instead of frequencies. Hence:

$$\text{Weighted average} = \frac{\Sigma wx}{\Sigma w}$$

where *x* denotes the values being averaged and w denotes the weights.

Illustration 6

Average exam marks of 40 per cent, 55 per cent and 58 per cent with weights of 2, 2 and 1.

Solution

$$\text{Weighted average} = \frac{(2 \times 40) + (2 \times 55) + (1 \times 58)}{2 + 2 + 1} = \frac{248}{5} = 49.6\%$$

Weights are a measure of the importance that we allocate to each item. In the above example, the first two exams are rated as twice as important as the third one. In the arithmetic mean, values are weighted by the frequency with which they occur; in price indices, similar weighting systems operate.

Test Your Understanding 7

The three types of bread sold by a shop have price indices of 107.0, 103.6 and 102.9 compared with last year. Find the weighted average index for bread, using quantities as weights if the quantities sold are in the ratio 10:2:1.

Test Your Understanding 8

A manufacturer produces four items (A–D) and wishes to find an overall index of their prices compared with three years ago. The quantities sold will be used as weights. Calculate the price index using the following price indices and quantities:

Product	*Price index base 3 years ago*	*Quantity sold per week*
A	114.5	25
B	109.7	48
C	106.6	59
D	110.7	32

9 Relative price indices

The notation commonly used for the construction of index numbers is as follows: the subscripts '0' and '1' are used, respectively, for the base year and the year under consideration, usually called the current year. Hence, for any given item:

P_0 = price in base year P_1 = price in current year
Q_0 = quantity in base year Q_1 = quantity in current year
$V_0 = P_0 Q_0$ = value in the base year $V_1 = P_1 Q_1$ = value in current year

where value means the total expenditure on the item, and other sorts of weights are denoted by *w* as before.

For a given item, the *price index* = 100 × (P_1/P_0), but quite often we work with the ratio called the price relative = P_1/P_0 and leave the multiplication by 100 to the end of the calculation.

The usual formula for a *relative price index* is therefore:

$$\text{Relative price index} = \frac{\Sigma[\text{w} \times (P_1/P_0)]}{\Sigma \text{w}} \times 100$$

This formula is given in your exam.

The weights could be base-year quantities (i.e. Q_0) or values (i.e. P_0Q_0), or current-year quantities or values (i.e. Q_1 or P_1Q_1), or they could simply be decided on some other basis such as the weighting of exam marks.

The index will be called *base-weighted* or *current-weighted*, depending on whether it uses base or current weights.

Illustration 7

A grocer wishes to index the prices of four different types of tea, with base year 1990 and current year 2010. The available information is as follows:

	1990		2010	
	Price *($)*	*Quantity* *(crates)*	*Price* *($)*	*Quantity* *(crates)*
Type	P_0	Q_0	P_1	Q_1
A	0.89	65	1.03	69
B	1.43	23	1.69	28
C	1.29	37	1.49	42
D	0.49	153	0.89	157

Calculate the base-weighted relative price index using as weights (a) quantities; and (b) values (i.e. revenue for each item).

Solution

	Price relative *(Rel)* P_1/P_0	*Base-year quantity* *(Q_0)*	*Base-year value* *(V_0)* P_0Q_0	*Rel ×* Q_0	*Rel ×* V_0
A	1.157	65	57.85	75.22	66.95
B	1.182	23	32.89	27.19	38.88
C	1.155	37	47.73	42.74	55.13
D	1.816	153	74.97	277.85	136.15
Total		278	213.44	423.00	297.11

Base-weighted relative price indices are:

Weighted by quantity: $\frac{\Sigma(\text{Rel} \times Q_0)}{\Sigma Q_0} \times 100 = \frac{423}{278} \times 100 = 152.2$

Weighted by value: $\frac{\Sigma(Rel \times V_0)}{\Sigma V_0} \times 100 = \frac{297.11}{213.44} \times 100 = 139.2$

The first index tells us that prices have risen on average by 52 per cent; the second that they have risen by 39 per cent. Why might this be so?

The really big price rise is D's 82 per cent. The size of the index will be very strongly influenced by the weight given to D. In the first case, the quantity 153 is bigger than all the other quantities put together. D gets more than half of the total weight and so the index strongly reflects D's price rise and is very high. However, when we use value for weighting, D's value is only about one-third of the total because its price is low, so the price index is rather smaller.

Now it is your turn to see what happens if we use current quantities and values as weights.

Test Your Understanding 9

Using the data of Illustration 7, calculate the current-weighted relative price index with weights given by (a) quantities; and (b) values.

10 Choice of base weighting or current weighting

- In general, current weighting will seem better because it remains up to date.
- In particular, current-weighted indices reflect shifts away from goods subject to high price rises.
- Base-weighted indices do not do this and hence exaggerate inflation.
- However, current quantities can be very difficult to obtain – some considerable time may elapse after a year ends before a company knows what quantity it sold, whereas base quantities are known and remain steady for the lifetime of the index.
- So, current-weighted price indices are usually much more costly and time-consuming to calculate than are base-weighted ones.
- The stability of base weights means that the index for each year can be compared with that of every other year which, strictly speaking, a current-weighted index cannot.

- There can be no general guidance on the choice: it depends on the resources available and on the degree to which prices and quantities are changing. The only other consideration is that, as always, you must compare like with like. The retail price index (RPI), as we shall see, is a current-value-weighted relative index weighted by (almost) current values, and that method of construction should be used if at all possible if comparison with the RPI is a major function of the index being constructed.

11 Quantity indices

Although it is the most important and most frequently encountered, price is not the only financial factor measured by index numbers. Quantity indices constitute another category. They show how the amounts of certain goods and commodities vary over time or location. They are of importance when one is considering changes in sales figures, volumes of trade and so on.

When considering price indices, quantities emerged as the best weighting factor. Here, the converse is true: prices are considered the most appropriate weights when calculating quantity indices.

A relative quantity index will take the form:

$$\frac{\Sigma\,[w \times (Q_1/Q_0)]}{\Sigma w} \times 100$$

An aggregative quantity index will take the form:

$$\frac{\Sigma w Q_1}{\Sigma w Q_0} \times 100$$

where in both cases the weights could be prices, either base year or current, or values or some other measure of the importance of the items. P_0, P_1, Q_0 and Q_1 have the same meanings as earlier in this chapter.

The calculation of quantity indices and their application involve no new arithmetical techniques, as the following example illustrates.

Test Your Understanding 10

A company manufactures three products, A, B and C, and the quantities sold in 2008 and 2009 were as follows:

Product	*Quantity sold*		*Weights*
	2008	*2009*	
A	7	10	85
B	12	15	68
C	25	25	45

Find the index of the quantity sold in 2009 with 2008 as a base using the weights given by using the relatives method.

12 Inflation

One of the most common areas indices are used is in measuring and dealing with inflation.

Terminology

When describing cash flows it is important to clarify whether inflation is included in the figures.

- 'Money' cash flows include predicted inflation and other price rises – they are the actual cash flows that take place. If I am awarded a 3% pay rise, then my gross salary will increase by 3% in money terms.
- 'Real' cash flows have had general inflation taken out of them. If general inflation is 3% per annum, then a 3% pay rise leaves me no better off in real terms – I cannot buy any more goods than before. If inflation is only 2% then I am approximately 1% better off in real terms (Note: this is a simplification)

Some payments are 'index linked', meaning that they automatically increase in line with inflation. (Strictly speaking, they increase in line with a specific index used to measure inflation)

Measuring UK inflation

The Retail Prices Index (RPI) was the UK's main indicator of inflation before 2003. Since then, the Government has focused policy on the Consumer Prices Index (CPI), although RPI figures are still widely quoted and used.Like the RPI, the CPI measures the average change from month to month in the prices of consumer goods and services. However it differs in the particular households it represents, the range of goods and services included, and the way the index is constructed.

The most useful way to think about both the CPI and RPI indices is to imagine a 'shopping basket' containing those goods and services on which people typically spend their money. As the prices of the various items in the basket change over time, so does the total cost of the basket. Movements in the CPI and RPI indices represent the changing cost of this representative shopping basket.

In principle, the cost of the basket should be calculated with reference to all consumer goods and services purchased by households, and the prices measured in every shop or outlet that supplies them. In practice, both the CPI and RPI are calculated by collecting a sample of prices for a selection of representative goods and services in a range of UK retail locations. Currently, around 120,000 separate price quotations are used every month in compiling the indices, covering some 650 representative consumer goods and services for which prices are collected in around 150 areas throughout the UK.

Within each year, the RPI and CPI are calculated as fixed quantity price indices – only the prices of goods affect the index from month to month.

However, the contents of the baskets of goods and services and their associated weights are updated annually. This is important in helping to avoid potential biases in consumer price indices that might otherwise develop over time, for example, due to the development of entirely new goods and services, or the tendency for consumers to substitute purchases away from those particular goods and services for which prices have risen relatively rapidly. For example, frozen chicken nuggets were included in the basket for the first time in 2005.

One major source of information comes from the diaries filled in by people taking part in the Office of National Statistics (ONS) 'Expenditure and Food Survey', a continuous survey of over 6000 households each year.

Adjusting for inflation (deflation)

There are many situations, business and other, where it is important to make adjustments for inflation.

For example, a company may wish to adjust its Revenue figures to reveal the real change in sales, or an employee may wish to adjust his/her salary to hopefully reveal a real increase in income and purchasing power. The Government and many employers often use inflation as a guide to pay increases and taxation changes.

Illustration 8

An inflation index and an index for a company's wages are given below:

Year	*2003*	*2004*	*2005*
Inflation index	110	114	119
Wages index	100	106	109

Determine what has happened to wages in real terms between 2003 and 2005 (you do not have to look at each year separately)

Solution

To compare two sets of index numbers, it is often useful to rebase both sets of figures to the same base. Here rebasing the inflation figures to 2003 will enable the index numbers to be compared directly:

Year	*2003*	*2004*	*2005*
Inflation index (rebased to 2003)	100	103.6	108.2
Wages index	100	106	109

This shows that wages have gone up by 9% over the two years while inflation by 8.2%. To get a wages index in real terms we can then divide the wages index by the inflation index

Year	*2003*	*2004*	*2005*
Inflation index (rebased to 2003)	100	103.6	108.2
Wages index (money terms)	100	106.0	109.0
Wages index (real terms)	100	102.3	100.7

Overall wages have increased in real terms by 0.7%

Test Your Understanding 11

At the start of a year, the RPI stood at 340. At that time, a certain person's index-linked pension was $4,200 per annum and she had $360 invested in an index-linked savings bond. At the start of the following year, the RPI had increased to 360. To what level would the pension and the bond investment have risen?

Test Your Understanding 12

Use the data given below to compare average earnings from 2008 to 2011.

	Average weekly earnings (male manual workers, 21 years+)	*RPI (January 1994 = 100)*
2008	$83.50	201.1
2009	$96.94	235.6
2010	$113.06	271.9
2011	$125.58	303.7

Test Your Understanding 13

The following are the annual salaries of trainee accountants employed by a particular firm over the period 1988–93, and the corresponding values of the RPI with base 1987.

Year	*Salary ($)*	*RPI*
1988	18,100	106.9
1989	18,600	115.2
1990	19,200	126.1
1991	19,700	133.5
1992	20,300	138.5
1993	20,900	140.7

A Express the salaries at constant 1988 prices.

B Index the results with 1988 = 100.

C Comment on your results.

Chapter Summary

- In general, index number:

$$\frac{\text{Current value}}{\text{Value in base year}} \text{ x } 100$$

- If we denote base-period prices by P_0; current prices by P_1; base-period quantities by Q_0; current quantities by Q_1; and weights in general by w, the two main types of price index can be expressed as:

$$\text{Relatives: } \frac{[\text{w x } (P_1/P_0)]}{\text{w}} \text{ x } 100$$

$$\text{Aggregative : } \frac{(\text{w x } P_1)}{(\text{w x } P_0)} \text{ x } 100$$

- The two types of quantity index are:

$$\text{Relatives: } \frac{[\text{w x } (Q_1/Q_0)]}{\text{w}} \text{ x } 100$$

$$\text{Aggregative : } \frac{(\text{w x } Q_1)}{(\text{w x } Q_0)} \text{ x } 100$$

The summation is over all items in the index.

As well as being able to calculate and interpret the above, you should also be able to:

- change the base of a series of index numbers
- splice together two series
- understand the factors influencing the choice of base year
- understand the advantages and disadvantages of base weights and current weights
- understand the construction of the RPI
- be able to use the RPI in practice.

13 Further Practice Questions

Test Your Understanding 14

In 2004, a price index based on 1990 = 100 stood at 126. In that year it was rebased at 2004 = 100. By 2006, the new index stood at 109. For a continuous estimate of price changes since 1990, the new index may be expressed, to two decimal places, in terms of the old as

A 85.51

B 137.34

C 135.00

D 135.68

Test Your Understanding 15

Profits have been as follows ($m):

2000	*2001*	*2002*	*2003*	*2004*
4.1	3.7	3.5	3.8	3.9

When converted to index numbers with base 2000, the index for 2004 is

A 95

B 105

C 20.2

D 5

Test Your Understanding 16

In general, the relative sizes of current-weighted and base-weighted price indices are as follows:

A more or less equal.

B current-weighted bigger than base-weighted.

C base-weighted bigger than current-weighted.

D no regular pattern exists.

Test Your Understanding 17

In 2000, a price index based on 1990 = 100 had a value of x. During 2000, it was rebased at 2000 = 100, and in 2008 the new index stood at 112.

If the total price movement between 1990 and 2008 was an increase of 40 per cent, what was the value of x in 2000, that is, before rebasing?

A 125

B 128

C 136

D 140.

Test Your Understanding 18

If an index with 2000 = 100 has values of 108 in 2005 and 128 in 2009, find the index for 2009 if the base is changed to 2005.

A 84.4

B 136

C 118.5

D 120

Test Your Understanding 19

Which of the following is an advantage of base-weighting?

A The index remains up to date.

B The index is easy to calculate.

C The index gives relatively high results.

D The index is comparable with the RPI.

Test Your Understanding 20

In 2002 the retail price index was 133.5 with 1997 = 100. Convert weekly wages of $300 back to 1997 constant prices.

A $400.50

B $333.50

C $433.50

D $224.72.

Test Your Understanding 21

If the base year is 2005 and the current year is 2009, find the base-weighted quantity index for 2009 given the following totals:

	wQ_0	wQ_1
Total	230	245

A 93.9

B 104.2

C 106.5

D 150.

Test Your Understanding 22

How are the weights obtained for the retail price index? They are:

A The quantity of the item that the average household bought.

B The amount the average household spent on the item.

C The quantity of the items that were sold by a sample of retail outlets.

D The expenditure on the item at a sample of retail outlets.

Test Your Understanding 23

Use the following data to calculate a current quantity-weighted relative price index:

Item	*P0*	*P1*	*w*
F	8	12	14
G	4	9	13

A 186.1

B 187.5

C 173.8

D 175.0.

Test Your Understanding 24

In which one or more of the following ways could a price index of 235 be interpreted?

A There has been a 35 per cent increase since the base year.

B There has been a 135 per cent increase since the base year.

C There has been a 235 per cent increase since the base year.

D Prices now are 2.35 times what they were in the base year.

Test Your Understanding 25

Which of the following statements about the base year is/are correct?

A The base year has to be changed from time to time.

B The base year is fixed and cannot be changed.

C The base year should be one in which there were important changes regarding the variable of interest.

D The base year should be the one in which the variable of interest took its lowest value.

Test Your Understanding 26

Complete the following table which shows two index number series being spliced together to give a single series based on 2008. Give your answers correct to one decimal place.

Year	*Price index (2000 = 100)*	*Price index (2008 = 100)*
2005	238	?
2006	242	?
2007	247	?
2008	250	100
	(2008 = 100)	
2009	104	104
2010	109	109
2011	111	111

Test Your Understanding 27

Complete the following table in which values are being expressed as a chain-base index, giving your answers to the nearest whole number.

Year	*2007*	*2008*	*2009*	*2010*	*2011*
Value	72	75	81	84	89
Chain index	?	?	?	?	?

Test Your Understanding 28

Complete the following table in which a chain-base index is being converted to one with fixed base 2006. Give your answers correct to the nearest whole number.

Year	*2006*	*2007*	*2008*	*2009*
Chain index	102.1	103.4	101.9	103.7
2006 = 100	?	?	?	?

Test Your Understanding 29

Exam marks of 40, 58 and 65 per cent are combined as a weighted average of 51 per cent. What does this tell you about the weighting system used?

A The exam with the lowest mark had a relatively high weight.

B The exam with the highest mark had a relatively high weight.

C The exam marks have not been given equal weights.

Test Your Understanding 30

The following table shows four items with their individual price indices and their relative weights. Calculate the weighted relative price index for the four items combined, giving your answer to the nearest whole number.

Item	*Price index*	*Weight*
A	102	42
B	130	22
C	114	30
D	107	65

Test Your Understanding 31

Which of the following statements about the UK Retail Price Index (RPI) is/are correct?

A The RPI covers the expenditures of all households in the UK.

B The RPI is published annually.

C The weights in the RPI are derived from the *Family Expenditure Survey*.

D The RPI now includes tax payments.

Test Your Understanding 32

Complete the table below in which annual salaries are being converted to their values at 2000 prices using the RPI. Give your answers to the nearest whole number.

Year	*Salary* *$*	*RPI*	*Salary at 2000 prices* *$*
2000	25,500	126.1	25,500
2001	26,900	133.5	?
2002	28,100	138.5	?
2003	28,700	140.7	?

Test Your Understanding 33

Some of the following comments are advantages of current weights over base weights and some are advantages of base weights compared to current weights. Delete answers accordingly.

	Advantage of
A Current weights are expensive to obtain	current/base/incorrect
B Base-weighted indexes are preferable in times of high inflation.	current/base/incorrect
C Current-weighted indexes remain up to date	current/base/incorrect
D Current weights may be very difficult to obtain	current/base/incorrect
E Base weights are always out of date	current/base/incorrect
F Current-weighted indexes reflect changes in demand following price rises	current/base/incorrect
G Base weights need only be obtained once	current/base/incorrect
H Bases-weighted indexes can be meaningfully compared from one year to the next	current/base/incorrect

Test Your Understanding 34

Which of the following are reasons why it is usual to weight the constituent parts of a price index?

A Weights reflect the prices of the constituent parts.

B Prices are always the price per some weight or other.

C Weights reflect the relative importance of the constituent parts.

D Weights must be known so that the entire 'shopping basket' will weigh 100.

Test Your Understanding 35

Price relatives and base-weighted index

A company buys and uses five different materials. Details of the actual prices and quantities used for 2005, and the budgeted figures for 2006, are as follows:

Material	*Weight*	*Actual 2005 Unit price $*	*Budgeted 2006 Unit price $*
A	21	11	12
B	56	22	26
C	62	18	18
D	29	20	22
E	31	22	23

Calculate the missing values in the following table, taking 2005 as the base year and giving your answers correct to two decimal places where appropriate.

Material	*Price relative*	*Price relative × Weight*
A	109.09	2,290.89
B	118.18	6,618.08
C	100	F
D	G	H
E	104.55	3,241.05
Total		I

Test Your Understanding 36

If the total of the price relatives × weights was 21,000, calculate the relative price index for the above data with base 2005, giving your answer to the nearest whole number.

Test your understanding answers

Test Your Understanding 1

	Year	*2001*	*2002*	*2003*	*2004*	*2005*	*2006*	*2007*
A (i)	*2001* = 100	100	125	150	158	133	125	142
(ii)	*2004* = 100	63	79	95	100	84	79	89

B The index of 133 means there has been a 33 per cent increase in profits from *2001* to *2005*. The index of 84 means that profits in *2005* are 16 per cent below their level in *2004*.

C 100 × (1.7/1.5) = 113 so there has been a 13 per cent increase from *2006* to *2007*.

D An index of 2,500 means that values now are 2,500/100 = 25 times their value in the base year, *1999*.

Test Your Understanding 2

Divide through by 140.3 and multiply by 100:

Year	*2005*	*2006*	*2007*	*2008*	*2009*
2006 = 100	91.9	100	105.8	110.5	116.3

The index of 163.2 tells us that values in 2009 were 63.2 per cent higher than in 1999; the index of 116.3 tells us that they were 16.3 per cent higher than in 2006.

Test Your Understanding 3

Year	*Price index*	*Price index*
	(1995 = 100)	(2005 = 100)
2002	141	86.5
2003	148	90.8
2004	155	95.1
2005	163	100
	(2005 = 100)	
2006	106	106
2007	110	110
2008	116	116

The technique used in this example is quite generally applicable. Regardless of which year you eventually want as base, the first step in splicing together two index number series should always be to take as the new overall base the year in which the base changes. (2005 in this example).

Test Your Understanding 4

In each case we divide by the index for the previous year and multiply by 100. We cannot do this for 2005 since we do not have the 2004 figure. We shall round to the nearest whole number to try to avoid rounding errors.

Year	*2005*	*2006*	*2007*	*2008*	*2009*
1999 =100	n/a	109	106	104	105

Over the period 2005–9, there were annual percentage increases of 9, 6, 4 and 5, respectively.

Test Your Understanding 5

Year	*2000*	*2001*	*2002*	*2003*	*2004*
Chain index	105.4	105.0	104.5	104.1	103.9
2000 = 100	100	105.0	109.725	114.224	118.7

First, let 2000 = 100 as instructed. We already have the index for 2001 with 2000 as base – it is 105.0. To get the index for 2002, we start with that for 2001 (i.e. 105.0) and increase it by 4.5 per cent. We do this by multiplying by the ratio 104.5/100 = 1.045, so the index for 2002 = 105.0 × 1.045 = 109.725. For the present we shall keep the spurious accuracy. The next index is given by multiplying 109.725 by 104.1/100 = 1.041, and the last by multiplying the result by 1.039.

Rounding gives the fixed-base index with 2000 = 100 to one decimal place:

Year	*2000*	*2001*	*2002*	*2003*	*2004*
2000 = 100	100	105.0	109.7	114.2	118.7

If you want to change a chain index into a fixed-base index with a middle year as the base, the easiest way is probably to start by expressing it with the first year as base and then to change to the base that you want.

Test Your Understanding 6

Year	*2006*	*2007*	*2008*	*2009*	*2010*	*2011*
Chain index	106.1	103.7	103.6	104.2	105.7	108.1
2006 = 100	100	103.7	107.4	111.9	118.3	127.9
2008 = 100	93	97	100	104	110	119

The index with 2006 = 100 is obtained by setting the 2006 figure = 100 and then multiplying consecutively by 1.037, 1.036, 1.042, 1.057 and 1.081.

The index with 2008 = 100 is then obtained from the 2006 = 100 index by dividing throughout by 107.4 and multiplying by 100.

We have only shown figures rounded to one decimal place but actually worked to about five decimal places in calculating the 2006 = 100 index. We worked from rounded figures to find the 2008 = 100 index.

Test Your Understanding 7

$$\text{Weighted average} = \frac{(10 \times 107.0) + (2 \times 103.6) + (1 \times 102.9)}{10 + 2 + 1} = \frac{1{,}380.1}{13} = 106.2$$

Because the first type of bread has such a high weighting (10), its index (107) has had a major impact in increasing the value of the composite index.

Test Your Understanding 8

We need to multiply each price index by its weight, add them together and divide by the total weight. A table may help to show the method:

Product	*Price index base 3 years ago*	*Quantity sold per week*	*Index × weight*
A	114.5	25	2,862.5
B	109.7	48	5,265.6
C	106.6	59	6,289.4
D	110.7	32	3,542.4
		164	17,959.9

$$\text{Weighted average} = \frac{17{,}959.9}{164} = 109.5$$

Test Your Understanding 9

As before, we need the price relatives which have already been calculated. This time, however, they will be multiplied first by Q_1 and second by the value Q_1P_1.

Note: Unrounded values used to calculate Q, Rel column and V, x Rel column

The calculations are as follows:

	Q1	$Rel = P_1/P_0$	$V_1 = P_1Q_1$	$Q_1 \times Rel$	$V_1 \times Rel$
A	69	1.157	71.07	79.85	82.25
B	28	1.182	47.32	33.09	55.92
C	42	1.155	62.58	48.51	72.28
D	157	1.816	139.73	285.16	253.80
Total	296		320.70	446.61	464.25

(a) Using Q1 as weights, the price index is:

$$\frac{\Sigma(\text{Rel x } Q_1)}{\Sigma Q_1} \text{ x } 100 = \frac{446.61}{296} \text{ x } 100 = 150.9$$

(b) Using V_1 as weights, the price index is:

$$\frac{\Sigma(Rel \text{ x } V_1)}{\Sigma V_1} \text{ x } 100 = \frac{464.25}{320.7} \text{ x } 100 = 144.8$$

Can you explain these further index numbers, compared with the ones we got using base weighting? Here they are in table form:

	Base-weighted	*Current*-weighted
Weighted by quantity	152.2	150.9
Weighted by value	139.2	144.8

Although the quantity of D purchased has dropped a little, presumably because of its high price rise, it still remains the cheapest and most popular brand. In fact, using quantities, it still accounts for over half the total weight. So its price index continues to be high, albeit slightly smaller than with base weighting.

The opposite has occurred with values. Although the quantity of D purchased has dropped, this is more than compensated by its increase in price and so it has increased its proportion of the total value (from 35 to 44 per cent). Consequently, the current-value-weighted index increasingly reflects D's big price rise and so is greater than the base-value-weighted index.

Test Your Understanding 10

Product	Q_1/Q_0	*w*	$w \times (Q_1/Q_0)$
A	1.4286	85	121.4
B	1.25	68	85
C	1	45	45
Total		198	251.4

Relative quantity index $= 100 \times \frac{251.4}{198} = 127.0$

Test Your Understanding 11

First of all, the RPI has risen by 20 from 340. As a percentage, this is

$$\frac{20}{340} \times 100 = 5.88\%$$

The pension and the investment, being index-linked, would increase by the same percentage. The pension thus increases by 5.88% of \$4,200 = \$247 (nearest \$), and the investment by 5.88% of \$360 = \$21.17. Hence, at the start of the year in question, the pension would be \$4,447 per annum, and the investment would stand at \$381.17.

Test Your Understanding 12

The value of the RPI in 2008 shows that average prices were 2.011 times higher then than in January 1994. The purchasing power of $1 will therefore have decreased by this factor in the time. A 2008 wage of $83.50 was therefore 'worth'

$$\frac{83.50}{2.011}$$

in January 1994. This is known as the *real wage*, at January 1994 prices. Applying this process to all the figures, we obtain:

		Real wages, January 1994 prices
2008		$41.52
2009	96.94/2.356	= $41.15
2010		$41.58
2011		$41.35

The average wages of this section of society can thus be seen not to have changed appreciably in real terms over this time period. The apparent rises in wages have been almost exactly cancelled out by similarly sized price rises.

Test Your Understanding 13

A Each value must be multiplied by

$$\frac{\text{1988 RPI}}{\text{RPI of year in Q}} = \frac{106.9}{\text{RPI of year in Q}}$$

B (Each adjusted salary will then be divided by the 1988 salary and multiplied by 100. The results are:

Year	*Salary ($)*	*RPI*	*Salary at 1988 prices*	*Index 1988 = 100*
1988	18,100	106.9	18,100	100
1989	18,600	115.2	17,260 ÷ 18,100 =	95
1990	19,200	126.1	16,277	90
1991	19,700	133.5	15,775	87
1992	20,300	138.5	15,668	87
1993	20,900	140.7	15,879	88

C The real salary paid to trainees, which tells us what they can purchase with their salary, has fallen steadily until 1993 when it increased a little. The decline over the entire 5-year period is 12 per cent.

We should hasten to add that this is an imaginary firm!
The RPI is not the only index used in deflation, particularly if there is a more suitable index available. For instance, an exporting company interested in its real level of profits might well deflate its actual profit figures by an index of export prices.

Test Your Understanding 14

B

Prices in 2004 were 1.26 times those in 1990 and prices in 2006 were 1.09 times those in 2004. Hence prices in 2006 were 1.09 × 1.26 = 1.3734 times those in 1990. This corresponds to a price index of 137.34.

Test Your Understanding 15

A

$$\text{Index} = \frac{3.9}{4.1} \times 100 = 95 \text{ (to the nearest whole number)}$$

Test Your Understanding 16

C

Base-weighted index numbers do not reflect the fact that customers buy less of items that are subject to high price rises. They subsequently exaggerate inflation and tend to be greater than current-weighted index numbers.

Test Your Understanding 17

A

The overall increase of 40 per cent has resulted from (x = 100) per cent followed by 12 per cent. Hence, using ratios, 1.12 × (x/100) = 1.40, giving x = 125.

Test Your Understanding 18

C

The index is given by dividing the 2009 value by the base-year value and multiplying by 100, that is, 100 × (128/108) = 118.5.

The ratio of values is upside down in A – this is the index for 2005 with 2009 as base. In B you seem to have added the 8 of the 108 to 128 and in D you seem to have translated the difference of 20 into an index of 120 without realising that the start point is 108, not 100.

Test Your Understanding 19

B

Base-weighted indices do not remain up to date, and since the RPI is current-weighted they are not really comparable. Base-weighted indices do exaggerate inflation but this is not an advantage. However, they are easy to calculate since the same weights are used year after year and this is an advantage.

Test Your Understanding 20

D

The value at constant 1997 prices is given by multiplying by the RPI for 1997 (i.e. 100) and dividing by the RPI for 2002.

A has the correct method but the ratio is upside down. B adds the increase of 33 in the RPI to the $300 and C adds the entire RPI to it. Both are wrong. You cannot add an index to a quantity in units such as $.

Test Your Understanding 21

C

The quantity index is given by 100 × (wQ_1/ wQ_0), which gives 100 × (245/230) = 106.5.

All the other answers involved the wrong ratio or, in the case of (D), the difference between the two totals

Test Your Understanding 22

B

The expenditure per $1,000 spent by the average household is given by the *Family Expenditure* Survey. The quantity bought would not be applicable because the household may only have one car and lots of baked beans, but the car is more significant than the beans. (C) would not be appropriate for the same reason. It might be possible to use a system similar to (D) but this is not the method used.

Test Your Understanding 23

A

The two price relatives 1.5 and 2.25 must be multiplied by the values of *w1*, that is, 14 and 13 and totalled. Then divide by 27 and multiply by 100. B has averaged the relatives without weights. (C) is correctly calculated but uses the aggregative rather than the relatives method and (D) has simply totalled the P_1 values and expressed them as a percentage of the total of the P_0 values, without any weighting.

Test Your Understanding 24

The correct answers are (B) and (D). If you subtract 100 from an index number, it gives the percentage increase since the base year. Equally, if you divide an index number by 100, it gives the ratio of current values to base-year values.

Test Your Understanding 25

The correct answer is (A). A base year will be fixed for several years but will eventually have to be changed to keep it relevant. The base year should be a very typical year in which there are no big changes or specially high or low values in the variable.

Test Your Understanding 26

The completed table is as follows:

Year	*Price index (2000 = 100)*	*Price index (2008 = 100)*
2005	238	95.2
2006	242	96.8
2007	247	98.8
2008	250	100
	(2008 = 100)	
2009	104	104
2010	109	109
2011	111	111

Test Your Understanding 27

The completed table is as follows:

Year	*2007*	*2008*	*2009*	*2010*	*2011*
Value	72	75	81	84	89
Chain index		104	108	104	106

Test Your Understanding 28

The completed table is as follows:

Year	*2006*	*2007*	*2008*	*2009*
Chain index	102.1	103.4	101.9	103.7
2006 = 100	100	103	105	109

Test Your Understanding 29

Answers (A) and (C) are correct. The low weighted average requires the low mark to have a relatively high weight and the high mark a relatively low weight. Equal weighting would have resulted in a considerably higher average.

Test Your Understanding 30

The relative index is given by Σindex × weight/Σweight = 17,519/159. Hence, the relative price index = 110.

Test Your Understanding 31

Only statement (C) is correct. Very rich and very poor households are not covered by the RPI, it does not include tax and it is published monthly.

Test Your Understanding 32

The method is to multiply each salary by the 2000 RPI and to divide by the RPI for the year in question.

Year	*Salary* $	*RPI*	*Salary at 2000 prices* $
2000	25,500	126.1	25,500
2001	26,900	133.5	25,409
2002	28,100	138.5	25,584
2003	28,700	140.7	25,722

Test Your Understanding 33

With base-year quantities as weights, the denominator will remain constant from year to year. However, since current weights change each year, their denominator constantly changes.

The base-weighted index is therefore easier to calculate and enables meaningful comparisons with previous years. It is also relatively cheap because the weights need to be obtained only once. However, in volatile conditions the base weights become dated and can give misleading indices. Another disadvantage is that base-weighted price indices do not reflect the tendency of consumers to buy fewer of those items that have undergone high price rises. They consequently give unrealistically high weighting to such items and tend to overstate inflation.

Current weights are much more suitable when conditions are volatile, since they remain up to date and reflect changes in demand following price rises. Their drawback is that meaningful comparisons with previous periods may not be possible because of the continually changing weights. Additionally, it can be very difficult and costly to obtain current weights and, in practice, the most recent weights available may have to be used instead.

Answers:		Advantage of
A	Current weights are expensive to obtain	base
B	Base-weighted indexes are preferable in times of high inflation	incorrect
C	Current-weighted indexes remain up to date	current
D	Current weights may be very difficult to obtain	base
E	Base weights are always out of date	incorrect
F	Current-weighted indexes reflect changes in demand following price rises	current
G	Base weights need only be obtained once	base
H	Bases-weighted indexes can be meaningfully compared from one year to the next	base

Test Your Understanding 34

Weights do not reflect prices so (A) is incorrect; (B) is basically correct but is not a reason for using weighting; (D) is simply incorrect.

Answer: (C) Weights reflect the relative importance of the constituent parts.

Test Your Understanding 35

F $100 \times 62 = 6{,}200$

G $100 \times 22/20 = 110$

H $110 \times 29 = 3{,}190$

I 21,540.02 (This is just the column total)

Test Your Understanding 36

Relative price index

$$\text{Relative price index} = 100 \times \frac{\Sigma[w \times (P_1 / P_0)]}{\Sigma w}$$

Answer: 106

chapter

5

Inter-relationships between variables

Chapter learning objectives

On completion of their studies students should be able to:

- prepare a scatter diagram
- calculate the correlation coefficient and the coefficient of determination between two variables
- calculate the regression equation between two variables
- apply the regression equation to predict the dependent variable, given a value of the independent variable.

1 Introduction

This session examines the **strength** and **nature** of the relationship between two sets of figures.

For example,

- How **strong** is the link between advertising spend and sales revenue in our industry? Is advertising a key driver of sales or a minor one?

  To explore the strength of the relationship between two sets of figures we will look at the subject of **correlation**.

- What is the **nature** of this relationship? Can we quantify it by determining an equation linking sales and advertising? If we can do this, then we could use such an equation to help forecast future sales.

  This will involve us looking at the subject of **regression**.

Obviously these two concepts are linked – regression may give us an equation to use for forecasting but correlation will tell us how useful the equation is.

Supplementary reading – Causal and extrapolative approaches

In the next two chapters we look at one of the major applications of statistics, namely forecasting. Although there are a number of ways of producing forecasts that involve little or no mathematics, we shall concentrate here on two of the most important quantitative approaches, causal and extrapolative.

- A *causal* approach is based on the assumption that changes in the variable that we wish to forecast are *caused* by changes in one or more other variables.
- With an *extrapolative* approach, we examine past data on the variable that is to be forecast, in order to determine any patterns the data exhibits. It is then assumed that these patterns will continue into the future: in other words, they are *extrapolated*.

2 Correlation

Two variables are said to be *correlated* if they are related to one another, or, more precisely, if changes in the value of one tend to accompany changes in the other.

For example, if children take higher vitamin C supplements, does that result in higher intelligence or is there no relationship between the two?

Scatter diagrams

With a scatter diagram the data points (*x, y*) are plotted on a graph.

- While strictly not essential for correlation (but it is for regression) it is good practice to set the variables so that the x-axis always shows the independent variable, i.e. that variable which is not affected by the other variable.
- The y-axis should always represent the dependent variable, i.e. that variable which depends on the other. A change in the value of the independent variable will cause the dependent variable to change.

For example, we believe that advertising spend influences sales revenue, not the other way round, so we would set

- x = advertising spend
- y = sales revenue

The result is known as a *scatter diagram*, *scatter graph* or sometimes a *scatter plot* and is a visual way of determining if there might be a (linear) relationship between the variables x and y. If it looks as though there is such a relationship, we can then go on to calculate the correlation coefficient (see section 3 below).

Illustration 1 – Scatter diagrams

A company is investigating the effects of its advertising on sales. Consequently, data on monthly advertising and sales in the following month are collated to obtain:

Advertising expenditure in month ($000)	*Total sales in following month ($000)*
1.3	151.6
0.9	100.1
1.8	199.3
2.1	221.2
1.5	170.0

Plot these data on a scatter diagram.

Solution

Since the company is interested in how advertising affects sales, it is clear that sales should be the dependent variable, *y*, and advertising the independent, *x*.

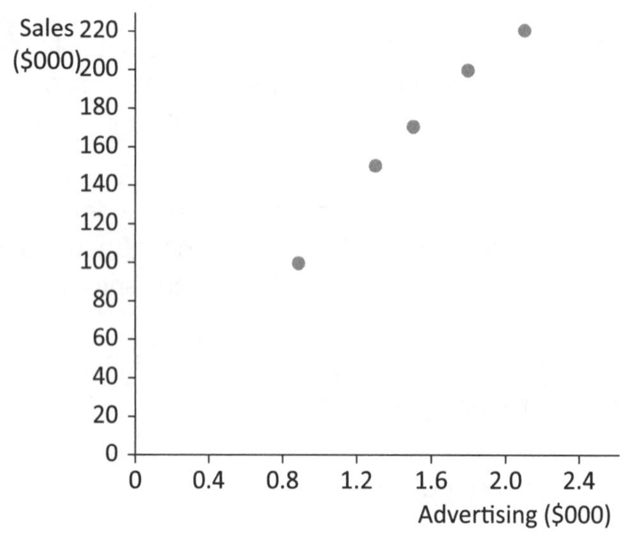

Scatter diagram

The five pairs of data points are marked as points on the graph.

The scatter diagram seems to show a case where the two variables are related to one another. Further, the relationship seems to be of an approximately *linear nature*: it is an example of linear correlation. Since the approximation is so good, and the points are close to a straight line, we talk of *strong* linear correlation.

Finally, as the gradient of the 'line' is positive, it is *positive linear* (or direct) correlation.

A scatter diagram can reveal a range of different types and degrees of correlation:

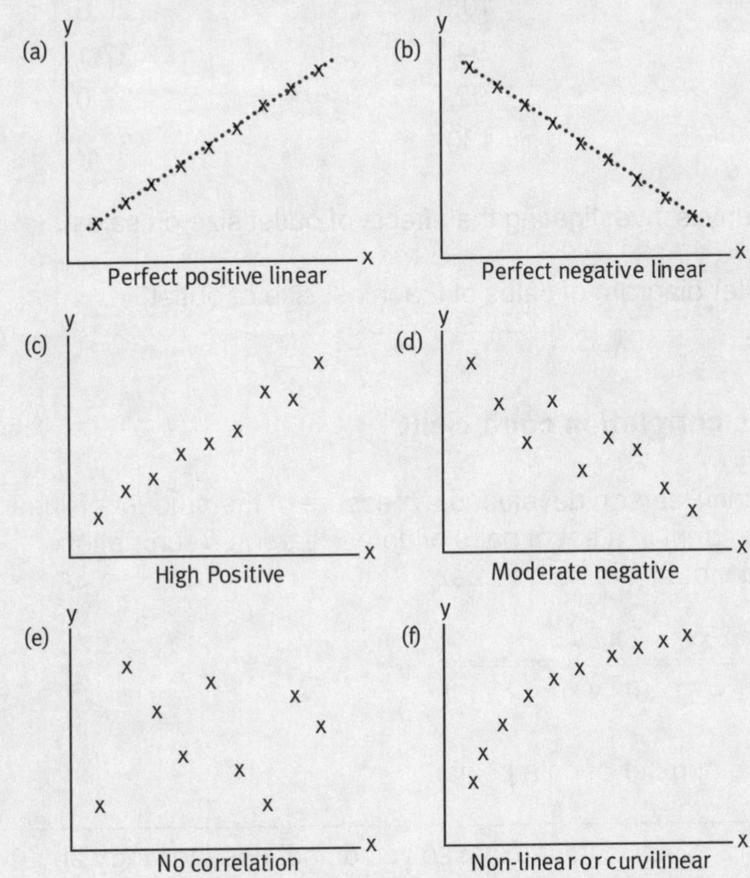

Test Your Understanding 1

From your own experience, try to think of pairs of variables that might have the different degrees of correlation, from weak to strong and from negative to positive.

Test Your Understanding 2

Most of the examples in this chapter relate to the following table. A company owns six sales outlets in a certain city. The sales last year of one of its key products is given below, together with the sizes of each outlet.

Outlet	*Floor space* m^2	*Sales of L* *'000 units*
A	75	22.4
B	60	21.1
C	108	29.6
D	94	27.1
E	92	27.0
F	130	36.9

The company is investigating the effects of outlet size on sales.

Plot a scatter diagram of sales of L against size of outlet.

3 Pearson's correlation coefficient

The statistician Pearson developed a measure of the amount of linear correlation present in a set of pairs of data. Pearson's correlation coefficient, denoted *r*, is defined as:

$$r = \frac{n\Sigma xy - \Sigma x \Sigma y}{\sqrt{(n\Sigma x^2 - (\Sigma x)^2)(n\Sigma y^2 - (\Sigma y)^2)}}$$

where *n* is the number of data points.

This formula is given in your exam so you do not need to worry about remembering it

This measure has the property of always lying in the range –1 to +1, where:

- *r* = +1 denotes *perfect positive* linear correlation (the data points lie *exactly* on a straight line of positive gradient);
- *r* = –1 denotes *perfect negative* linear correlation (again the data points lie on a straight line but with a negative gradient); and
- *r* = 0 denotes no *linear* correlation.

The strength of a correlation can be judged by its proximity to +1 or –1: the nearer it is (and the further away from zero), the stronger is the linear correlation. A common error is to believe that negative values of *r* cannot be strong. They can be just as strong as positive values except that *y* is decreasing as *x* increases.

Illustration 2 – Pearson's correlation coefficient

Evaluate Pearson's correlation coefficient for the data on sales and advertising spend in the table below, and interpret its value.

Advertising expenditure in month ($000)	*Total sales in following month ($000)*
1.3	151.6
0.9	100.1
1.8	199.3
2.1	221.2
1.5	170.0

Solution

With calculations involving summations, we facilitate the calculations by setting them out in columns:

x	y	x^2	y^2	xy
1.3	151.6	1.69	22,982.56	197.08
0.9	100.1	0.81	10,020.01	90.09
1.8	199.3	3.24	39,720.49	358.74
2.1	221.2	4.41	48,929.44	464.52
1.5	170.0	2.25	28,900.00	255.00
7.6	842.2	12.40	150,552.50	1,365.43

Using

$$r = \frac{n\Sigma xy - \Sigma x \Sigma y}{\sqrt{(n\Sigma x^2 - (\Sigma x)^2)(n\Sigma y^2 - (\Sigma y)^2)}}$$

Gives

$$r = \frac{(5 \times 1{,}365.43) - (7.6 \times 842.2)}{\sqrt{[(5 \times 12.4) - 7.6^2][(5 \times 150{,}552.5) - 842.2^2]}} = \frac{426.43}{\sqrt{4.24 \times 43{,}461.66}} = 0.993$$

The value of Pearson's correlation coefficient in this case is 0.993.

The arithmetic in such a calculation can be seen to be potentially very tedious. It is worthwhile investigating the availability of any computer packages or special functions on a calculator in order to ease the computation of correlation coefficients. Note that a simple check is that your calculated value for the correlation coefficient must be between –1 and 1.

The value of the coefficient in this case is clearly very close to the value 1, indicating a very strong positive linear correlation.

Test Your Understanding 3

Using the data on floor space and sales from TYU 2, evaluate Pearson's correlation coefficients for sales of L and the size of outlets.

Test Your Understanding 4

If $\Sigma x = 440$, $\Sigma y = 330$, $\Sigma x^2 = 17{,}986$, $\Sigma y^2 = 10{,}366$, $\Sigma xy = 13{,}467$ and $n = 11$, then the value of r, the coefficient of correlation, to two decimal places, is:

A 0.98

B 0.63

C 0.96

D 0.59

4 The coefficient of determination

We have already seen how Pearson's correlation coefficient allows us to discuss the strength of the relationship between two sets of figures. However, the interpretation of the figure is made slightly easier if we square the correlation coefficient, r, to give the *coefficient of determination, r^2*.

The coefficient of determination, r^2, gives the proportion of changes in y that can be explained by changes in x, assuming a **linear** relationship between x and y.

For example:

If the correlation coefficient were +0.7, say, then $r^2 = 0.49$ and we could state that 49% of the observed changes in y can be explained by the changes in x but that 51% of the changes must be due to other factors.

Spurious correlation

However, one must always watch out for 'spurious' correlation where there is a high value for the correlation coefficient but no direct 'cause and effect' relationship between the sets of data. Often a third 'hidden' factor is influencing both sets of data.

For example, suppose we assume that:

(1) intelligent parents have intelligent children and that

(2) intelligent parents give their children more vitamins.

A study examining the link between quantities of vitamins taken as children and intelligence would probably yield a high correlation, even if there was no scientific link between the two, because of this hidden third factor.

Supplementary reading – Interpreting correlation coefficients

In general, it is not always straightforward to interpret a value of r. Although it would be inappropriate for the purpose of this text to go into detailed theory, it must be noted that the sample size (n) has a crucial effect: the smaller the value of n, the 'easier' it is for a large value of r to arise purely by accident.

Very rough guidelines are that, with a sample of ten data points, a minimum correlation of about 0.6 is needed before you can feel confident that any sort of linear relationship holds. With twenty data points, the minimum correlation needed is about 0.4.

Extrapolation is a further danger in the interpretation of r. If your x-values range from 0.9 to 2.1, then $r = 0.993$ tells you that there is a near-perfect linear relationship between x and y in that range. However, you know nothing at all about the relationship outside that range. It may or may not continue to be linear. The process of drawing conclusions outside the range of the data is called extrapolation. It often cannot be avoided but it leads to unreliable conclusions.

It is possible that an apparently high correlation can occur *accidentally* or *spuriously* between two unconnected variables. There is no mathematical way of checking when this is the case, but common sense can help. In the case under discussion, it seems plausible that sales and the advertising spend *are* connected, and so it would seem reasonable to assume that this is not an accidental or spurious correlation.

More importantly here, two variables can be correlated because they are separately correlated to a *hidden third variable*. The size of the region could well be such a variable: larger regions would tend to have larger sales figures and the management of larger regions would tend to have larger advertising budgets. It is therefore *possible* that this high correlation coefficient may have arisen because the variable 'sales' is highly correlated with size of region, advertising expenditure is highly correlated with size of region, but sales and advertising spend are not themselves directly connected.

Even if this third variable effect is not present, we still cannot conclude that y depends on x. The strong correlation lends support to the *assumption* that this is so, but does not prove it. *Correlation cannot be used to prove causation*.

In your assessment, interpreting correlation is as important as calculating the coefficient.

Test Your Understanding 5

The correlation between x and y is 0.85. This means that:

A x is 85 per cent of y.

B y is 85 per cent of x.

C there is a strong relationship between x and y.

D there is a weak relationship between x and y.

Test Your Understanding 6

If the correlation coefficient is 0.8, what is the coefficient of determination?

A 0.64

B 89

C 20.8

D 0.4

5 Rank correlation: Spearman's coefficient

There are occasions when the degree of correlation between two variables is to be measured but one or both of them is not in a suitable quantitative form.

For example if a student comes top in their mathematics exam, does that mean they will also come top in their economics exam. Here we are interested in their rank rather than their absolute mark.

In such circumstances, Pearson's coefficient cannot be used, but an alternative approach – rank correlation – might be appropriate. The most common measure of this type is *Spearman's rank correlation coefficient, R:*

$$R = 1 - \frac{6\Sigma d^2}{n(n^2 - 1)}$$

where d denotes the difference in ranks, and n the sample size.

You do not need to remember this formula because it will be given in your exam.

The arithmetic involved in calculating values of this coefficient is much easier than that for Pearson's coefficient, as the following example illustrates.

Illustration 3 – Rank correlation, R

As part of its recruitment procedures, a company awards applicants ratings from A (excellent) to E (unsatisfactory) for their interview performance, and marks out of 100 for a written test. The results for five interviewees are as follows.

Interviewee	*Interview grade*	*Test score*
a	A	60
b	B	61
c	A	50
d	C	72
e	D	70

Calculate the Spearman's rank correlation coefficient for this data, and comment on its value.

Solution

In order to apply the formula, the grades and scores are ranked, with the best scores given a rank of 1. Notice how interviewees a and c share the best interview grade. They therefore share the ranks 1 and 2 to give 1.5 each.

Interviewee	*Rank of interview grade*	*Rank of test score*	*d*	d^2
a	1.5	4	–2.5	6.25
b	3	3	0	0.00
c	1.5	5	–3.5	12.25
d	4	1	3	9.00
e	5	2	3	9.00
				36.50

Hence:

$$R = 1 - \frac{6\Sigma d^2}{n(n^2 - 1)} = 1 - \frac{6 \text{ x } 36.50}{5(25-1)} = -0.825$$

The high negative value (near to –1) indicates that interview grades and test scores almost totally disagree with each other – good interview grades go with the lowest test scores and vice versa. This should concern the company, as it may mean that one or both methods of judging applicants is faulty. The interpretation of *R*-values (and warnings!) is similar to that for *r*.

Test Your Understanding 7

An expert was asked to rank, according to taste, eight wines costing below $4. Her rankings (with 1 being the worst taste and 8 the best) and the prices per bottle were as follows:

Sample	*Rank of taste*	*Price*
$		$
A	1	2.49
B	2	2.99
C	3	3.49
D	4	2.99
E	5	3.59
F	6	3.99
G	7	3.99
H	8	2.99

Calculate Spearman's rank correlation coefficient for this data and interpret your result. What result would you expect if the best-tasting wine were ranked 1 and the worst 8?

Supplementary reading – Which correlation coefficient to use?

If the data have already been ranked, there is no option but to use the rank correlation coefficient (*R*). Where actual values of *x* and *y* are given, Pearson's coefficient (*r*) should generally be used since information is lost when values are converted into their ranks. In particular, Pearson's coefficient must be used if you intend to use regression for forecasting (see later). The only advantages in converting actual data into ranks and using Spearman's coefficient are:

(1) that the arithmetic is easier, but this is a minor point given computers and scientific calculators;

(2) that Spearman checks for a linear relationship between the ranks rather than the actual figures. If you simply want to confirm, say, that the variables increase together but have no concern about the linearity of the relationship, you might prefer to use the rank correlation coefficient.

6 Regression

The preceding sections give us a way of checking on whether it may be valid to assume that one variable, *y*, may depend on another, *x*. We now proceed to consider how, after making such an assumption, y can be forecast from *x (for appropriate values of x)*. This involves establishing an equation linking *y* and *x* of the form:

$$y = \text{a function of } x$$

For simplicity, we restrict our attention to instances of **linear** correlation. Thus, we are interested in situations where the dependence is in the form of a straight line. As we saw in Chapter 1, this involves equations of the type:

$$y = a + bx$$

where *a* and *b* are numbers.

While this could be done by estimating the line using a scatter diagram, a formula-based method is quicker and involves less judgement. Within C03 the method you need to understand is "least squares regression".

7 Least-squares regression

Regression analysis finds the line of best fit computationally rather than by estimating the line on a scatter diagram. It seeks to minimise the distance between each point and the regression line.

The regression line has the equation:

$$y = a + bx$$

where:

$$b = \frac{n\Sigma xy - (\Sigma x)(\Sigma y)}{n\Sigma x^2 - (\Sigma x)^2}$$

and

$a = \bar{y} - b\bar{x}$ *($\bar{y}$, $\bar{x}$: are the means of y and x, respectively)*

e.g

Illustration 4 – Regression

A company has the following data on its sales during the last year in each of its regions and the corresponding number of salespersons employed during this time:

Region	*Sales (units)*	*Salespersons*
A	236	11
B	234	12
C	298	18
D	250	15
E	246	13
F	202	10

Develop a linear model for forecasting sales from the number of salespersons.

Solution

As we wish to forecast sales, we shall make this the dependent variable, y, and the number of sales persons the independent variable, *x*.

The next step is to evaluate the parameters *a* and *b*:

x	y	x^2	xy
11	236	121	2,596
12	234	144	2,808
18	298	324	5,364
15	250	225	3,750
13	246	169	3,198
10	202	100	2,020
79	1,466	1,083	19,736

Thus

$$b = \frac{(6 \times 19{,}736) - (79 \times 1{,}466)}{(6 \times 1{,}083) - 79^2} = \frac{2{,}602}{257} = 10.12$$

$$\bar{x} = \frac{79}{6} = 13.17$$

$$\bar{y} = \frac{1{,}466}{6} = 244.33$$

and so

$$a = 244.33 - (10.12 \times 13.17) = 111.05$$

Thus, the least-squares regression line in this case is

$$y = 111.05 + 10.12x$$

Interpreting *a* and *b*

You may remember from Chapter 1 that in the equation of a straight line, $y = a + bx$, a is the intercept on the y-axis and b is the gradient or slope of the line. Expressed slightly differently, that means that a is the value of y when $x = 0$, and b is the increase in y for each unit increase in x.

The b-value of 10.12 tells us that each extra salesperson generates an extra 10.12 sales (on average), while the a-value of 111.05 means that 111.05 units will be sold if no salespeople are used.

Note: The latter conclusion may well be non-sensical because $x = 0$ is outside the range of the data, but we return to this later.

Forecasting

Once the equation of the regression line has been computed, it is a relatively straightforward process to obtain forecasts.

For example, forecast the number of sales that would be expected next year in regions that employed (a) 14 salespersons; and (b) 25 salespersons.

Solution

As we have the 'best' line representing the dependence of sales on the number of salespersons we shall use it for the forecasts. The values could be read off the line drawn on the scattergraph, but it is more accurate to use the equation of the line.

(a) The regression line is $y = 111.05 + 10.12x$ so, when $x = 14$:

$$y = 111.05 + 10.12 \times 14 = 252.73$$

Rounding this to a whole number, we are forecasting that 253 units will be sold in a region employing 14 salespersons.

(b) Substituting $x = 25$ into the formula:

$$y = 111.05 + 10.12 \times 25 = 364.05$$

Hence the forecast is sales of 364 units in a region employing 25 salespersons.

Note: we will have more confidence with the forecast for 14 staff than we do for 25 staff as the latter is within the original range of measurements (between 10 and 18).

Supplementary reading – Least squares regression

The linear correlation coefficient between these two variables can be shown to be 0.948. This high value encourages us to assume that sales, y, might depend on the number of salespersons, x, in a linear way.

The scatter diagram for the data is shown below. For convenience of drawing, the scales on the axes do not start from zero. However, this has the effect of exaggerating the divergences from linearity. A truer impression would be obtained from a graph containing the origin, but this would not be so easy to draw.

In the upper part of the figure, a straight line has been gauged or 'guessed' by using a ruler to draw a line that appears to be 'close' to all five data points. We have deliberately fitted a very poor guessed line so that the errors are clear. If you do have to fit a line 'by eye', the aim is to follow the slope of the points and to draw the line as far as possible through the centre of the points with roughly equal numbers either side. The lower part shows the best possible fitted line.

This approximate approach may well be accurate enough in many instances, but it is certainly arbitrary. A number of different, equally plausible, lines could be drawn in: the question is, how can you judge whether one line is 'better' than another? Indeed, which is the 'best'?

If we look at the 'guessed' line, it is clear that there are discrepancies between actual y-values and those obtained from the line. There are *y*-errors present, and the sizes of these enable us to judge one line against another.

Examples of *y*-errors in this instance are:

- $x = 13$:

  Actual $y = 246$, y from line = 239

  Difference = –7

- $x = 15$

  Actual $y = 250$, y from line = 266

  Difference = +16

Some errors are positive and some negative. Simply adding the errors to judge the 'goodness' of the line, therefore, would not be a sensible idea, as positive errors would tend to be cancelled out by negative ones. To eliminate this effect, we square the errors, and deem one line 'better' than another if its sum of squared errors is lower. The 'best' line is thus the one with the least sum of squared errors: the so-called least-squares regression line of *y* on *x*.

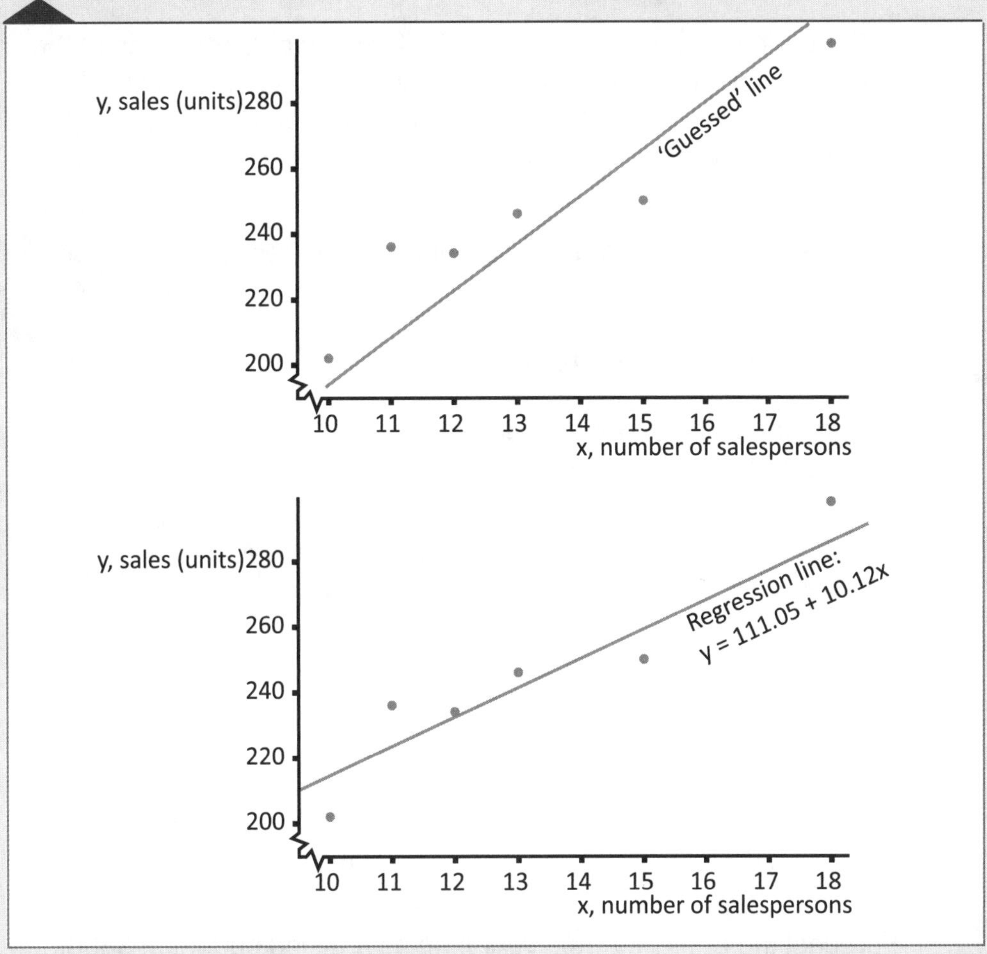

Limitations over the use of linear regression

Just because we have generated an equation of a straight line, it does not mean that it is useful for forecasting.

- Firstly, the actual relationship between the two sets of figures may not be linear. This can be investigated by calculating the coefficient of determination described earlier.

  For example, if $r^2 = 0.6$, then we can say that 60% of the variation in y can be explained using our regression line equation and variations in x. However, this means that 40% of the variation in y cannot be explained by our regression line equation.

- Secondly, even if we have a high level of correlation (and coefficient of variation), then this may be due to "spurious" correlation and the presence of other causal factors
- Finally we need to be careful using the regression line to make forecasts outside of the range of the original data ("extrapolation").

For example, a straight line may be a reasonable reflection of the link between height and age of people between the ages of 10 and 16. However, if we use this to predict the height of a 90 year old, then we will probably predict that they should be 4m tall!

Forecasting using the regression equation is a frequent exam question.

Test Your Understanding 8

A company has the following data on its profits and advertising expenditure over the last 6 years:

Profits $m	*Advertising expenditure* $m
11.3	0.52
12.1	0.61
14.1	0.63
14.6	0.70
15.1	0.70
15.2	0.75

Forecast the profits for next year if an advertising budget of $800,000 is allocated.

Test Your Understanding 9

All of the following except one will adversely affect the reliability of regression forecasts. Which is the exception?

A Small sample

B Low correlation

C Extrapolation

D Negative correlation

Test Your Understanding 10

The regression equation $y = 50 - 2x$ has been obtained from fifteen pairs of x- and y-values, with the x-values ranging from 0 to 20. Which of the following is/are correct?

A When $x = 0$, y is estimated to be 25.

B y decreases by 2 whenever x increases by 1.

C The equation cannot be relied upon for x-values greater than 20.

D The correlation between x and y must be negative.

Chapter summary

Pearson's coefficient of linear correlation, r, is:

$$r = \frac{n\Sigma xy - \Sigma x \Sigma y}{\sqrt{(n\Sigma x^2 - (\Sigma x)^2)(n\Sigma y^2 - (\Sigma y)^2)}}$$

where n is the sample size (number of data points). The linear relationship between x and y is strong if r is close to +1 or –1 and is weak if r is close to 0.

The *coefficient of determination* is given by r^2 and it gives the percentage of the variations observed in the y-values that can be explained by the linear relationship and the corresponding variations in the x-values.

When interpreting the value of correlation coefficients or coefficients of determination, care should be taken over:

- how representative (or otherwise) is the sample
- the sample size
- whether the correlation is spurious or accidental
- whether a hidden third variable is present
- that the interpretation is not generalised beyond the range of the data.

The *least-squares y-on-x regression line* is

$$y = a + bx$$

and

$$a = y - bx$$

In using this line to forecast values of y, the following points/questions must be considered:

- is the correlation coefficient, r (or the coefficient of determination, r^2), large enough to support the assumption that y depends on x?
- is there a hidden third variable?
- does y depend on x, or is it the case that x depends on y?
- interpolated forecasts are more reliable than extrapolated ones
- ensure that the y-on-x line is used only to forecast y
- are there any other variables that might affect y?
- have there been, or are there likely to be, any changes in background circumstances that might invalidate the forecast?
- is the sample sufficiently representative and sufficiently large for reliable results?

8 Further Practice Questions

Test Your Understanding 11

In a forecasting model based on $Y = a + bX$, the intercept on the Y–axis is \$234. If the value of Y is \$491 and X is 20, then the value of the slope, to two decimal places, is:

A 224.55

B 212.85

C 12.85

D 24.85

Test Your Understanding 12

If the coefficient of determination is 0.49, which of the following is correct?

A $y = 0.49x$

B $y = a + 0.49x$

C 49% of the variation in y can be explained by the corresponding variation in x.

D 49% of the variation in x can be explained by the corresponding variation in y.

Test Your Understanding 13

Find the value of a in a regression equation if $b = 7$, $\Sigma x = 150$, $\Sigma y = 400$ and $n = 10$.

A 145

B – 65

C $y – 7x$

D – 650

Test Your Understanding 14

If the regression equation (in $'000) linking sales (y) and advertising expenditure (x) is given by $y = 5{,}000 + 10x$, forecast the sales when $100,000 is spent on advertising.

A $1,005,000

B $501,000

C $4m

D $6m

Test Your Understanding 15

If the regression equation linking costs ($m) to number of units produced ('000s) is $y = 4.3 + 0.5x$, which of the following is correct?

A For every extra unit produced, costs rise by $500,000.

B For every extra 1,000 units produced, costs rise by $500,000.

C For every extra 1,000 units produced, costs rise by $4.3m.

D For every extra unit produced, costs rise by $4,300.

Test Your Understanding 16

The prices of the following items are to be ranked prior to the calculation of Spearman's rank correlation coefficient. What is the rank of item G?

Item	E	F	G	H	I	J	K	L
Price	18	24	23	23	19	23	19	25

A 5

B 4

C 3

D 3.5

Test Your Understanding 17

If $n = 8$, Σx 10, $\Sigma y = 800$, $\Sigma xy = 1{,}500$ $\Sigma x^2 = 20$ and $\Sigma y^2 = 120{,}000$, calculate Pearson's correlation coefficient, giving your answer correct to three decimal places.

Test Your Understanding 18

If n = 10, $\Sigma x = 90$, $\Sigma y = 1{,}500$, $\Sigma x^2 = 1{,}000$ and $\Sigma xy = 20{,}000$, calculate the value of *b* in the regression line $y = a + bx$, giving your answer correct to three significant figures.

Test Your Understanding 19

If the Pearson correlation coefficient between *x* and *y* is + 0.9, which of the following is/are true?

A There is a strong linear relationship between *x* and *y*.

B *y* increases as *x* increases.

C Ninety per cent of the changes in *y* can be explained by the corresponding changes in *x*.

D The slope of the regression line of *y* on *x* is positive.

Test Your Understanding 20

Over a period of 12 months, in which monthly advertising expenditure ranges from \$20,000 to \$50,000, the correlation between monthly advertising expenditure and monthly sales is 0.8. Which of the following is/are true on the basis of the information given?

A Higher sales are caused by higher expenditure on advertising.

B If advertising expenditure is increased to \$100,000, sales will increase.

C Sixty-four per cent of the changes in sales from one month to the next can be explained by corresponding changes in advertising expenditure.

D A correlation coefficient derived from 24 months' data would be more reliable than that given above.

Test Your Understanding 21

Two wine tasters ranked eight bottles of wine as follows:

Wine	A	B	C	D	E	F	G	H
Taster X	3	7	1	8	5	2	4	6
Taster Y	3	8	2	7	4	1	5	6

Find Spearman's rank correlation coefficient for this data, giving your answer to three decimal places.

Test Your Understanding 22

Determine the ranks of the following data, with the *smallest* being ranked 1.

Values	3.21	3.49	3.99	4.05	3.49	4.49	4.99	4.05	3.49

Test Your Understanding 23

In the calculation of the regression equation $y = a + bx$ using ten pairs of x– and y–values, $\Sigma x = 80$, $\Sigma y = 500$ and $b = -1.59$. Calculate the value of a correct to three significant figures.

Test Your Understanding 24

The correlation coefficient for ten pairs of x- and y-values, with x ranging from \$500 to \$700, is calculated to be 0.79, and the regression equation is y = 620 + 4.3x. Which of the following is/are correct?

A When x = \$600, the estimate of y = 3,200.

B When x = \$550, the estimate of y from the regression equation is likely to be reliable.

C When x = 0, the estimate of y from the regression equation is likely to be reliable.

D When x increases by \$1, y increases by 0.79.

Test Your Understanding 25

Scatter diagram; line of best fit

An ice-cream supplier has recorded some sales data that he believes shows a relationship between temperature and sales. The results shown below are for ten sample days in the summer:

Temperature (°C)	*Cartons sold*
x	y
13	10
16	11
17	14
19	15
20	16
21	19
23	24
26	25
27	26
28	27

Using the intermediate totals given below, calculate the coefficient of correlation giving your answer correct to two d.p.

$\sum x = 210$ $\sum y = 187$

$\sum x^2 = 4{,}634$ $\sum y^2 = 3{,}865$

$\sum xy = 4{,}208$

Test Your Understanding 26

Using the data in TYU 25, if the correlation coefficient was 0.95 calculate the coefficient of determination as a percentage, giving your answer to the nearest whole per cent.

Test Your Understanding 27

Using the data in TYU 25, if the correlation coefficient was 0.95, which of the following statements would be correct?

A The positive sign tells us that there is a strong relationship between temperature and sales.

B The positive sign tells us that as temperature rises, so do sales.

C The value of the correlation coefficient tells us that there is a strong linear relationship between temperature and sales.

D The value of the correlation coefficient tells us that for each increase of 1 degree in temperature, sales increase by 0.95 cartons.

E The value of the correlation coefficient tells us that for each decrease of 1 degree in the temperature, sales decrease by 5 per cent.

F The value of correlation coefficient tells us that high temperatures cause high sales.

Test Your Understanding 28

Using the data in TYU 25, if the coefficient of determination was 85 per cent, which of the following statements would be correct?

A When temperature increases by 1°C, sales increase by 85 per cent.

B When temperature increases by 1°C, sales increase by 15 per cent.

C On 85 per cent of days it is possible to accurately predict sales if an accurate prediction of temperature exists.

D 85 per cent of the changes in sales from one day to the next can be explained by corresponding changes in temperature.

Test Your Understanding 29

The following graph displays the data in TYU 25. What type of graph is it?

A Scattergram

B Histogram

C Pictogram

D Ogive

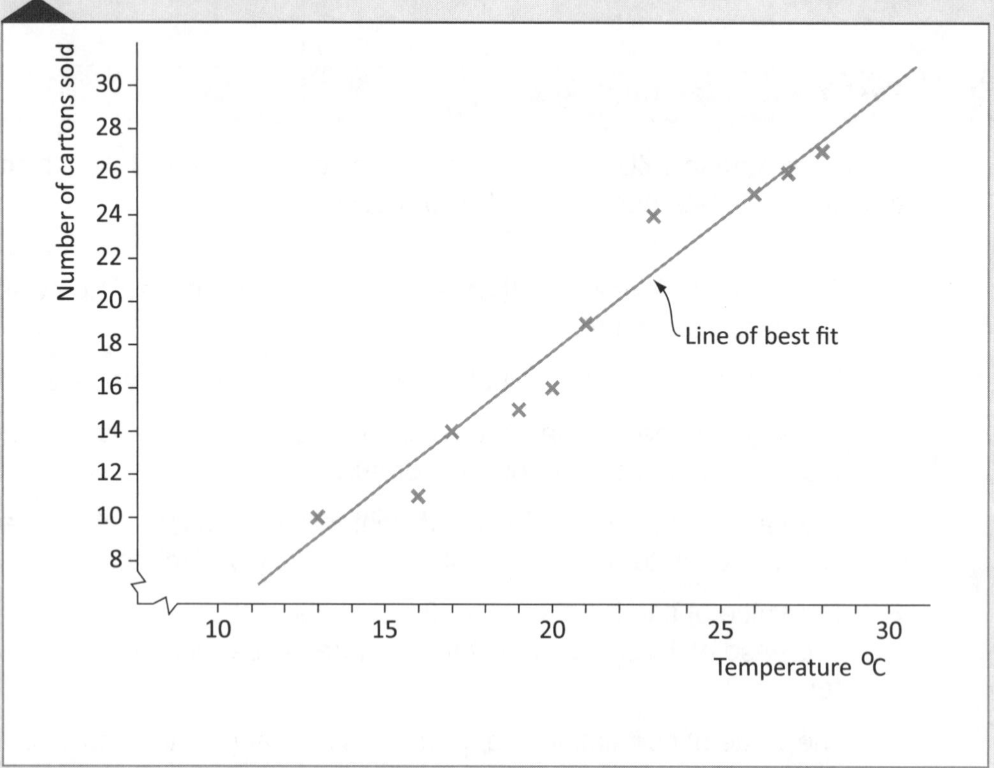

Test Your Understanding 30

A A freehand line of best fit has been fitted to the graph of the data. Estimate the likely sales when the temperature is 15°C, giving your answer to the nearest whole number.

B Estimate the likely sales when the temperature is 30°C, giving your answer to the nearest whole number.

Test Your Understanding 31

Which of the following statements about the reliability of the estimates made in TYU 25 are correct, assuming that the correlation is 0.95.

A The estimate for a temperature of 15°C should be reliable because it involves interpolation.

B Both estimates are less reliable than they otherwise would be because the sample is small.

C The estimate for 30°C should be reliable because it involves extrapolation.

D Both estimates are more reliable than they would otherwise be because the correlation is high.

Test Your Understanding 32

Least-squares analysis

A travel agency has kept records of the number of holidays booked and the number of complaints received over the past ten years. The data is as follows:

Year	*1*	*2*	*3*	*4*	*5*	*6*	*7*	*8*	*9*	*10*
Number of holidays booked	246	192	221	385	416	279	343	582	610	674
Number of complaints received	94	80	106	183	225	162	191	252	291	310

The agency suspects there is a relationship between the number of bookings and the volume of complaints and wishes to have some method of estimating the number of complaints, given the volume of bookings. Denoting number of holidays by X and number of complaints by Y, the following summations are given:

- $\Sigma X = 3,948$,
- $\Sigma Y = 1,894$,
- $\Sigma X^2 = 1,828,092$,
- $\Sigma Y^2 = 417,596$,
- $\Sigma XY = 869,790$

Calculate the value of the correlation coefficient '*r*', giving your answer correct to three d.p.

Test Your Understanding 33

The agency now wants to determine the equation of the regression line. If the value of '*b*' is taken to be 0.4 calculate the value of the regression coefficient '*a*', giving your answer correct to two d.p.

Test Your Understanding 34

If the regression equation was y = 31 + 0.4*x* forecast the likely number of complaints if 750 holidays are booked, giving your answer to the nearest whole number.

Test Your Understanding 35

Which of the following methods could be used to check whether there is in fact a linear relationship between the variables.

A Scatter diagram

B Time series analysis

C Coefficient of variation

D Regression analysis

E Correlation coefficient

Test Your Understanding 36

Which of the following comments about the likely reliability of the estimate of complaints arising from 750 holidays is/are correct?

A The estimate is likely to be reliable because the value of 'a' is positive.

B The estimate is likely to be reliable because it lies outside the range of the data.

C The estimate is likely to be unreliable because the sample is small.

D The estimate is not likely to be reliable because the value of *'b'* is not close to 1.

E The estimate is likely to be unreliable because it was obtained by extrapolation.

Test Your Understanding 37

Correlation

A company is building a model in order to forecast total costs based on the level of output. The following data is available for last year:

Month	*Output '000 units [x]*	*Costs $000 [y]*
January	16	170
February	20	240
March	23	260
April	25	300
May	25	280
June	19	230
July	16	200
August	12	160
September	19	240
October	25	290
November	28	350
December	12	200

If output is denoted by X and costs by Y, you are given that $\Sigma X = 240$, $\Sigma Y = 2{,}920$, $\Sigma XY = 61{,}500$, $\Sigma X^2 = 5{,}110$ and $\Sigma Y^2 = 745{,}200$. Calculate the correlation coefficient between output and costs, giving your answer to three d.p.

Test Your Understanding 38

If the correlation coefficient was 0.9, which of the following comments are correct?

A The correlation coefficient shows that there is a strong linear relationship between output and costs.

B The correlation coefficient shows that high output causes high costs.

C The correlation coefficient shows that costs rise as output rises.

D Costs rise by 0.9 in $1000 for every extra 1000 units of output.

E The high value of the correlation coefficient means that estimates made using regression are likely to be reliable.

Test Your Understanding 39

If the regression equation linking output and costs is $Y = 43 + 10X$, which of the following comments is/are correct?

A For every extra unit produced, costs will rise by $43.

B Even with zero output there will be costs of $43,000.

C For every extra 1000 units produced, costs will rise on average by $10,000.

D For every extra unit produced, costs are likely to increase by $53.

E When 1000 units are produced, costs are likely to be $10,043.

Test your understanding answers

Test Your Understanding 1

These are just some examples:

- costs probably have a strong positive correlation with the number of units produced
- number of deaths on the roads probably has a middling positive correlation with traffic levels
- the level of street crime is often thought to relate to the level of visible policing, so the correlation would be negative but probably not strong
- a strong negative correlation would probably be found if almost any measure of bodily function, such as the condition of the heart, were compared with age in adults, although the graph is unlikely to be perfectly linear.

Test Your Understanding 2

We are investigating the effect of size on sales, so sales must be the dependent variable.

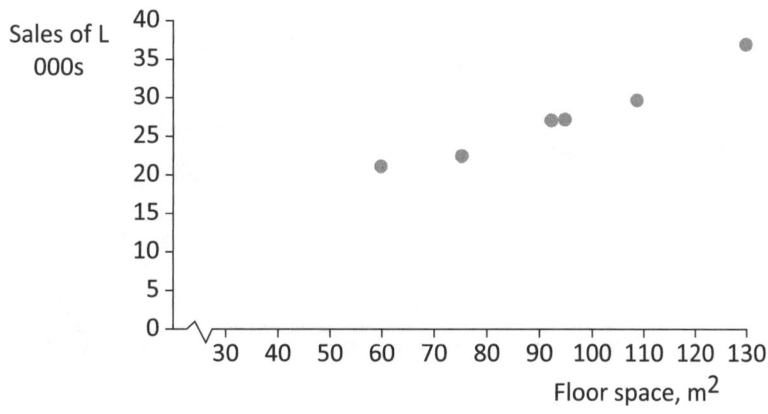

The scatter diagram indicates that there is a positive linear correlation between outlet size and sales: larger outlets have higher sales figures.

Test Your Understanding 3

The necessary summations are

- $n = 6$
- $\Sigma x = 559$
- $\Sigma y = 164.1$
- $\Sigma x^2 = 55{,}089$
- $\Sigma y^2 = 4{,}648.15$
- $\Sigma xy = 15{,}971.2$

Hence:

$$r = \frac{(6 \times 15{,}971.2) - (559 \times 164.1)}{\sqrt{(6 \times 55{,}089 - 559^2)(6 \times 4{,}648.15 - 164.1^2)}}$$

$$= \frac{4{,}095.3}{\sqrt{18{,}053 \times 960.09}} = \frac{4{,}095.3}{\sqrt{(17{,}332{,}504.77)}} = \frac{4{,}095.3}{4{,}163.23} = 0.984$$

This is a very strong positive correlation between outlet size and sales of L.

Many students initially find these calculations very difficult. Even if you got the right answer, you may find it useful to run through the calculations once more. Correlation is a very important topic in business mathematics.

Test Your Understanding 4

B

$$r = \frac{(11 \times 13{,}467) - (440 \times 330)}{\sqrt{(11 \times 17{,}986 - 440^2)(11 \times 10{,}366 - 330^2)}} = \frac{2{,}937}{\sqrt{4{,}246 \times 5{,}126}} = 0.63$$

Test Your Understanding 5

C

Correlation coefficients measure the strength of the linear relationship between two variables. They vary numerically between –1 and 1, being weak when close to 0 and strong when close to 1 or –1.

Test Your Understanding 6

A

The coefficient of determination is given by squaring the correlation coefficient. Often it is also multiplied by 100.

Test Your Understanding 7

Sample	*Rank of taste*	*Rank of price*	*d*	d^2
A	1	1	0	0
B	2	3	–1	1
C	3	5	–2	4
D	4	3	1	1
E	5	6	–1	1
F	6	7.5	–1.5	2.25
G	7	7.5	–0.5	0.25
H	8	3	5	25
				34.50

Hence

$$R = 1 - \frac{6\Sigma d^2}{n(n^2-1)} = 1 - \frac{6 \times 34.5}{8(64-1)} = 1 - \frac{207}{504} = 1 - 0.41 = 0.59$$

There seems to be some positive correlation between price and taste, with the more expensive wines tending to taste better. Given the sample size the result is not really reliable and it cannot be extrapolated to wines costing more than $4. Had the taste rankings been allocated in the opposite order, the correlation would be negative indicating that the cheaper wines tasted worse.

Students often find this calculation difficult and it is worth running through it again if you had problems. Probably the most common errors are either forgetting to subtract from 1 or subtracting the numerator from 1 prior to dividing by the denominator.

Tied rankings can also be difficult. B, D and H all cost $2.99. Had they been marginally different they would have been ranked 2, 3 and 4. Since they are identical, they each have the rank of 3 (the average of 2, 3 and 4). Similarly F and G share the ranks 7 and 8 by giving them an average 7.5 each.

The *d* column is obtained by subtracting rank of taste minus rank of price, but it would be equally correct the other way round.

Test Your Understanding 8

First of all, to justify our assumption that there is a relationship between the two variables, the correlation coefficient should be computed. It is left as an exercise for you to verify that its value is 0.936. This high correlation encourages us to proceed with the regression approach.

As we wish to forecast profits, we shall make this the dependent variable, y, and advertising expenditure the independent variable, *x*.

The next step is to evaluate the parameters *a* and *b*:

x	y	x^2	xy
0.52	11.3	0.2704	5.876
0.61	12.1	0.3721	7.381
0.63	14.1	0.3969	8.883
0.70	14.6	0.4900	10.220
0.70	15.1	0.4900	10.570
0.75	15.2	0.5625	11.400
3.91	82.4	2.5819	54.330

Thus

$$b = \frac{(6 \text{ x } 54.33) - (3.91 \text{ x } 82.4)}{(6 \text{ x } 2.5819) - 3.91^2} = \frac{3.796}{0.2033} = 18.67$$

$$\bar{x} = \frac{3.91}{6} = 0.652$$

$$\bar{y} = \frac{82.4}{6} = 13.73$$

and so:

$$a = 13.73 - (18.67 \times 0.652) = 1.56$$

The least-squares regression line relating profits to advertising expenditure therefore has equation

$$y = 1.56 + 18.67x$$

Hence each extra million dollars of advertising generates an extra \$18.67 million profits. Also, profits would be \$1.56 million without any advertising.

If advertising expenditure is to be \$800,000 ($x = 0.8$), then:

$$y = 1.56 + 18.67 \times 0.8 = 16.496$$

Rounding this value off to a sensible level of apparent accuracy, we are forecasting profits of \$16.5 million next year, if advertising expenditure is \$800,000.

Test Your Understanding 9

D

It is the strength of the correlation but not its sign that influences the reliability of regression forecasts. Correlation can be negative but still very strong so (D) is the exception. Small samples, low correlation and extrapolation all tend to give unreliable forecasts.

Test Your Understanding 10

A Incorrect: when $x = 0$, $y = 50 - 0 = 50$.

B Correct.

C Correct.

D Correct.

Test Your Understanding 11

C

$$Y = a + bX$$
$$491 = 234 + 20b$$
$$257 = 20b$$
$$12.85 = b$$

Test Your Understanding 12

C

The coefficient of determination gives the percentage of the variation in y which can be explained by the regression relationship with *x*. Answers (A) and (B) are confusing this with the actual regression equation, while answer (D) has x and y the wrong way round.

Test Your Understanding 13

B

$$a = \frac{\Sigma y}{n} - b\frac{\Sigma x}{n} = 40 - (7 \times 15) = -65$$

Solution (A) has added instead of subtracting and (D) has failed to divide by *n*. Solution (C) correctly states that, since $y = a + bx$, then $a = y - bx$. However, this is an equation satisfied by a and is not the value of *a*.

Test Your Understanding 14

D

y = 5,000 + 10x, and x = 100 when advertising is $100,000.

Hence y = 5,000 + 10 × 100 = 6,000 (in $'000). Hence sales forecast is $6m.

A is wrong because x = 100,000 has been used and the units of y ignored.

B In (B) 5,000 + 10 has been calculated before multiplication by 100 and in

C the 10x has been wrongly subtracted.

Test Your Understanding 15

B

In the equation y =a + bx, if x increases by one unit, y will increase by b units. In this case if x increases by 1 unit, y increases by 0.5 units, which translates into production increasing by 1,000 units and costs by $500,000. All the other answers have either confused a and b or confused the units of x and y.

Test Your Understanding 16

A

Item	E	F	G	H	I	J	K	L
Price	18	24	23	23	19	23	19	25
Rank	1	7	5	5	2.5	5	2.5	8

The two 19s occupy ranks 2 and 3 with an average of 2.5, and the three 23 s occupy ranks 4, 5 and 6 with an average of 5. It is essential to count both the 19s and the fact that item G happens to be the first of the 23s listed does not give it a lower rank. Answer D seems to be misled by item G's position as third in the list but adjacent to another 23.

Test Your Understanding 17

$$r = \frac{n\Sigma xy - \Sigma x\Sigma y}{\sqrt{\{(n\Sigma x^2 - (\Sigma x)^2)(n\Sigma y^2 - (\Sigma y)^2)\}}}$$

$$= \frac{8 \times 1,500 - 10 \times 800}{\sqrt{\{(8 \times 20 - 10^2)(8 \times 120,000 - 800^2)\}}}$$

$$= \frac{4,000}{\sqrt{(60 \times 320,000)}} = 0.913$$

Test Your Understanding 18

$$b = \frac{n\Sigma xy - (\Sigma x)(\Sigma y)}{n\Sigma x^2 - (\Sigma x)^2}$$

$$= \frac{10 \times 20,000 - 90 \times 1,500}{10 \times 1,000 - 90^2}$$

$$= \frac{65,000}{1,900} = 34.2$$

Test Your Understanding 19

A True: the correlation is close to 1 in value.

B True: the correlation is positive.

C Untrue: the correct percentage would be 81.

D True: the correlation is positive.

Test Your Understanding 20

A Untrue on the basis of this information. Causation cannot be deduced from high correlation.

B Untrue on the basis of this information. We cannot be sure that the positive correlation will continue for advertising greater than $50,000.

C True.

D True.

Test Your Understanding 21

	A	B	C	D	E	F	G	H
d	0	–1	–1	1	1	1	–1	0
d^2	0	1	1	1	1	1	1	0

$\Sigma d^2 = 6;\ n = 8$

$$\text{Rank correlation} = 1 - \frac{6 \times \Sigma d^2}{n(n^2 - 1)}$$

$$= 1 - \frac{6 \times 6}{8 \times 63} = 0.929$$

Test Your Understanding 22

Values	3.21	3.49	3.99	4.05	3.49	4.49	4.99	4.05	3.49
Ranks	1	3	5	6.5	3	8	9	6.5	3

Test Your Understanding 23

$$a = \frac{\Sigma y}{n} - b\frac{\Sigma x}{n}$$

$$= \frac{500}{10} - (-1.59) \times \frac{80}{10} = 50 + 12.72 = 62.7 \text{ to three s.f}$$

Test Your Understanding 24

A Correct.

B Correct.

C Incorrect: $x = 0$ is outside the range of the data.

D Incorrect: when x increases by 1, y increases by 4.3 from the regression equation.

Test Your Understanding 25

$$r = \frac{n\Sigma xy - \Sigma x \Sigma y}{\sqrt{((n\Sigma x^2 - (\Sigma x)^2)(n\Sigma y^2 - (\Sigma y)^2)}}$$

$$= \frac{(10 \times 4{,}208) - (210 \times 187)}{\sqrt{(10 \times 4{,}634 - 210^2)(10 \times 3{,}865 - 187^2)}}$$

$$= \frac{2{,}810}{\sqrt{(2{,}240 \times 3{,}681)}} = 0.98$$

Answer: 0.98

Test Your Understanding 26

Coefficient of determination = $(r^2) \times 100 = (0.95^2) \times 100 = 90$ per cent.

Test Your Understanding 27

B and C

The positive sign tells us that as temperature rises, so do sales but it tells us nothing about the strength of the relationship. So (B) is correct and (A) is incorrect.

The value of the correlation coefficient tells us that there is a strong linear relationship between temperature and sales (C) but it cannot prove cause and effect, so (F) is wrong. Equally it doesn't enable us to estimate likely changes in sales corresponding to known changes in temperature and hence (D) and (E) are both incorrect.

Test Your Understanding 28

(A), (B) and (C) are all incorrect because predictions cannot be made on the basis of the coefficient of determination.

Answer: (D).

Eighty-five per cent of the changes in sales from one day to the next can be explained by corresponding changes in temperature.

Test Your Understanding 29

Answer: (A) Scattergram

Test Your Understanding 30

A Answer: 11

B Answer: 30

Test Your Understanding 31

A and B

Estimation within the range of the data is called interpolation and, all other things being equal, tends to give reliable estimates. Extrapolation – estimating outside the range of the data – is not reliable, although in this instance a temperature of 30°C is only just outside the range and would not therefore constitute so much of a problem. The high correlation coefficient will make both estimates more reliable, while the small sample of ten points will reduce the reliability of both.

The estimate for 30°C is not reliable because it involves extrapolation and the fact that correlation is high does not strictly speaking render it more reliable because it lies outside the range of the data for which the correlation has been calculated. The small sample reduces the reliability of all estimates.

Test Your Understanding 32

$$r = \frac{n\Sigma xy - \Sigma x\Sigma y}{\sqrt{(n\Sigma x^2 - (\Sigma x)^2)(n\Sigma y^2 - (\Sigma y)^2}}$$

$$r = \frac{10 \times 869{,}790 - 3948 \times 1894}{\sqrt{(10 \times 1{,}828{,}092 - 3948^2)(10 \times 417{,}596 - 1894^2)}}$$

$$= \frac{1{,}220{,}388}{\sqrt{2{,}694{,}216 \times 588{,}724}}$$

$= 0.969$ (to 3dp)

This would suggest a strong linear relationship here.

Test Your Understanding 33

$a = \Sigma Y/n - b\Sigma X/n = 1{,}894/10 - 0.4 \times 3{,}948/10 = 31.48$

Test Your Understanding 34

The number of complaints for 750 holidays booked:

$y = 31 + 0.4 \times 750 = 331$

Test Your Understanding 35

A and E

Time series analysis and the coefficient of variation are not related to this question at all. Regression analysis is concerned with finding the best possible line to fit the data when it has been established that there is in fact an approximately linear relationship. Hence (B), (C) and (D) are incorrect.

Test Your Understanding 36

C and E

The sample has only 10 points and the estimate was obtained by extrapolation. For both these reasons it is not likely to be reliable.

Test Your Understanding 37

$$r = \frac{12 \times 61{,}500 - 240 \times 2{,}920}{\sqrt{(12 \times 5{,}110 - 240^2)(12 \times 745{,}200 - 2{,}920^2)}} = \frac{37{,}200}{\sqrt{(3{,}720)(416{,}000)}}$$

$$= \frac{37{,}200}{39{,}338.53} = 0.946$$

Test Your Understanding 38

A, C and E

There is a strong linear relationship because the value of the correlation coefficient is close to 1 and the positive sign means that costs rise as output rises. The high value of the correlation coefficient does means that estimates made using regression are likely to be reliable. However correlation cannot prove causation and it tells us nothing about the changes in costs resulting from particular levels of output. So (B) and (D) are incorrect.

Test Your Understanding 39

B and C

It is important to remember that X is 1000 units of output and Y is $1,000 of costs. When $X = 0$, $Y = 43$ so costs are $43,000 and B is correct. When X increases by 1 (i.e. 1,000 units), Y increases by 10 (i.e. $10,000 in costs) so C is also correct. All the other statements are incorrect.

chapter

6

Forecasting

Chapter learning objectives

On completion of their studies students should be able to:

- prepare a time series graph
- identify trends and patterns using an appropriate moving average
- identify the components of a time series model
- prepare a trend equation using either graphical means or regression analysis
- calculate seasonal factors for both additive and multiplicative models and explain when each is appropriate
- calculate predicted values, given a time series model
- identify the limitations of forecasting models.

1 Introduction

In the last chapter we looked at linear regression as a method for forecasting. However, one limitation of this was that we only incorporated one causal factor (shown as the independent variable, x). In reality forecasting scenarios are more complex than this.

Time series analysis is one approach to forecasting more complex scenarios.

2 Components and models of time series

There are considered to be four *components of variation* in time series:

- the trend, *T*
- the seasonal component, *S*
- the cyclical component, *C*; and
- the residual (or irregular, or random) component, *R*.

The *trend* in a time series is the general, overall movement of the variable, with any sharp fluctuations largely smoothed out. It is often called the underlying trend, and any other components are considered to occur around this trend.

The *seasonal* component accounts for the regular variations that certain variables show at various times of the year. Thus, a newly formed ice-cream manufacturing company may have sales figures showing a rising trend. Around that, however, the sales will tend to have peaks in the summer months and troughs in the winter months. These peaks and troughs around the trend are explained by the seasonal component. In general, if a variable is recorded weekly, monthly or quarterly, it will tend to display seasonal variations, whereas data recorded annually will not.

The *cyclical* component explains much longer-term variations caused by business cycles. For instance, when a country's economy is in a slump, most business variables will be depressed in value, whereas when a general upturn occurs, variables such as sales and profits will tend to rise. These cyclical variations cover periods of many years and so have little effect in the short-term.

The *residual* component is that part of a variable that cannot be explained by the factors mentioned above. It is caused by random fluctuations and unpredictable or freak events, such as a major fire in a production plant. If the first three components are explaining the variable's behaviour well, then, subject to rare accidents, the irregular component will have little effect.

The four components of variation are assumed to combine to produce the variable in one of two ways: thus we have two mathematical models of the variable. In the first case there is the additive model, in which the components are assumed to add together to give the variable, Y:

$$Y = T + S + C + R$$

The second, multiplicative, model considers the components as multiplying to give Y:

$$Y = T \times S \times C \times R$$

It will be noted that, in the additive model, all components are in the same units as the original variable. In the multiplicative model, the trend is in the same units as the variable and the other three components are just multiplying factors.

Inflation and growth can erode the validity of the figures used in an additive model, so most firms use the multiplicative approach.

Illustration 1

Suppose we have a monthly sales figure of $21,109.

Addititive model

Thus, under the additive model, the figure might be explained as follows:

- the trend might be $20,000
- the seasonal factor: + $1,500 (the month in question is a good one for sales, expected to be $1,500 over the trend)
- the cyclical factor: – $800 (a general business slump is being experienced, expected to depress sales by $800 per month); and
- the residual factor: + $409 (due to unpredictable random fluctuations).

The model gives:

$$Y = T + S + C + R$$

$$21{,}109 = 20{,}000 + 1{,}500 + (-800) + 409$$

Multiplicative model

The multiplicative model might explain the same sales figures in a similar way:

- trend: \$20,000
- seasonal factor: 1.10 (a good month for sales, expected to be 10 per cent above the trend)
- cyclical factor: 0.95 (a business slump, expected to cause a 5 per cent reduction in sales) and
- residual factor: 1.01 (random fluctuations of 1 per cent).

The model gives:

$$Y = T \times S \times C \times R$$

$$21{,}109 = 20{,}000 \times 1.10 \times 0.95 \times 1.01$$

Test Your Understanding 1

The component parts of a time series model are:

A the trend

B the cyclical component

C the seasonal component

D the residual component.

Associate each of the following with the appropriate component.

P The impact of a strike.
Q An economic cycle of ups and downs over 5 years.
R A long-term increase of 5 per cent per annum.
S An increase in sales over Christmas.

Test Your Understanding 2

In a time series analysis using the multiplicative model, at a certain time actual, trend and seasonal values are 523, 465 and 1.12 respectively.

Assuming there is no cyclical element to be incorporated, find the residual element at this point.

A 1.2597

B 56.88

C 1.0042

D 51.7857

3 Establishing the underlying trend

There are many ways of forecasting time series variables. Within the C03 syllabus you need to be aware of two methods for determining the trend.

(1) If we assume a linear trend, then we can determine the trend line using linear regression

(2) For situations where the assumption of a linear trend is not reasonable, then the alternative is to use moving averages.

Both of these will be used in this chapter.

Illustration 2 – McNamee Ltd

The following table gives the quarterly sales figures for McNamee Ltd, a small company, for the last 3 years.

	Time period	*Sales* *$000*
20X2	quarter 1 (t = 1)	42
	quarter 2 (t = 2)	41
	quarter 3 (t = 3)	52
	quarter 4 (t = 4)	39
20X3	quarter 1 (t = 5)	45
	quarter 2 (t = 6)	48
	quarter 3 (t = 7)	61
	quarter 4 (t = 8)	46
20X4	quarter 1 (t = 9)	52
	quarter 2 (t = 10)	51
	quarter 3 (t = 11)	60
	quarter 4 (t = 12)	46

Forecast the next four values of the trend in the series.

Solution

Let us start by looking at a graph of the data:

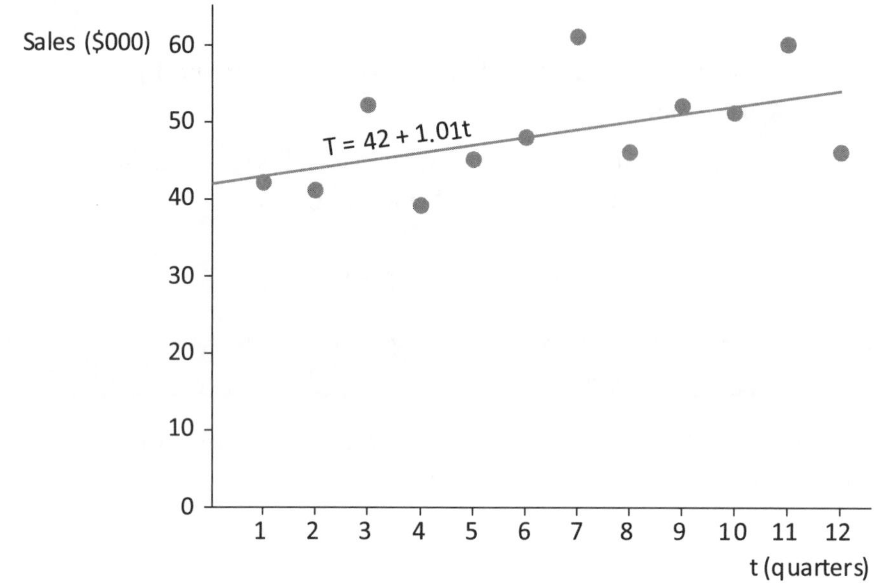

The graph of these data, the time series graph, shows that the company's sales are following an upward trend, of a more or less linear shape, and that there is a definite seasonal pattern:

- each third quarter is a peak; and
- each fourth quarter is a trough.

The approach and model being used here are therefore appropriate.

It will be noted that the twelve quarters for which we have data have been numbered from one to twelve, for ease of reference and to facilitate the computation of the regression line. It is left as an exercise for you to verify that this has equation:

$$T = 42.0 + 1.01t$$

where T is the assumed linear trend in sales ($000) and t is the number of the quarter (20X2, quarter 1: t = 1, and so on). This line has been superimposed on the graph.

The process of calculating the trend, whether by regression or by moving averages (see later), is often described as 'smoothing the data'. As you can see from the above graph, the original ups and downs of the data have been smoothed away.

20X5, quarter 1:	*t = 13, giving*
	T = 42.0 + 1.01 x 13 = 55.1 ($,000)
20X5, quarter 2:	*t = 14, so*
	T = 56.1 ($,000)
20X5, quarter 3:	*t = 15:*
	T = 57.2 ($,000)
20X5, quarter 4:	*t = 16:*
	T = 58.2 ($,000)

The next four trend values are therefore forecast to be $55,000, $56,000, $57,000 and $58,000 (nearest $'000), respectively.

Test Your Understanding 3 – Bates plc

Bates plc has the following sales results for the last 4 years for product B, broken down by quarter.

Sales of article B ('000 units)

	Q1	Q2	Q3	Q4
20X3	24.8	36.3	38.1	47.5
20X4	31.2	42.0	43.4	55.9
20X5	40.0	48.8	54.0	69.1
20X6	54.7	57.8	60.3	68.9

(Note: a number of the TYUs in this chapter relate to this data.)

Required

(a) Look at the data. What sort of trend and seasonal pattern do you expect to emerge from the analysis of this data?

(b) Numbering 20X3 Q1 as t = 1, through to 20X6 Q4 as t = 16, calculate the equation of the trend (T) using linear regression.

Test Your Understanding 4 – Bates plc (continued)

Use the regression equation $T = 28.54 + 2.3244t$ calculated in TYU 1 to forecast the trend in sales for the four quarters of 20X7.

Test Your Understanding 5

The regression equation of a linear trend is given by $T = 43 + 5.9t$ where the time $t = 1$ in the first quarter of 2011.

Estimate the trend for the fourth quarter of 2015, giving your answer correct to three significant figures.

4 Forecasting seasonal components

Up to now, we have not had to concern ourselves with the choice of model. Since the nature of the seasonal component is so different in the two models, we now have to make a choice.

- The multiplicative model is usually considered the better, because it ensures that seasonal variations are assumed to be a constant *proportion* of the sales.
- The additive model, in contrast, assumes that the seasonal variations are a constant *amount*, and thus would constitute a diminishing part of, say, an increasing sales trend.

Because there is generally no reason to believe that seasonality does become a less important factor, the multiplicative model is adopted more frequently, as demonstrated here.

The arithmetic involved in computing seasonal components is somewhat tedious but essentially simple. Assuming a very simple model in which there are no cyclical or residual variations:

Actual value, $Y = T \times S$

so $S = \dfrac{Y}{T}$

The seasonal component, S, is therefore found as the ratio of the actual values to the trend, averaged over all available data (so as to use as much information as possible). For forecasting purposes, the same degree of seasonality is assumed to continue into the future, and so the historical seasonal components are simply projected unaltered into the future.

Illustration 3 – McNamee Ltd (continued)

Calculate the seasonal components from the sales data and trend of Illustration 1.

Solution

The first, tedious step is to calculate the ratio of sales to trend for each of the twelve quarters given. We show the first and last here, leaving the intermediate ten calculations as exercises:

First

- When $t = 1$, $T = 42.0 + (1.01 \times 1) = 43.01$
- $S = Y/T = 42/43.01 = 0.9765$

Last

- When $t = 12$, $T = 42.0 + (1.01 \times 12) = 54.12$
- $S = Y/T = 46/54.12 = 0.8500$

The complete set of ratios, arranged by quarter, is:

	Quarter 1	*Quarter 2*	*Quarter 3*	*Quarter 4*
20X2	0.9765	0.9314	1.1548	0.8471
20X3	0.9564	0.9988	1.2431	0.9185
20X4	1.0178	0.9789	1.1297	0.8500
Total	2.9507	2.9091	3.5276	2.6156
Mean	0.9836	0.9697	1.1759	0.8719

When arranged like this, the averaging process for each quarter is facilitated. The resulting values constitute the mean seasonal component for each quarter from the given data: they show that, on average in the past, quarter 1 sales have been 98 per cent (approximately) of the trend, quarter 2 sales 97 per cent of the trend, and so on. These values are now adopted as the required forecast seasonal components (denoted S). In this case the forecasts for the four quarters of 20X5 are thus:

0.9836, 0.9697, 1.1759 and 0.8719, respectively.

Tidying up the seasonal adjustments

As the four seasonal components under this model should, on average, cancel out over a year, an extra step is often taken here, to ensure they add up to 4 (an average of 1 each).

The arithmetic is straightforward:

Total = 0.9836 + 0.9697 + 1.1759 + 0.8719 = 4.0011

To reduce this to 4, we will have to subtract from each one

$$\frac{(4.0011 - 4)}{4} = 0.0003 \text{ (to four d.p.)}$$

This gives the seasonal components as:

0.9833, 0.9694, 1.1756 and 0.8716, respectively.

In this instance, the adjustment has had scarcely any effect and so can be ignored. In fact, the original data seems to have been rounded to three s.f. so giving the seasonal components to four d.p. cannot really be justified. They would be better rounded to 0.98, 0.97, 1.18 and 0.87.

We have used arithmetic averaging to find the average seasonal variation and to adjust the averages so that our estimated components add to 4. An alternative method that is more mathematically 'correct' is to use geometric means and to adjust the average ratios so they multiply to 1. However, in practice it makes virtually no difference and the geometric mean is off-syllabus.

Note: had we used an additive model, then the four seasonal adjustments should add up to zero.

Test Your Understanding 6 – Bates plc (continued)

Using the original sales data and the regression line calculated for Bates plc

$T = 28.5425 + 2.324411765 \times t$,

find the seasonal component (S) as the arithmetic mean of Y/T for each quarter, where Y denotes the actual sales and T the trend given by the regression equation. Adjust your average seasonal variations so that they add to 4.

Test Your Understanding 7

In the additive model, four seasonal components initially calculated as +25, –54, –65 and +90 are to be adjusted so that they total zero.

Calculate the values of the adjusted seasonal components, giving your answers to the nearest whole number.

5 Producing the final forecast

We must now consider the final two components of variation. Isolating the *cyclical* component of time series has proved to be a controversial area in economics and statistics. There is no consensus on an approach to the problem. Also, as we have already mentioned, cyclical variations have little effect in the short-term. For these reasons, we shall omit the factor C from this first treatment.

The *residual* component is by nature unpredictable. The best that we can do is to hope that any random fluctuations are small and that no freak events occur, so that the factor R has no overall effect.

For a component to be omitted or to have no effect, it must have the value 1 in the multiplicative model, since multiplying anything by 1 leaves it unchanged. We have thus simplified our model, for the purposes of forecasting, to

$$Y = T \times S$$

Illustration 4 - McNamee Ltd (continued)

In the illustration used so far, forecast the sales during 20X5.

Solution

We have already found values for the underlying trend T and the seasonal variation S , and so it is now a matter of pulling these values together to find Y:

20X5 quarter 1: $Y = T \times S$

$= 55.1 \times 0.9833 = 54.18$

20X5 quarter 2: $Y = 56.1 \times 0.9694 = 54.38$

20X5 quarter 3: $Y = 57.2 \times 1.1756 = 67.24$

20X5 quarter 4: $Y = 58.2 \times 0.8716 = 50.73$

The forecast sales for the four quarters of 20X5 are thus $54,000, $54,000, $67,000 and $51,000, respectively (to the nearest $'000).

Test Your Understanding 8 – Bates plc (continued)

Using the results of TYUs so far that relate to Bates plc, forecast the sales of B for the four quarters of 20X7.

Test Your Understanding 9

Based on the last fifteen periods, the underlying trend of sales is:

345.12 – 1.35x

If the sixteenth period has a seasonal factor of –23.62, assuming an additive forecasting model, then the forecast for that period, in whole units, is:

A 300

B 343

C 347

D 390

Test Your Understanding 10

Based on twenty past quarters, the underlying trend equation for forecasting is: y = 23.87 + 2.4x. If quarter 21 has a seasonal factor of times 1.08, using a multiplicative model, then the forecast for the quarter, in whole units, is:

A 75

B 80

C 83

D 85.

6 Seasonal adjustment

Before proceeding we digress slightly to look at a closely related topic, *seasonal adjustment*. This is important, because we are often presented with a single figure for weekly revenue, monthly profit, or whatever, and it is difficult to make judgements without some idea of the extent to which the figure has been distorted by seasonal factors and consequently does not give a good indication of the trend. One approach is to *deseasonalise* or remove the seasonal effects from the figure. In the multiplicative model, in which the factor S *multiplies* with all the other components, seasonal adjustment consists of *dividing* by S. In other words, from:

$$Y = T \times S$$

we estimate:

$$T = \frac{Y}{S}$$

Effectively, the seasonally adjusted figure is an estimate of the trend.

Illustration 5 – McNamee Ltd (continued)

McNamee Ltd, the company in our illustrations, reports sales of $50,000 during the fourth quarter of a certain year.

Seasonally adjust this figure.

Solution

We saw earlier that the seasonal component for the fourth quarter in this series is 0.8716. Dividing by this:

$$\frac{50,000}{0.8716} = \$57,365.$$

we see that the seasonally adjusted sales for the quarter in question are $57,365.

Test Your Understanding 11 – Bates plc (continued)

Bates plc has forecast sales of $60,000 in the first quarter of a year.

Seasonally adjust this figure.

7 Moving average trends

The above approach is based on an assumption of a linear trend. Although this may appear plausible or 'appropriate', there are many occasions where such an assumption might not be made. An alternative approach that does not depend on linearity, but that also has some relative disadvantages discussed later, involves using *moving averages* as the trend.

We use averages to eliminate seasonal and random fluctuations to isolate the trend.

The arithmetic involved in this approach is still voluminous but essentially simpler than that of regression analysis, and can just as easily be computerised. To illustrate the method, we continue to look at the example discussed above.

Illustration 6 – McNamee Ltd (continued)

For McNamee Ltd, the company in our illustrations, compute the trend as a centred four-point moving average.

Solution

		Sales ($000) (Y)	*Four-quarterly total*	*Centred eight-quarterly total*	*Moving average (T)*
20X2	Q1	42			
	Q2	41			
			174		
	Q3	52		351	43.88
			177		
	Q4	39		361	45.13
			184		
20X3	Q1	45		377	47.13
			193		
	Q2	48		393	49.13
			200		
	Q3	61		407	50.88
			207		
	Q4	46		417	52.13
			210		

20X4	Q1	52		419	52.38
			209		
	Q2	51		418	52.25
			209		
	Q3	60			
	Q4	46			

The table is constructed as follows:

The 'four-quarterly total' column

This is simply the sum of each set of four consecutive quarterly sales figures. The first is thus:

42 + 41 + 52 + 39 = 174

The second is:

41+ 52 + 39 + 45 = 177

and so on.

The important question is where these totals should go. As they are to represent a four-quarterly period, the usual convention is to place them in the middle of that period, that is, between Q2 and Q3 for the first one, between Q3 and Q4 for the second, and so on. You will find that the table looks neater and is easier to read if you leave an empty line between the quarters, but there is often insufficient space to do this.

The 'centred eight-quarterly total' column

A small problem now arises because we wish each value of the trend to be eventually associated with a specific quarter. To overcome this, the figures are 'centred' – that is, each pair of values is added to give the 'centred eight-quarterly totals'

174 + 177 = 351 opposite 20X2 Q3

177 + 184 = 361 opposite 20X2 Q4 ... and so on

The 'trend' column

Dividing the eight quarterly totals by 8 now gives the trend values shown.

We now complete the process of forecasting from these trend values. There are no new techniques involved.

Test Your Understanding 12 – Bates plc (continued)

Using the data for Bates plc, repeated below, calculate the trend for the sales of article B as a centred four-point moving average.

Sales of article B ('000 units)

	Q1	Q2	Q3	Q4
20X3	24.8	36.3	38.1	47.5
20X4	31.2	42.0	43.4	55.9
20X5	40.0	48.8	54.0	69.1
20X6	54.7	57.8	60.3	68.9

Test Your Understanding 13 – McNamee Ltd (continued)

Using the data for the company McNamee Ltd in the illustrations:

A find the seasonal components from the new trend values, assuming the multiplicative model

B forecast sales for the four quarters of 20X5

C deseasonalise fourth-quarterly sales of $50,000.

Test Your Understanding 14 – Bates plc (continued)

Using the data for Bates plc in the TYUs to date:

A evaluate the seasonal component for each quarter based on the moving average trend obtained in TYU 6

B forecast the sales of B for the four quarters of 20X7 using trend forecasts of 66.7, 68.8, 70.9 and 73.

Supplementary reading – Article

This extract from an article by Gripaios advocates caution when using forecasts – even from so-called 'reliable' sources – and the adoption of 'think-tank' scenario planning as detailed support for forecasts. You should consider how an organisation would integrate practically 'official' forecasts with think-tank scenarios into routine forecasting.

The use and abuse of economic forecasts

Peter Gripaios, *Management Decision*, Vol. 32, No. 6, 1994. Republished with permission, Emerald Group Publishing Limited

Why firms use them

One obvious possibility is that businesses believe the results. This seems unlikely, so that more realistically it may be considered that businesses have to have something for strategic planning purposes and believe that econometric forecasts, though flawed, are better than even the best alternatives. If so, they may be wrong, for there is little evidence, certainly for some variables such as exchange rates, that complex econometric simulations are more accurate than graphical extrapolation techniques (chartism) or simple statistical models including 'random walk'. The latter work on the assumption that, as you have no idea about the future, you might as well take the present as the best guide.

Moreover, many econometric forecasters are themselves unhappy with the accuracy of their results, some so much so that they are experimenting with other types of models. One type is vector autogressive models (VAR), which do not attempt to explain how economic variables are causally related to one another. Instead, each variable is regressed on a lagged series of all the other variables in the model to form a basis for forecasting.

Perhaps many managers are comfortable with the single outcomes suggested by the individual forecasting teams and prefer them to the difficult thought processes involved in 'scenario planning' or, as practised in France, the similar 'prospective analysis'. These try to identify what fundamental economic relationships may change, the starting point for an effective consideration of sensible business strategy.

Conclusion

Though widely used in business, macroeconometric forecasts should be used with considerable caution. It may be 'comfortable' to do what others are doing in paying the economists and blaming them if they turn out to be wrong. Unfortunately, they very often are wrong, particularly at times such as turning points in the economic cycle when accurate information is most required for sensible business strategy-making. Of course, economic forecasts do have some use as an input in the strategic planning process, but the likelihood of error should be recognised from the start. One sensible approach would be to input a range of forecast output which, as individual forecasters still produce single estimates of, say, household consumption, will involve using the output of various forecasting teams. Even then, it would be prudent to carry out sensitivity analysis of the impact of different economic variables on the profits of the business in question, so that key variables can be watched with particular care.

The important point is surely that econometric forecasts should only ever be considered as one approach to formulating strategy. They should never be used as an alternative to fundamental scenario planning in which managers set up 'think tanks' to work out respective middle- and long-term scenarios on, for example, the prospects for their business in the light of such changed circumstances as the conclusion of the GATT talks, new entry into the EU, changes in European legislation, a strengthening dollar, destabilising in Russia and so on. It should also be emphasised that economic forecasts are no substitute for risk management strategies with regard to, say, movement in interest or exchange rates. Such strategies should sensibly encompass a range of operations, including holding a diversified portfolio of assets through the liquidity spectrum in a number of different currencies. Use of the forward foreign exchange markets should also be considered, as should other hedging strategies, including options.

Of course, companies may not wish to hedge all of their exposure to exchange rate risk and may partially rely on economic forecasts (or guesses) of future currency movements and gamble that these will be favourable. However, this can be a very costly policy if the gamble fails, as recent evidence for Japanese motor companies in the American market demonstrates. The safest option, which is only likely to be available to large firms, is investment in foreign subsidiaries. In that way, sales can be matched with costs in a particular country or trading bloc and profits remitted to the host country at the most appropriate time.

Discussion points
Discuss these within your study group

In this chapter and the one preceding it we have considered only the most simple forecasting models, in which the variable to be forecast depends on only one other variable or simply on time. As you have seen from this article, even quite complicated models cannot guarantee accurate forecasts.

(1) Try to list the reasons why forecasts are so often unreliable.

(2) Spend some time evaluating how economic forecasting is (or might be) used in your organisation. Is there any laid-down system using models, etc., or is it simply guesswork?

(3) On the basis of this article, does it matter if managers use only guesswork?

Chapter Summary

We are modelling the values, *Y*, in a time series by

$$Y = T \times S \times C \times R$$

where *T* is the trend component of variation, *S* is the seasonal component, *C* is the cyclical component, and *R* is the residual component. If we ignore the cyclical component and omit the unpredictable, residual component, the model becomes, for forecasting purposes:

$$Y = T \times S$$

Assuming constant seasonality, *T* can be found from a linear regression analysis or as a centred moving average, and *S* can be found as the average past ratio of actual value to trend (i.e. Y = T). A numerical check on the validity of the model can be obtained by inspecting the past values of the residual component, found from:

$$R = \frac{Y}{T \times S}$$

In the case of the additive model:

$$Y = T + S + C + R$$

For forecasting purposes:

$$Y = T + S$$

where *S* is found as the average past differences between actual value and trend (i.e. *Y* – *T*). The residuals are found from:

$$R = Y - T - S$$

8 Further Practice Questions

Test Your Understanding 15

In a time series analysis, the trend equation for a particular product is given by:

Trend = (0.0004 × YEAR^2) + (0.2 × YEAR) + 80.2

Owing to the cyclical factor, the forecast for 2016 is estimated at 1.87 times trend. In whole units, the forecast for 2016 is:

A 2,109

B 3,794

C 3,944

D 31,305

Test Your Understanding 16

Unemployment numbers actually recorded in a town for the second quarter of 2012 were 2,200. The underlying trend at this point was 2,000 people and the seasonal factor is 0.97. Using the multiplicative model for seasonal adjustment, the seasonally adjusted figure (in whole numbers) for the quarter is:

A 1,940

B 2,061

C 2,134

D 2,268

Test Your Understanding 17

In December, unemployment in a region is 423,700. If the seasonal factor using an additive time series model is + 81,500, find the seasonally adjusted level of unemployment to the nearest whole number.

A 342,200

B 505,200

C 345,316

D 519,877.

Test Your Understanding 18

In a multiplicative time series analysis, the seasonal variations given by averaging the *Y/T* values are 1.06, 1.13, 0.92 and 0.94. They are subsequently adjusted so that their total is 4. What is the new value of the average currently valued at 1.06?

A 0.2975

B 1.01

C 1.0725

D 1.0475

Test Your Understanding 19

In a time series analysis using the additive model, at a certain time actual, trend and seasonal values are 85, 91, –6.4. Find the residual at this point.

A –0.6

B 0.4

C –0.4

D –12.4.

Test Your Understanding 20

In an additive time series analysis, the seasonal variations given by averaging the $(Y - T)$ values are 22, 15, –8, –33. They are subsequently adjusted so that their total is 0. What is the new value of the average currently valued at –33?

A –34

B –37

C –29

D –32

Test Your Understanding 21

All except one of the following are conditions that should be met if time series forecasts are to be reliable. Which is the odd one out?

A Residuals should be numerically small.

B Extrapolation should be avoided.

C The trend should continue as in the past.

D The seasonal pattern should continue as in the past.

Test Your Understanding 22

In an additive model, at a certain time point, the actual value is 32,080 while the trend is 27,076 and the seasonal factor is 4,508. If there is no cyclical variation, calculate the residual variation to the nearest whole number.

Test Your Understanding 23

In the additive model $A = T + S + R$, which of the following is/are correct?

A S is estimated by averaging A/T values for the particular season.

B T may be estimated by a moving average.

C T may be estimated from an appropriate regression equation.

D R is estimated from $A - T$.

E The seasonally adjusted value is given by $A - S$.

Test Your Understanding 24

If the trend is estimated to be 45.8 for a quarter with a seasonal component of 0.96, estimate the actual value using the multiplicative model and giving your answer correct to three decimal places.

Test Your Understanding 25

Unemployment figures are given as 1,897,000 but after seasonal adjustment (using the multiplicative model) they are down to 1,634,000. Calculate the seasonal factor for the particular season, giving your answer to three decimal places.

Test Your Understanding 26

Data showing a 5-day cycle has a trend estimated using a 5-day moving average. For how many days will it not be possible to estimate the trend?

Test Your Understanding 27

The following statements all refer to time series analysis beginning with the estimation of the trend using a centred moving average. Which of the following is/are true?

A Centring must be used when the data has a cycle with an even number of points.

B When the data has a cycle with an even number of points, centering may be omitted but gives more accurate results.

C When the data has a four-point cycle, each centred moving average utilises five actual values.

Test Your Understanding 28

Which of the following comments regarding the validity of forecasts is/are correct?

A Regression trends give more accurate trend forecasts than those obtained using moving averages.

B Forecasts depend on the previous trend continuing.

C Forecasts depend on the previous seasonal and cyclical patterns continuing.

D Forecasts made with the multiplicative model are better than those made with the additive model.

E Checking the fit of the model by examining the values of residuals can help in judging the validity of forecasts.

F Provided the model is a good fit, forecasts should be accurate even if there are unexpected events.

Time series

The managers of a company have observed recent demand patterns of a particular product line in units. The original data, which has been partially analysed, is as follows:

Year	*Quarter*	*Data*	*Sum of fours*	*Sum of twos*
20X3	2	31		
	3	18	94	190
	4	20	96	193
20X4	1	25	97	195
	2	33	98	197
	3	19	99	198
	4	21	99	198
20X5	1	26	99	199
	2	33	100	201
	3	19	101	
	4	22		
20X6	1	27		

You have been commissioned to undertake the following analyses and to provide appropriate explanations. (Work to three d.p.)

Test Your Understanding 29

In the following table, find the missing values of the underlying four-quarterly moving average trend.

Year	*Quarter*	*Sum of twos*	*Moving average*
20X3	4	190	A
20X4	1	193	B
	2	195	24.375
	3	197	24.625
	4	198	24.750
20X5	1	198	24.750
	2	199	24.875
	3	201	C

Test Your Understanding 30

Calculate the seasonally adjusted demand (to three d.p.) for the four quarters of 20X4 based on the multiplicative model if the seasonal factors are as follows:

Quarter 1	1.045
Quarter 2	1.343
Quarter 3	0.765
Quarter 4	0.847

Test Your Understanding 31

Which of the following statements about seasonal adjustment is/are correct?

D Seasonally adjusted data has had the seasonal variations removed from it.

Correct/incorrect

E Seasonally adjusted data has had the seasonal variations included in it.

Correct/incorrect

F Seasonal adjustment is the process by which seasonal components are adjusted so that they add to zero.

Correct/incorrect

G Seasonal adjustment is the process by which estimates of the trend can easily be obtained.

Correct/incorrect

Test Your Understanding 32

If the seasonally adjusted values are increasing, which of the following would you deduce?

H The trend is upwards.

I The trend is downwards.

J No deductions about the trend are possible from the information given.

K Seasonal variability is increasing.

L Seasonal variability is decreasing.

M No deductions are possible about seasonal variability.

Test Your Understanding 33

If *A* denotes the actual value, *T* the trend and *S* the seasonal component, write down the formula for the seasonally adjusted value if an additive model is being used.

Forecasting

You are assisting the management accountant with sales forecasts of two brands – Y and Z – for the next three quarters of 20X3. Brand Y has a steady, increasing trend in sales of 2 per cent a quarter and Brand Z a steadily falling trend in sales of 3 per cent a quarter. Both brands are subject to the same seasonal variations, as follows:

Quarter	*Q1*	*Q2*	*Q3*	*Q4*
Seasonality	–30%	0	–30%	+60%

The last four quarter's unit sales are shown below:

	20X2 Q2	*20X2 Q3*	*20X2 Q4*	*20X3 Q1*
Brand Y	331	237	552	246
Brand Z	873	593	1,314	558

Test Your Understanding 34

Which of the following statements about the seasonal variations is/are correct?

A Actual sales are on average 30 per cent below the trend in the third quarter.

B Actual sales in the first and third quarters are identical on average.

C Average sales in the second quarter are zero.

D Actual sales in the fourth quarter are on average 60 per cent above the trend.

E Actual sales in the first quarter are 1.3 times the trend.

F Actual sales in the fourth quarter are 1.6 times the trend.

Test Your Understanding 35

Seasonally adjust the sales figures for 20X3 Q1, giving your answers to one d.p.

Test Your Understanding 36

Forecast the trend for brand Y for 20X3 Q4, giving your answer to one d.p.

Test Your Understanding 37

If the trend forecast in Quarter 4 was 370, forecast the actual sales of brand Y for 20X3 Q4, giving your answer to the nearest whole number.

Test Your Understanding 38

Forecast the trend for brand Z for 20X3 Q3, giving your answer to one d.p.

Test Your Understanding 39

If the trend forecast in quarter 3 was 770, forecast the actual sales of brand Z for 20X3 Q3, giving your answer to the nearest whole number.

Test Your Understanding 40

Which of the following are assumptions on the basis of which time series forecasts are made?

A That there will be no seasonal variation.

B That the trend will not go up or down.

C That there will be no change in the existing seasonal pattern of variability.

D That the model being used fits the data.

E That there will be no unforeseen events.

Forecasting

The quarterly sales of a product are monitored by a multiplicative time series model. The trend in sales is described by

$$Y = 100 + 5X$$

where Y denotes sales volume and X denotes the quarterly time period.

The trend in sales for the most recent quarter (first quarter 20X1, when X = 20) was 200 units. The average seasonal variations for the product are as follows

Quarter	*First*	*Second*	*Third*	*Fourth*
Seasonal effect	0	–20%	+40%	–20%

The price of a unit was $1,000 during the first quarter of 20X1. This price is revised every quarter to allow for inflation, which is running at 2 per cent a quarter.

Test Your Understanding 41

Forecast the trend in the number of units sold for the remaining three quarters of 20X1.

Test Your Understanding 42

Forecast the actual number of units sold (to the nearest whole number) for the remaining three quarters of 20X1.

Test Your Understanding 43

Forecast the price per unit for the remaining quarters of 20X1, giving your answers correct to two d.p.

Test Your Understanding 44

If the prior forecasts were as follows, forecast the sales revenue for the remaining quarters of 20X1, giving your answers to the nearest $.

Quarter of 20X1	*Forecasts*	*Price per unit*
	Numbers sold	($)
2	150	1010
3	300	1030
4	170	1050

Test your understanding answers

Test Your Understanding 1

The component parts of a time series model are:

A	The trend	R
B	The cyclical component	Q
C	The seasonal component	S
D	The residual component	P

Test Your Understanding 2

C

In the full multiplicative model $Y = T \times S \times C \times R$, so if we can ignore cyclical elements (a common simplification in exam questions), this reduces to give:

$$Y = T \times S \times R$$

$R = Y/(T \times S) = 523/(465 \times 1.12) = 1.0042$ (to four decimal places).

Note: In A the $Y = T$ ratio has been multiplied by 1.12 instead of divided, while in both B and D the additive model has been used.

Test Your Understanding 3 – Bates plc

A For every quarter, each year shows an increase in sales, so an increasing trend is expected. Also, there is a regular seasonal pattern with a steady increase in sales from Q1 to Q4.

B Letting $x = t$ and $y = T$, the necessary summations are n = 16; Σx = 136; Σy = 772.8; Σxy = 7,359.1; Σx^2 = 1,496.

$$b = \frac{n\Sigma xy - \Sigma x \Sigma y}{n\Sigma x^2 - (\Sigma x)^2} = \frac{(16 \times 7{,}359.1) - (136 \times 772.8)}{(16 \times 1{,}496) - 136^2} = 2.3244 \text{ (to 4 dp)}$$

$$a = \bar{y} - b\bar{x} = \frac{772.8}{16} - 2.324411765 \times \frac{136}{16} = 28.54 \text{ (to 2dp)}$$

The trend equation is thus:

$T = 28.54 + 2.3244t$

Test Your Understanding 4 – Bates plc (continued)

In 20X7, t takes values 17–20, giving trend forecasts as follows:

Q1	$t = 17$	$T = 28.54 + 2.3244 \times 17 = 68.0548$
Q2	$t = 18$	$T = 70.3792$
Q3	$t = 19$	$T = 72.7036$
Q4	$t = 20$	$T = 75.028$

Test Your Understanding 5

In the fourth quarter of 2015, $t = 20$, so

$T = 43 + 5.9 \times 20 = 161.$

Test Your Understanding 6 – Bates plc (continued)

Year	*Quarter*	*t*	*T*	*Sales, Y*	*Y/T*
20X3	1	1	30.8669	24.8	0.8034
	2	2	33.1913	36.3	1.0937
	3	3	35.5157	38.1	1.0728
	4	4	37.8401	47.5	1.2553
20X4	1	5	40.1646	31.2	0.7768
	2	6	42.4890	42.0	0.9885
	3	7	44.8134	43.4	0.9685
	4	8	47.1378	55.9	1.1859
20X5	1	9	49.4622	40.0	0.8087
	2	10	51.7866	48.8	0.9423
	3	11	54.1110	54.0	0.9979
	4	12	56.4354	69.1	1.2244
20X6	1	13	58.7599	54.7	0.9309
	2	14	61.0843	57.8	0.9462
	3	15	63.4087	60.3	0.9510
	4	16	65.7331	68.9	1.0482

Year	*Q1*	*Q2*	*Q3*	*Q4*	
20X3	0.8034	1.0937	1.0728	1.2553	
20X4	0.7768	0.9885	0.9685	1.1859	
20X5	0.8087	0.9423	0.9979	1.2244	
20X6	0.9309	0.9462	0.9510	1.0482	
Total	3.3198	3.9707	3.9902	4.7138	*Total*
Average	0.8300	0.9927	0.9976	1.1785	3.9988
+	0.0003	0.0003	0.0003	0.0003	0.0012
Comp.	0.8303	0.9930	0.9979	1.1788	4.0000

Quite a few rounding errors will have built up by now, so do not worry if your results differ a little from these.

To two decimal places, the seasonal components are

0.83	0.99	1.00	1.18

Test Your Understanding 7

Start by adding the seasonal components together:

25 – 54 – 65 + 90 = –4.

To sum to zero we thus need to add 4 in total, equivalent to adding 1 to each component.

- First = 25 + 1 = 26;
- second = –54 + 1 = –53;
- third = –65 + 1 = –64;
- fourth = 90 + 1 = 91.

Test Your Understanding 8 – Bates plc (continued)

The model is $Y = T \times S$ so the forecast sales *(Y)* in '000 units are given by multiplying the trend forecasts *(T)* by the seasonal factors (S).

Using a regression equation and seasonal components to forecast is a very common assessment question.

Forecast trend	68.0548	70.3792	72.7036	75.028
Seasonal	0.8303	0.993	0.9979	1.1788
Forecast sales	56.5	69.9	72.6	88.4

Test Your Understanding 9

A

For the sixteenth period, put x = 16:

Trend = 345.12 – (1.35 × 16) = 323.52

Forecast is 23.62 below the trend:

Forecast = 323.52 – 23.62 = 299.9 = 300(to nearest unit).

Test Your Understanding 10

B

$$\text{Trend forecast} = 23.87 + 2.4 \times 21 = 74.27$$

$$\text{Forecast} = \text{trend} \times \text{seasonal factor}$$

$$= 74.27 \times 1.08$$

$$= 80.$$

Test Your Understanding 11 – Bates plc (continued)

The seasonally adjusted figure is an estimate of the trend and so is given by Y/S = 60,000/0.8303 = 72,263 units.

Seasonal adjustment is another common exam question.

Test Your Understanding 12 – Bates plc (continued)

Year	*Quarter*	*Sales (Y)*	*Four-point moving total*	*Eight-point moving total*	*Four-point moving ave. trend (T)*
20X3	1	24.8			
	2	36.3			
			146.7		
	3	38.1		299.8	37.4750
			153.1		
	4	47.5		311.9	38.9875
			158.8		
20X4	1	31.2		322.9	40.3625
			164.1		
	2	42.0		336.6	42.0750
			172.5		
	3	43.4		353.8	44.2250
			181.3		
	4	55.9		369.4	46.1750
			188.1		
20X5	1	40.0		386.8	48.3500
			198.7		
	2	48.8		410.6	51.3250
			211.9		
	3	54.0		438.5	54.8125
			226.6		
	4	69.1		462.2	57.7750
			235.6		
20X6	1	54.7		477.5	59.6875
			241.9		
	2	57.8		483.6	60.4500
			241.7		
	3	60.3			
	4	68.9			

Test Your Understanding 13 – McNamee Ltd (continued)

A First of all, in order to find S-values, we have to compute the individual values of $Y \div T$, and tabulate and average them as before.

For example 20X2 quarter 3 = 52 ÷ 43.88.

	Quarter 1	*Quarter 2*	*Quarter 3*	*Quarter 4*
20X2			1.1851	0.8642
20X3	0.9548	0.9770	1.1989	0.8824
20X4	0.9927	0.9761	0.0000	0.0000
Total	1.9475	1.9531	2.3840	1.7466

					Total
Mean	0.9738	0.9766	1.1920	0.8733	4.0157
Adjustment	– 0.0039	– 0.0039	– 0.0039	– 0.0039	– 0.0156
Seasonal component	0.9699	0.9727	1.1881	0.8694	4.0001

B To produce sales forecasts, we need values of T. The graph below shows the sales figures with the moving average trend superimposed. We are not using a linear trend, and so an estimate of where the trend appears to be going has been included, without the benefit of a straight-line assumption. (See the next section for a discussion of this.) As before, we assume that S remains at its average values for each quarter, as computed above.

20X5 quarter 1: $Y = T \times S$

$= 51.8 \times 09699 = 50.24$

20X5 quarter 2: $Y = 51.6 \times 0.9727 = 50.19$

20X5 quarter 3: $Y = 51.5 \times 1.1881 = 61.19$

20X5 quarter 4: $Y = 51.4 \times 0.8694 = 44.69$

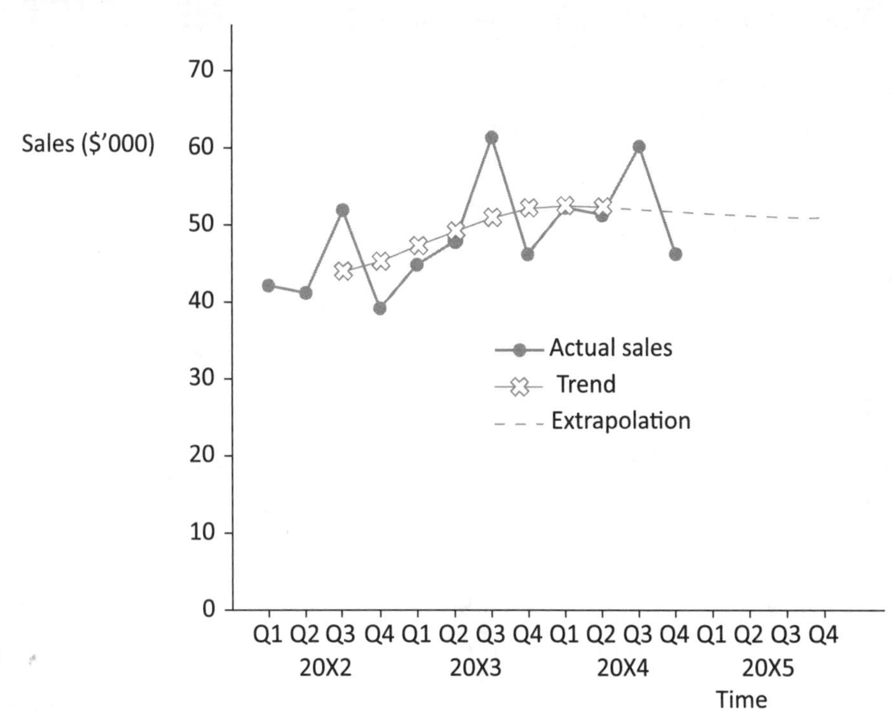

Time series graph and moving average trend

The forecast sales for the four quarters of 20X5 are thus $50,000, $50,000, $61,000 and $45,000, respectively (to the nearest $'000).

C As before, these seasonal components imply that, for example, quarter 4 sales are, on average, 87.33 per cent of the trend. A fourth-quarterly figure of $50,000 will therefore be deseasonalised to

$$\frac{50,000}{0.8694} = 57,511$$

With this approach to the trend, therefore, the seasonally adjusted sales figure will be $57,500 (approximately).

Test Your Understanding 14 – Bates plc (continued)

Calculating $Y = T$ in the solution to TYU6 and arranging the $Y = T$ values according to their quarters gives:

	Q1	*Q2*	*Q3*	*Q4*	
20X3			1.017	1.218	
20X4	0.773	0.998	0.981	1.211	
20X5	0.827	0.951	0.985	1.196	
20X6	0.916	0.956			
Total	2.516	2.905	2.983	3.625	Total
Average	0.839	0.968	0.994	1.208	4.009
–	0.002	0.002	0.002	0.002	0.008
Comp.	0.837	0.966	0.992	1.206	4.001

Rounding to two decimal places gives seasonal components of:

0.84	0.97	0.99	1.21

Forecast for 20X7

	Q1	*Q2*	*Q3*	*Q4*
Trend	66.70	68.80	70.90	73.00
Comp.	0.84	0.97	0.99	1.21
Sales	56.028	66.736	70.191	88.33

Hence the sales forecasts for the four quarters of 20X7 are (in ‘000 units):

56	67	70	88

Test Your Understanding 15

C

$$\text{Trend} = 0.0004 \times 2016^2 + 0.2 \times 2016 + 80.2$$
$$= 2{,}109.1024$$
$$\text{Forecast} = 1.87 \times \text{trend}$$
$$= 3{,}944 \text{ to nearest whole number.}$$

Test Your Understanding 16

D

$$\text{Actual value} = \text{trend} \times \text{seasonal factor}$$
$$\text{Seasonally adjusted figure} = \text{estimate of the trend}$$
$$= \text{actual value} \div \text{seasonal factor}$$
$$= 2{,}200/0.97 = 2{,}268$$

It seems likely that the stated trend of 2000 is incorrect.

Test Your Understanding 17

A

In the additive model, value Y = trend T + seasonal S. The seasonally adjusted value estimates the trend $Y - S = 423{,}700 - 81{,}500 = 342{,}200$ in this case.

The errors were: in B, adding instead of subtracting S, and in C and D, getting confused with the multiplicative model and multiplying or dividing by 0.81500.

Test Your Understanding 18

D

Total = 1.06 + 1.13 + 0.92 + 0.94 = 4.05, hence we adjust by subtracting 0.05/4 = 0.0125 from each average. The adjusted first average = 1.06 – 0.0125 = 1.0475.

(C) is almost correct but the excess 0.0125 has been added instead of subtracted. In (A) the averages have been adjusted to total to 1, while in (B) the entire 0.05 has been subtracted from the 1.06.

Test Your Understanding 19

B

In the additive model $Y = T + S + R$, so $R = Y - T - S = 85 - 91 - (-6.4) = 0.4$.

(C) was almost correct but the wrong way round, while in (D) the 6.4 was subtracted rather than added, giving a very large residual. Answer (A) looks to be an arithmetical error.

Test Your Understanding 20

D

Total = 22 + 15 – 8 – 33 = – 4, hence we adjust by adding 4/4 = 1 to each average. The average currently at -33 becomes –33 + 1 = –32.

In (A) the 1 has been subtracted rather than added; in (B) the entire 4 has been subtracted; and in (C) the entire 4 has been added.

Test Your Understanding 21

B

It is true that extrapolation leads to unreliable forecasts but, by definition, it is totally unavoidable in time series analysis.

Test Your Understanding 22

Residual variation = 496.

$$Y = T + S + R$$
$$32080 = 27076 + 4508 + R$$

Test Your Understanding 23

A Incorrect: *S* is estimated by averaging A÷T values and not A/T or *A* ÷ *T* values when the additive model is used.

B Correct.

C Correct.

D Incorrect: *R* is estimated from *A* – *T* – *S*.

E Correct.

Test Your Understanding 24

Estimate = 43.968.

Test Your Understanding 25

A = *T* × *S* and the seasonally adjusted value is an estimate of *T*. Hence S = 1,897,000/1,634,000 = 1.16

Test Your Understanding 26

The first trend figure will be located at time point three, so two days at the start and a similar two days at the end of the data will not be able to have their trends estimated using this method. The number of days is therefore four.

Test Your Understanding 27

A Correct.

B Incorrect: centering is not optional since *A* and *T* values must be associated if seasonal components are subsequently to be estimated.

C Correct.

Test Your Understanding 28

A Incorrect: regression trends would be more accurate only if the trend was linear.

B Correct.

C Correct.

D Incorrect: although it is generally the case that the multiplicative model gives better estimates than the additive model, one can really only tell by examining the data to see whether seasonal variation actually increases or decreases with the trend.

E Correct.

F Incorrect: forecasts cannot be expected to be accurate if there are unexpected events.

Test Your Understanding 29

A 23.750

B 24.125

C 25.125

All the moving averages are given by dividing the 'sum of twos' by 8.

Test Your Understanding 30

Seasonally adjusted demand is given by dividing the actual demand by the corresponding seasonal factor.

Quarter	*Actual demand*	*Seasonal factor*	*Seasonally adjusted demand*
1	25	1.045	23.923
2	33	1.343	24.572
3	19	0.765	24.837
4	21	0.847	24.793

Test Your Understanding 31

The ‘seasonal adjustment’ described in F is used when initially calculating the seasonal components.

D correct
E incorrect
F incorrect
G correct.

Test Your Understanding 32

H, the trend is upwards, and, **M,** No deductions are possible about seasonal variability.

Increasing seasonally adjusted values tell us that the trend is increasing. They provide no information about seasonal variability.

Test Your Understanding 33

A* – *S

Ignoring residuals, the model is given by $A = T + S$. Seasonal adjustment is about estimating the trend and so is given by $T = A - S$.

Test Your Understanding 34

A Actual sales are on average 30 per cent below the trend in the third quarter.

D Actual sales in the fourth quarter are on average 60 per cent above the trend.

F Actual sales in the fourth quarter are 1.6 times the trend.

The values of the average seasonal variations tell us that the actual values have been on average 30 per cent below the trend in the first and third quarters, identical with the trend in the second quarter and 60 per cent above it in the fourth.

Test Your Understanding 35

Brand Y 246/0.7 = 351.4
Brand Z 558/0.7 = 797.1

Test Your Understanding 36

The trend rises at 2 per cent per quarter and so, after three quarters, reaches the value $351.4 \times 1.02^3 = 372.9$

Test Your Understanding 37

Actual sales forecast is 60 per cent greater than the trend, that is, 370 × 1.6 = 592 to the nearest whole number.

Test Your Understanding 38

Trend forecast is given by reducing the initial trend value of 797.1 by 3 per cent a quarter over two quarters, i.e. by $797.1 \times 0.97^2 = 750.0$

Test Your Understanding 39

Actual sales forecast is 30 per cent below the trend forecast, that is, 770.0 × 0.7 = 539.

Test Your Understanding 40

C That there will be no change in the existing seasonal pattern of variability.

D That the model being used fits the data.

E That there will be no unforeseen events.

The assumptions on the basis of which time series forecasts are made are really that everything will continue in the future as it has in the past. In other words the same trend and seasonal variability will apply and there will be no unforeseen events. All of this presupposes that an appropriate model is being used.

Test Your Understanding 41

2nd quarter	205
3rd quarter	210
4th quarter	215

In the first quarter of 20X1, $X = 20$ and so X must take the values 21–23 in the remaining quarters. For example, the trend in the 2nd quarter will be = $100 + 5 \times 21 = 205$ units.

Test Your Understanding 42

2nd quarter	164
3rd quarter	294
4th quarter	172

Actual forecasts are given by changing the trend by the appropriate seasonal per cent. For example, the forecast of actual numbers sold in the 2nd quarter will be $205 \times 0.8 = 164$.

Test Your Understanding 43

Price per unit is given by increasing 1,000 at 2 per cent per quarter, that is, by multiplying by 1.02 for each quarter.

Answers to 2 d.p.:

2nd quarter	1,000 × 1.02 = 1,020.00
3rd quarter	1,020 × 1.02 = 1,040.40
4th quarter	1,040.4 × 1.02 = 1,061.21

Note: always check the question to see how the answer should be given (here to 2 d.p.).

Test Your Understanding 44

Quarters of 20X1	Sales revenue forecast ($)
2	150 × 1010 = 151,500
3	300 × 1030 = 309,000
4	170 × 1050 = 178,500

Sales revenue is given by multiplying together the forecasts for unit price and sales volume.

chapter

7

Financial Mathematics

Chapter learning objectives

On completion of their studies students should be able to:

- calculate future values of an investment using both simple and compound interests
- calculate an annual percentage rate of interest given a monthly or quarterly rate
- calculate the present value of a future cash sum
- calculate the present value of an annuity and a perpetuity
- calculate loan/mortgage repayments and the value of the loan/mortgage outstanding
- calculate the future value of regular savings and/or the regular investment needed to generate a required future sum
- calculate the net present value (NPV) and internal rate of return (IRR) of a project and explain whether and why it should be accepted.

1 Introduction

Perhaps the most important part of the C03 syllabus is the use of mathematics to solve investment appraisal decisions.

In this chapter we shall start by looking at the calculations surrounding interest payments and equivalent rates of interest, before moving on to cover the highly important but less well-known concept of net present value in investment appraisal.

As well as investments, the practical applications dealt with in this chapter also include loans, mortgages and regular saving plans.

2 Simple interest

One of the most basic uses of mathematics in finance concerns calculations of *interest*, the most fundamental of which is *simple interest*.

With simple interest the interest is paid only on the original principal (i.e. the original amount borrowed/saved), not on the interest accrued.

Illustration 1 – Simple interest

Suppose I invest $200 for 3 years at an annual interest rate of 5% and that interest is calculated by reference to the original sum invested.

How much will I have at the end of the investment?

- The annual interest will be 200 × 5% = $10
- At the end of three years the total interest will be 3 × 10 = $30
- The final sum will thus be $230

Formula

More generally , suppose $\$P$ is invested at a fixed rate of interest of r per annum (where r is a proportion) The interest earned each year is calculated by multiplying the rate of interest r by the amount invested, $\$P$, giving an amount $\$r \times P$. After n years the sum of $\$r \times P \times n$ will be credited to give a total at the end of the period, $\$V$, of:

$$V = P + r \times P \times n$$

or:

$$V = P(1 + r \times n)$$

This well-known formula is often referred to as the *simple interest* formula.

Note: this formula can be applied to non-annual time periods as long as an interest rate is used to match the timescales.

Illustration 2 – Simple interest

Suppose I invest $2,000 in a deposit account paying 0.1% per month.

Calculate the final value in the account after two years, assuming simple interest.

- P = 2,000
- r = 0.001 (remember to express the interest rate as a decimal)
- n = 24

$V = P(1 + r \times n) = 2{,}000 \times (1 + 0.001 \times 24) = 2{,}000 \times 1.024 = \$2{,}048$

Test Your Understanding 1

An amount of $5,000 is invested at a rate of 8 per cent per annum. What will be the value of the investment in 5 years' time, if simple interest is added once at the end of the period?

Test Your Understanding 2

Calculate the value of the following, assuming that simple interest is added:

A $20,000 invested for 5 years at 5 per cent per annum;

B $50,000 invested for 3 years at 6 per cent per annum;

C $30,000 invested for 6 years with 1 per cent interest per quarter.

3 Compound interest

In practice, simple interest is not used as often as *compound interest.*

With compound interest the interest is paid on both the original principal plus any interest accrued. This means that the interest is calculated on the total balance brought forward rather than on the initial amount.

Illustration 3 – Compound interest

Suppose \$200 is invested for 3 years at 5% compound interest - i.e. interest is added at the end of each year based on the brought forward balance and so affects the interest for the next year.

- For year 1 the interest will be 5% × 200 = \$10. The total sum carried forward will thus be

  200 + 10 = \$210.

- For year 2 the interest will be 5% × 210 = \$10.50. The total sum carried forward will thus be

  210 + 10.50 = \$220.50.

- For year 3 the interest will be 5% × 220.50 = \$11.025. The total sum at the end of the investment will thus be

  220.50 + 11.025 = \$231.525.

Notice that each year the sum grows by a factor of (1.05). As a short cut we could calculate the value at the end of year 3 as

$$200 \times (1.05) \times (1.05) \times (1.05) = 200 \times (1.05)^3 = \$231.525$$

Formula

Suppose \$*P* is invested for *n* years at a fixed rate of interest of *r* per annum compounded annually. After *n* years the value, \$*V*, will be given by

$V = P(1 + r)^n$, where *r* is expressed as a decimal

This well-known formula is often referred to as the compound interest formula and is given in your exam.

As you will see, in financial mathematics we work with an annual ratio denoted by $(1 + r)$ rather than with the rate of interest.

Test Your Understanding 3

An amount of $5,000 is invested at a fixed rate of 8 per cent per annum. What amount will be the value of the investment in 5 years' time, if the interest is compounded:

A annually?

B every 6 months?

Test Your Understanding 4

Calculate the value of the following, assuming compound interest

A $20,000 invested for 5 years at 5 per cent per annum

B $50,000 invested for 3 years at 6 per cent per annum

C $30,000 invested for 6 years with 1 per cent interest per quarter.

4 Equivalent rates of interest

Suppose the rate of interest on a loan was stated to be 8 per cent per annum with payments made every 6 months. This means that 4 per cent would be paid every 6 months.

We can find the effective annual rate of interest by considering the impact of two 4 per cent increases on an initial value of $1:

Value at the end of 1 year = 1 × 1.04 × 1.04 = $1.0816

This is the annual ratio that results not from 8 per cent per annum but from 8.16 per cent.

Hence, the effective annual rate of interest is 8.16 per cent in this case.

Note: In some respects quoting the cost of the loan as 8% per annum is misleading and understates the real effective rate. This is why, in the UK, lenders have to quote the 'APR' of any loans or financing deals they want you to use, as this gives the effective annual percentage rate. This is the most useful figure to use when comparing different financing deals.

Test Your Understanding 5

An investor is considering two ways of investing $20,000 for a period of 10 years:

- option A offers 1.5 per cent compounded every 3 months
- option B offers 3.2 per cent compounded every 6 months.

Which is the better option?

Test Your Understanding 6

Find the effective annual rates of interest corresponding to the following:

A 3 per cent every 6 months

B 2 per cent per quarter

C 1 per cent per month.

Test Your Understanding 7

Over 5 years a bond costing $1,000 increases in value to $1,250. Find the effective annual rate of interest.

Test Your Understanding 8

If house prices rise by 20 per cent per annum, find:

A the equivalent percentage rise per month

B the percentage rise over 9 months.

Test Your Understanding 9

A Find the effective annual rate if an investment of $500 yields $600 after 4 years.

B If prices rise by 5.8 per cent over a year, find the percentage rise over 6 months.

5 Depreciation

Within financial accounting you will meet the concept of depreciation, in which the value of an item goes down at a certain rate reflecting its usage and reduction in useful economic life. There are many ways to calculate depreciation but one is called "reducing balance", where the book value goes down by a constant rate each year.

The same basic formula for compound interest can be used to deal with such depreciation. We simply ensure that the rate of 'interest' is negative.

Illustration 4 – Depreciation

An asset was bought for $120,000 and is to be depreciated at 40% each year on a reducing balance basis. Determine the net book value after 5 years.

In C02 you might be tempted to set out a calculation as follows:

		$
Purchase price		120,000
Year 1 depreciation	40% × 120,000	(48,000)
NBV at end of year 1		72,000
Year 2 depreciation	40% × 72,000	(28,800)
NBV at end of year 2		43,200
etc		

Notice that the NBV goes down by 40% each, equivalent to an annual interest rate of –40%. We can then use our compound interest rate formulae as follows

- "r" = –0.4
- $(1 + r) = (1 - 0.4) = 0.6$
- Value after 5 years = $120,000 \times 0.6^5$ = $9,331

Test Your Understanding 10

A company buys a machine for $20,000. What will its value be after 6 years, if it is assumed to depreciate at a fixed rate of 12 per cent per annum reducing balance?

Test Your Understanding 11

A piece of capital equipment is purchased for $120,000 and is to be scrapped after 7 years. What is the scrap value if the depreciation rate is 8 per cent per annum?

Illustration 5 – More complex example of depreciation

In practice, rates of depreciation change over the lifetime of an item. A motor car costing $21,000 may depreciate by 15 per cent in the first year, then by 10 per cent per annum in each of the next three years, and by 5 per cent per annum thereafter. Find its value after 8 years.

Solution

$P = 21{,}000$, $r = 0.15$ for *one year*, then $r = 0.10$ for $n = 3$ years, and finally $r = 0.05$ for $n = 4$ years

$V = 21{,}000 \times 0.85^1 \times 0.90^3 \times 0.95^4 = \$10{,}599$

Test Your Understanding 12

A machine depreciates by 20 per cent in the first year, then by 10 per cent per annum for the next 5 years, and by 2 per cent per annum thereafter. Find its value after 7 years if its initial price is $720,000.

6 More complex investments and terminal values

We can return now to the evaluation of investments, but now considering situations where there are several different investments spread over a period of time.

One approach is to work out the terminal value at the end of the investment for each cash flow.

Illustration 6 – Terminal values

A man invests $3,000 initially and then $1,800 at the end of the first, second and third years, and finally $600 at the end of the fourth year. If interest is paid annually at 6.5 per cent, find the value of the investment at the end of the fifth year.

Solution

The diagram shows when the investments and evaluation take place.

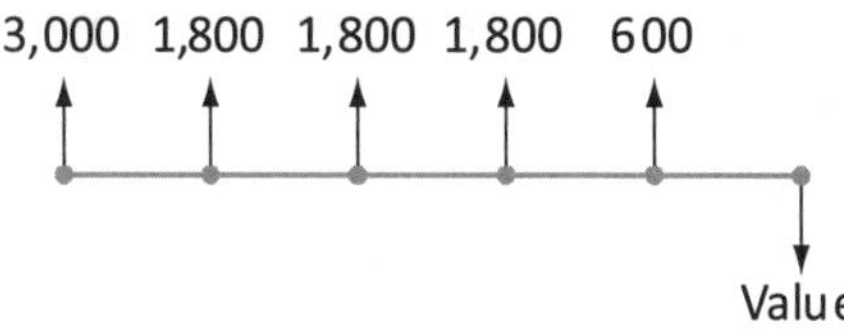

The $3,000 is invested for 5 years and grows to:

$$3{,}000 \times (1.065^5) = 4{,}110.26$$

The three sums of $1,800 are invested for 4, 3 and 2 years, and grow in total to:

$$1800 \times (1.065^4 + 1.065^3 + 1.065^2) = 6{,}531.55$$

Finally, the $600 is invested for just 1 year and grows to:

$$600 \times 1.065 = 639$$

The total value at the end of 5 years is $11,280.81.

A *sinking fund* is a special type of investment in which a constant amount is invested each year, usually with a view to reaching a specified value at a given point in the future. Questions need to be read carefully in order to be clear about exactly when the first and last instalments are paid.

Illustration 7 – Sinking funds

Suppose a company needs to replace a machine costing $50,000 in 6 years' time. To achieve this it will make six annual investments, starting immediately, at 5.5 per cent.

Find the value of the annual payment.

Solution

To ensure you have understood the question it is always worth drawing a timeline diagram showing, in this case the payments (denoted by P) and asset replacement:

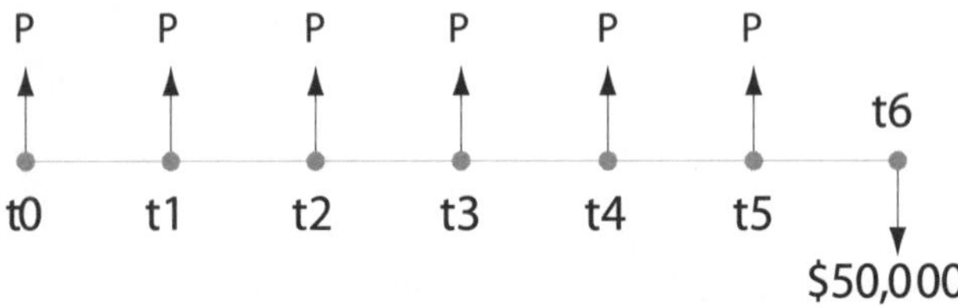

Note:

- t0 means 'now'. We normally start the clock with the first cash flow.
- t1 is a point in time one year from now, so is at the end of the first year
- t2 is a point in time two years from now, etc

The first investment grows for 6 years and its final value is $P(1.055)^6$. The second amounts to $P(1.055)^5$, the third to $P(1.055)^4$, etc. until the sixth, which amounts to only $P(1.055)^1$.

We thus need to solve the following

$$50,000 = P(1.055)^6 + P(1.055)^5 + P(1.055)^4 + P(1.055)^3 + P(1.055)^2 + P(1.055)$$

$$50,000 = P(1.055^6 + 1.055^5 + 1.055^4 + 1.055^3 + 1.055^2 + 1.055)$$

$$50,000 = P \times 7.267, \text{ giving}$$

$$P = 50,000/7.267 = \$6,880 \text{ per annum (to the nearest \$)}$$

Test Your Understanding 13

Three annual instalments of $500 are to be paid, starting immediately, at 4.9 per cent per annum.

Find the value of the investment **immediately after** the third instalment.

7 Geometric progressions

In the examples so far we have worked out the final values for the sinking fund questions simply by using calculators and taking each payment in turn.

However, a sinking fund could easily run for 20 years or more – in fact, the endowment element of some mortgages is a very common example of a sinking fund that would typically run for 20–25 years. So it is useful to be aware of *geometric progressions* and how they can help with all this arithmetic.

A geometric progression (GP) is a series of numbers of the form

$$A, AR, AR^2, AR^3, \ldots$$

where A and R are numbers.

The particular feature that defines a GP is that, after an initial term, A, each term in the progression is a constant multiple (R) (or ratio) of the preceding one.

We shall need to know the sum of the first n terms of such a series. Denoting this by S

$$S = A + AR + AR^2 + AR^3 + \ldots + AR^{n-1}$$

$$S = \frac{A(R^n - 1)}{(R - 1)}$$

Illustration 8 – Geometric progressions

If six annual instalments of $800 are made, starting immediately, at 5 per cent per annum, the value of the investment immediately after the sixth instalment is given by the following expression.

$$\$800 \times (1.05^5 + 1.05^4 + 1.05^3 + 1.05^2 + 1.05 + 1)$$

Use GP theory to evaluate it.

Solution

The series in the brackets, viewed back to front, is a GP with $A = 1$, $n =$ 6 and $R = 1.05$, so its sum is:

$$S = 1 \times \frac{1.05^6 - 1}{1.05 - 1} = 6.8019$$

Hence, the value of the fund is \$800 × 6.8019 = \$5,442 (to the nearest \$).

Notice that n is given by the number of terms, not by the greatest power of R.

Test Your Understanding 14

Use GPs to find the following totals:

A $\$500 (1.042^4 + 1.042^3 + 1.042^2 + 1.042 + 1)$;

B $\$650 (1.03^4 + 1.03^3 + 1.03^2 + 1.03)$.

8 Investment appraisal

Introduction

Firms often have investment appraisal decisions that involve looking at forecast cash flows occuring many years into the future. The long term nature of such projects raises potential problems when comparing cash flows at different times. Consider the following illustration.

Illustration 9 – Long term projects

Suppose you have a very simple project that involves the following:

- Invest \$10,000 now
- Based on your best estimates you expect to receive \$11,000 in the future.

Would you accept this project?

Even though it gives you a gain of \$1,000 and a return of 10%, the answer is not clear cut because it depends on **when** you receive the \$11,000 and what else you could do with the \$10,000 now.

Suppose the $11,000 is to be received in 2 year's time (t2) and that you could invest your current funds in a deposit account paying interest at 6% per annum.

If you invest your cash for two years, then in two year's time you would end up with

$$10,000 \times (1.06)^2 = 11,236$$

This is greater than the $11,000 expected through the project, so you would therefore reject the project and invest the money in the bank instead.

Effectively you are saying that $10,000 now (t0) is worth more to you than $11,000 in two year's time (t2), illustrating the concept that money has a *time value.*

The time value of money

Money received today is worth more than the same sum received in the future, i.e. it has a **time value.**

This occurs for three reasons:

- potential for earning interest/cost of finance
- impact of inflation
- effect of risk.

The time value of money can be expressed as an annual interest rate for calculation purposes. Different terminology is used to describe this rate, depending on the exam paper and the context:

- discount rate
- required return
- cost of capital

Suppose we have a 'cost of capital' of 10% per annum:

- If this related just to a deposit rate at a bank, say, then we could invest $100 now and end up with 100 × 1.10 = $110 in one year's time
- This means that $100 now and $110 in one year's time have the same value to us for decision making purposes when assessing other potential projects.
- Equivalently, we could say that the offer of $110 in a year's time is only worth 110/1.10 = $100 in today's terms.

Supplementary reading – The time value of money

Potential for earning interest

Cash received sooner can be invested to earn interest, so it is better to have $1 now than in one year's time. This is because $1 now can be invested for the next year to earn a return, whereas $1 in one year's time cannot. Another way of looking at the time value of money is to say that $1 in six years' time is worth less than $1 now.

Impact of inflation

In most countries, in most years prices rise as a result of inflation. Therefore funds received today will buy more than the same amount a year later, as prices will have risen in the meantime. The funds are subject to a loss of purchasing power over time.

Risk

The earlier cash flows are due to be received, the more certain they are – there is less chance that events will prevent payment. Earlier cash flows are therefore considered to be more valuable.

Discounted cash flows

In a potential investment project, cash flows will arise at many different points in time. To make a useful comparison of the different flows, they must all be converted to a common point in time, usually the present day, i.e. the cash flows are discounted.

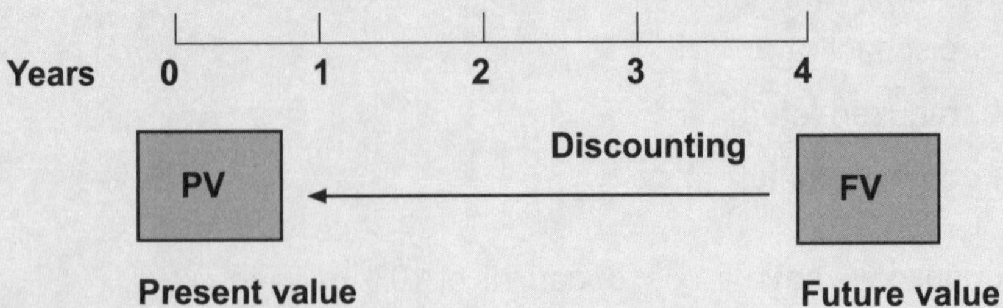

The process of converting future cash flows into present values is known as "discounting" and is effectively the opposite of compound interest.

Illustration 10 – Discounting

Find the present value of:

(a) \$200 payable in 2 years' time, assuming that an investment rate of 7 per cent per annum, compounded annually, is available;

(b) \$350 receivable in 3 years' time, assuming that an annually compounded investment rate of 6 per cent per annum, is available.

Solution

(a) From the definition, we need to find that sum of money that would have to be invested at 7 per cent per annum and have value \$200 in 2 years' time. Suppose this is \$*X*, then the compound interest formula gives:

$$V = P(1 + r)^n$$

Thus:

$$200 = X(1 + 0.07)^2$$

$$X = \frac{200}{1.1449} = 174.69$$

Thus, the present value is \$174.69: that is, with an interest rate of 7 per cent, there is no difference between paying \$174.69 now and paying \$200 in 2 years' time.

(b) Using the compound interest formula again:

$$350 = X(1 + 0.06)^3$$

$$X = \frac{350}{1.191016} = 293.87$$

The present value is thus \$293.87.

Discounting a single sum

The present value (PV) is the cash equivalent now of money receivable/payable at some future date.

The PV of a future sum can be calculated using the formula:

$$P = \frac{F}{(1+r)^n} = F \times (1+r)^{-n}$$

This is just a re-arrangement of the formula we used for compounding.

$(1 + r)^{-n}$ is called the discount factor (DF). To find the DF, for example if r = 10% and n = 5, you can either use the formula or the tables:

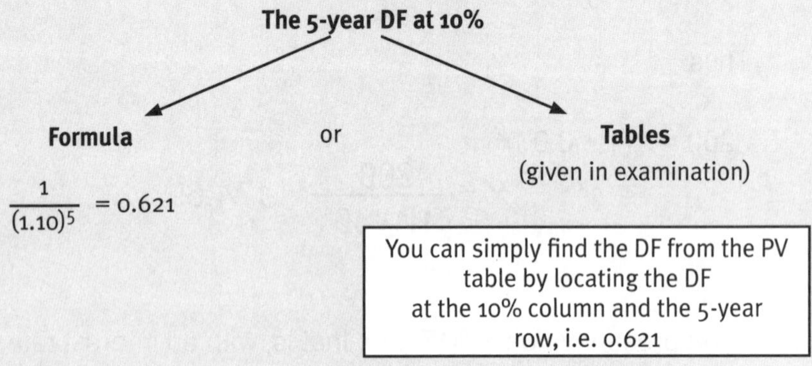

The 5-year DF at 10%
Formula
or
Tables
(given in examination)
$\frac{1}{(1.10)^5} = 0.621$
You can simply find the DF from the PV table by locating the DF at the 10% column and the 5-year row, i.e. 0.621

Test Your Understanding 15

Calculate the present values of the following amounts:

A $12,000 payable in 6 years' time at a rate of 9 per cent

B $90,000 payable in 8 years' time at 14 per cent

C $80,000 payable in 5 years' time at 6.3 per cent

D $50,000 payable in 4 years and 3 months' time at 10 per cent.

9 Net present value (NPV)

In many situations, there are a number of financial inflows and outflows involved, at a variety of times. In such cases, the *net present value* (NPV) is the total of the individual present values, after discounting each, as above.

The NPV represents the net gain or loss on the project after taking into account the timing of cash flows and the time value of money (i.e. incorporates the cost of finance, investment opportunities, inflation and risk), therefore:

- if the NPV is positive – the project is financially viable
- if the NPV is zero – the project breaks even
- if the NPV is negative – the project is not financially viable
- if the company has two or more mutually exclusive projects under consideration it should choose the one with the highest NPV
- the NPV gives the impact of the project on shareholder wealth.

NPV is a hugely important topic that will be revisited again at higher level papers.

Illustration 11 – Net Present Value

A company can purchase a machine now for $10,000. The company accountant estimates that the machine will contribute $2,500 per annum to profits for five years, after which time it will have to be scrapped for $500.

Find the NPV of the machine if the interest rate for the period is assumed to be 5 per cent.

(Assume, for simplicity, that all inflows occur at year ends.)

Solution

We set out the calculations in a systematic, tabular form:

Timing	*Cash flow ($)* *($)*	*Discount factor* *@5%*	*Present value* *($)*
0	(10,000)	1.000	–10,000.00
1	2,500	0.952	2,380.00
2	2,500	0.907	2,267.50
3	2,500	0.864	2,160.00
4	2,500	0.823	2,057.50
5	3,000	0.784	2,352.00
			1,217.00

Hence, the NPV is $1,217.

Test Your Understanding 16

The cash flows for a project have been estimated as follows:

Year	$
0	(25,000)
1	6,000
2	10,000
3	8,000
4	7,000

The cost of capital is 6%.

Calculate the net present value (NPV) of the project to assess whether it should be undertaken.

Test Your Understanding 17

Evaluate the net present values of the following potential purchases (figures, all in $000, show net inflows/(outflows)):

		A	*B*
		r = 6%	*r* = 8%
After:	Year 0	(35)	(55)
	Year 1	(10)	0
	Year 2	20	15
	Year 3	30	25
	Year 4	40	35

Are either of the above purchases worth making, on financial grounds alone?

Supplementary reading – Using NPV in practice

Problems using NPV in practice

One of the major difficulties with present values is the estimation of the 'interest rates' used in the calculations. Clearly, the appropriate rate(s) at the start of the time period under consideration will be known, but future values can be only estimates. As the point in time moves further and further into the future, the rates become more and more speculative.

Many situations in which NPV might be involved are concerned with capital investments, with the capital needing to be raised from the market. For this reason, the 'interest rate(s)' are referred to as the *cost of capital*, since they reflect the rate(s) at which the capital market is willing to provide the necessary money.

Another problem with calculating net present value is the need to estimate annual cash flows, particularly those that are several years in the future, and the fact that the method cannot easily take on board the attachment of probabilities to different estimates. Finally, it is a usual, although not an indispensable, part of the method to assume that all cash flows occur at the end of the year, and this too is a potential source of errors.

With easy access to computers it is now possible to calculate a whole range of NPVs corresponding to worst-case and best-case scenarios as well as those expected, so to some extent some of the problems mentioned above can be lessened.

10 Annuities

An *annuity* is an arrangement by which a person receives a series of constant annual amounts. The length of time during which the annuity is paid can either be until the death of the recipient or for a *guaranteed* minimum term of years, irrespective of whether the annuitant is alive or not. In other types of annuity, the payments are *deferred* until sometime in the future, such as the retirement of the annuitant.

When two or more annuities are being compared, they can cover different time periods and so their net present values become relevant. In your exam you will be given the following formula for the NPV of a $1 annuity over n years at interest rate r, with the first payment 1 year after purchase.

$$\frac{1}{r} - \frac{1}{r(1+r)^n} \quad \text{OR} \quad \frac{1}{r}\left(1 - \frac{1}{(1+r)^n}\right)$$

The cumulative present value tables can also be used.

Illustration 12 – Annuities

Let us revisit the last illustration:

A company can purchase a machine now for $10,000. The company accountant estimates that the machine will contribute $2,500 per annum to profits for five years, after which time it will have to be scrapped for $500.

Find the NPV of the machine using annuity discount factors if the interest rate for the period is assumed to be 5 per cent.

Solution

We can set out the calculations highlighting the annuity as follows:

After year	*Total inflow ($)*	*Discount factor @5%*	*Present value ($)*
0	(10,000)	1.000	(10,000)
1–5	2,500 per year	4.329 (W)	10,823
5	500	0.784	392
			1,215

This table gives the NPV as $1,215. Before we got $1,217, the difference being due to rounding.

(W) This figure can be obtained using the tables or the formulae above

Illustration 13 – Annuities

An investor is considering two annuities, both of which will involve the same purchase price.

- Annuity A pays $5,000 each year for 20 years, while
- Annuity B pays $5,500 each year for 15 years.

Both start payment 1 year after purchase and neither is affected by the death of the investor.

Assuming a constant interest rate of 8 per cent, which is the better?

Solution

Using tables, the cumulative PV factors are 9.818 for A and 8.559 for B. This gives:

- PV of annuity A = 5,000 × 9.818 = 49,090
- PV of annuity B = 5,500 × 8.559 = 47,075

You will only be able to use the tables given in your exam if the period of the annuity is 20 years or less and if the rate of interest is a whole number. It is, therefore, essential that you learn to use the formula as well. You will notice that there is some loss of accuracy, due to rounding errors, when tables are used.

Using the above formula:

$$\text{Factor for the NPV of A} = \frac{1}{0.08} - \frac{1}{0.08(1+0.08)^{20}} = 9.818147$$

and so the NPV of A is:

5,000 × 9.818147 = $49.090 (to the nearest $)

Similarly:

$$\text{Annuity factor for the NPV of B} = \frac{1}{0.08} - \frac{1}{0.08(1+0.08)^{15}} = 8.559479$$

and so the NPV of B is:

5,500 × 8.559479 = $47,077 (to the nearest $)

From the viewpoint of NPVs, therefore, *annuity* A is the better choice. As we have already seen, however, there are two further considerations the investor may have. Assuming constant interest rates for periods of 15 or 20 years is speculative, so the NPVs are only approximations: they are, however, the best that can be done and so this point is unlikely to affect the investor's decision. More importantly, although any payments after the investor's death would go to their estate, some people may prefer more income 'up front' during their lifetime.

Unless the investor is confident of surviving the full 20 years of annuity A, they may prefer annuity B – especially as the two NPVs are relatively close to each other.

A further example will demonstrate an NPV being expressed as an equivalent annuity.

Test Your Understanding 18

A payment of $3,600 is to be made every year for seven years, the first payment occurring in one year's time. The interest rate is 8%. What is the PV of the annuity.

Test Your Understanding 19

A payment of $11,400 is to be made every year for 13 years, the first payment occurring in one year's time. The interest rate is 5%. What is the PV of the annuity.

Test Your Understanding 20

An annuity pays $12,000 at the end of each year until the death of the purchaser. Assuming a rate of interest of 6 per cent, what is the PV of the annuity if the purchaser lives for:

A 10 years; and

B 20 years after purchase?

In order to practise both methods, use the tables in (a) and the formula in (b).

Test Your Understanding 21

An investor is considering three options, only one of which she can afford. All three have the same initial outlay, but there are different income patterns available from each.

- Investment A pays $2,000 each year at the end of the next 5 years.
- Investment B pays $1,000 at the end of the first year, $1,500 at the end of the second year, and so on until the final payment of $3,000 at the end of the fifth year.
- Investment C pays $4,000 at the end of the first year, $3,000 at the end of the second year, and $2,000 at the end of the third.

The investor estimates a constant rate of interest of 10 per cent throughout the next 5 years: which investment should she choose?

Test Your Understanding 22

Compare the following three potential investments, assuming the investor has a maximum of $15,000 to deploy, if the prevailing rate of interest is 11 per cent:

	Investment A	*Investment B*	*Investment C*
	$000	*$000*	*$000*
Initial outlay	14	14	12
Inflow at end of:			
Year 1	0	7	10
Year 2	6	7	8
Year 3	8	7	5
Year 4	10	7	5
Year 5	10	7	5
Year 6	10	7	5

None of the investments brings any income after year 6.

Perpetuities

Finally, there is the concept of *perpetuity*. As the name implies, this is the same as an annuity except that payments go on forever. It is therefore of interest to those who wish to ensure continuing payments to their descendants, or to some good cause. It must be recognised, however, that constant payments tend to have ever-decreasing value, owing to the effects of inflation, and so some alternative means of providing for the future may be preferred.

As *t* becomes very large, the second term in the formula for the PV of an annuity gets smaller and smaller, to the point where it becomes zero, and the factor for the NPV of a perpetuity simplifies considerably to:

$$\frac{1}{r}$$

Test Your Understanding 23

Bob has won a competition that pays him $12,000 per annum for life. Using an interest rate of 6%, calculate the present value of the income, assuming he lives forever.

11 Internal rate of return

We have seen that if the NPV is positive, then it means that the project is more profitable than investing at the discount rate, whereas if it is negative, then the project is less profitable than a simple investment at the discount rate.

For most projects the NPV falls as the discount rate increases. When the NPV becomes zero we have a breakeven discount rate, defined as the *internal rate of return* (IRR) of the project.

This now gives us two ways of appraising an investment:

(1) Accept if NPV > 0 as this means the project will increase shareholder wealth

(2) Accept if actual discount rate < project IRR, as this means we should have a positive NPV

Calculating IRR

The *internal rate of return* (IRR) is the discount rate at which NPV is zero. It is obtained generally by a trial and error method as follows.

(1) find a discount rate at which NPV is small and positive;

(2) find another (larger) discount rate at which NPV is small and negative;

(3) use linear interpolation between the two to find the point at which NPV is zero.

Illustration 14 – IRR

Find the IRR for the following project.

Time	*Cash flow ($000)*
0	(80)
1	40
2	30
3	20
4	5

The question offers no guidance as to what discount rates to try, so we will select 5 per cent randomly. Since 5 per cent turns out to give a positive NPV we now randomly select 10 per cent in the hope that it will give a negative NPV.

Time	*Cash flow* $000	*PV (5%)* $000	*PV (10%)* $000
0	(80)	(80.000)	(80.000)
1	40	38.095	36.364
2	30	27.211	24.793
3	20	17.277	15.026
4	5	4.114	3.415
Net present value:		6.697	(0.402)

We can now use either (a) a graphical method or (b) a calculation based on proportions.

(a) *Graphical method*

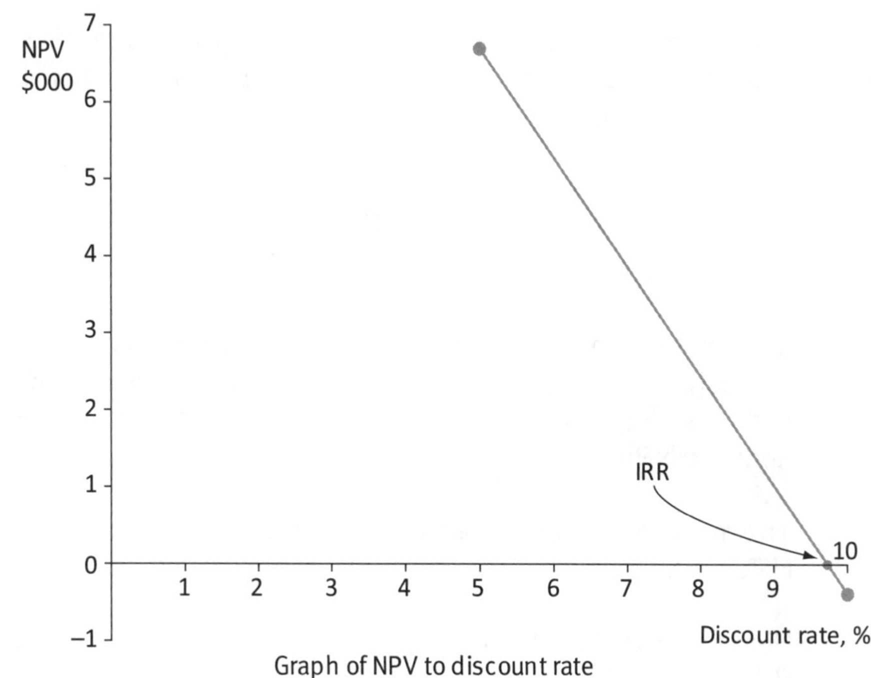

Graph of NPV to discount rate

From the graph the estimated IRR is 9.7 per cent.

(b) *Calculation method using proportions*

The NPV drops from 6.697 to –0.402, that is, a drop of 7.099, when the discount rate increases by 5 percentage points (from 5 to 10 per cent).

NPV will therefore drop by 1 when the discount rate increases by 5/7.099 = 0.7043 percentage points.

The NPV will reach zero if, starting at its 5 per cent level, it drops by 6.697.

This requires an increase of 6.697× 0.7043 = 4.7 percentage points in the discount rate.

Hence, the IRR (the discount rate at which NPV is zero) is 5 + 4.7 = 9.7 per cent.

Calculation method using formula

In general, if you have calculated two NPVs (NPV_1 and NPV_2) for two discount rates (R_1 and R_2 respectively), then the IRR will be given by the formula:

$$R_1 + (R_2 - R_1) \times \frac{NPV_1}{NPV_1 - NPV_2}$$

This formula works whether or not one of the NPVs is positive and one negative, or both are negative or both are positive, so don't bother having a third guess if the first two don't give a positive and negative NPV.

The main calculation aspect to be careful with is if either of the NPVs is negative.

Here we have the following:
$R_1 = 0.05$, $NPV_1 = 6.697$
$R_2 = 0.10$, $NPV_2 = -0.402$

Using the formula gives:
IRR = 0.05 + (0.10 - 0.05) × 6.697/(6.697 + 0.402)
IRR = 0.05 + 0.0472 = 0.0972 or 9.7% as before.

Test Your Understanding 24

Use both the graphical and calculation methods to estimate the IRR for the following project, and interpret your result.

The calculation method is most likely to be useful in your assessment.

Time	*Cash flow ($000)*
0	(100)
1	50
2	50
3	20

12 Interest calculations revisited

Introduction

When performing complex calculations using interest rates, it may be simpler to recognise that two sets of cash flows are equivalent if they have the same NPV.

Illustration 15 – Equivalent annuities

An investment is due to give payoffs with an NPV calculated at $20,000 and an assumed constant interest rate of 6 per cent per annum.

What annuity lasting for 10 years is equivalent to the investment, in that it has the same NPV?

Solution

The two sets of cash flows are equivalent if they have the same NPV.

If the annuity pays $$x$ at the end of each of the next 10 years, then tables give its NPV as $7.360x$. Hence:

$$7.360x = 20,000$$
$$x = 2,717.39$$

The equivalent annuity is thus $2,717.39 per annum.

Loans in general

When setting up any loan, the

PV of amount to be borrowed at t_0= PV of future repayments.

Repayment mortgages

Most people will be aware that, when a mortgage is taken out on a property over a number of years, there are several ways of repaying the loan. We shall concentrate here on *repayment mortgages*, because they are among the most popular, and because they are the only ones that involve complex mathematical calculations.

The features of a repayment mortgage are:

- a certain amount, $*M,* is borrowed to be repaid over *n* years;
- interest (at a rate *r*) is added to the loan retrospectively at the end of each year; and
- a constant amount, $*P*, is paid back each year by the borrower, usually in equal monthly instalments.

Viewed from the standpoint of the lender, a repayment mortgage is an **annuity**.

To perform any calculations with mortgage style loans simply involves working out the present value of the appropriate annuity:

PV of amount to be borrowed at t_0 = PV of future (annuity) repayments

If a mortgage was set up a number of years ago and something changes, such as the interest rate or remaining term of the loan, then the equivalent statement would be:

PV of amount outstanding at t = PV of future (annuity) repayments

Illustration 16 – Mortgages

(a) A \$30,000 mortgage is taken out on a property at a rate of 12 per cent over 25 years. Using annuity discount factors calculate the annual repayment and hence determine the gross monthly repayment.

(b) After 2 years of the mortgage, the interest rate increases to 14 per cent: recalculate the monthly repayment figure.

Solution

(a) Equating present values:

Amount to be borrowed = PV of future repayments

Amount to be borrowed = Annual payment × annuity discount factor

Here, the annuity discount factor = $(1 - 1/1.12^{25}) \times 1/0.12 =$ 7.843139

Thus 30,000 = annual payment × 7.843139, giving

Annual payment = 30,000/7.843139 = \$3,825 per annum (nearest \$).

Dividing by 12 gives a monthly repayment of \$318.75 (to two d.p.).

(b) Suppose we imagine ourselves two years into the future and equate PVs at that point:

PV of amount outstanding = PV of remaining annuity

After 2 years, immediately after the second annual repayment, the amount still owing is:

$30{,}000 \times 1.12^2 - 3{,}825 \times 1.12 - 3{,}825 = \$29{,}523$

The mortgage now has 23 years still to run and at 14 per cent interest we have:

$$29{,}523 = P\frac{1}{0.14}\left(1 - \frac{1}{1.14^{23}}\right) = 6.792056P$$

giving P = 29,523/6.792056 = \$4,346.70 per annum and a monthly repayment of \$362.22 (two d.p.).

Test Your Understanding 25

A property is mortgaged over 20 years at a rate of 8 per cent per annum. If the mortgage is $70,000, what are the annual repayments? If, after 5 years, the rate is reduced to 7.5 per cent, to what are the annual payments reduced?

Sinking funds revisited

Some students prefer to solve sinking fund questions using annuities and equating PVs rather than geometric progressions:

PV of sinking fund (annuity) = PV of final target payment required

Illustration 17 – Sinking funds

Suppose a company needs to replace a machine costing $50,000 in 6 years' time. To achieve this it will make six annual investments, starting immediately, at 5.5 per cent.

Find the value of the annual payment.

Solution

As stated before, it may help to draw a timeline diagram showing the timings of cash flows, in this case the payments (denoted by P) and asset replacement:

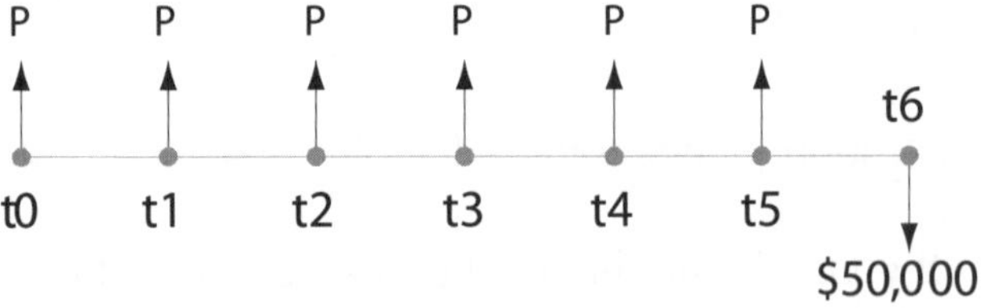

The PV of the future target payment for the machine is given by:

- PV of 50,000 at t6 = 50,000 × $1/1.055^6$ = 50,000 × 0.725 = 36,250

The PV of the sinking fund annuity has two components:

- The payment at t0 does not need discounting - it has a discount factor of 1
- The payments for t1-t5 have a DF = $(1 – 1.055^{-5})$ × 1/0.055 = 4.270

This give a combined discount factor for all the payments t0 – t5 of (1 + 4.270) = 5.270

The PV of the sinking fund is thus = annual payment × 5.270

Equating PVs we get

- 36,250 = annual payment × 5.270
- Annual payment = 36,250/5.270 = **$6,879 pa**

Test Your Understanding 26

Which of the following statements is/are true of a sinking fund?

A A sinking fund is an investment of a constant annual amount.

B A sinking fund is an investment of a declining annual amount.

C A repayment mortgage is a type of sinking fund.

D A sinking fund is a type of annuity.

Chapter Summary

The value, $\$V$, of a sum, $\$P$, invested for n years at a *simple* rate of r per annum is:

$$V = P(1 + rn)$$

The value, $\$V$, of a sum, $\$P$, invested for n years at a *compound* rate of *r* per annum is:

$$V = P(1 + r)^n$$

The same formula can be used to calculate the value of *depreciating* quantities by using a negative value of *r*.

The *present value* (PV) of a sum of money payable/receivable in the future is that sum that would have to be invested now (at a given rate of interest) to reach the target sum at the required future point in time. The PV can be calculated from the appropriate table or from first principles, using the compound interest formula:

$$V = P(1 + r)^n$$

giving the PV of *X* as:

$$PV = \frac{X}{(1 + r)^n}$$

The *net present value* (NPV) of an investment is the total of the present values of all the inflows and outflows involved in the investment.

An annuity is a series of equal cash flows occurring at regular intervals of time. The factor giving the NPV of an annuity paying $1 per annum for t years at a rate of *r* is:

$$\frac{1}{r} - \frac{1}{r(1 + r)^t}$$

This is equivalent to applying tables of cumulative present values of a constant amount. The factor giving the NPV of a perpetuity paying $1 per annum at a rate of *r* is:

$$\frac{1}{r}$$

A geometric progression is a series of numbers, each one a constant multiple of the one preceding it:

$$A, AR, AR^2, AR^3, \ldots$$

The sum, S, of the first n terms of such a progression is:

$$S = \frac{A(R^n - 1)}{R - 1}$$

13 Further Practice Questions

Test Your Understanding 27

A leasing agreement is for 5 years. A sum of $10,000 must be paid at the beginning of the first year, to be followed by four equal payments of $x at the beginning of years two, three, four and five. At a discount rate of 8 per cent, the present value of the four equal payments is $26,496. The total amount to be paid during the lease period is

A $32,000

B $40,000

C $42,000

D $44,000

Test Your Understanding 28

A building society adds interest monthly to investors' accounts even though interest rates are expressed in annual terms. The current rate of interest is 6 per cent per annum.

An investor deposits $1,000 on 1 January. How much interest will have been earned by 30 June?

A $30.00

B $30.38

C $60.00

D $61.68

Test Your Understanding 29

A company charges depreciation at the rate of 25 per cent per annum on the reducing balance method on an asset that cost $20,000.

At the end of year three the written-down value will be

A $5,000.00

B $8,437.50

C $11,560.50

D $12,500.00

Test Your Understanding 30

An individual placed a sum of money in the bank and left it there for 12 years at 5 per cent per annum. The sum is now worth $1,705.56.

Using PV tables, the original principal was found (to the nearest whole $) to be

A $948

B $949

C $950

D $951

Test Your Understanding 31

A firm has arranged a 10-year lease, at an annual rent of $8,000. The first rental payment has to be paid immediately, and the others are to be paid at the end of each year.

What is the present value of the lease at 12 per cent?

A $50,624

B $53,200

C $45,200

D $65,288

Test Your Understanding 32

If a single sum of $12,000 is invested at 8 per cent per annum with interest compounded quarterly, the amount to which the principal will have grown by the end of year three is approximately

A $15,117

B $14,880

C $15,219

D $15,880

Test Your Understanding 33

It is estimated that a particular cost will decline by 5 per cent per annum on a compound basis. If the cost now is $10,000, by the end of year four the cost will be approximately

A $7,500

B $8,000

C $8,145

D $8,500

Test Your Understanding 34

A person is to receive a 10-year annuity of $5,000 per year, received at the end of each year. At what interest rate does this have a present value of $33,550?

A 2 per cent

B 4 per cent

C 8 per cent

D 16 per cent

Test Your Understanding 35

An investor is to receive an annuity of $1,360 for 6 years commencing at the end of year one. It has a present value of $6,101. What is the rate of interest?

A 6 per cent

B 9 per cent

C 12 per cent

D 15 per cent

Test Your Understanding 36

A bond increases in value from $400 to $500 over a 6-year period. Find the percentage increase per annum.

A 25 per cent

B 4.17 per cent

C 3.79 per cent

D 3.81 per cent

Test Your Understanding 37

A sum of $40,000 is invested for 10 years at 7 per cent per annum. What is its final value (to the nearest $) if interest is (a) simple; and (b) compound?

Test Your Understanding 38

A sum of $10,000 is invested at a nominal rate of 12 per cent per annum. What is its value (to the nearest $) after 4 years if interest is compounded (a) annually; (b) every 6 months; and (c) every month?

Test Your Understanding 39

The following is a calculation in which a rate of interest of 2 per cent per month is converted into an effective annual rate of interest. For each line of the calculation, (A)–(D), identify whether it follows correctly from the line immediately preceding it (regardless of whether you believe the immediately preceding line to be correct).

Monthly rate is 2 per cent

A Monthly ratio is 1.2

B Annual ratio is 1.2 × 12

C 14.4

D Annual rate is 44 per cent

Test Your Understanding 40

A bond increases from $5,000 to $8,500 over 6 years. Complete the following calculation of the effective rate of interest:

Six-year ratio = ?
Annual ratio = ?
Effective annual rate = ?% (to one decimal place)

Test Your Understanding 41

Equipment costing $100,000 depreciates by 20 per cent in its first year and thereafter by 10 per cent per annum. The following calculation aims to find how many years it will take for its value to drop to $20,000. For each line of the calculation, (A)–(I), say whether or not it follows correctly from the line immediately preceding it (regardless of whether you believe the immediately preceding line to be correct).

Value of equipment at end of 1 year:
A 100,000 × 0.8
B 80,000

Value after a further *n* years
C 80,000 – *n* × 80,000 × (10/100)
D 80,000 (1 – 0.1*n*)

When value reaches $20,000, we have:
E 20,000 = 80,000 (1 – 0.1*n*)
F 2/8 = 1 – 0.1n
G 0.1*n* = 1.25
H *n* = 1.25/0.1 = 12.5

The value would drop to $20,000:
(I) In 12 years.

Test Your Understanding 42

Find the present value of $100,000 receivable in five years, giving your answer to the nearest $, if the discount rate is 7 per cent: (a) using the present value table and (b) by exact calculation.

Test Your Understanding 43

Complete the following net present value calculation, using a 6 per cent discount rate.

Time	*Cash flow* $	*Discount factor* 6%	*Present value* $
0	(5,000)	1.000	(5,000)
1	3,000	0.943	?
2	1,000	0.890	?
3	2,000	?	?
Net present value			?

Test Your Understanding 44

The net present value (NPV) of a project is $3,000 when the discount rate is 5 per cent. Which of the following statements is/are correct on the basis of the information given?

A The initial investment in this project is $3,000.

B If $3,000 were invested at 5 per cent, it would generate the cash flows of this project.

C If the discount rate were to increase to 7 per cent, the NPV would increase.

D The project is viable compared with investing at 5 per cent.

Test Your Understanding 45

Calculate the present value of an annuity of $10,000 per annum, payable at the end of each year for 20 years at a discount rate of 5 per cent, giving your answer correct to the nearest $: (a) using the cumulative present value table and (b) by exact calculation.

Test Your Understanding 46

A $50,000 repayment mortgage is taken out at 10 per cent over 20 years. Use tables to calculate the annual repayment (to the nearest $), assuming that payments are made at the end of each year.

Test Your Understanding 47

Which of the following is true of the internal rate of return (IRR)?

A The IRR is the current cost of borrowing.

B The IRR is the discount rate.

C The IRR is the discount rate for which net present value is zero.

D All other things being equal, a project with a low IRR will always be preferable to one with a high IRR.

Test Your Understanding 48

Percentages and discounting

A company is planning a new product for which a 10-year life is anticipated. The product is expected to follow a typical life cycle of growth, maturity and decline with a cash flow of $56,000 in year 1. Estimates of cash flows expected from years 2 – 10 are as follows:

Year	*Percentage rate of change expected on the previous year's cash flow*
2	+2
3	+5
4	+10
5	+10
6	+10
7	+5
8	–1
9	–3
10	–5

Assume all cash flows arise at year ends. Work throughout to the nearest $. Calculate the cash flow expected in the tenth year.

Test Your Understanding 49

Supposing that the expected cash flows are as follows, complete the following table, to calculate the net present value of the expected cash flows, by filling in the appropriate numerical values in the spaces indicated by the letters. Use a discount rate of 8 per cent per annum and use CIMA tables.

Year	*Cash flow ($)*	*Discount factor*	*Present value ($)*
1	56,000	...	...
2	57,000	...	A
3	60,000	...	...
4	66,000	...	...
5	72,000	...	B
6	79,000	...	...
7	84,000	...	...
8	82,000	...	C
9	80,000	...	...
10	75,000	...	...
Net present value			

Test Your Understanding 50

If the net present value at 8% was $450,000, what is the maximum amount that the company could invest now in the product if it is to meet a target of an 8% return?

Test Your Understanding 51

If the net present value was $450,000 and, if the company needs to borrow at 8 per cent in order to finance the project, which of the following statements is/are correct?

A $450,000 is the profit that the company expects to make if they can borrow at 8 per cent.

B $450,000 is the maximum profit that the company might make if they borrow at 8 per cent.

C $450,000 is the maximum that the company should borrow if they wish to make a profit.

D $450,000 is the present value of the profit that the company expects to make if they borrow at 8 per cent.

Test Your Understanding 52

Annual equivalent costs

To carry out identical tasks, a company uses several machines of the same type, but of varying ages. They have a maximum life of five years. Typical financial data for a machine are given below:

Time	*Now*	*After 1 year*	*After 2 years*	*After 3 years*	*After 4 years*	*After 5 years*
Initial cost	$10,000	–	–	–	–	–
Maintenance 1 service costs	$1,000	$1,500	$2,000	$2,500	$3,000	$5,000
Resale value if sold	–	$7,000	$5,000	$3,500	$2,500	$2,000

The rate of interest is 15 per cent.

These machines are assumed to produce flows of revenue that are constant.

Complete the following table, to calculate the net present value of the costs if the machine is kept for 5 years, by filling in the appropriate numerical values in the spaces indicated by the letters. Work to the nearest $ throughout.

Time (years)	Outflows ($)	Discount factor	Present value ($)
0	A	D	...
1	B	...	...
2	...	E	...
3	...	...	F
4	...	...	...
5	C	...	...

Test Your Understanding 53

The present values of the costs of keeping the machine for between 1 and 4 years are given below. Convert each of these into an annual equivalent amount and write them in the final column of the table, for one mark each.

Year of scrapping	Present value of cost ($)	Annuity equivalent ($)
1	6,215	...
2	10,037	...
3	13,159	...
4	15,748	...
5	18,669	...

Test Your Understanding 54

If the annual equivalent amounts calculated above were as follows, what would be the most economical age at which to replace the machines?

Year of scrapping	Annual equivalent ($)
1	7,000
2	6,000
3	5,800
4	5,500
5	5,600

Test Your Understanding 55

NPV and IRR

A company is planning capital investment for which the following cash flows have been estimated:

Time	*Net cash flow ($)*
Now	(10,000)
At the end of year 1	500
At the end of year 2	2,000
At the end of year 3	3,000
At the end of year 4	4,000
At the end of year 5	5,000
At the end of year 6	2,500
At the end of year 7	2,000
At the end of year 8	2,500

The company has a cost of capital of 15 per cent.

Complete the following table by filling in the appropriate numerical values in the spaces indicated by the letters. Work to the nearest £ throughout. Cash flows are all at the ends of years unless stated otherwise.

Year end	*Net cash flow ($)*	*Discount factor at 15%*	*Present value ($)*
Now	(10,000)	A	C
1	500	B	...
2	2,000	...	...
3	3,000	...	...
4	4,000	...	...
5	5,000	...	...
6	2,500	...	...
7	2,000	...	...
8	2,500	...	D

Test Your Understanding 56

Which of the following defines the 'internal rate of return'.

A The current discount rate used by a company.

B The discount rate at which net present value is zero.

C The discount rate recommended by a trade association or similar.

D The discount rate at which cash flows total zero.

Test Your Understanding 57

A project has a net present value of $(543) when the discount rate is 20 per cent and $3,802 when it is 15 per cent.

Which of the following statements about the value of the internal rate of return (IRR) is correct in this case?

A The IRR must be below 10 per cent.

B The IRR must lie between 10 per cent and 15 per cent.

C The IRR must lie between 15 per cent and 20 per cent.

D The IRR must be greater than 20 per cent.

E None of the above statements is correct.

Test Your Understanding 58

A project has a net present value of $(543) when the discount rate is 20 per cent and $1,344 when it is 15 per cent.

Calculate the approximate internal rate of return (to the nearest whole per cent point) of this investment without calculating any further net present values.

Test Your Understanding 59

If the internal rate of return was 12 percent in this case, and ignoring any other considerations, would you recommend acceptance of the project?

Answer: Yes/No

Test Your Understanding 60

Sinking funds and mortgages

A retailer is facing increasing competition from new shops that are opening in his area. He thinks that if he does not modernise his premises, he will lose sales. A local builder has estimated that the cost of modernising the shop will be $40,000 if the work is started now. The retailer is not sure whether to borrow the money and modernise the premises now, or to save up and have the work carried out when he has sufficient funds himself. Current forecasts show that if he delays the work for 3 years, the cost of the modernisation is likely to rise by 4 per cent per annum.

Investigations have revealed that, if he borrows, he will have to pay interest at the rate of 3 per cent per quarter, but if he saves the money himself he will only earn 2 per cent per quarter.

Use tables to find the cumulative discount factor appropriate to quarterly payments of $1 at 3 per cent per quarter over 2 years.

Test Your Understanding 61

Calculate the equal amounts that would need to be paid at the end of each quarter if the retailer borrows the $40,000 now and repays it at 3 per cent per quarter over 3 years. Give your answer to two d.p.

Test Your Understanding 62

Calculate the likely cost of modernisation if it is delayed by 3 years. Give your answer to two d.p.

Test Your Understanding 63

If the retailer decides to delay modernisation and to save at 2 per cent per quarter, use tables to find the present value of his savings of $\$x$ per quarter, with 12 payments in total and the first being made immediately.

Test Your Understanding 64 – Net present value

An organisation is considering a capital investment in new equipment. The estimated cash flows are as follows.

Year	Cash flow
	$
0	(240,000)
1	80,000
2	120,000
3	70,000
4	40,000
5	20,000

The company's cost of capital is 9%.

Calculate the NPV of the project to assess whether it should be undertaken.

Test your understanding answers

Test Your Understanding 1

The interest rate in the formula needs attention: it is assumed that r is a proportion, and so, in this case, we must convert r = 8 per cent into a proportion:

$$r = 0.08$$

Also, we have

$$P = 5{,}000 \text{ and } n = 5$$

So

$$V = P(1 + r \times n) = 5{,}000(1 + 0.08 \times 5) = 5{,}000 \times 1.4 = 7{,}000$$

Thus, the value of the investment will be $7,000.

Test Your Understanding 2

A $r = 0.05$, $n = 5$, $P = 20{,}000$:
$V = 20{,}000(1 + 0.25) = \$25{,}000$

B $r = 0.06$, $n = 3$, $P = 50{,}000$:
$V = 50{,}000(1 + 0.18) = \$59{,}000$

C $r = 0.01$, $n = 6 \times 4 = 24$, $P = 30{,}000$:
$V = 30{,}000(1 + 0.24) = \$37{,}200$

Test Your Understanding 3

A The only part of this type of calculation that needs particular care is that concerning the interest rate. The formula assumes that r is a proportion, and so, in this case:

$r = 0.08$

In addition, we have $P = 5{,}000$ and $n = 5$, so:

$V = P(1 + r)^5 = 5{,}000 \times (1 + 0.08)^5 = 5{,}000 \times 1.469328 = 7{,}346.64$

Thus, the value of the investment will be $7,346.64.
It will be noted that compound interest gives higher values to investments than simple interest.

B With slight modifications, the basic formula can be made to deal with compounding at intervals other than annually. Since the compounding is done at 6-monthly intervals, 4 per cent (half of 8 per cent) will be added to the value on each occasion. Hence, we use $r = 0.04$. Further, there will be ten additions of interest during the five years, and so $n = 10$. The formula now gives:

$V = P(1 + r)^{10} = 5{,}000 \times (1.04)^{10} = 7{,}401.22$

Thus, the value in this instance will be $7,401.22.
In a case such as this, the 8 per cent is called a nominal annual rate, and we are actually referring to 4 per cent per 6 months.

Test Your Understanding 4

A $r = 0.05$, $n = 5$, P = 20,000
$V = 20{,}000(1.05)^5 = \$25{,}525.63$

B $r = 0.06$, $n = 3$, $P = 50{,}000$
$V = 50{,}000(1.06)^3 = \$59.550.80$

C $r = 0.01$, $n = 6 \times 4 = 24$, $P = 30{,}000$
$V = 30{,}000(1.01)^{24} = \$38{,}092.04$

Test Your Understanding 5

We have, for option *A*, $P = 20{,}000$; $n = 10 \times 4 = 40$; $r = 0.015$ and so:

$$V = 20{,}000(1 + 0.015)^{40} = \$36{,}280.37$$

For option *B*, $P = 20{,}000$; $n = 10 \times 2 = 20$; $r = 0.032$ and so:

$$V = 20{,}000(1+0.032)^{20} = \$37{,}551.21$$

Hence, option B is the better investment.
In this case, $P = 20{,}000$ was given but it is not necessary to be given an initial value because \$1 can be used instead.

Test Your Understanding 6

A For \$1, value at the end of 1 year = $1 \times 1.03^2 = 1.0609$. Hence, the effective annual rate is 6.09 per cent.

B For \$1, value at the end of 1 year = $1 \times 1.02^4 = 1.0824$. Hence, the effective annual rate is 8.24 per cent.

C For \$1, value at the end of 1 year = $1 \times 1.01^{12} = 1.1268$. Hence, the effective annual rate is 12.68 per cent.

Test Your Understanding 7

The 5-year ratio = 1,250/1,000 = 1.25 = annual ratio^5. Hence, the annual ratio = $1.25^{1/5} = 1.0456$, giving an effective annual rate of 4.56 per cent.

Test Your Understanding 8

The annual ratio = 1.2 = monthly ratio^{12}

A Monthly ratio = $1.2^{1/12} = 1.0153$, and the monthly rate is 1.53 per cent.

B Nine-month ratio = $1.2^{9/12} = 1.1465$, and the 9-month rate = 14.65 per cent.

Test Your Understanding 9

A The 4-year ratio = 600/500 = 1.2 = annual ratio^4. Hence, the annual ratio is $1.2^{1/4}$ = 1.047, so the effective annual rate is 4.7 per cent.

B The annual ratio is 1.058 = 6-month ratio^2. So the 6-month ratio √(1.058) = 1.0286 and the 6-monthly rate is 2.86 per cent.

Test Your Understanding 10

We have P = 20,000; n = 6; r = –0.12, hence:

$$V = P(1 + r)^6 = 20{,}000(1 - 0.12)^6 = 20{,}000 \times 0.4644041 = 9{,}288.08$$

The machine's value in 6 years' time will therefore be $9,288.08.

Test Your Understanding 11

P = 120,000, n = 7, r = –0.08, so

$$V = 120{,}000(1 - 0.08)^7 = 120{,}000(0.92)^7 = \$66{,}941.59$$

Test Your Understanding 12

P = 720,000, r = 0.2 for n = 1, r = 0.1 for n = 5 and r = 0.02 for n = 1

$$V = 720{,}000 \times 0.08^1 \times 0.9^5 \times 0.98^1 = \$333{,}319.80$$

Test Your Understanding 13

The diagram shows when the investments and evaluation take place:

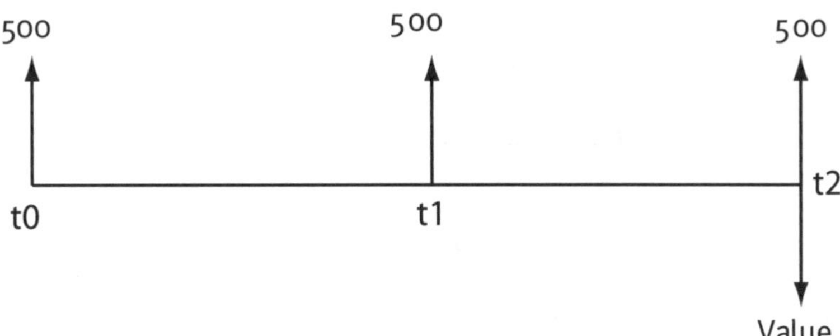

Note that the final instalment has no time to grow at all. The value is:

$500 \times (1.049^2 + 1.049 + 1) = 500 \times 3.1494 = \$1,575$ to the nearest $

Test Your Understanding 14

A Inside the bracket, $A = 1$, $n = 5$, $R = 1.042$:

$$s = 500 \times \frac{(1.042^5 - 1)}{1.042 - 1} = \$2,719 \text{ (to the nearest \$)}$$

B Inside the bracket, $A = 1.03$, $n = 4$, $R = 1.03$:

$$s = 650 \times \frac{1.03(1.03^4 - 1)}{1.03 - 1} = \$2,801 \text{ (to the nearest \$)}$$

Test Your Understanding 15

A Discount factor at 9 per cent for 6 years = $1/(1.09)^6$ = 0.596 (or use tables)

PV = 12,000 × 0.596 = $7,152

B Discount factor at 14 per cent for 8 years = $1/(1.14)^8$ = 0.351 (or use tables)

PV = 90,000 × 0.351 = $31,590

C Discount factor at 6.3 per cent for 5 years = $1/(1.063)^5$ = 0.737 (have to use calculator)

PV = 80,000 × 0.737 = $58,960

D Discount factor at 10 per cent for 4.25 years = $1/(1.10)^{4.25}$ = 0.667 (have to use calculator)

PV = 50,000 × 0.667 = $33,350

Test Your Understanding 16

Year	**Cash flow**	**DF**	**PV**
	$	**at 6%**	$
0	(25,000)	1.000	(25,000)
1	6,000	0.943	5,658
2	10,000	0.890	8,900
3	8,000	0.840	6,720
4	7,000	0.792	5,544
			1,822

The NPV of the project is positive at $1,822. The project should therefore be accepted.

Test Your Understanding 17

Time	A $000	Discount factor	PV $000
0	(35)	1.000	(35.00)
1	(10)	0.943	(9.43)
2	20	0.890	17.80
3	30	0.840	25.20
4	40	0.792	31.68
Net present value:			30.25 (i.e. $30,250)

Time	B $000	Discount factor	PV $000
0	(55)	1.000	(55.00)
1	0	0.926	–
2	15	0.857	12.86
3	25	0.794	19.85
4	35	0.735	25.73
Net present value:			3.44 (i.e. $3,440)

Both investments have positive NPVs and so both are worthwhile.

The idea of NPV enables us to compare two or more options, as illustrated below.

Test Your Understanding 18

Using the formula:

$$\frac{1-(1+r)^{-n}}{r} = \frac{1-(1.08)^{-7}}{0.08} = 5.206$$

$3,600 × 5.206 = $18,741.60

Note that the AF could have been taken straight from the tables.

Test Your Understanding 19

Using the formula:

$$\frac{1-(1+r)^{-n}}{r} = \frac{1-(1.05)^{-13}}{0.05} = 9.394$$

$11,400 × 9.394= $107,091.60

Note that the AF could have been taken straight from the tables.

Test Your Understanding 20

A If $n = 10$ and rate is 6 per cent, from tables the annuity factor is 7.360:

PV = 12,000 × 7.360 = $88,320

B If $n = 20$, from the formula:

$$PV = 12{,}000 \times \left(\frac{1}{0.06} - \frac{1}{0.06 \times 1.06^{20}}\right) = \$137{,}639.05$$

Test Your Understanding 21

From tables, the cumulative present value factor for a constant inflow at 10 per cent for 5 years is 3.791; hence the NPV of investment A is

2,000 × 3,791 = $7,582

The other two investments do not involve constant inflows, and so the PVs for individual years have to be summed.

Year (end)	PV factor	Investment B Inflow ($)	PV ($)	Investment C Inflow ($)	PV ($)
1	0.909	1,000	909	4,000	3,636
2	0.826	1,500	1,239	3,000	2,478
3	0.751	2,000	1,502	2,000	1,502
4	0.683	2,500	1,707.50	–	–
5	0.621	3,000	1,863	–	–
			7,220.50		7,616

In summary, the NPVs of investments A, B and C are $7,582, $7,220.50 and $7,616, respectively.

The investor should choose C as it has the highest NPV.

Test Your Understanding 22

Time	Discount factor	A $000	PV $000	B $000	PV $000	C $000	PV $000
0	1.000	(14)	(14.000)	(14)	(14,000)	(12)	(12.000)
1	0.901	0	0.000	7	–	10	9.010
2	0.812	6	4.872	7	–	8	6.496
3	0.731	8	5.848	7	–	5	–
4	0.659	10	6.590	7	–	5	–
5	0.593	10	5.930	7	–	5	–
6	0.535	10	5.350	7	29.61	5	12.590
Net present values:			14.590		15.617		16.096

In the case of B we have multiplied 7 by the cumulative PV factor for 6 years at 11 per cent, giving 7 × 4.231 = 29.617

For C we have subtracted the 2-year cumulative PV factor from the 6-year factor and then multiplied the result by 5.

All the investments are worthwhile since they have positive NPVs. Investment C costs the least initially and yet has the highest NPV and so is to be preferred.

Test Your Understanding 23

For a perpetuity of $12,000 per annum, discounted at 6 per cent, the present value is 12,000/0.06 or $200,000.

You can check this easily. At 6 per cent, the interest on $200,000 is $12,000 per annum, so the annuity can be paid indefinitely without touching the capital.

Test Your Understanding 24

Time	*Cash flow* *$000*	*PV (5%)* *$000*	*PV (15%)* *$000*
0	(100)	(100.000)	(100.000)
1	50	47.619	43.478
2	50	45.351	37.807
3	20	17.277	13.150
	Net present value:	10.247	(5.565)

A Graphical method

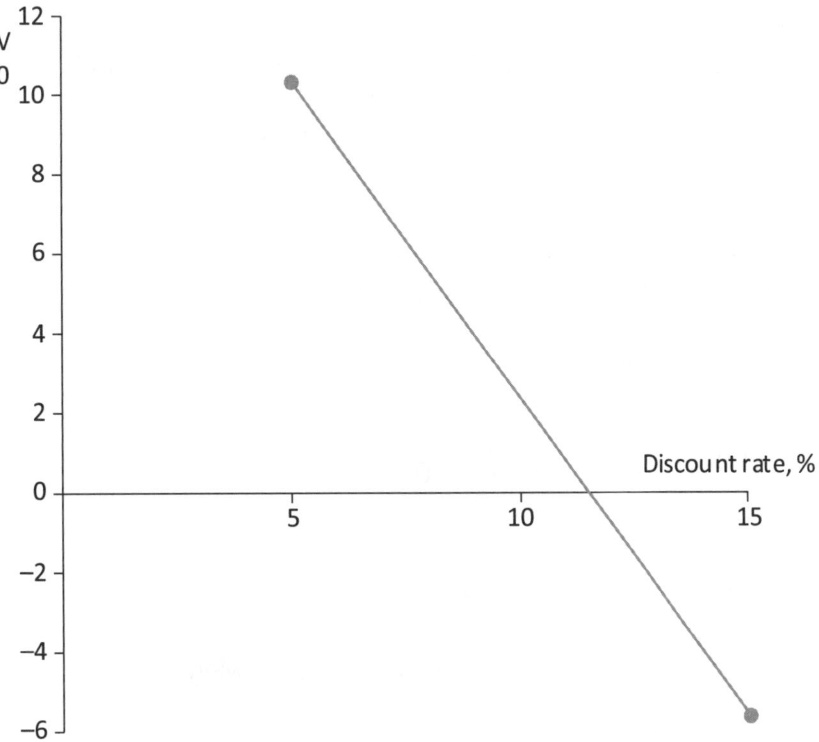

From the graph the estimate of the IRR is 11.5 per cent.

B Using proportions:

The NPV drops by 10.247 + 5.565 = 15.812 when discount rate increases by 10 percentage points.

The NPV will drop by 1 ($'000) when discount rate increases by 10/15.812 = 0.6324 percentage points.

For IRR, NPV must drop by 10.247, which requires an increase in the discount rate of 10.247 × 0.6324 = 6.5 percentage points.

Hence, the IRR = 5 + 6.5 = 11.5 per cent.

Alternatively, using the formula:

R_1 = 0.05, NPV_1 = 10.247

R_2 = 0.15, NPV_2 = -5.565

Using the formula gives:

IRR = 0.05 + (0.15 - 0.05) × 10.247/(10.247 + 5.565)

IRR = 0.05 + 0.0648 = 0.1148 or 11.5% as before.

Test Your Understanding 25

Equating PVs:

$$70{,}000 = P\left(\frac{1}{0.08} - \frac{1}{0.08 \times 1.08^{20}}\right) = 9.818147P$$

giving P = $7,129.65 per annum.

After the fifth annual payment, the amount owing is:

$70{,}000 \times 1.08^5 - 7{,}129.65(1.08^4 + 1.08^3 + 1.08^2 + 1.08 + 1)$
$= 102{,}852.97 - 7{,}129.65 \times 1 \times (1.08^5 - 1) \div 0.08$
$= 102{,}852.97 - 41{,}826.81$
$= 61{,}026.16$

At 7.5 per cent for the remaining 15 years, equating PVs gives:

$$61{,}026.16 = P\left(\frac{1}{0.075} - \frac{1}{0.075 \times 1.075^{15}}\right)$$

giving P = $6,913.49.

Test Your Understanding 26

A True

B False

C False

D False

Test Your Understanding 27

C

Using tables, the annuity factor of \$1 over 4 years at 8 per cent = 3.312
Let x = the annual sum payable at the beginning of years two, three, four and five.

Thus:

$$3.312\ x = 26{,}496$$
$$x = 26{,}496/3.312$$
$$x = 8{,}000$$

Thus, the total amount payable:

= \$10,000 + (4 × \$8,000)
= \$10,000 + \$32,000
= \$42,000

Test Your Understanding 28

B

Assuming the rate of interest stated is nominal, that is, 6 per cent per annum in this case means ½ per cent per month, monthly ratio = 1 + (0.5/100) = 1.005

Value after 6 months = 1,000 × 1.005^6 = 1,030.38

That is, interest = \$30.38

Test Your Understanding 29

B

Each year, the value at the end is 0.75 times the value at the beginning. So the value after three years is 20,000 × 0.75^3 = 8,437.5

Test Your Understanding 30

C

The present value of 1,705.56 discounted at 5 per cent p.a. for 12 years is 1,705.56 × 0.557 = 949.99692 = $950 to the nearest whole $.

Test Your Understanding 31

A

Present value = $8,000 + present value of an annuity of $8,000 for 9 years at 12 per cent.

Present value = $50,626

Test Your Understanding 32

C

Three years is equal to twelve quarters, at an interest rate of 2 per cent per quarter.

The principal will have grown to $12,000 × 1.02^{12}$ = $15,219

Test Your Understanding 33

C

Cost at end of year 4 = $10,000 × 0.95^4$ = $8,145

Test Your Understanding 34

C

Present value 5 annual amount 3 annuity factor. So, annuity factor = 33,550/5,000 = 6.71

From the 10-year row in the cumulative present value tables, 6.71 corresponds to a discount rate of 8 per cent.

Test Your Understanding 35

B

Present value = annual amount × annuity factor
6,101 = 1.360 × annuity factor
Annuity factor = 6,101/1,360 = 4,486

From tables, over 6 years this factor corresponds to a rate of 9 per cent.

Test Your Understanding 36

C

The 6-year ratio = 500/400 = 1.25, and its sixth root = the annual ratio = 1.038

Hence the rate is 3.8 per cent per annum.

A gives the 25 per cent increase over the entire period and B gives 25 per cent divided by 6. D presumably comes from raising 1.25 to the power 6 instead of taking the sixth root.

Test Your Understanding 37

A $68,000 (= 40,000 + 10 × 40,000 × 7/100)

B $78,686 (= 40,000 × 1.07^{10})

Test Your Understanding 38

A $15,735 (= 10,000 × 1.12^{4})

B $15,938 (= 10,000 × 1.06^{8})

C $16,122 (= 10,000 × 1.01^{48})

Test Your Understanding 39

Monthly rate is 2 per cent.

A Monthly ratio is 1.2	Incorrect: it is 1.02
B Annual ratio is 1.2 × 12	Incorrect: it would be 1.2^{12}
C 1 4.4	Correct
D Annual rate is 44 per cent.	Incorrect: it would be 1,340 per cent.

Test Your Understanding 40

Six-year ratio = 1.7

Annual ratio = $1.7^{1/6}$ = 1.092

Effective annual rate 9.2 per cent.

Test Your Understanding 41

Value of equipment at end of 1 year:

A 100,000 × 0.8	Correct
B 80,000	Correct
Value after a further *n* years	
C 80,000 – *n* × 80,000 × 10/100	Incorrect: it is 80,000 × 0.9^n
D 80,000 (1 – 0.1*n*)	Correct
When value reaches $20,000, we have:	
E 20,000 = 80,000 (1 – 0.1*n*)	Correct
F 2/8 = 1 – 0.1n	Correct
G 0.1*n* = 1.25	Incorrect: it is 0.1*n* = 0.75
H *n* = 1.25/0.1 = 12.5	Correct
The value would drop to $20,000:	
I In 12 years.	Incorrect: after 12 years the value would still be above $20,000 on the basis of this calculation.

Test Your Understanding 42

A $71,300 (=100,000 × 0.713)

B $71,299 (=100,000/$1.07^5$)

Test Your Understanding 43

Time	*Cash flow* $	*Discount factor* 6%	*Present value* $
0	(5,000)	1.000	(5,000)
1	3,000	0.943	2,829
2	1,000	0.890	890
3	2,000	0.840	1,680
Net present value			399

Test Your Understanding 44

A Incorrect.

B Incorrect – it would generate cash flows with the same value in present value terms as the project flows, but not necessarily the exact flows.

C Incorrect.

D Correct.

Test Your Understanding 45

A $124,620 (= 10,000 × 12.462)

B $124,622 (= 10,000/0.05(1 – 1/1.05^{20}))

Test Your Understanding 46

$5,873 (= 50,000/8.514)

Test Your Understanding 47

A False

B False

C True

D False

Test Your Understanding 48

Beginning with 56,000 at the end of year one, increase by 2 per cent by multiplying by 1.02, then by 5 per cent (multiply by 1.05) and so on. To decrease by 1 per cent, multiply by 0.99 (i.e. by 1–1/100).

Year	*Cash flow ($)*
1	56,000
2	57,120
3	59,976
4	65,974
5	72,571
6	79,828
7	83,819
8	82,981
9	80,492
10	76,467

Test Your Understanding 49

The discount factors are given by present value tables at the rate of 8 per cent and years 1–10. The present value is given by multiplying the cash flow by the appropriate discount factor and the net present value is the total of the present values.

NPV of cash flows at 8 per cent

Year	*Cash flow* *($)*	*Discount factor* *($)*	*DCF*
1	56,000		
2	57,000	0.857	48,849
3	60,000		
4	66,000		
5	72,000	0.681	49,032
6	79,000		
7	84,000		
8	82,000	0.540	44,280
9	80,000		
10	75,000		
NPV			

Test Your Understanding 50

The net present value is the amount which if invested now at 8 per cent would result in the cash flows listed and hence it gives the maximum amount which should be invested if a return of 8 per cent is required.

Test Your Understanding 51

C

$450,000 is the maximum that the company should borrow if they wish to make a profit.

Test Your Understanding 52

The outflows are given in the question apart from the first and last which need minor arithmetic. Discount factors are given by the 15 per cent column in present value tables up to 5 years and present value is given by multiplying each outflow by the corresponding discount factor. The following table then gives the values required:

Time (years)	*Outflows ($)*	*Discount factor*	*Present value ($)*
0	11,000	1,000	11,000
1	1,500	0.870	1,305
2	2,000	0.756	1,512
3	2,500	0.658	1,645
4	3,000	0.572	1,716
5	3,000	0.497	1,491

Test Your Understanding 53

In order to compare these five NPV figures which span five different time periods, we need to convert each of them into a regular annual payment; to do this we divide the net present value by the corresponding cumulative present value factor taken from tables.

Answers

Year of Scrapping	*Present value of cost ($)*	*Cum PV factor*	*Annuity equivalent ($)*
1	6,215	0.870	7,144
2	10,037	1.626	6,173
3	13,159	2.283	5,764
4	15,748	2.855	5,516
5	18,669	3.352	5,570

Test Your Understanding 54

The lowest annual cost occurs if the machines are scrapped after 4 years

Test Your Understanding 55

Discount factors are obtained from present value tables, using the 15 per cent column and the years up to 8. Present value is given by multiplying the net cash flow by the corresponding discount factor.

Year end	*Net cash flow ($)*	*Discount factor at 15%*	*Present value ($)*
0	–10,000	1.000	–10,000
1	500	0.870	435
2	2,000	0.756	1,512
3	3,000	0.658	1,974
4	4,000	0.572	2,288
5	5,000	0.497	2,485
6	2,500	0.432	1,080
7	2,000	0.376	752
8	2,500	0.327	818

Test Your Understanding 56

B

It is the discount rate at which net present value is zero.

Test Your Understanding 57

If the net present value is positive at 15 per cent and negative at 20 per cent, it must be zero somewhere between the two, so (C) is the correct answer.

Test Your Understanding 58

At 15 per cent NPV is +1,344 and at 20 per cent it is -543.

Using the formula

- $IRR = R_1 + (R_2 - R_1) \times NPV_1 /(NPV_1 - NPV_2)$
- $IRR = 0.15 + (0.20 - 0.15) \times 1{,}344/(1{,}344 + 543)$
- $IRR = 0.15 + 0.0356 = 0.1856$ or 19% to the nearest per cent.

Using proportions

- Discount rate increases by 5 per cent the NPV drops by 1,344 + 543 = 1,887.
- Starting at 15 per cent, the NPV must drop by 1,344 to reach zero. A \$1,887 drop corresponds to a 5 per cent increase; a \$1 drop corresponds to a 5/1,887 per cent increase; and so a \$1,344 drop corresponds to a 1,344 × 5/1,887 = 3.56 per cent increase.
- Rounding to the nearest whole per cent point gives an IRR of 15 + 4 = 19 per cent.

Test Your Understanding 59

Yes.

The project is acceptable, because the cost of capital is less than the IRR, so should deliver a positive NPV.

This ignores the fact that the cash flows are almost all estimates, the applicable discount rate may change, there may be even more profitable projects available elsewhere, etc.

Test Your Understanding 60

Total number of payments is 8; first payment occurs at time 1; discount rate is 3 per cent. From tables the cumulative discount value is 7.020.

Test Your Understanding 61

From the tables, the cumulative discount factor at 3 per cent for 12 time periods is 9.954. The present value of $\$x$ paid at the end of each of 12 quarters at 3 per cent per quarter is $9.954x$ and this must equal the initial debt of $40,000.

If $9.954x = 40{,}000$, then $x = 40{,}000/9.954 = \$4{,}018.49$

Test Your Understanding 62

Likely cost is 40,000 compounded at 4 per cent for 3 years, that is $40{,}000 \times 1.04^3 = \$44{,}994.56$.

Test Your Understanding 63

From the tables, the cumulative present value of $1 at the ends of 11 time periods at 2 per cent per period is 9.787. If we include an immediate payment of $1, this PV becomes 10.787. Hence the present value required is $10.787x$.

Test Your Understanding 64 – Net present value

Year	Cash flow	DF at 9%	PV
	$		$
0	(240,000)	1.000	(240,000)
1	80,000	0.917	73,360
2	120,000	0.842	101,040
3	70,000	0.772	54,040
4	40,000	0.708	28,320
5	20,000	0.650	13,000
NPV			+ 29,760

The PV of cash inflows exceeds the PV of cash outflows by $29,760, which means that the project will earn a DCF return in excess of 9%, i.e. it will earn a surplus of $29,760 after paying the cost of financing. It should therefore be undertaken.

chapter

8

Probability

Chapter learning objectives

On completion of their studies students should be able to:

- calculate a simple probability
- demonstrate the addition and multiplication rules of probability
- calculate a simple conditional probability
- calculate an expected value
- demonstrate the use of expected value tables in decision making
- explain the limitations of expected values
- explain the concepts of risk and uncertainty
- prepare graphs/diagrams of normal distribution, explain its properties and use tables of normal distribution.

1 Introduction

Most people have an intuitive, common-sense understanding of probabilities.

For example, consider the following statements:

- "If I flick a coin, then there is a 50:50 chance of getting heads or tails."
- "If I am playing a board game and need to roll a die, then there is a one in six probability of rolling a four"
- "You are more likely to be hit by lightning, then win the lottery"
- "Experience suggests we have a one in ten chance of winning a tender for a new contract"

All of these statements relate to the idea of probabilities.

This session covers the basic rules of probability, in some cases develops it beyond the realms of common sense and finally looks at the concept of expected values.

2 Definitions of probability

Definition

A probability expresses the likelihood of an event occurring.

Note the terminology here. The 'event' referred to is simply what we want to calculate the probability for, such as 'winning the tender' or 'rolling a six'.

Basic ideas

- If an event is certain to occur, then it has a probability of one.
- If an event is impossible, then it has a probability of zero.
- For any event, the probability of it occuring must lie between zero and one. If you calculate a probability bigger than one, then you have made a mistake!
- The higher the probability is, then the more likely it is that the event will happen.
- In any given scenario, the probabilities associated with all possible outcomes must add up to one.

  For example, if trying to win a particular tender for new work, then there are only two possible outcomes - either you win or you don't. If the probability of winning the tender is 0.4, then the probability of not winning must be 0.6 as the two probabilities must add up to one.

Notation

The probability of event 'A' occurring is written as P(A).

This allows us to write down some of the above rules more concisely, for example:

P(NOT A) = 1 – P(A), where P(NOT A) means the probability of event A not occurring.

This is known as the "complementary rule".

3 Simple probabilities

In situations where it is possible to compile a *complete* list of all the *equally likely* outcomes, we can define the probability of an event, denoted *P* (event), in a way that agrees with intuition.

$$P(\text{event}) = \frac{\text{Total number of outcomes which constitute the event}}{\text{Total number of possible outcomes}}$$

Illustration 1 – Simple probabilities

An ordinary six-sided die is rolled. What is the probability that it will show a number less than three?

Solution

Here it is possible to list all the possible equally likely outcomes of rolling a die, namely the whole numbers from one to six inclusive:

1, 2, 3, 4, 5, 6

The outcomes that constitute the 'event' under consideration, that is, 'a number less than three' are:

1, 2

Hence the proportion of outcomes that constitute the event is 2/6 or 1/3, which is therefore the desired probability.

We could write this as P(Getting a number < 3) = 1/3

Note: Most people would have arrived at this answer using intuition.

Test Your Understanding 1

Background

A standard pack of playing cards has 52 cards (excluding 'jokers').

These are split into four 'suits':

- 'hearts'
- 'clubs'
- 'diamonds'
- 'spades'

Each 'suit' has 13 cards - the Ace, 2, 3, 4, 5, 6, 7, 8, 9, 10, Jack, Queen and King

Hearts and diamonds are red cards whereas clubs and spades are black.

Required

Suppose I pick one card at random. Determine the probability for each of the following:

(a) The card I pick is a king
(b) The card I pick is red
(c) The card I pick is a club
(d) The card is the Ace of Spades.

Test Your Understanding 2

A tennis club organises the draw for its annual men's singles tournament by picking names from a hat. There are 32 men in the draw this year.

In the last two years Johann has had to play Petr, his arch rival in the first round.

What is the probability that Johann will have to play Petr in the first round this year?

Constructing a discrete probability distribution

We use the word discrete here to describe a variable that can assume only certain values, regardless of the level of precision to which it is measured.

For example, the number of errors made on an invoice is a discrete variable as it can be only 0 or 1 or 2 or . . .and never 2.3, for example.

A *discrete probability distribution* consists of a list of all the values the variable can have (in the case of exact probabilities) or has had (in the case of empirical probabilities), together with the appropriate corresponding probabilities.

Probabilities can be used in an *exact* sense when applied to the population of outcomes, or in an *empirical*, approximate sense when applied to a sample. *Subjective* probabilities arise from individuals' or a group's judgement.

There are thus three ways of constructing the probability distribution:

1. Using theory to determine exact probabilities

Suppose we are looking at throwing two dice and adding their scores. What are the probabilities of the different outcomes?

Firstly we need to assume that both dice are fair and that each of the numbers 1 to 6 has an equal chance of being rolled for each dice.

We can then use our approach to simple probabilities described above. For example out of the 36 possible outcomes for the two dice (1 and 1, 1 and 2, 1 and 3,..., 1 and 6, 2 and 1, 2 and 2, ..., 2 and 6, 3 and 1,..., 6 and 6) only one outcome (6 and 6) sums to 12.

Thus the probability of getting 12 is 1/36.

2. Using past data to determine empirical probabilities

The key assumption here is that the past is a good indicator of the future.

A simple example will illustrate.

The records of a shop show that, during the previous 50 weeks' trading, the number of sales of a certain item have been

Number of sales/week	*Number of weeks*
0	4
1	16
2	22
3	6
4 or more	2

Construct the corresponding probability distribution.

Probabilities can be based on the empirical data given.

$$P(\text{0 sales in a week}) = \frac{4}{50} = 0.08$$

Proceeding in this way, we can build up the distribution:

Number of sales/week	*P(number of sales/week)*
0	0.08
1	0.32
2	0.44
3	0.12
4 or more	0.04
	1.00

Note that the total probability sums to 1.

One reason firms carry out market research is to obtain data to allow empirical probabilities to be estimated. For example, a supermarket may be planning to release a new food product. Before attempting a national launch, they may trial it in a limited number of stores. Suppose in the sample of stores selected that 10% of customers said they would buy it. The firm could then estimate that 10% of its national customers would buy it if launched in all stores, assuming the sample was representative.

Such data gathering may involve either

- "primary" research – this generates new, "primary" data, such as through the trial above. This also known as "field research".
- "secondary research", where existing research findings are reviewed. This is also known as "desk research" and the data referred to as "secondary data".

3. Estimation of subjective probabilities

Based on a mixture of past experience, hunches and pure guess work, a sales manager may believe that the firm has a 1 in 3 chance of winning a forthcoming sales pitch to a potential new client. Even though the basis of this probability may be suspect, it still allows the firm to plan accordingly.

Test Your Understanding 3

A quality controller wishes to estimate the probability of a component failing within 1 year of installation. How might she proceed?

Using tables with simple probabilities

In some exam questions you have to do some detective work on the information given before you can apply the above rule. This is often easier if you use a table to set out the different possibilities.

Illustration 2 – Using tables

A sample of 100 companies has been analysed by size and whether they pay invoices promptly.

The sample has been broken down as follows:

- *large* v *small* companies
- *fast* v *slow* payers

Suppose that

- Sixty of the companies analysed are classified as *large*, of which forty are *slow payers*.
- In total, thirty of all the companies are *fast payers*.

The probability that a company chosen at random is a *fast paying*, *small* company is:

A 0.10

B 0.20

C 0.30

D 0.40

Solution

If we try to set up a table covering all possibilities, then we know the following:

	Fast	*Slow*	*Total*
Large	?	40	60
Small	?	?	?
	—	—	—
	30	?	100
	—	—	—

We now need to deduce the missing figures.

For example

- Looking at the final column, there must be 40 small firms as we have 100 in total and 60 are large
- Looking at the top row, out of the 60 large firms, 20 must be fast

Once we have filled in the easier figures, we can deduce others until we end up with

	Fast	*Slow*	*Total*
Large	20	40	60
Small	10	30	40
	—	—	—
	30	70	100
	—	—	—

Now we can answer the question: P(fast and small) = 10/100 = 0.1

Answer: (A)

Test Your Understanding 4

In a group of 100 CIMA students, thirty are male, fifty-five are studying Certificate level, and six of the male students are not studying Certificate level. A student chosen at random is female. What is the probability that she is **not** studying Certificate level?

A 0.80

B 0.56

C 0.44

D 0.20

4 Combining probabilities to answer more complex questions

Multiple events

In principle, it is possible to find any probability by the methods discussed above. In practice, however, there are many complex cases that can be simplified by combining simpler probabilities, especially if there are two or more events in the question.

For example, at some airports you will find a game of chance where you pay $10, say, and get to roll 5 dice. If you roll them all at the same time and get all sixes, then you win a sports car.

What is the probability of winning the car with your first attempt?

To answer this we need to recognise that there are five 'events' here - each dice roll is a separate event and we need all of them to give the desired result (a six) to win. We know that the probability of getting a six with a particular die is 1/6 but how do we combine this to get our desired probability?

We can determine such probabilities using the so-called *rules* of probability.

Rules of probability

These can take two forms:

- P(A **and** B both happening)

  Here we want **all** of our desired events to happen together - for example, all of our five dice need to land with a six to win the car.

- P(A **or** B happening)

  Here we want **one** or more of a number of different possible events to happen. For example, what is the probability of **either** being struck by lightning **or** hit by a meteor on my birthday?

It is vital in questions that you distinguish between the two.

5 P(A or B) – The "addition rules" of probability

If the question asks for P(A **or** B), then there are three ways of calculating the answer:

(1) **Basic rules**

Use the basic rules by looking at how many possible outcomes there are.

(2) **Simple version of addition rule**

If A and B are 'mutually exclusive' events, then you can simply add probabilities together, which is why it is referred to as the 'addition' rule:

$$P(A \text{ or } B) = P(A) + P(B)$$

Mutually exclusive events cannot both occur at the same time.

For example, a particular employee cannot simultaneously be aged both over 50 and below 21.

This can be shown as $P(A \text{ and } B) = 0$

(3) **More complex version of addition rule**

The more general rule is

$$P(A \text{ or } B) = P(A) + P(B) - P(A \text{ and } B)$$

This allows us to calculate probabilities when both events can happen simultaneously.

For example, an employee could be both over 50 and female.

It is vital in questions that you can identify whether the two events described are mutually exclusive or not.

Note

These rules are given in your CIMA assessment in the forms:

- *P(A or B)* = *P*(A U B) = *P*(A) + *P*(B)
- *P(A or B)* = *P*(A U B) = *P*(A) + *P*(B) – *P*(A ∩ B)

Test Your Understanding 5

Identify which of the following pairs of events, if any, are mutually exclusive:

(a) Roll one die. A = get a six, B = get a five

(b) Pick a card from a standard 52 card pack. A = get an ace, B = get a red card

(c) Sitting two exams (C03 and C04) at Certificate level. A = pass C03, B = pass C04

(d) Bidding for an item on an online auction site. A = win the auction, B = lose the auction.

Illustration 3 – P(A or B)

Suppose I roll a fair die. What is the probability of getting a 2 or a 3?

Using simple approach

- There are two favourable outcomes (2 or a 3) out of six possible outcomes
- Thus P(2 or 3) = 2/6 = 1/3

Using addition rule

- P(get a 2) = 1/6
- P(get a 3) = 1/6
- P(2 or 3) = P(2) + P(3) = 1/6 + 1/6 = 1/3

Note: adding the two probabilities in this case only works because you cannot simultaneously get a 2 and a 3 - the two events are mutually exclusive.

Illustration 4 – P(A or B)

Suppose I roll a fair die. What is the probability of getting a multiple of three or an even number?

Using simple approach

- There are four favourable outcomes (2, 3, 4 or 6) out of six possible outcomes
- Thus P(multiple of three or even) = 4/6 = 2/3

Using the simple version of the addition rule:

P(A or B) = P(A) + P(B)

- Event A is "get a multiple of 3", so P(A) = P(3 or 6) = 2/6
- Event B is "get an even number", so P(B) = P(2, 4 or 6) = 3/6
- P(multiple of 3 or even) = P(multiple of 3) + P(even) = 2/6 + 3/6 = 5/6, which is the wrong answer!

Note: adding the two probabilities in this case does not work because you **can** have both events happening at the same time - rolling a 6 means both events A and B have happened - 6 is both even and a multiple of 3. The two events are not mutually exclusive.

Effectively we have double counted so need to use the more complex version of the addition rule.

using the full version of the addition rule:

P(A or B) = P(A) + P(B) – P(A and B)

- P(A) = P(multiple of 3) = P(3 or 6) = 2/6
- P(B) = P(get an even number) = P(2, 4 or 6) = 3/6
- P(A and B) = P(multiple of 3 **and** even) = P(6) = 1/6
- P(A or B) = P(A) + P(B) – P(A and B) = 2/6 + 3/6 – 1/6 = 4/6, the correct answer.

Test Your Understanding 6

Calculate the following probabilities using the addition rules:

(a) *P*(Roll one die – get a six or a five)

(b) *P*(Pick a card from a standard 52 card pack – get an ace or a red card)

Using tables

As with simple probabilities, some more complex questions can be solved more easily using tables.

Illustration 5 – P(A or B) – using a table

According to personnel records, the 111 employees of an accountancy practice can be classified by their workbase (A, B or C) and by their professional qualifications thus:

	Office A	*Office B*	*Office C*	*Total*
Qualified	26	29	24	79
Not qualified	11	9	12	32
	—	—	—	—
Total	37	38	36	111
	—	—	—	—

What is the probability that a randomly selected employee will:

(a) work at office A or office B?

(b) work at office A or be professionally qualified or both?

Solution

(a) **Using simple probability techniques.**

There are 37 people working in A and 38 in B, making 75 out of 111 who work in either A or B.

Hence, P(Office A or B) = 75/111.

Using the rules of probability

An employee is not based in office A and office B so we have mutually exclusive events:

P(A or B) = P(A) + P(B)

P(Office A) = 37/111, P(Office B) = 38/111 giving

P(Office A or B) = 37/111 + 38/111 = 75/111

(b) Using simple probability techniques

Examining the table: 37 are employed at office A, and 79 are qualified, making a total of 116. It is clear, however, that we have 'double counted' the 26 employees who both work at office A and are qualified.

Subtracting this double-counted amount, we see that 116 – 26 = 90 employees have the desired property. Hence:

P(Office A or qualified) = 90/111

Using the rules of probability

Suppose we try using P(A or B) = P(A) + P(B)

P(Office A or qualified) = P(Office A) + P(Qualified) = 37/111 + 79/111 = 116/111

Not only is the answer wrong but it is greater than one!

The problem is the double counting highlighted above. Our two events are not mutually exclusive - it is possible to be both qualified and work in office A. Thus we have to use:

P(A or B) = P(A) + P(B) – P(A and B)

P(Office A or qualified) = P(Office A) + P(qualified) – P(Office A and qualified)

P(Office A or qualified) = 37/111 + 79/111 – 26/111 = 90/111 as before

Test Your Understanding 7

The following table relates to a check on the quality of all the items produced by three shifts at a factory during a certain day.

	Shift X	*Shift Y*	*Shift Z*	*Total*
Grade I	65	72	71	208
Grade II	56	72	33	161
Faulty	9	16	6	31
Total	130	160	110	400

If an item is selected at random from the day's production, what is the probability that:

A it is Grade I?

B it was produced by Shift X?

C it was produced by Shift Y or Shift Z?

D it was produced by Shift Y or is Grade II?

E it is faulty or was produced by Shift Z?

6 P(A and B) – The "multiplication" rules of probability

If the question asks for P(A **and** B both happening), then there are three ways of calculating the answer:

(1) **Basic rules**

Using the basic rules by looking at how many possible outcomes there are.

(2) **Simple version of multiplication rule**

If the two events are 'independent', then you can just multiply the individual probabilities together, which is why we refer to it as the multiplication rule:

P(A and B) = P(A) × P(B)

Two events are said to be 'independent' if the occurrence of one event **does not** affect the probability of the other event occurring.

For example the probability of finding an employee with an IQ above 120 is independent of whether the employee is male or female.

(3) **More complex version of multiplication rule**

More generally the multiplication rule has to be adapted as follows:

P(A and B) = P(A) × P(B|A) for 'conditional' events

Two events are said to be 'conditional' if the occurrence of one event **does** affect the probability of the other event occurring.

P(B|A) means the probability of B occuring, **given** that A has occurred

For example the probability of finding an employee with a height above 170cm **is** affected by whether the employee is male or female.

Note:

These rules are given in your CIMA assessment in the forms:

$P(A \cap B) = P(A) \times P(B)$ and

$P(A \cap B) = P(A) \times P(B|A)$

Test Your Understanding 8

Which of the following events is/are likely to be independent?

A Successive tosses of a coin.

B Successive selections of a card from a pack without replacement.

C Gender and shoe size.

D Breakdown of machines of different types and ages.

Illustration 6 – P(A and B)

Consider an earlier example, where you had to roll five sixes in order to win a car.

How likely is it that you will succeed?

Solution

Each of the five dice are independent so we can multiply the probabilities together:

P(five sixes) = P(6 on first die) × P(6 on second die) × ... × P(6 on fifth die)

P(five sixes) = 1/6 × 1/6 × 1/6 × 1/6 × 1/6 = 1/7,776

i.e. you have a roughly one in 8,000 chance of winning the car.

Illustration 7 – P(A and B)

In an earlier illustration we had the following table concerning the 111 employees of an accountancy practice:

	Office A	*Office B*	*Office C*	*Total*
Qualified	26	29	24	79
Not qualified	11	9	12	32
Total	37	38	36	111

What is the probability that a randomly selected employee will come from office B and not be qualified?

Solution

Using simple probabilities by looking at the number of possibilities:

A reading from the table shows that nine of the 111 employees come under the required category. Hence:

- P(employed at office B and not qualified) = 9/111, or approximately 0.080

Using the simple version of the multiplication rule

- P(Office B) = 38/111
- P(Not professionally qualified) = 32/111

- P(Office B and not qualified) = P(office B) × P(not qualified)
= 38/111 × 32/111 = 1,216/12,321,
or approximately 0.099, which is the wrong answer.

The reason this doesn't work is because the two events given (Office B and not qualified) are conditional. The probability of being qualified or not **does** depend on whether we are picking generally from the whole organisation or just office B.

Using the general version of the multiplication rule:

The two events given are conditional. so use P(A and B) = P(A) × P(B|A)

- P(Office B) = 38/111
- P(Not professionally qualified if from office B) = 9/38
- P(Office B and not qualified) = P(office B) × P(not qualified given from office B)
= 38/111 × 9/38 = 9/111,
or approximately 0.08, which is the correct answer.

Constructing a discrete probability distribution II

Multiplication rules can be used with conditional probabilities to construct probability distributions.

Example

For example, suppose a firm is considering a new project and has estimated the following:

- In the first year there is a 60% probability that sales will be 10,000 units and a 40% probability that sales will be 6,000 units
- If sales are high in the first year, then in the second year there is a 70% chance of sales of 12,000 units and a 30% chance of sales of 8,000 units
- If sales are low in the first year, then in the second year there is a 50% chance of sales of 7,000 units and a 50% chance of sales of 5,000 units

Construct the probability distribution for the sales in each year.

Solution:

Year 1

Sales	*Probability*
10,000	0.6
6,000	0.4
	1.0

Year 2

Sales	Working	Probability
12,000	0.6 × 0.7	0.42
8,000	0.6 × 0.3	0.18
7,000	0.4 × 0.5	0.20
5,000	0.4 × 0.5	0.20
		1.00

Example working:

P(12,000 in year 2) = P(10,000 in year 1) × P(12,000 in year 2 | high sales in year 1) = 0.6 × 0.7 = 0.42

Test Your Understanding 9

Past data show that the probability of a married woman of age 32 being alive in 30 years' time is 0.69. Similarly, the probability of a married man of age 35 being alive in 30 years' time is 0.51. Calculate, for a married couple (woman aged 32, man aged 35), the probabilities that in 30 years' time:

A they are both alive

B only (exactly) one is alive

C neither is alive.

Test Your Understanding 10

The following table relates to a check on the quality of all the items produced by three shifts at a factory during a certain day.

	Shift X	*Shift Y*	*Shift Z*	*Total*
Grade I	65	72	71	208
Grade II	56	72	33	161
Faulty	9	16	6	31
Total	130	160	110	400

If an item is selected at random from the day's production, what is the probability that:

A it was produced by Shift X and is faulty?

B it was produced by Shift Y and is Grade II?

C it is faulty, given that it was produced by Shift Z? – that is, P (faulty|from Shift Z)

D it is from Shift Z, given that it is Grade I? – that is, P (from Shift Z | Grade I)

E it is not Grade II?

Test Your Understanding 11

A manufacturing company's accountant wishes to estimate the costs arising from faults in a new product, which is soon to be launched. Tests show that:

- Two per cent of the product is faulty; and, independently of this,
- Six per cent of the packaging is faulty.

Further, it is known from past experience of similar items that customers always return faulty products. However, they return items with faulty packaging (product not faulty) only *half* the time.

Since costs associated with defective products differ from those relating to packaging, the accountant wishes to estimate the percentage of products that will be returned owing to:

A faulty product;

B faulty packaging, but no problems with the product itself;

C any fault.

Test Your Understanding 12

A mass-produced article can exhibit two types of fault, A or B. Past records indicate that 1 per cent of production has fault A, 2 per cent has fault B. Further, the presence of fault A has no effect on whether fault B is present or not. Find the following probabilities:

A *P*(an article has both faults)

B *P*(an article has no fault)

C *P*(an article has only fault A)

D *P*(an article has precisely one fault)

E *P*(an article has fault A, given that it does not have fault B).

Using tables

As we have seen before, some conditional probability problems are easier to solve if we construct a table showing all possibilities.

Illustration 8 – Conditional probabilities and tables

A firm produces 55 per cent of items on production line A and 45 per cent on line B. In general, 3 per cent of the products of line A and 5 per cent of that of line B are found to be defective but, once a product is packaged and sold, it is not possible to tell by which line it was manufactured. If an item is subsequently returned as faulty, what is the probability that it was made on line A?

Solution

The easiest way to calculate this type of conditional probability is to set out the information in table form, taking a total of 100 for convenience. We shall show the process in several steps, though in practice you would only produce one table:

	Defective	*OK*	*Total*
A			55
B			45
Total			100

This table shows the information about A and B having 55 per cent and 45 per cent of production respectively.

Next we shall incorporate the fact that 3% of A's 55 items are defective, giving 55 × 0.03 = 1.65. Similarly, the percentage of defective items for B is 5% of 45 = 0.05 × 45 = 2.25.

	Defective	*OK*	*Total*
A	1.65		55
B	2.25		45
Total			100

Finally, complete the rest of the table by addition and subtraction:

	Defective	*OK*	*Total*
A	1.65	53.35	55
B	2.25	42.75	45
Total	3.90	96.10	100

We can now find the conditional probability required:

P(A|defective) = 1.65/3.9 = 0.42

Test Your Understanding 13

Three accountancy training establishments, A, B and C, have numbers of CIMA students in the ratio 4:3:3 and their pass rates are 35, 68 and 53 per cent, respectively. What is the probability that a successful student, who is known to have been at one of these establishments, was in fact at B?

Supplementary reading – Venn diagrams

Venn diagrams were first developed in the 19th century by John Venn. They are a graphic device useful for illustrating the relationships between different elements or objects in a set. A Venn diagram is a picture that is used to illustrate intersections, unions and other operations on sets. Venn diagrams belong to a branch of mathematics called set *theory*. They are sometimes used to enable people to organise thoughts prior to a variety of activities. Using Venn diagrams enables students to organise similarities and differences in a visual way.

A set of elements is a group which has something in common. Such a group could be all the children in a school:

Venn Diagram representing the set of all the children in a Village School

A second Venn diagram shows all the boys and the girls at the school.

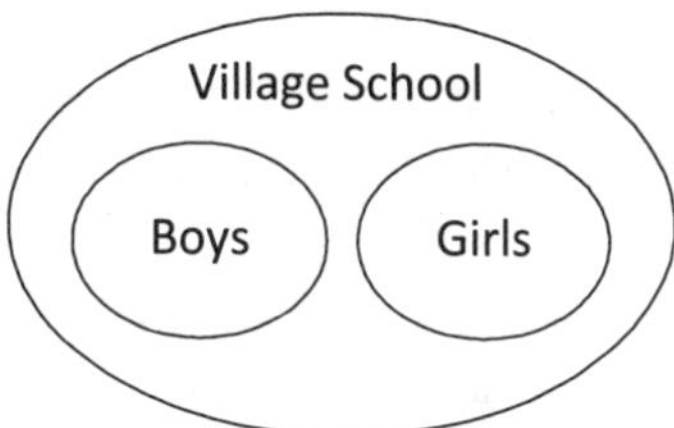

Venn Diagram representing the boys and girls in a Village School

A third Venn diagram could be the children who play for the village football team.

Venn Diagram representing the children from the Village who play in the football team

So, if we want to represent the children in a village school who also play football for the village team we would draw the following Venn diagram. Then the area of intersection between the two ellipses is a pictorial representation of the children from the Village School who are in the Village football team.

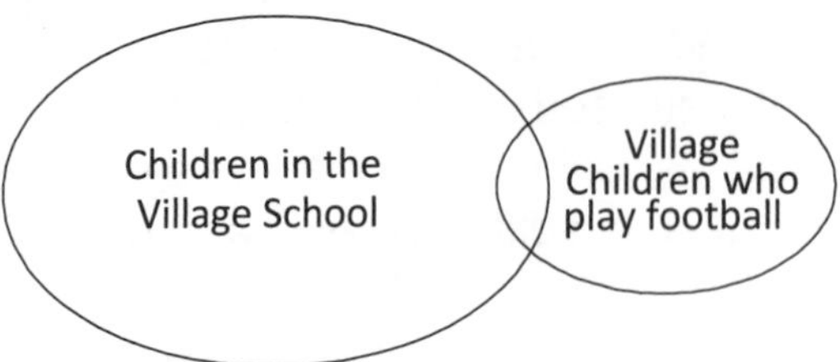

The intersection of the Venn diagrams represents the children from the Village School who play in the football team

Using Venn diagrams to assist with probability

Venn diagrams can be a useful way of understanding calculations of probability. This will be explained through the use of an example.

Illustration

The probability that a woman drinks wine is 0.4.

The probability that a woman drinks gin and tonic is 0.7. The probability that a woman does not drink wine nor gin and tonic is 0.1. This example will show how a Venn diagram will assist in obtaining the probability that a woman selected at random drinks wine and gin and tonic.

The first step is to draw a Venn diagram showing the two sets of women, that is those that drink wine and those that drink gin and tonic The group that drink wine will be referred to as set W and the set that drink gin and tonic will be referred to as G&T.

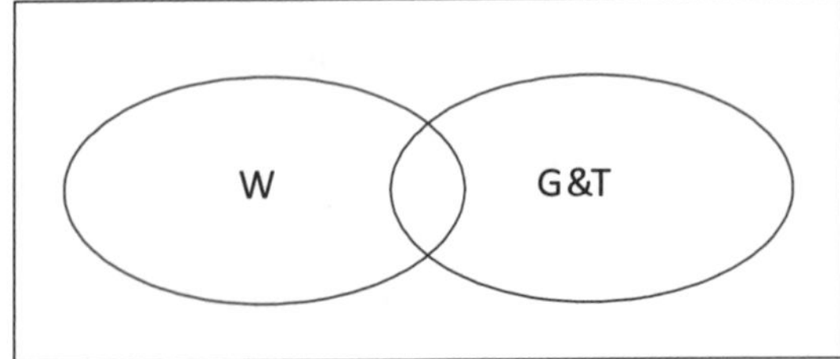

Two sets of women who drink wine, and gin and tonic

The next step in the process is to insert the probabilities in the Venn diagram and to start the calculations. Let x be the probability that a woman drinks both wine and gin and tonic. This is represented by the intersection of the two ellipses. This assumption now allows us to say that the area of the set W, which represents the women who only drink wine and not gin and tonic is 0.4–x. In the same way we can say that the area of the set G&T, which represents women who only drink G&T and not wine is 0.7–x. We also know from our data that the probability of a woman not drinking wine and not drinking gin and tonic is 0.1. These are all represented as:

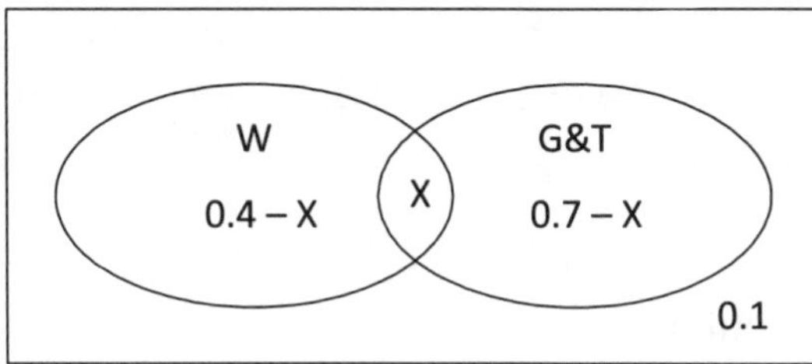

Venn diagram showing the sum of all the probabilities

It is known that the sum of all the probabilities in the diagram equals 1. Therefore the following equation can be constructed.

$$(0.4 - x) + x + (0.7 - x) + 0.1 = 1$$
$$1.2 - x = 1$$
$$-x = -0.2$$
$$x = 0.2$$

From this calculation it is possible to ascribe the probabilities to each part of the Venn diagram:

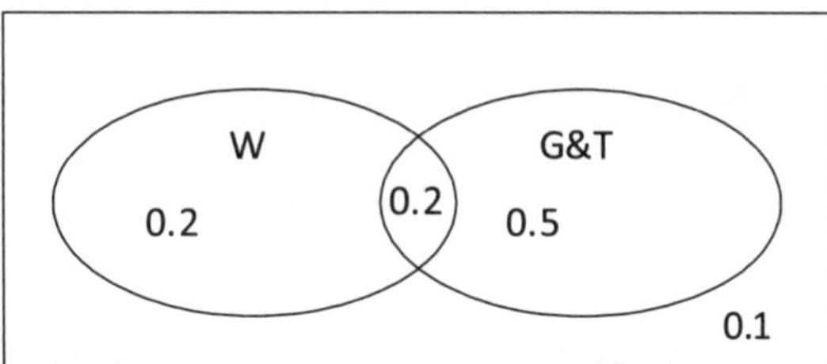

Venn diagram showing the final results

7 Expected values

Many business situations require a choice between numerous courses of action whose results are uncertain. Clearly, the decision-maker's experience and judgement are important in making 'good' choices in such instances. The question does arise, however, as to whether there are objective aids to decision-making that, if not entirely replacing personal judgement, can at least assist it. In this section, we look at one such possible aid in the area of *financial* decision-making.

In order to introduce a degree of objectivity, we begin by seeking a criterion for classing one option as 'better' than another. One commonly accepted criterion is to choose the option that gives the highest expected financial return. This is called the *expected value* (EV) criterion.

An expected value is a long run average. It is the weighted average of a probability distribution.

Supplementary reading – Risk and Uncertainty

Business planning is rarely certain.

For example, we may budget for sales of 100,000 units per annum but could anticipate sales being anywhere between 50,000 and 130,000 units.

Dealing with risk and uncertainty is a major topic in your future studies.

In everyday speech most people use the terms "risk" and "uncertainty" as though they were interchangeable. As far as your CIMA studies are concerned, however, there is a distinction.

- The term "**risk**" is used to describe a scenario when we know the different possible outcomes and can estimate their associated probabilities. This is the context for using expected values, for example.
- The term "**uncertainty**" is used when we do not know the possible outcomes and/or their associated probabilities – uncertainty is essentially a matter of ignorance. The future cannot be predicted because there is insufficient information about what the future outcomes might be. Decisions under conditions of uncertainty are often a matter of guesswork

Understanding probabilities is thus essential to fully understanding risk and uncertainty.

Illustration 9 – Expected values

A company has recorded the following daily sales over the last 200 days:

Daily Sales (units)	Number of days
100	40
200	60
300	80
400	20

What will be the expected sales level in the future?

Solution

Firstly we will assume that the past is a good indicator of the future.

Next we can convert the above results into a probability distribution (i.e. show the range of possible outcomes and their associated probabilities):

Daily Sales (units)	Probability
100	40/200 = 0.2
200	60/200 = 0.3
300	80/200 = 0.4
400	20/200 = 0.1

(Note that the probabilities add up to one.)

The expected value ('EV') of the future sales is then given by

EV = 0.2 × 100 + 0.3 × 200 + 0.4 × 300 + 0.1 × 400 = 240 units

So what does this mean?

- On average we will sell 240 units a day.
- On a particular day we will sell 100 or 200 or 300 or 400, so the average cannot actually happen.
- While this worries some, most managers are happy to make decisions based on expected values.

Test Your Understanding 14

A decision has to be made between three options, A, B and C. The possible profits and losses are:

- Option A: a profit of $2,000 with probability 0.5 or otherwise a loss of $500
- Option B: a profit of $800 with probability 0.3 or otherwise a profit of $500
- Option C: a profit of $1,000 with probability 0.8, of $500 with probability 0.1 or otherwise a loss of $400

Which option should be chosen under the EV criterion?

Test Your Understanding 15

A decision-maker is faced with the following options, which can result in the profits shown:

	High sales	*Medium sales*	*Low sales*
	P = 0.5	*P* = 0.4	*P* = 0.1
Option 1	$50,000	$10,000	–$60,000
Option 2	$40,000	$10,000	–$20,000
Option 3	$30,000	$15,000	$0

If the intention is to maximise expected profit, which option should be taken?

Comment on the riskiness of the choice facing the decision-maker.

Payoff tables

Payoff tables (also known as expected value tables) can be useful in more complex scenarios.

Illustration 10 – Payoff tables

A storeholder has to decide how many units of the perishable commodity X to buy each day. Past demand has followed the distribution:

Demand (units)	*Probability*
1	0.2
2	0.4
3	0.4

Each unit is bought for $10 and sold for $20, and, at the end of each day, any unsold units must be disposed of with no financial return.

Using the EV criterion, how many units should be bought daily?

Solution

If we assume that the past demand pattern will obtain in the future, we see that, logically, the store-holder has only three initial choices: buy one, two or three units per day. There are also only three possible outcomes each day, a demand of one, two or three units. We can therefore construct a payoff table showing the financial effects of the nine possible combinations (three choices by three outcomes).

		Daily order number		
		1	2	3
Daily demand	1	$10	$0	–$10
	2	$10	$20	$10
	3	$10	$20	$30

The monetary values in each case show the daily profit: we give three examples here and leave the others to be calculated as an exercise:

- order 1, demand 1: cost = $10, revenue = $20; so profit = $10;
- order 2, demand 1: cost = $20, revenue $20; so profit = $0 (in this case, one valueless unit would be left at the end of the day);
- order 2, demand 2: cost = $20, revenue = $40; so profit = $20 (in this case, the demand for the third unit would be unsatisfied).

Using the probabilities for the various levels of demand, we can now calculate the expected daily profit for each order number:

- EV (order 1) $10 (no need for calculations here, as the profit is $10, regardless of the outcome)
- EV (order 2) $(0.2 \times 0) + (0.4 \times 20) + (0.4 \times 20) = \$16$
- EV (order 3) $(0.2 \times -10) + (0.4 \times 10) + (0.4 \times 30) = \$14$

Thus, in order to maximise daily profit, the storeholder should order two units per day.

It should be noted that the feature that makes the construction of the table possible is that the outcomes (demand) are independent of the decision taken (number of units ordered).

Test Your Understanding 16

A shopkeeper buys an item at $10 and sells it at $50 but if it is not sold by the end of the day it will be thrown away. If demand is as shown below, use the EV criterion to advise the shopkeeper on how many he should stock per day.

Demand (units)	*Probability*
0	0.3
1	0.4
2	0.3

Supplementary reading – Limitations of expected values

Limitations of this approach

We are not advocating that the above approach is ideal: merely an *aid* to decision-making. Indeed, many texts that develop so-called *decision theory* further address at some length the limitations we shall discuss here. Suffice it to say, at this point, that attempts to overcome these problems meet with varying degrees of success, and so it is inconceivable that an 'objective' approach can ever replace the human decision-maker.

Another limitation that this approach shares with most other attempts to model reality is that the outcomes and probabilities need to be estimated. The subsequent analysis can never be more reliable than the estimations upon which it is based. There is also often a considerable degree of simplification with very limited discrete probability distributions being used when more complex ones or perhaps continuous distributions might be more appropriate.

When the probabilities are empirical, arising from past experience, then they have some degree of reliability unless demand patterns change dramatically. In other cases only subjective estimates of probabilities may be available, and their reliability may be open to question. There is therefore a doubt over this approach when *subjective* probabilities are used.

If the scenario is a *repeated* decision, made every day, then the expected values have a commercial meaning: they are long-term *average* profits. In many cases, however, individuals or companies are faced with *one-off* decisions. An analysis of expected values would give the best average profits over a long run of many *repeats* of the decision, a circumstance that does not obtain in a one-off situation. One must question the use of the EV criterion in the latter case.

Finally, expected values take no account of the decision-makers' attitude to risk. Avoiding significant downside exposure may be more important than possible gains, although expected values consider each equally. Particularly with one-off decisions, it can only give a guide to decision-makers.

Even with objective testing it is still important to be aware of the limitations of methods. The failure to take account of risk is a key criticism of this approach.

8 Normal distributions

8.1 Discrete and continuous variables revisited

We saw in chapter 2 that variables could be discrete or continuous

Discrete variables

Discrete variables can only consist of certain values. For example the number of invoices could be

	0 or 1 or 2 or …
but never	1.6, 2.3 and so on.

Continuous variables

On the other hand, the time taken to undertake a certain operation can theoretically take a value to any level of precision:

20.2 minutes
20.19 minutes
20.186 minutes
20.1864 minutes and so on.

In practice the issue it the degree of accuracy to which management want to measure.

However, a number of invoices *cannot* be measured any more accurately than in whole numbers.

Probabilities

With discrete variables we can talk about the probability of a particular value occuring

e.g. P(we have 5 invoices)

However, with continuous variables we cannot do this

e.g. P(someone is **exactly** 1.9m tall) is probably zero if we could measure to a sufficiently small scale.

Instead it makes more sense to specify a *range* of values

e.g. P(height is >1.9m but <2.0m) could be determined.

8.2 Characteristics of the normal distribution

The normal distribution is a continuous probability distribution. The values of probabilities relating to a normal distribution come from a normal distribution curve, in which *probabilities* are *represented by areas*: An immediate consequence of probabilities being equated to areas is that *the total area under the normal curve is equal to 1.*

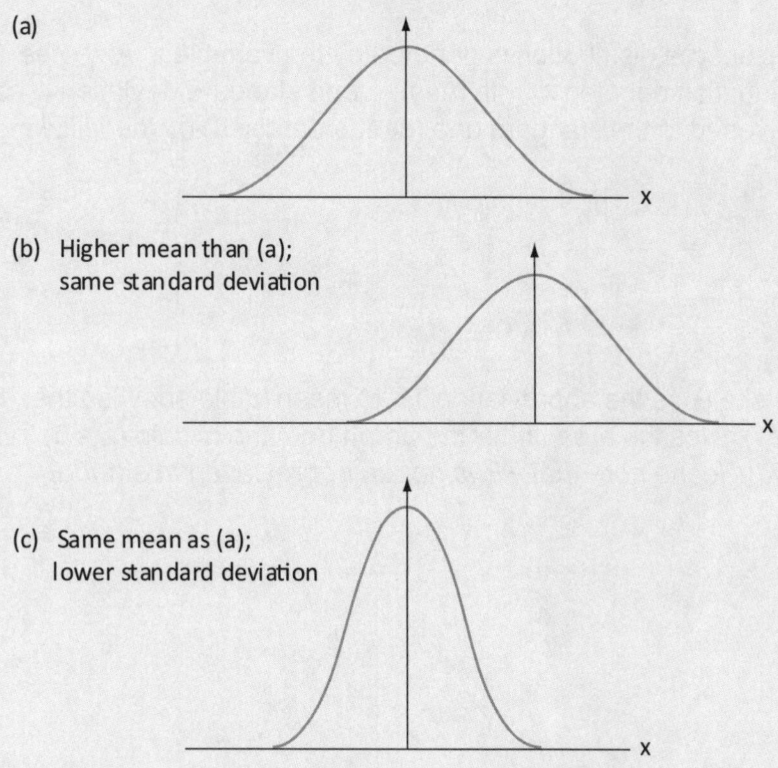

Examples of the normal distribution

As the diagram illustrates, there are many examples of the normal distribution. Any one is completely defined by its mean (μ) and its standard deviation (σ). The curve is bell-shaped and symmetric about its mean, and, although the probability of a normal variable taking a value far away from the mean is small, it is never quite zero. The examples in the figure also demonstrate the role of the mean and standard deviation. As before, the mean determines the general position or *location* of the variable, whereas the standard deviation determines how *spread* the variable is around its mean.

8.3 Use of the tables of normal distribution

The preceding section describes the normal distribution but is insufficient to enable us to calculate probabilities based upon it, even though we know that the total area under the curve is one. To evaluate normal probabilities, we must use tables such as those given in your exam. These tables convert normal distributions with different means and standard deviations to a *standard* normal distribution, which has

a mean of 0
a standard deviation of 1

This special distribution is denoted by the variable z. Any other normal distribution denoted x, with mean μ and standard deviation σ can be converted to the standard one (or standardised) by the following formula:

$$z = \frac{x - \mu}{\sigma}$$

We shall use the abbreviation TE to mean 'table entry' so that, for example, TE(1) gives the area under the graph from the middle (z = 0) to the value z=1. (*Please note that TE is not an abbreviation in standard usage.*)

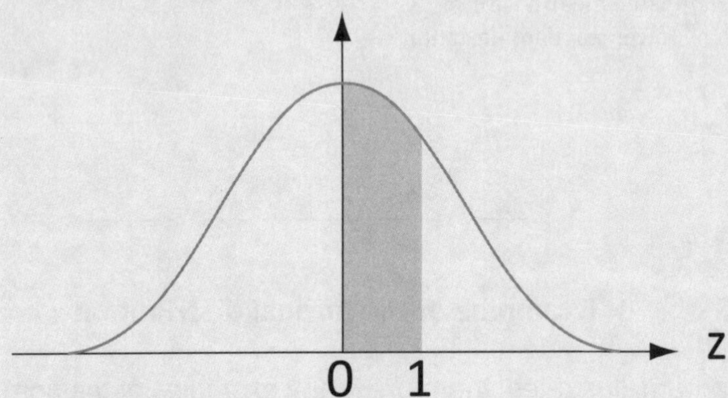

In the table "Area under the Normal Curve" the column on the left is the value you are looking up to one decimal place. The row across the top represents the value's second decimal place.

If a and b are positive values then you find probabilities from the table as follows:

$P(a < z < b)$ = TE (b) – TE (a)

$P(z < b)$ = 0.5 + TE (b)

$P(z > b)$ = 0.5 – TE (b)

$P(z < -b)$ = $P(z > b)$ = 0.5 – TE (b)

$P(z > -b)$ = $P(z > b)$ = 0.5 + TE (b)

$P(-a < z < 0)$ = $P(z < a)$ = 0.5 + TE (a)

$P(-a < z < b)$ = TE (a) + TE (b)

$P(-a < z < -b)$ = $P(b < z < a)$ = TE (a) – TE (b)

Illustration 11 – Normal distributions

Use normal distribution tables to find the following:

(a) $P(0 < z < 1)$;

(b) $P(0 < z < 1.25)$;

(c) $P(z < 2.1)$;

(d) $P(0.7 < z < 1)$;

(e) $P(z > 1.96)$;

(f) $P(z < -1.96)$;

(g) $P(-1.96 < z < 1.96)$;

(h) $P(-1.2 < z < 2.8)$;

(i) $P(z > 3)$.

Solution

(a) $P(0 < z < 1)$ = TE(1.00) = 0.3413. In the table this is the entry in row 1.0 and column 0.00.

(b) $P(0 < z < 1.25)$ = TE(1.25) = 0.3944. In the table this is the entry in row 1.2 and column 0.05.

(c) $P(z < 2.1)$ = 0.5 + TE(2.1) = 0.5 + 0.4821 = 0.9821. This probability includes all the negative values of z, which have a probability of 0.5, as well as those between 0 and 2.1 which are covered by the table entry.

(d) $P(0.7 < z < 1)$ = TE(1) – TE(0.7) = 0.3413 – 0.2580 = 0.0833. This is given by the small area under the curve from 0 to 0.7 subtracted from the larger area from 0 to 1.

(e) $P(z > 1.96)$ = 0.5 – TE(1.96) = 0.5 – 0.475 = 0.025. This tail-end area is given by the area under half the curve (i.e. 0.5) minus the area from 0 to 1.96.

(f) $P(z < -1.96) = P(z > 1.96)$ = 0.025 by symmetry.

(g) $P(-1.96 < z < 1.96) = 1 - 2 \times 0.025 = 0.95$, which is the total area of 1 minus the two tail-ends. This symmetrical interval which includes 95 per cent of normal frequencies is very important in more advanced statistics.

(h) $P(-1.2 < z < 2.8)$ = TE(1.2) + TE(2.8) = 0.3849 + 0.4974 = 0.8823. We have split this area into two. That from 0 to 2.8 is simply the table entry and that from –1.2 to 0 equals the area from 0 to +1.2 by symmetry, so it too is given by the table entry.

(i) $P(z > 3) = 0.5 - 0.49865 = 0.00135$. The method here is the standard one for tail-end areas but we wanted to make two points. The first is that virtually all normal frequencies lie between three standard deviations either side of the mean. The second is that, for symmetrical data, the standard deviation will be approximately one-sixth of the range.

Graphs showing the areas concerned are as follows:

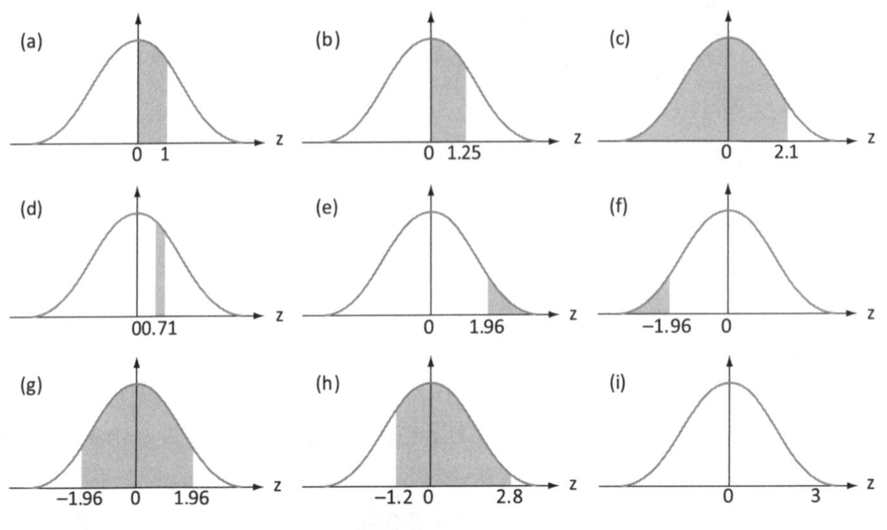

Test Your Understanding 17

Evaluate the following probabilities from the standard normal distribution (mean = 0; standard deviation = 1):

A $P(0 < z < 2.03)$;

B $P(-1.27 < z < 0)$;

C $P(z > 0.55)$;

D $P(z < -1.55)$;

E $P(z > -1.23)$;

F $P(z < 0.88)$;

G $P(-0.91 < z < 1.08)$;

H $P(0.23 < z < 0.34)$.

Test Your Understanding 18

A machine produces components with diameter of mean 5 cm and standard deviation 0.1 cm. Knowing that the dimensions of many such products follow a normal distribution, the production manager of the manufacturing company decides to use a normal model for the machine's production.

What proportion of the production will have diameters

A between 5 and 5.2 cm;

B between 4.9 and 5 cm

C over 5.15 cm

D between 4.8 and 5.1 cm;

E between 5.1 and 5.2 cm?

Test Your Understanding 19

Evaluate the following probabilities from the normal distribution stated:

A $P(2 < x < 3)$ when $\mu = 2, \sigma = 4$

B $P(x < 6)$ when $\mu = 10, \sigma = 5$

C $P(2 < x < 6)$ when $\mu = 3, \sigma = 4$

D $P(2 < x < 6)$ when $\mu = 1, \sigma = 4$

E $P(2 < x < 6)$ when $\mu = 8, \sigma = 5$.

Test Your Understanding 20

The finance department of a pharmaceutical company is concerned that the ageing machinery on its production line is causing losses by putting too much on average of a certain product into each container. A check on the line shows that the mean amount being put into a container is 499.5 ml, with a standard deviation of 0.8 ml

A Adopting a normal distribution, what percentage of containers will contain more than the notional contents of 500 ml?

B There are two courses of remedial action available: one would reduce the mean amount inserted (leaving the standard deviation unaltered), while the other would reduce the standard deviation (mean unaltered). If the manager wishes to reduce the percentage of containers containing over 500 ml to 10 percent, how could this be achieved by reducing (i) the mean; and (ii) the standard deviation amount inserted?

Test Your Understanding 21

The weights of a certain mass-produced item are known, over a long period of time, to be normally distributed with a mean of 8 kg and a standard deviation of 0.02 kg

A Any item whose weight lies outside the range 7.985–8.035 kg is deemed to be faulty. What percentage of products will be faulty?

B If it is required to reduce the percentage that is too heavy (i.e. with weight over 8.035 kg) to 2 per cent, to what value must the mean weight be decreased, leaving all other factors unchanged?

C If it is required to reduce the percentage that is too light (i.e. with weight below 7.985 kg) to 2 per cent, to what value must the standard deviation be decreased, leaving other factors unchanged?

Supplementary reading – Further discussion on risk

This chapter gives some background to the concepts of uncertainty and risk, and in particular, how probability can be used as a measure of risk. Although uncertainty and risk are connected concepts, they are sufficiently different to require separate explanations. Whilst a detailed understanding of uncertainty and risk is not required for your exam, it is useful to have an appreciation of these terms, and also the practical role that probability plays when assessing risks.

The terms uncertainty and risk are used in different ways by different commentators, researchers and professional practitioners in the business world, and it is useful to start with a discussion of what these words or terms mean.

Starting with risks, every business is said to face a series of risks, and as a result of these risks it is difficult to be able to say how the business will actually perform. These risks have a number of different origins or drivers and can include risks relating to marketing, production, technology, personnel, information systems and financial. (Note that this is not intended to be an exhaustive list of the sources of business risk.)

For example, the marketing risks which a business faces may include the chance that the product which they are selling goes out of fashion. It may include the chance that a large and powerful competitor may enter the market and take traditional customers away. Another risk might be that due to a recession and the corresponding reduction in buying power, clients, and as a result sales decline. There may also be the risk of new government legislation being aimed at market controls which make the product too expensive for its traditional customers. Thus, from these examples, it may be seen that a risk can be a threat to the business.

If we considered production risks, there would be a similar list of issues, which may, for example, include the risk of a disruption in the supply of raw materials, or the risk of substantial price increases in essential services such as electricity and gas costs. Another risk could be that new legislation might require a much more costly regime of waste disposal in order to protect the environment.

It is not difficult to list similar types of risks for technology, personnel and information aspects of the business and the reader may do that for himself/herself. The category of risks referred to as financial risks are sometimes perceived to be different. Financial risks include the availability of credit, the cost of borrowing, the value (price) of the business' shares if they are quoted on the stock market. The issues which are discussed under this heading are often thought to be more volatile than those under the other more general business risks. But financial risks pose essentially the same sort of problems as other risks.

It is important for every organisation to be aware of the risks which it faces and there are no organisations which do not have a set of business and financial risks which directly affect them. Businesses need to assess the risks which they face and to take appropriate action. The assessment of risk is not a trivial matter and it requires considerable skill. The first step is to list all the possible risks, preferably by the major activities and functions of the business. Once this list is complete then an assessment needs to be made to estimate the likelihood of the risk occurring, as well as the amount of damage which the business could sustain if the risk materialises. The likelihood of the risk occurring is normally expressed on a scale from 0 (zero) to 1 where 0 means the risk will not actually occur and 1 means the risk will certainly occur. You will recognise this as the description of probability. Thus, a score of 0.50 suggest that there is a 50% chance that the risk will occur. However, there is no rigorous way of assessing the likelihood of a risk. It is simply a question of management judgement.

With regard to the question of how much damage a risk could do to the business, it is possible to make a more detailed and objective assessment of this and the use of financial estimates play a large role in this activity.

Once these numbers have been estimated then they may be used to calculate the expected value of a given risk. The expected value (EV) of a risk is the product of the chance (probability) of it happening multiplied by the size of the damage it will do to the organisation if the risk occurs. The expected value combines the probability and the damage of the result of the risk to give a figure which represents the relative importance of the risk to the business.

The calculation of expected value for each item in the list of marketing risks is shown below. Note that the expected value of the individual risks may be summed to give a total expected value of the risks emanating out of the marketing activity of the business.

1 The zero and 1 positions are theoretically limits on a spectrum. If the possible threat is rated at 0 then it need not be included in risk analysis as it will not occur. If the possible threat is rated at 1 then it need not be included in risk analysis as it has either occurred or will certainly occur and therefore there is not the element of chance which is inherent in the definition of risk.

Example – Marketing risks

From the table below it may be seen that the most damaging risk which the business faces is the possibility of the entry of big competitor. If this occurs then the loss to the business is expected to be $375,000. The second greatest risk is the possibility that the product could go out of fashion. If this occurs then the loss to the business is expected to be $360,000. The size of the other risks may be read from the table.

In a similar way, analyses may be undertaken for other risks; production, technology, personnel, information systems and financial.

Type of risk	Probability of occurrence	Estimate of financial damage	Expected value
Product out of fashion	0.30	1,200,000	360,000
Entry of big competitor	0.25	1,500,000	375,000
Recession	0.10	2,000,000	200,000
Legislation changes	0.05	3,000,000	150,000
Total Marketing risks			1,085,000

Individual marketing risks and their total expected value

There are two courses of action which management may take in the face of these risks. The first is to initiate risk avoidance measures, and the second is to establish a programme which will mitigate the impact of the risk if it should occur. However, a detailed discussion of this is beyond the scope of this book.

The technique described above whereby the expected values are calculated, may also be applied to other business calculations in which it is appropriate to include risk assessments. There are two major approaches to this. Both approaches call for the use of a range of estimates of the projected values of cost and benefits for the production of budgets. These techniques are frequently used in capital investment appraisal or assessment. By using the maximum estimated and the minimum estimated values, a range of possible outcomes for the investment are calculated. The results of these calculations which will be a range of values themselves will show the result of the investment if the impact of the risks are minimal, i.e. few of the threats materialise, and also the result of the investment if the impact of the risks are large i.e. most of the threats materialise. Management judgement is then required to decide which of these scenarios is the most plausible.

There are sophisticated variations of this approach which use a technique known as Monte Carlo simulation, although this is beyond the scope of this book.

Before concluding this section it is appropriate to more comprehensively define risk in broad terms. The risk of a project is the inherent propensity of the estimates concerning the cost, time or benefits for the project not to be achieved in practice, due to foreseeable and unforeseeable circumstances.

Although risk is often spoken of in a negative context, i.e. the project will cost more than budgeted for, or take longer than originally believed, it is obviously the case that sometimes projects are completed below budget and before their deadlines. Thus risk may enhance the potential of a project as well as detract from it.

It is clear that risk is based on the fact that the future is always unknowable or uncertain in the sense that we are unable to be sure of anything before it happens.

With regard to the concept of uncertainty when it is not possible to make any estimate of the probability or the impact of a future event or threat we do refer to its risk – rather we refer to *uncertainty*. For example, we cannot state with any degree of confidence about the risk that any large banks will become insolvent. This is because we have neither a way of estimating the chance nor a probability of that happening (nor the ability of estimating the impact that such an event would have on our society). However, we can safely say is that at present, the future of banks is uncertain.

Thus uncertainty may be thought of as a sort of risk about which nothing may be estimated. While risk is a concept which is used extensively by business and management practitioners, the concept of uncertainty is employed by economists when they are referring more generally about business affairs in the economy.

Chapter Summary

Probability can be defined from a complete list of equally like outcomes as

$$P(\text{event}) = \frac{\text{Total number of outcomes that constitute the event}}{\text{Total number of possible outcomes}}$$

This can be used in an *exact* sense when applied to the population of outcomes, or in an empirical, approximate sense when applied to a sample. *Subjective* probabilities arise from individuals' or a group's judgement.

The *additive* law of probability states that

$$P(\text{X or Y}) = P(\text{X}) + P(\text{Y}) - P(\text{X and Y})$$

which becomes:

$$P(\text{X or Y}) = P(\text{X}) + P(\text{Y})$$

when X and Y are *mutually exclusive*.
The *multiplicative law* of probability states that:

$$P(\text{X and Y}) = P(\text{X}) \times P(\text{Y}|\text{X})$$

which becomes:

$$P(\text{X and Y}) = P(\text{X}) \times \text{P}(\text{Y})$$

when X and Y are *independent*.

Further, we saw the concept of a *discrete probability distribution* with its associated expected value:

$$E(X) = \Sigma\, XP$$

If, further, the probability of a certain outcome in a certain circumstance is *P*, then, in n independent repeats of the circumstance, the expected number of times the outcome will occur is *nP*.

The *expected value* (EV) criterion of decision-making consists of choosing the option giving the maximum expected return.

A *payoff table* is a method of setting out financial returns when faced with choosing between a number of options with a number of outcomes that are not dependent on the option chosen. A rectangular table can then be drawn to show the financial results of each combination of option and outcome.

A *normal distribution* is a bell-shaped continuous distribution, symmetric about its mean. It is completely defined by its mean, μ, and standard deviation, σ, and can be transformed to the standard normal distribution (mean 0 and standard deviation 1) by:

$$z = \frac{x - \mu}{\sigma}$$

If you know the variance of a distribution, the standard deviation can be found by taking its square root.

Venn diagrams may be used to assist in the calculation of probabilities.

9 Further Practice Questions

Test Your Understanding 22

A sales representative makes calls to three separate unrelated customers. The chance of making a sale at any one of them is 60 per cent. The probability that a sale is made on the third call only is:

A 0.096

B 0.216

C 0.36

D 0.4

Test Your Understanding 23

A normal distribution has a mean of 55 and a variance of 14.44. The probability of a score of 59 or more is approximately:

A 0.15

B 0.35

C 0.50

D 0.65

Test Your Understanding 24

A company has a normally distributed sales pattern for one of its products, with a mean of $110. The probability of a sale worth more than $120 is 0.0119. Using normal tables, the standard deviation, to two decimal places, associated with sales is:

A 4.41

B 4.42

C 4.43

D 4.44

Test Your Understanding 25

From past records it is known that 10 per cent of items from a production line are defective. If two items are selected at random, what is the probability that only one is defective?

A 0.09

B 0.10

C 0.18

D 0.20

Test Your Understanding 26

A project may result in profits of $20,000 or $12,000, or in a loss of $5,000, with probabilities 0.3, 0.5 and 0.2, respectively. What is the expected profit?

A $11,000

B $27,000

C $9,000

D $12,000

Test Your Understanding 27

Project S will result in profits of $2 m or $1.3 m, with probabilities 0.3 and 0.7, respectively. If Project T results in $1.5 m with probability *P* or alternatively $2.1 m, what is the value of *P* for which the projects are equally attractive under the expected value criterion?

A 0.3933

B 0.9167

C 0.9833

D 0.7

Test Your Understanding 28

If weights are normally distributed with mean 65 kg and standard deviation 8 kg, what is the probability of a weight being less than 70 kg?

A 0.2357

B 0.7357

C 0.7643

D 0.2643

Test Your Understanding 29

Associate each of the following rules of probability with one of the qualifying statements:

A P(not A) = 1 – P(A)

B P(A or B) = P(A) + P(B)

C P(A and B) = P(A) × P(B)

D P(A + B + C) = 1

Qualifying statements:

P provided that the events are mutually exclusive.

Q for all such events.

R provided that the events cover all possible outcomes.

S provided that the events are independent.

Test Your Understanding 30

Use the data about the production of faulty or acceptable items in three departments to answer the probability questions. All items referred to in the questions are randomly selected from this sample of 361 items. Give all answers correct to four decimal places.

	Department			
	P	*Q*	*R*	*Total*
Faulty	6	13	3	22
Acceptable	94	195	50	339
Total	100	208	53	361

A What is the probability that an item is faulty?

B What is the probability that an item is from either department P or Q?

C What is the probability that an item is either from P or is faulty or both?

D What is the probability that two items are both faulty?

E What is the probability that, of two items, one is faulty and the other is acceptable?

F If an item is known to be from department P, what is the probability that it is faulty?

G If an item is faulty, what is the probability that it is from department P?

Test Your Understanding 31

A firm produces 62 per cent of items in department A and the rest in department B. In A, 4 per cent of production is faulty whereas in B the proportion is 5 per cent. Complete the following table, giving answers correct to two decimal places.

	Department A	*Department B*	*Total*
Faulty	?	?	?
Acceptable	?	?	?
Total	?	?	100

Test Your Understanding 32

A project may result in the following profits with the probabilities stated.

Profit	*Probability*
$50,000	0.2
$22,000	0.5
($10,000)	0.3

Calculate the expected profit.

Test Your Understanding 33

A decision-maker must choose between three projects with profit distributions and expected values (EV) as shown below:

		State of the economy		
Profits ($'000)	*Good*	*Average*	*Poor*	*EV*
Probabilities	0.5	0.4	0.1	
Project P	26.0	6.0	(29.0)	12.5
Project Q	21.0	6.0	(9.0)	12.0
Project R	16.0	8.5	0.0	11.4

Which of the following comments is/are correct, if the decision-maker broadly follows the EV criterion?

A Using the EV criterion, project P should be chosen.

B A risk-averse decision-maker would probably choose option R.

C Option Q is much less risky than P and has only slightly less expected profit. It would be a good compromise choice.

D Project R should be chosen because it shows the highest profit when the economic situation is average.

Test Your Understanding 34

Which of the following is/are limitations of the expected value criterion for decision-making, as compared with other decision criteria or methods?

A Virtually no decisions can be based only on financial considerations.

B All the profits and probabilities need to be estimated.

C It does not take account of the fact that circumstances may change.

D The method takes no account of the decision-maker's attitude to risk.

Test Your Understanding 35

A variable, X, is normally distributed with mean 65 kg and standard deviation 8 kg.Find the following probabilities:

A $P(X > 69)$

B $P(X < 81)$

C $P(59 < X < 75)$

Test Your Understanding 36

If a normal distribution has a standard deviation of 10 kg and it is known that 20 per cent of the items concerned weigh more than 50 kg, what is the value of the mean?

Test Your Understanding 37

If 88.6 per cent of certain normally distributed items must have weights within 8 kg either side of the mean, what is the maximum allowable value of the standard deviation? (Give your answer correct to two decimal places.)

Conditional and simple probabilities

A pharmaceutical company has developed a new headache treatment that is being field-tested on 1,000 volunteers. In a test, some volunteers have received the treatment and some a placebo (a harmless neutral substance). The results of the test are as follows:

	Treatment received	*Placebo received*
Some improvement	600	125
No improvement	150	125

Calculate the probabilities required in 34 – 38, giving your answers correct to three d.p.

Test Your Understanding 38

The probability that a volunteer has shown some improvement.

Test Your Understanding 39

The conditional probability that the volunteer has shown some improvement, given that he or she has received the treatment.

Test Your Understanding 40

The conditional probability that the volunteer has received the treatment, given that no improvement has been observed.

Test Your Understanding 41

The conditional probability that the volunteer has received the placebo, given that some improvement has been observed.

Test Your Understanding 42

On the basis of this survey, does the treatment appear to be effective?

Normal distribution; stock control

The Bell Curve Company carries out repair work on a variety of electronic equipment for its customers. It regularly uses a circuit board, Part Number X216. To replenish its stock of Part Number X216 takes 3 weeks (lead time) and during this time the average demand is 950 boards with a standard deviation of eighty boards.

Evidence suggests that the distribution of usage is normal. It has been company policy to keep a safety stock of 100 boards, so they order new stocks when existing stock reaches 1,050 boards.

Test Your Understanding 43

Fill in the numerical values indicated by letters in the following calculation, giving your answers correct to two d.p. The standard normal variable is denoted by z.

The probability of not running out of stock of Part Number X216 during lead time
= *P*(demand in lead time < *A*)
= *P*(z < *B*)
= *C*

Test Your Understanding 44

If the company wishes to improve the probability of not running out of stock to 99 per cent, they will need a higher level of safety stock. Fill in the numerical values indicated by letters in the following calculation of the necessary level of safety stock. Answers should be given correct to two d.p.

From Normal tables, the z-value which is greater than 99 per cent of Normal values is D. This corresponds to a demand level of E.

So safety stock = F

Test Your Understanding 45

If the standard deviation of the distribution of usage were to increase, would the company need to hold more or less safety stock in order to satisfy the same level of service?

Test Your Understanding 46

If a coin is tossed three times, the resulting number of heads is given by the following probability distribution:

No. of heads (X)	*Probability* (P)
0	1/8
1	3/8
2	3/8
3	1/8
Total	1

Find:

A the expected number of heads in three throws of a coin

B the expected number of heads in 30 throws of a coin.

Test Your Understanding 47

Using Venn diagrams

Given a probability of 0.4 that a man has trained as an accountant, and a probability of 0.5 that a man has trained as a salesperson, and a probability of 0.3 that a man has trained neither as an accountant nor as a salesman, what is the probability that he is both an accountant and a salesman?

Test your understanding answers

Test Your Understanding 1

(a) The card I pick is a king

There are 4 kings in a pack of 52 cards, so the probability = 4/52 = 1/13

(b) The card I pick is red

There are 26 red cards (hearts + diamonds) in a pack of 52 cards, so the probability = 26/52 = 1/2

(c) The card I pick is a club

There are 13 clubs in a pack of 52 cards, so the probability = 13/52 = 1/4

(d) The card is the Ace of Spades.

There is only one Ace of Spades in a pack of 52 cards, so the probability = 1/52

Test Your Understanding 2

Assuming that the draw is fair, then Johann has an equal likelihood of playing any of the 31 other players in the draw in the first round.

Thus P(playing Petr) = 1/31

Note: the results of previous draws is irrelevant, unless it indicates that in some way the method of picking names is biased or unfair.

Test Your Understanding 3

To find this probability from an exact approach would necessitate obtaining a list of the lifetimes of all the components, and counting those of less than 1 year. It is clearly impossible to keep such a detailed record of every component, after sale.

An alternative, feasible approach is to take a sample of components, rather than the whole population, and test them under working conditions, to see what proportion fail within one year. Probabilities produced in this way are known as empirical and are essentially approximations to the true, but unobtainable, exact probabilities. In this case, the quality controller may choose to sample 1,000 components. If she then finds that 16 fail within 1 year:

$$P(\text{Component failing within 1 year}) = \frac{16}{1{,}000} \text{ or } 0.016$$

For this approximation to be valid, it is essential that the sample is representative. Further, for a more accurate approximation, a larger sample could be taken, provided that the time and money are available.

Test Your Understanding 4

B

The classifications we need in the table are

- *certificate* v *not certificate*
- *male* v *female*

Table (note figures in bold are those given in the question)

	Male	*Female*	*Total*
Certificate level	24	31	**55**
Not Certificate level	**6**	39	45
Total	**30**	70	**100**

P(female but not studying Certificate) = 39/70 = 0.56

Test Your Understanding 5

(a) Roll one die. A = get a six, B = get a five

These events **are** mutually exclusive - you cannot get a five and a six at the same time with one die.

(b) Pick a card from a standard 52 card pack. A = get an ace, B = get a red card

These events **are not** mutually exclusive – drawing either the ace of hearts or the ace of diamonds satisfies both events simultaneously. There is an overlap.

(c) Sitting two exams (C03 and C04) at Certificate level. A = pass C03, B = pass C04

These events **are not** mutually exclusive – it is quite possible to pass both exams!

(d) Bidding for an item on an online auction site. A = win the auction, B = lose the auction.

These events **are** mutually exclusive – you cannot simultaneously win and lose the same auction.

Test Your Understanding 6

(a) P(Roll one die and get a six or a five)

The two options are mutually exclusive so we can add probabilities:

P(six or five) = P(6) + P(5) = 1/6 +1/6 = 2/6, or 1/3

(b) P(Pick a card from a standard 52 card pack and get an ace or a red card)

The two options are not mutually exclusive (the ace of hearts and ace of diamonds satisfy both events), so we must use the more general form of the addition rule:

P(ace or red card) = P(ace) + P(red card) - P(red ace) = 4/52 + 26/52 – 2/52 = 28/52

Test Your Understanding 7

A P(Grade I) = 208/400 = 0.52

B P(Shift X) = 130/400 = 0.325

C P(Shift Y or Z) = P(Y) + P(Z) because they are mutually exclusive
= (160 + 110)/400 = 270/400 = 0.675

D P(shift Y or Grade II) = P(Y) + P(Grade II) – P(both)
= 160/400 + 161/400 – 72/400
= 249/400 = 0.6225

E P(Faulty or Shift Z) = P(Faulty) + P(Z) – P(both)
= 31/400 + 110/400 – 6/400
= 135/400 = 0.3375

Test Your Understanding 8

The events that are likely to be independent are (A) and (D).

Successive selections of a card from a pack without replacement will involve probabilities changing as the number of cards is reduced and, in general, gender and shoe sizes tend to be related.

Test Your Understanding 9

If we consider the woman first, there are two possibilities: she will be alive (probability 0.69) or she will not (probability 0.31). Independently of these, there are two possibilities concerning the man: alive (probability 0.51) or not (0.49). There are thus four possible combinations:

A	woman alive and man alive;	P = 0.69 × 0.51	= 0.3519
B	(i) woman not alive and man alive;	P = 0.31 × 0.51	= 0.1581
	(ii) woman alive and man not;	P = 0.69 × 0.49	= 0.3381
C	both not alive;	P = 0.31 × 0.49	= 0.1519
	Total		1.0000

Note that, as we are listing every possibility, there is the check that the probabilities must add to 1.

A This is the case A above. The probability is thus 0.3519.

B This possibility consists of cases B or C above. The two are mutually exclusive and so the probability is

$$P(\text{B or C}) = P(\text{A}) + P(\text{C}) = 0.1581 + 0.3381 = 0.4962$$

The probability that only (exactly) one of the couple will be alive is 0.4962.

C This is simply D, so the probability that neither will be alive is 0.1519.

Test Your Understanding 10

A P (X and faulty) = 9/400 = 0.0225

B P (Y and Grade II) = 72/400 = 0.18

C P (faulty|Z) = 6/110 = 0.0545 (to four d.p.)

Notice that in this case we only consider the 110 items produced by Shift Z because that information was given.

D P (Z|Grade I) = 71/208 = 0.3413 (to four d.p.)

E P (not Grade II) = 1 – (161/400) = 0.5975

Test Your Understanding 11

Before proceeding, we point out that this is essentially a problem on probabilities. For example, 2 per cent of the product being faulty is the same as:

$$P(\text{product is faulty}) = 0.02$$

A Two per cent of products are faulty and all of these will be returned, so 2 per cent will be returned owing to the product being faulty.

B P(faulty package and satisfactory product) = 0.06 × 0.98 = 0.0588 = 5.88 per cent. Half of these, that is, 2.94 per cent, will be returned.

C The two outcomes described above are mutually exclusive and cover all the circumstances in which the product might be returned, hence the percentage of products returned for any reason = 2 + 2.94 = 4.94 per cent.

It should be emphasised that these estimates are valid only if the test results are representative of the actual product performance and if this product does resemble the previous 'similar items' regarding return rates of faulty product (100 per cent) and faulty packaging (50 per cent).

Test Your Understanding 12

A and B are independent and so the special multiplication rule can be used.

$$P(\text{A}) = 0.01$$
$$P(\text{not A}) = 1 - 0.01 = 0.99$$
$$P(\text{not B}) = 0.98$$

A P(both A and B) = 0.01 × 0.02 = 0.0002

B P(neither) = 0.99 × 0.98 = 0.9702

C P(A but not B) = 0.01 × 0.98 = 0.0098

D. P(precisely one fault) = P(A but not B) + P(B but not A)
= 0.0098 + 0.02 × 0.99
= 0.0296

E P(A not B) = P(A) since A and B are independent = 0.01

Test Your Understanding 13

	Pass	*Fail*	*Total*
A	14.0	26.0	40
B	20.4	9.6	30
C	15.9	14.1	30
Total	50.3	49.7	100

P(B|passed) = 20.4 ÷ 50.3 = 0.4056

Test Your Understanding 14

The expected value of each option is:

EV(A) = (2000 × 0.5) + (–500 × 0.5) = $750
EV(B) = (800 × 0.3) + (500 × 0.7) = $590
EV(C) = (1000 × 0.8) + (500 × 0.1) + (–400 × 0.1) = $810

Thus, we would choose option C in order to maximise expected profit. However, it is arguable that a person or organisation that cannot afford a loss would opt for the 'safe' option B, which guarantees a profit in all circumstances.

Test Your Understanding 15

Option 1	*Probability*	*Profit*	*EV*
		$'000	
	0.5	50	25
	0.4	10	4
	0.1	–60	–6
	——		—
	1.0		23
	——		—

Option 2	*Probability*	*Profit*	*EV*
		$'000	
	0.5	40	20
	0.4	10	4
	0.1	–20	–2
	——		—
	1.0		22
	——		—

Option 3	*Probability*	*Profit*	*EV*
		$'000	
	0.5	30	15
	0.4	15	6
	0.1	0	0
	——		—
	1.0		21
	——		—

Using the EV criterion, option 1 should be taken since it has the largest expected profit at $23,000.

Notice that option 1 is very risky, with a 10 per cent chance of making a loss greater than the maximum possible profit. Many decision-makers who are not specially averse to risk would nevertheless choose option 2 as having a very similar expected profit with considerably lower risk.

Test Your Understanding 16

Payoff table (in $ per day)

		Probability	Order		
			0	1	2
Demand	0	0.3	0	–10	–20
	1	0.4	0	40	30
	2	0.3	0	40	80

Expected values:

EV of order of 0 = $0
EV of order of 1 = (–10 × 0.3) + (40 × 0.40) 1 (40 × 0.3) = $25
EV of order of 2 = (–20 × 0.3) + (30 × 0.4) 1 (80 × 0.30) = $30

Hence, the optimal order is two units per day, on the basis of the EV criterion. The shopkeeper risks a loss of $20 a day compared with $10 a day on an order of one, but in the long term this strategy gives an improved expected profit of $5 per day.

Test Your Understanding 17

A $P(0 < z < 2.03)$ = TE(2.03) = 0.4788

B $P(-1.27 < z < 0)$ = TE(1.27) = 0.3980 by symmetry

C $P(z > 0.55)$ = 0.5 – TE(0.55) = 0.5 – 0.2088 = 0.2912

D $P(z < -1.55) = P(z > 1.55)$ = 0.5 – TE(1.55) = 0.5 – 0.4394 = 0.0606

E $P(z > -1.23) = P(z < 1.23)$ = 0.5 + TE(1.23) = 0.5 + 0.3907 = 0.8907

F $P(z < 0.88)$ = 0.5 + TE(0.88) = 0.5 + 0.3106 = 0.8106

G $P(-0.91 < z < 1.08)$ = TE(0.91) + TE(1.08) = 0.3186 + 0.3599 = 0.6785

H $P(0.23 < z < 0.34)$ = TE(0.34) – TE(0.23) = 0.1331 – 0.0910 = 0.0421

Test Your Understanding 18

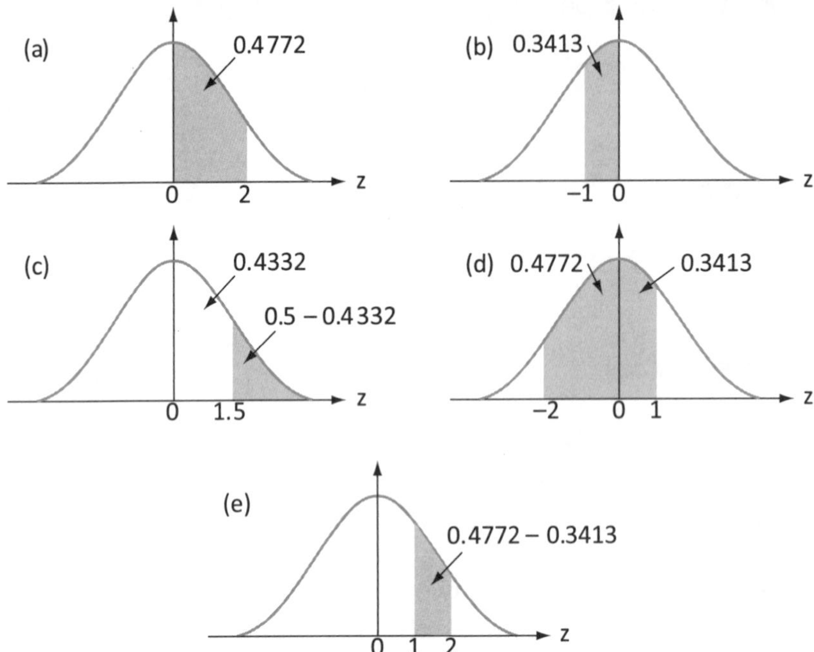

Although this question concerns proportions, it is essentially a problem on probabilities. We are dealing with a normal distribution with μ = 5 and σ = 0.1. The values in the tables are for a normal distribution with μ = 0 and standard deviation = 1 so we will need to standardise the values in this question.

A Denoting the components' diameters by x, we need

$$P(5 < x < 5.2)$$

which reads as 'the probability of x being between 5 and 5.2'.

Standardising the x-values in this expression:

$$x = 5: z = \frac{5-5}{0.1} = 0$$

$$x = 5.2: z = \frac{5.2-5}{0.1} = 2$$

To standardise you subtract the mean and divide the standard deviation. Then we get the equivalent probability involving z:

$$P(0 < z < 2)$$

This probability (area) is depicted as the shaded area in graph (a) below. This is a direct reading from the tables, giving 0.4772.

Hence 0.4772 (47.72 per cent) of components produced will have diameters between 5 and 5.2 cm

B The probability involved here is:

$P(4.9 < x < 5)$

Standardising:

$$x = 4.9\text{: } z = \frac{4.9 - 5}{0.1} = -1$$

$$x = 5\text{: } z = 0 \text{ (see above)}$$

We get:

$P(-1 < z < 0)$

This is the area shown in graph (b). However, we recall that the normal curve is *symmetric* about its mean; hence the shaded area is the same as the corresponding area to the *right* of the central dividing line, between the z-values 0 and 1. Tables give this area to be 0.3413.

Thus, 0.3413 (34.13 per cent) of components produced will have diameters between 4.9 and 5 cm

C We want:

$P(x > 5.15)$

which standardises, as before, to:

$P(z > (5.15 - 5)/0.1) = P(z > 1.5)$

This area, shown in graph (c), cannot be read directly from the table of probabilities. However, the area immediately to its left (between z-values 0 and 1.5) can: it is 0.4332. Now, as the total area under the curve is 1, and the central dividing line splits the area into two symmetrical halves, the area to the right of the dividing line is 0.5. Hence the area required is

$0.5 - 0.4332 = 0.0668$

and so 0.0668 (6.68 per cent) of components produced will have diameters over 5.15 cm

D In this case, the probability is:

$$P(4.8 < x < 5.1)$$

which standardises to:

$$P\left(\frac{4.8-5}{0.1} < z < \frac{5.1-5}{0.1}\right) = P(-2 < z < 1)$$

which is the shaded area in graph (d). The central dividing line splits this area into two parts, convenient for direct readings from the table:

z from −2 to 0 = 0.4772 (the symmetry prooperty has been used here, as in part (b) of this example
z from 0 to 1 = 0.3413
total = 0.8185

That is, 0.8185 (81.85 per cent) of components produced will have diameters between 4.8 and 5.1 cm

E The final case is:

$$P(5.1 < x < 5.2)$$

or

$$P(1 < z < 2)$$

The tables show that the area between:

z-values 0 and 1 = 0.3413

z-values 0 and 2 = 0.4772

Now, the shaded area in graph (e) can be seen to be the difference between these:

0.4772 – 0.3413 = 0.1359

So 0.1359 (13.59 per cent) of components produced will have diameters between 5.1 and 5.2 cm.

The crucial role of the diagrams above should be noted. Such graphs need not be drawn very accurately, but their use is strongly advised in order to make correct use of the probabilities taken from the table.

Test Your Understanding 19

A $P(2 < x < 3) = P[(2-2)/4 < z < (3-2)/4] = P(0 < z < 0.25) = TE(0.25) = 0.0987$

B $P(x < 6) = P[z < (6-10)/5] = P(z < -0.8) = P(z > 0.8) = 0.5 - TE(0.8) = 0.5 - 0.2881 = 0.2119$

C $P(2 < x < 6) = P[(2-3)/4 < z < (6-3)/4] = P(-0.25 < z < 0.75) = TE(0.25) + TE(0.75) = 0.0987 + 0.2734 = 0.3721$

D $P(2 < x < 6) = P[(2-1)/4 < z < (6-1)/4] = P(0.25 < z < 1.25) = TE(1.25) - TE(0.25) = 0.3944 - 0.0987 = 0.2957$

E $P(2 < x < 6) = P[(2 \text{ v } 8)/5 < z < (6-8)/5] = P(-1.2 < z < -0.4) = P(0.4 < z < 1.2) = TE(1.2) - TE(0.4) = 0.3849 - 0.1554 = 0.2295$

Test Your Understanding 20

A Initially, we are working with a normal distribution having $\mu = 499.5$ and $\sigma = 0.8$, and we want:

$P(x > 500)$

Standardising, we get:

$$P\left(z > \frac{500 - 499.5}{0.8}\right)$$

$P(z > 0.63)$

which is the shaded area in graph (a) and equals:

$0.5 - 0.2357 = 0.2643$

Thus, 26.43 per cent of containers have contents over 500 ml

B This problem is different from the earlier ones: we now know the probability (10 per cent or 0.1) and we need to 'work backwards' to find a new value for μ and σ.

Graph (b) shows the standard normal distribution, with the upper 10 per cent of area shaded. To find the unknown z-value marked, we must look through the body of the table to find the z-value corresponding to an area of 0.4. The nearest to this is z = 1.28.

Before moving on, we point out that all we have done is use the table 'backwards' to see that

$P(z > 1.28) = 0.5 - 0.4 = 0.1$

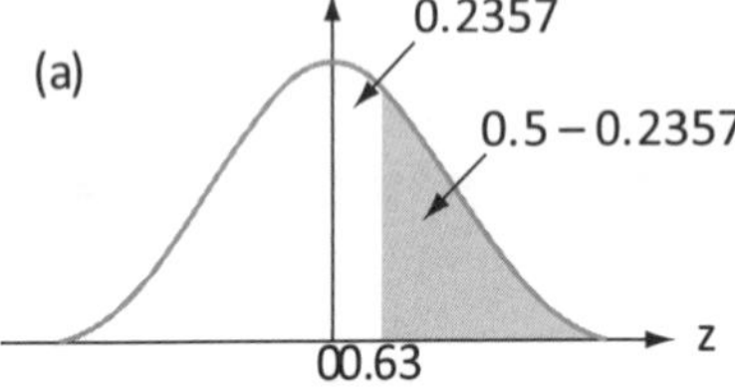

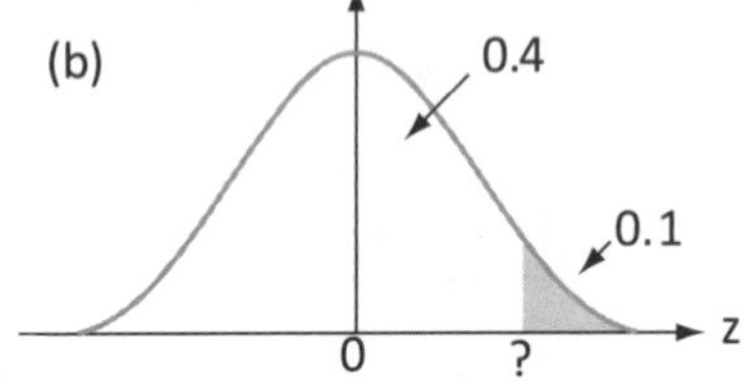

(i) Now we have:

$$z = \frac{x - \mu}{\sigma}$$

So, using the value of z we have found:

$$1.28 = \frac{500 - \mu}{0.8}$$

Therefore:

$$1.28 \times 0.8 = 500 - \mu$$

$$\mu = 499.0 \text{ (to one d.p)}$$

Hence, reducing the mean input to 499.0 ml would reduce the percentage of containers with over 500 ml to 10 per cent.

(ii) Similarly, if we regard μ as fixed and change σ:

$$1.28 = \frac{500 - 499.5}{\sigma}$$

so:

$1.28\sigma = 0.5$

$\sigma = 0.39$ (to two d.p.)

Thus, the standard deviation input must be reduced to 0.39 ml to achieve the reduction to 10 per cent of containers with contents over 500 ml.

Test Your Understanding 21

A $P(7.985 < W < 8.035) = P[(7.985 - 8)/0.02 < z < (8.035 - 8)/0.02] = P(-0.75 < z < 1.75) = TE(0.75) + TE(1.75) = 0.2734 + 0.4599 = 0.7333$

Faulty items are outside this range so the probability that an item is faulty is 1 – 0.7333 = 0.2667. Hence 26.67 per cent of products will be faulty.

B The tail-end probability of 2 per cent corresponds to the table entry 48% = 0.48, and so to the z-value 2.05.

Hence $z = 2.05 = (8.035 - \text{mean})/0.02$, giving mean = $8.035 - 2.05 \times 0.02 = 7.994$. So the mean weight must be decreased to 7.994 kg

C The z-value must now be $-2.05 = (7.985 - 8)/\sigma$ giving $\sigma = -0.015/-2.05 = 0.0073$ (to four d.p.). Hence, the standard deviation must fall to 0.0073 kg.

Test Your Understanding 22

A

If *P*(sale) = 0.6 then P(no sale) = 1 – 0.6 = 0.4. Thus:

P(two no sales then one sale) = 0.4 × 0.4 × 0.6 = 0.096

Test Your Understanding 23

Standard deviation = $\sqrt{14.44} = 3.8$

$$P(score > 59) = \text{P } z > \left(\frac{59 - 55}{3.8}\right) = P(z > 1.05)$$

$$\begin{aligned} &= 0.5 - \text{normal table entry for } 1.05 \\ &= 0.5 - 0.3531 \\ &= 0.15 \text{ (two d.p)} \end{aligned}$$

Test Your Understanding 24

B

$$\begin{aligned} \text{P(sale} > 120) &= 0.0119 \\ \text{P}(110 < \text{sale} < 120) &= 0.5 - 0.0119 \\ &= 0.4881 \end{aligned}$$

which corresponds to z = 2.26 from normal tables. Hence the gap of $10 between $110 and $120 corresponds to 2.26 standard deviations.

Standard deviation = 10/2.26

= $4.42

Test Your Understanding 25

C

P(defective) = 0.1
P(satisfactory) = 0.9
P(first defective, second not) = 0.1 x 0.9 = 0.09
P(second defective, first not) = 0.9 x 0.1 = 0.09
P(only one defective) = 0.18

Test Your Understanding 26

A

Expected profit = 20 × 0.3 + 12 × 0.5 – 5 × 0.2 = 11 ($000)

Answer (B) has simply totalled all possible profits, whereas (C) has averaged them without reference to their probabilities. (D) has selected the profit with the highest probability.

Test Your Understanding 27

C

EV(S) = 2 × 0.3 + 1.3 × 0.7 = 1.51 ($m)
EV(T) = 1.5*P* + 2.1(1 – *P*) = 2.1 – 0.6*P*

so the projects are equally attractive when 1.51 = 2.1 – 0.6P, that is, when P = 0.9833 (four d.p.). In answer (A), the probability 1 has been taken instead of (1 × P). Answer (B) divided the profits of S by those of T, while answer (D) selected the higher of the two probabilities of S.

Test Your Understanding 28

B

$P(W < 70) = P[z < (70 - 65)/8] = P(z < 0.63) = 0.5 + TE(0.63)$
$= 0.5 + 0.2357 = 0.7357$

The other answers have all correctly arrived at 0.2357 but have not added the 0.5 that covers all the negative z-values.

Test Your Understanding 29

Associate each of the following rules of probability with one of the qualifying statements:

A	*P*(not A) = 1 × *P*(A)	Q
B	*P*(A or B) = *P*(A) + *P*(B)	P
C	*P*(A and B) = *P*(A) × *P* (B)	S
D	*P*(A + B + C) = 1	R

Test Your Understanding 30

A P(faulty) = 22/361 = 0.0609

B P(P or Q) = (100 + 208)/361 = 0.8532

C P(P or faulty or both) = (100 + 22 – 6)/361 = 0.3213

D P(two items both faulty) = P(1st faulty) × P(2nd faulty) = (22/361) × (21/360) = 0.0036

E P(one faulty and other OK) = 2 × P(1st faulty) × P(2nd OK) = 2 × (22/361) × (339/360) = 0.1148

F P(faulty | from P) = 6/100 = 0.06

G P(from P | faulty) = 6/22 = 0.2727

Test Your Understanding 31

The table should look as follows:

	Department A	*Department B*	*Total*
Faulty	2.48	1.90	4.38
Acceptable	59.52	36.10	95.62
Total	62.00	38.00	100.00

Test Your Understanding 32

Expected profit = 50 × 0.2 + 22 × 0.5 + (–10) × 0.3 = 18 ($'000).

Test Your Understanding 33

A Correct.

B Correct.

C Correct.

D Incorrect: there is no commonly used decision criterion that would argue as in option (D), and the EV criterion would not do so.

Test Your Understanding 34

A Yes.

B,C No: both would be limitations regardless of which decision criterion or method was used.

C Yes.

Test Your Understanding 35

A $P(X > 69) = P[Z > (69 - 65)/8] = P(Z > 0.5) = 0.5 - 0.1915 = 0.3085$

B $P(X < 81) = P[Z < (81 - 65)/8] = P(Z < 2) = 0.5 + 0.4772 = 0.9772$

C $P(59 < X < 75) = P[(59 - 65)/8 < Z < (75 - 65)/8] = P(-0.75 < Z < 1.25)$

$= 0.2734 + 0.3944 = 0.6678$

Test Your Understanding 36

A total of 29.95 per cent of Z-values lie between 0 and 0.84, so 20 per cent of Z-values exceed 0.84. Hence 50 = mean + 0.84 standard deviations. Therefore, mean = 50 – 0.84 × 10 = 41.6.

Test Your Understanding 37

A total of 44.3 per cent of Z-values lie between 0 and 1.58, so 88.6 per cent of weights are within 1.58 standard deviations either side of the mean. Hence 8 = 1.58 standard deviations.

Maximum standard deviation = 8/1.58 = 5.06

Test Your Understanding 38

Initial workings

	Treatment received	*Placebo received*	*Total*
Some improvement	600	125	725
No improvement	150	125	275
	–––	–––	–––
Total	750	250	1,000
	–––	–––	–––

Prob. (some improvement) = 725/1,000 = 0.725

Test Your Understanding 39

Prob. (some improvement | treatment received) = 600 improved/750 treated = 0.8

Test Your Understanding 40

Prob. (treatment received | no improvement observed) = 150 treated/275 no improvement = 0.545

Test Your Understanding 41

Prob. (placebo received | improvement observed) = 125 had placebo/725 improved = 0.172

Test Your Understanding 42

Yes

Test Your Understanding 43

The probability of not running out of stock during lead time

= P(demand in lead time < 1,050)
= P(z < [1050 – 950]/80)
= P(z < [1.25)
= 0.5 + Normal table entry for z = 1.25
= 0.5 + 0.3944
= 0.8944

A 1,050

B 1.25

C 0.89

Test Your Understanding 44

D 2.33
E 1,136.4
F 186.4

From Normal tables, the z-value which is greater than 99 per cent of Normal values is 2.33. This corresponds to a demand level of 950 + 2.33 × 80 = 1,136.4. So safety stock = 1136.4 – 950 = 186.4

P (demand < x) = 0.5 + 0.49

Table entry for 0.49 = 2.33

$$\frac{x - 950}{80} = 2.33$$

x = 1136.4

Test Your Understanding 45

More

If the standard deviation of demand gets larger it means that demand will become more variable and, specifically, that there will be higher levels of demand. Safety stock will have to be increased to cover these increased levels. Another way of looking at it is to say that safety stock = 2.33 × standard deviation and so must increase as standard deviation increases.

Test Your Understanding 46

A.

No. of heads (X)	Probability (P)	PX
0	1/8	0
1	3/8	3/8
2	3/8	6/8
3	1/8	3/8
Total	1	12/8 i.e. 1.5

As expected, if a coin is tossed three times the expected (or average) number of heads is 1.5.

B If a coin is tossed 30 times we would intuitively expect 30/2 = 15 heads. Notice that 30 throws = 10 repeats of the three-throw trial and the expected number of heads is 10 × 1.5 = 15.

Test Your Understanding 47

Draw a Venn diagram showing the two sets of men, i.e. those who have trained as accountants (A) and those who have trained as salesmen (S).

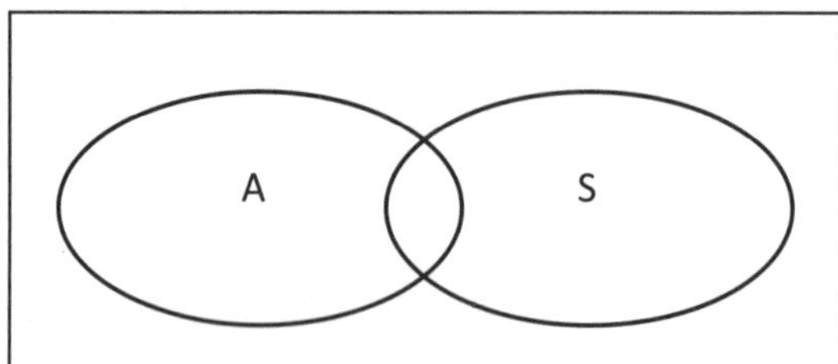

Insert the probabilities in the Venn diagram and begin calculations.

Let x be the probability that a man is trained as both an accountant and a salesman. This is represented by the intersection of the two ellipses.

Therefore A, which represents the men who are only trained as accountants is 0.4–x and S, which represents the mean who are only trained as salesmen is 0.5–x.

We also know from our data that the probability of a man not being trained as an accountant nor as a salesman is 0.3.

This information can be added to the Venn Diagram.

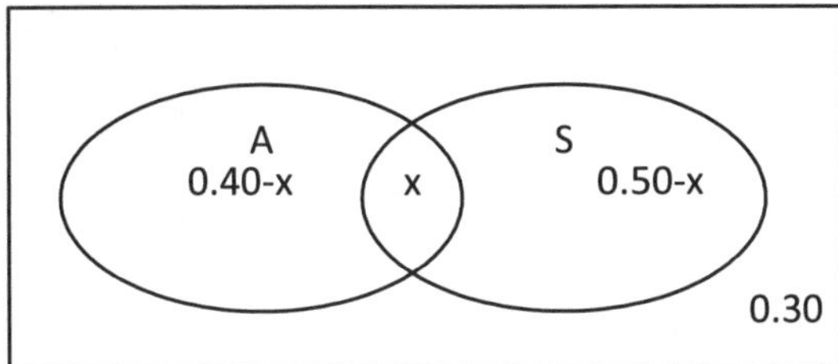

It is known that the sum of all the probabilities in the example is 1. Therefore the following equation can be constructed.

$(0.4 - x) + x + (0.5 - x) + 0.3 = 1$
$1.2 - x = 1$
$-x = -0.2$
$x = 0.2$

From this calculation the Venn diagram can be completed.

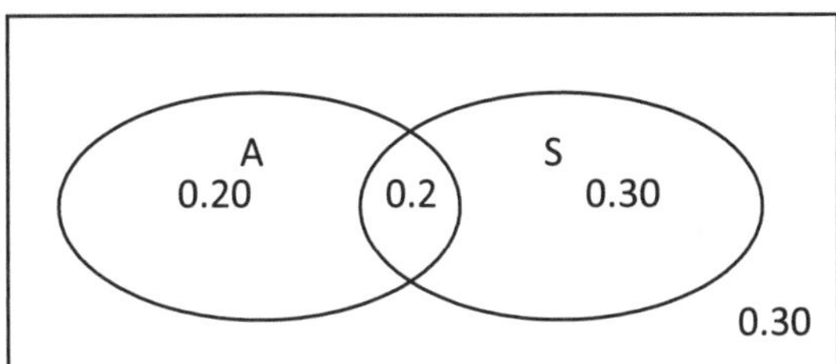

chapter

9

Spreadsheet Skills using Excel

Chapter learning objectives

The objective of this chapter is to help you improve your understanding of how to use a spreadsheet in the business environment, especially with regards to financial forecasting and planning. This chapter assumes that you are familiar with the more basic operation of Excel and focuses on how to produce professional spreadsheets that minimise the amount of potential error that can occur.

On completion of their studies students should be able to:

- explain the features and functions of spreadsheet software
- explain the use and limitations of spreadsheet software in business
- apply spreadsheet software to the normal work of a Chartered Management Accountant.

Please note that this chapter takes a different approach to the other chapters. In previous sections of the book, where appropriate we discussed the detailed use of Excel to perform specific tasks. In this chapter we look at how to design and maintain a higher standard of spreadsheet. Concepts in this chapter are addressed without using examples and solutions. Instead by working through this chapter you can develop a spreadsheet which incorporates all the good practices highlighted here.

1 Introduction

A spreadsheet is a multipurpose piece of software which may be used for calculations, drawing graphs or handling data in a way similar to a database program. All these functions are available in most spreadsheets at both an elementary level and a highly sophisticated level. In a spreadsheet like Excel, complex problems may be handled by using macros.

A spreadsheet may also be described as a computer program that allows data to be entered and formulae to be created in a tabular format. It was designed to mimic a large paper-based worksheet with many rows and columns. Spreadsheet information is stored in *cells* and the power of this technology lies in the way each cells can store numerical or alphabetical data or a formula for operating on other cells. A *cell* can also hold references to other spreadsheets or objects (such as graphics).

Excel has become the de facto spreadsheet in use today. For any readers using an alternative, the basic functionality of most spreadsheets is pretty similar and the exercises and examples used in this book can still largely be followed.

In your exam, it is important that you input your answer exactly how you would enter it into Excel, for example, including the leading $ sign. It is, of course, possible to enter alternative, but equivalent correct formulae; the assessment software will handle this, although the question will indicate how you should input your answer.'

2 Spreadsheet terminology

It is worth clarifying the different application areas within the spreadsheet.

Workbooks and Worksheets

An Excel file is referred to as a *workbook*. A workbook can consist of a single *worksheet* or can be a combination of multiple worksheets, charts, databases etc. An Excel file is saved on disk with a .xls or .xlsx file extension, depending on which version you are using.

Cells

A worksheet is described by column letters and row numbers and each row/column co-ordinate is referred to as a *cell*. In Excel there are 256 columns labelled A through IV and 65,536 rows. This in theory provides 16,777,216 cells into which information can be placed! In actual fact the number of cells that can really be used is restricted by the specification of the computer and the complexity of the data and formulae being worked on.

3 A note on macros and application development

It is possible in Excel to *record* a series of keystrokes and/or mouse clicks which can be stored in a *macro*. The macro can then be run whenever that series of keystrokes and/or mouse clicks is required. For example, to print a specific area of a spreadsheet, or to save a file with a particular name.

In addition to recordable macros, Excel has a powerful computer language called Visual Basic for Applications (VBA). With VBA it is possible to program the spreadsheet to perform in very individualistic ways.

The development and use of macros requires a substantial understanding of the spreadsheet and is thus beyond the scope of this book.

4 Getting started with Excel

When the Excel program is launched a blank spreadsheet is displayed:

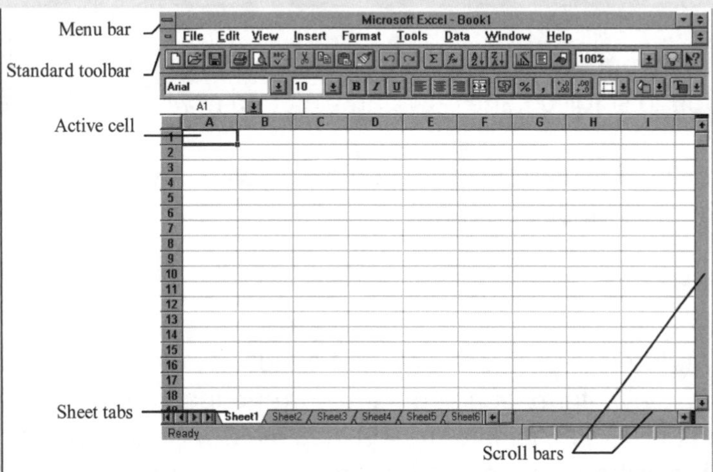

Note: *This figure assumes that Excel has not been customised in any way. If your system has been installed with customised toolbars the screen may not look the same. It would be preferable to re-install Excel without customisation for the purposes of working with this book.*

Workbooks of files

When Excel is loaded a new, blank *workbook* is displayed as shown above. This workbook is called BOOK1 and consists of a number of blank *worksheets*. Each worksheet is labelled on a tab at the bottom of the workbook. You will be able to customise the name of these worksheets as you use them, but at this stage they are labelled *Sheet 1*, *Sheet 2* etc. Sheets can be moved or copied between workbooks, and you can reorganise sheets within a workbook. In addition you can have several workbooks open at the same time, each in its own window.

Worksheets

Most of the work you do will use worksheets. As you can see in the image above, a worksheet is a grid of rows and columns, forming a series of *cells*. Each *cell* has a unique address. For example, the cell where column C and row 8 intersect is referred to as cell C8. You use cell references when you create formulae or reference cells in command instructions.

The *active* cell is the one into which data will be placed when you start typing. You can determine the active cell by the bold border it has around it. When you open a new workbook this will be cell A1 on Sheet1.

To change the active cell you can either use the directional arrow keys on the keyboard to move one cell at a time to the left, right, up or down, or you can use the mouse to move the pointer into the required cell and then click once on the left mouse button.

Scroll bars

To the right and the bottom right of the screen there are scroll bars which allow you to scroll up and down and left and right around the active window.

Click on the down arrow in the vertical scroll bar which will scroll the worksheet down by one row.

Status bar

At the bottom of the screen are the horizontal scroll bar and the status bar which display information about the current document or the task you are working on. The exact information displayed will vary according to what you are doing. When you open a new workbook there are indicators to the right of the status bar that are highlighted if the CAPS LOCK key, NUM LOCK key or SCROLL LOCK key is activated.

Toolbars

As in all Windows applications the toolbars allow quick access to commonly used commands. On starting Excel the Standard and Formatting toolbars are displayed.

Move the pointer over one of the toolbar buttons and notice the name is displayed in a small box below the selected button. This is called a *ToolTip*. A brief description of what the button does is displayed.

5 Good spreadsheet design

Whether a spreadsheet is being developed for specific business mathematical calculations or as a forecasting plan, a profit and loss account or a marketing plan, it is essential that due care and attention be given to its design and structure. Establishing some rules as to how all the spreadsheets in a department or organisation are developed enables different people to look at different plans and feel familiar with the layout, style, reports, charts, etc. This is in much the same way as users feel familiar with software applications that have a similar interface such as those in the Microsoft Office suite of products.

The objectives of good design in spreadsheet terms are exactly the same as those required for any other software development:

(1) to ensure that the spreadsheet is as error free as possible;

(2) to ensure that the spreadsheet can be used without much training or control;

(3) to minimise the work required to enhance or change the spreadsheet.

If care is taken to ensure sound structure and good design a spreadsheet will be straightforward to develop, easy to read, simple to use, not difficult to change and will produce the required results.

The plan developed over a number of stages in this chapter illustrates a variety of aspects of the principles of spreadsheet design and development. The series begins with a plan that has had little or no thought put into its design and layout and as the chapter proceeds ways of improving and enhancing the plan are identified and explained.

6 Getting started

The spreadsheet below is a simple profit projection that may be of use to the author, but is unlikely to be helpful to anyone else. This is clearly a quick one-off plan which has been prepared with very little care and which may well not even be saved on the disk.

	A	B	C	D	E
1	sales	150	173	198	228
2	price	12.55	12.55	12.55	12.55
3	revenue	1883	2165	2490	2863
4	costs	1185	1362	1567	1802
5	profit	698	803	923	1061
6					

Problems with this spreadsheet

The immediately obvious problems with this spreadsheet are that it has no title, it is not clear what the columns represent, i.e. are they different periods or perhaps different products, and the author is unknown.

With regards the data itself, the figures are hard to read as there are varying numbers of decimal places. Whilst perhaps there has been a growth in sales and price, the percentage has not been indicated. The costs line could be misleading as no indication of where the costs have been derived is supplied.

Positive aspects of this spreadsheet

If the author of the spreadsheet required a quick profit estimation based on known data and growth rates for sales units, price and costs then the spreadsheet has supplied that information quickly and in a more concise form than would have been achievable using a calculator and recording the results on paper.

7 Ownership and version

In the next image the three major shortfalls of the first spreadsheet have been remedied.

	A	B	C	D	E	F	G	H	I
1		Profit Projection for Widget Division for 20XX					Last updated:	Jan 20XX	
2		Written by P.A. Jones							
3		pajones@business.com							
4		0118 999 9999							
5									
6									
7		Qtr 1	Qtr 2	Qtr 3	Qtr 4				
8	sales	150	175	195	220				
9	price	12.55	12.55	12.55	12.55				
10	revenue	1882.5	2196.25	2447.25	2761				
11	costs	1184.55	1381.975	1539.915	1737.34				
12	profit	697.95	814.275	907.335	1023.66				
13									
14									
15									
16									

The plan has also been given a title and author details have been included. It is important that every business plan have a clear owner who is responsible for overseeing the accuracy and maintenance of the system. A name plus some form of contact details should always be included.

Problems with this spreadsheet

The construction of the data and results is still unclear and the lack of formatting makes the figures hard to read. The costs remain grouped together.

Positive aspects of this spreadsheet

In addition to the owner details having been added to the plan, the date when the plan was written is a useful feature. The date becomes particularly important when the question of spreadsheet versions arise. Note that the date has been entered here as text. If a DATE function had been used it would be continually updated each time the file is retrieved, whereas here it is the date of the last update that is required. The ruling lines above and below specific sections of the spreadsheet are also quite helpful. This can be quickly achieved using the automatic formatting features. These are accessed via the Format Autoformat command.

8 Formatting

In the next version the data for the four quarters is totalled and reported as an annual figure. The values in the plan have also been formatted with the majority of figures being formatted to zero decimal places and the price line to two decimal places.

One of the automatic formatting options has been selected to shade and outline the plan.

	A	B	C	D	E	F	G	H	I
1	Profit Projection for Widget Division for 20XX						Last updated:	Jan 20XX	
2	Written by P.A. Jones								
3	pajones@business.com								
4	0118 999 9999								
5									
6		Qtr 1	Qtr 2	Qtr 3	Qtr 4	Total			
7	sales	150	173	198	228	749			
8	price	12.55	12.55	12.55	12.55				
9	revenue	1883	2165	2490	2863	9400			
10	costs	1185	1362	1567	1802	5915			
11	*profit*	698	803	923	1061	3485			
12									
13									
14	Report Printed		22-Mar-05	12:29:57					
15									
16									
17									
18									
19									

Problems with this spreadsheet

It can be seen that the sales and the costs both increase over time. However it is not clear by how much because the sales growth factor and the increase in costs have been incorporated into the formulae as absolute references.

If we think we are likely to want to change the sales growth estimate later, then it is best if this is not included as an absolute value within formulae. In our spreadsheet to change the sales growth factor two processes are required. First, cell C7 is accessed and the edit key pressed. The growth factor is changed and enter is pressed. This has changed the formula in this one cell, but only once the formula has been extrapolated across into cells D7 and E7 is the amendment complete. It is not difficult to see that there is room for error here in a number of different ways.

Positive aspects of this spreadsheet

Having a current date and time indicator displayed on the spreadsheet ensures that a hard copy report will reflect the date, and perhaps more importantly the time it was printed. This is achieved through the NOW( ) function, which can be formatted with a range of different display options. Because it is likely that a spreadsheet will be recalculated, even if it is set to manual calculation, before printing, the date and time will always be up-to-date. It is of course possible to include the date and time in headers and footers, but during the development phase of a system the page layout is less relevant than printing the section being worked on and so thought should be given to the positioning of the NOW function.

The cells in this plan have now been formatted, which makes the data easier to read. When formatting a spreadsheet it is important to consider the entire plan and not just the cells that are currently being worked on. The entire spreadsheet should be formatted to the degree of accuracy required for the majority of the plan then those cells that need to be different, such as percentages, can be reformatted accordingly. This is quickly achieved by right clicking on the top left corner of the spreadsheet at the intersection between the column letters and row numbers and then select format cells. Whatever formatting is now applied will affect the entire worksheet.

It is important to understand that formatting cells only changes the display and does not affect the results of calculations that are still performed to the full degree of accuracy, which is usually 16 significant decimal places. This is why a cell containing the sum of a range of cells might display an answer that does not agree with the result of visually adding the values in the range.

The only safe way to ensure that the results of a calculation are actually rounded to a given number of decimal places the ROUND function is required.

	A	B	C	D	E	F
14	**Costs**					
15	Administration	1500	1576	1656	1739	6471
16	Depreciation	1500	1553	1607	1663	6322
17	Finance Charges	1200	1288	1382	1482	5352
18	Maintenance	600	630	662	696	2588
19	Salary Expenses	13000	13858	14773	15748	57378
20	***Total Other Costs***	17800	18904	20079	21328	78112
21						
22	**Net Profit B.T.**	200	1102	2060	3076	6438
23						

Table A

	A	B	C	D	E	F
14	**Costs**					
15	Administration	1500	1576	1656	1739	6471
16	Depreciation	1500	1553	1607	1663	6322
17	Finance Charges	1200	1288	1382	1482	5352
18	Maintenance	600	630	662	696	2588
19	Salary Expenses	13000	13858	14773	15748	57378
20	***Total Other Costs***	17800	18904	20079	21328	78111
21						
22	**Net Profit B.T.**	200	1102	2060	3076	6438
23						

Table B

The table now shows two tables representing the same extract from a profit and loss account. In both cases all the cells have been formatted to zero decimal places, but in Table B the ROUND function has been incorporated in the formulae for cells F15 through F20.

The formula entered into cell F15, which can then be copied for the other line items is: = ROUND(SUM(B15:E15),0)

The effect of the ROUND function can be seen in cell F20. By visually adding up the numbers in the range F15 through F19 the result is 78111 whereas the formatting of these cells without the use of the ROUND function in Table A returns a value of 78112 in cell F20. Having applied the ROUND function to a cell any future reference made to that cell will use the rounded value.

Excel does offer an alternative to the ROUND function in the Precision as displayed option within TOOLS:OPTIONS:CALCULATION. This command assumes that calculations will be performed to the level of accuracy currently displayed. The danger of using this command is that when data is changed or added to the spreadsheet the command is no longer valid and it is then necessary to repeat the command to update the spreadsheet – this is another invitation for problems to develop.

9 Documentation

Spreadsheet developers are notoriously bad at supplying documentation and other supporting information about the plan. There are a number of features offered by Excel to assist in the documenting of plans including the INSERT COMMENT command.

	A	B	C	D	E	F	G	H	I
1		Profit Projection for Widget Division for 20XX					Last updated:	Jan 20XX	
2		Written by P.A. Jones							
3		pajones@business.com							
4		0118 999 9999							
5									
6		Qtr 1	Qtr 2	Qtr 3	Qtr 4	Total			
7	sales	150	173	198	228	749			
8	price	12.55	12.55						
9	revenue	1883	2165			9400			
10	costs	1185	1362			5915			
11	profit	698	803			3485			
12									
13									
14	Report Printed		22-Mar-05	12:29:57					
15									
16									
17									

Sue Nugus:
This period should be watched

The spreadsheet now shows a comment being entered onto a plan – notice how the user name of the comment author is included. This is useful when a team of people are working on a system. The presence of a comment is indicated by a small red triangle on the cell – to read the comment move the cursor over the cell and it will automatically be displayed. A word of caution concerning the use of comment boxes – they take up a considerable amount of space and if used widely they can make a noticeable difference to the size of a file. To clear all the comments use the EDIT CLEAR COMMENTS command.

The provision of a hard copy report showing the logic used to create a plan is also helpful as this is the ultimate reference point if a formula has been overwritten and needs to be reconstructed.

In Excel there is a shortcut key to display the formulae which is CTRL + (accent grave). Alternatively this can be achieved through the TOOLS OPTIONS VIEW command and then check the Formulas box.

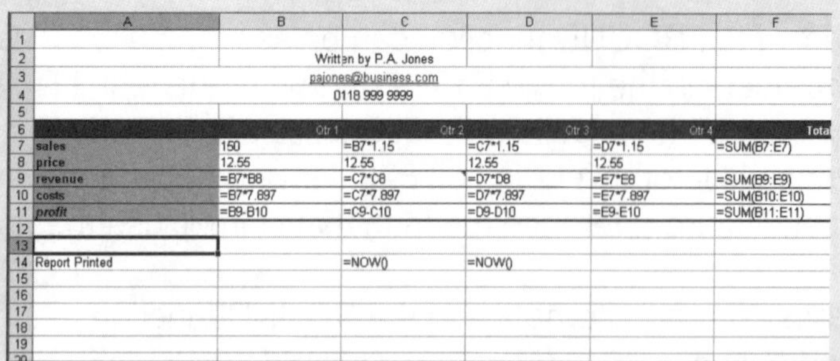

	A	B	C	D	E	F
1						
2			Written by P.A. Jones			
3			pajones@business.com			
4			0118 999 9999			
5						
6		Qtr 1	Qtr 2	Qtr 3	Qtr 4	Total
7	sales	150	=B7*1.15	=C7*1.15	=D7*1.15	=SUM(B7:E7)
8	price	12.55	12.55	12.55	12.55	
9	revenue	=B7*B8	=C7*C8	=D7*D8	=E7*E8	=SUM(B9:E9)
10	costs	=B7*7.897	=C7*7.897	=D7*7.897	=E7*7.897	=SUM(B10:E10)
11	profit	=B9-B10	=C9-C10	=D9-D10	=E9-E10	=SUM(B11:E11)
12						
13						
14	Report Printed		=NOW()	=NOW()		
15						
16						
17						
18						
19						

In addition to providing documentation for a spreadsheet system, looking at the contents of the cells as opposed to the results can also be a helpful auditing tool. For example, our table highlights the fact that there are still values embedded in formulae which is not good practice and is addressed in the next version of the plan.

A third form of documentation which can be particularly useful for large systems is the 'sentence at the end of the row' technique. Requiring less file space than comment boxes, and always on view it can be useful to have a brief description of the activity taking place in each row of a plan.

10 Minimising absolute values

One of the reasons that spreadsheets have become such an integral part of the way we do business is the fact that they facilitate quick, easy and inexpensive what-if analysis. What-if analysis may be defined as the process of investigating the effect of changes to assumptions on the objective function of a business plan.

Performing what-if analysis on the opening sales assumption or the opening price assumption is quite straightforward, involving placing the cursor on the figure and entering the new value. On pressing ENTER the spreadsheet is re-evaluated and all cells which refer to the changed values, either directly or indirectly are updated.

The success of performing even the simplest what-if analysis is dependent on the spreadsheet having been developed with the correct series of relationships.

	A	B	C	D	E	F
1						
2			Written by P.A. Jones			
3			pajones@business.com			
4			0118 999 9999			
5						
6		Qtr 1	Qtr 2	Qtr 3	Qtr 4	Total
7	sales	150	=B7*1.15	=C7*1.15	=D7*1.15	=SUM(B7:E7)
8	price	12.55	12.55	12.55	12.55	
9	revenue	=B7*B8	=C7*C8	=D7*D8	=E7*E8	=SUM(B9:E9)
10	costs	=B7*7.897	=C7*7.897	=D7*7.897	=E7*7.897	=SUM(B10:E10)
11	profit	=B9-B10	=C9-C10	=D9-D10	=E9-E10	=SUM(B11:E11)
12						
13						
14	Report Printed		=NOW()	=NOW()		
15						
16						
17						
18						
19						

For example, changing the opening sales value in the table would automatically cause the other quarter sales values to recalculate, as well as the revenue, costs and profit lines. This is because they relate, through the cell references in the formulae, either directly or indirectly to the sales value in cell B7.

However, as already mentioned this plan incorporates absolute values in the formulae for sales and costs growth. Furthermore, the price is a fixed value and has been entered once into cell B8 and the value has then been copied into the other periods. This presents problems when what-if analysis is required on any of these factors.

Problems with this spreadsheet

Because no growth in the price is required the opening value of 12.55 has been copied for the four quarters. Whilst this is fine all the time a price of 12.55 is required, it presents a problem when the price requires changing. With this spreadsheet it would be necessary to overwrite the price in the first quarter and then copy the new value for the remaining three quarters. The same applies if the sales growth or the cost factors required changing.

To prevent these problems arising, a different approach to the development of the plan needs to be taken.

In the first instance all growth and cost factors should be represented in a separate area of the spreadsheet – even on a different sheet altogether in the case of a large system with a lot of input. The factors can then be referenced from within the plan as and when they are required. The next table shows the adapted layout for this plan after extracting the sales growth and costs factors.

	A	B	C	D	E	F	G	H
1	Profit Projection for Widget Division for 20XX						Last updated:	Jan 20XX
2			Written by P.A. Jones					
3			pajones@business.com					
4			0118 999 9999					
5								
6								
7		Qtr 1	Qtr 2	Qtr 3	Qtr 4	Total		
8	sales	150	152	153	155	609		
9	price	12.55	12.61	12.68	12.74			
10	revenue	1883	1911	1940	1969	7703		
11	costs	1125	1136	1148	1159	4569		
12	profit	758	775	792	810	3134		
13								
14								
15	Growth in Sales Volume as %			1.01%				
16	Growth in Price as %			0.5%				
17	Cost per unit of production			7.50				
18								
19	Report Printed	22-Mar-05	13:00:00					
20								
21								
22								

Having the growth and cost factors in separate cells means that the formulae need to be changed to pick up this information. The next table shows the amended formulae for this plan.

	A	B	C	D	E	F	
1				Profit Projection for Widget Division for 20XX			Last
2				Written by P.A. Jones			
3				pajones@business.com			
4				0118 999 9999			
5							
6							
7		Qtr 1	Qtr 2	Qtr 3	Qtr 4	Total	
8	sales	150	=B8*(1+$D$15)	=C8*(1+$D$15)	=D8*(1+$D$15)	=SUM(B8:E8)	
9	price	12.55	=B9*(1+$D$16)	=C9*(1+$D$16)	=D9*(1+$D$16)		
10	revenue	=B8*B9	=C8*C9	=D8*D9	=E8*E9	=SUM(B10:E10)	
11	costs	=B8*$D$17	=C8*$D$17	=D8*$D$17	=E8*$D$17	=SUM(B11:E11)	
12	profit	=B10-B11	=C10-C11	=D10-D11	=E10-E11	=SUM(B12:E12)	
13							
14							
15	Growth in Sales Volume as %			0.01			
16	Growth in Price as %			0			
17	Cost per unit of production			7.5			
18							
19	Report Printed	=NOW()	=NOW()				
20							
21							

Note that the references to cells D15,D16 and D17 are fixed references. This is achieved by placing the $ symbol before the column letter and row number, i.e. $D$15, and means that when the formula is copied the reference to cell D15 remains fixed. A shortcut key to add the $ symbols to a cell reference is F4.

In this plan an option in the growth factors has been included for the price, despite the fact that in this plan the price does not change. It is important to always think ahead when developing any plan and although the price does not currently change, it might be necessary to include a percentage increase in the future. Having the facility for change built-in to the plan could save time later – and for the time being the growth factor is simply set to zero.

Removing the growth and cost factors from the main body of a business plan is the first step in developing a data input form which will ultimately separate all the input data from the actual logic of the spreadsheet. This separation of the data allows the logic cells to be protected from accidental damage. This is discussed further in the Template section of this chapter.

11 Charts

It is useful to support the information supplied in business plans with charts. In the profit and loss account used in this chapter various charts might be useful, for example to show the relative impact of price and sales volume figures. Although charts can be placed on the same worksheet as the plan, it is usually preferable to keep graphs on separate *chart sheets*. The exception might be if it is appropriate to view changes on a chart at the same time data in the plan is changed, or if a spreadsheet is to be copied into a management report being created in Word.

An example of the type of chart that might be produced from the plan used in this chapter is as follows:

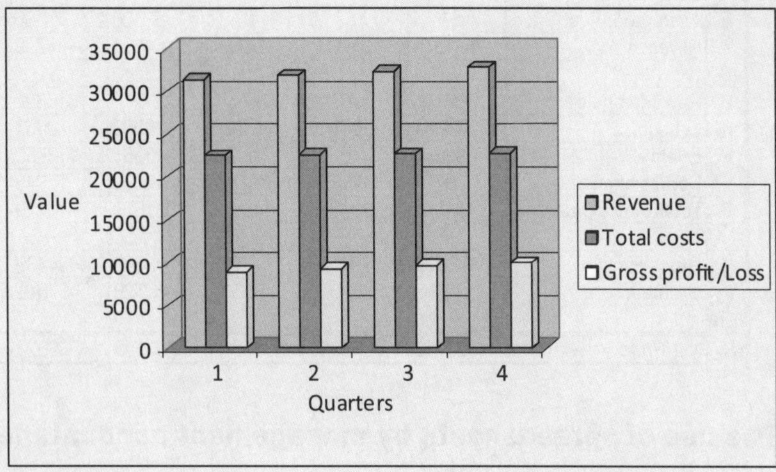

12 Tips for larger plans

The plan used in this chapter has been a simple quarterly plan, but in many cases business plans will be larger and more complex. The next diagram shows an extract from a five-year quarterly plan. Although it is not obvious by looking, each year in this report has been formatted with a different colour font. This is a useful technique when working with large models because it enables the user to quickly know which part of the plan is being viewed or worked on, without having to scroll around the spreadsheet to see the titles.

	A	B	C	D	E	F	G	H	I	J	K
1	Five Year Profit Projection for Widget Division for 1998										
2	Written by P.A. Jones 31 July 1997										
3											
4		Y1 Qtr 1	Y1 Qtr 2	Y1 Qtr 3	Y2 Qtr 4	Y1 Total	Y2 Qtr 1	Y2 Qtr 2	Y2 Qtr 3	Y2 Qtr 4	Y2 Total
5	Sales Volume	8000	8080	8161	8242	32483	12000	12000	12000	12000	48000
6	Price	50.00	50.75	51.51	52.28		67.00	67.00	67.00	67.00	
7	Revenue	400000	410060	420373	430945	1661378	804000	804000	804000	804000	3216000
8											
9	Raw Materials	96000	96960	97930	98909	389798	180000	180000	180000	180000	720000
10	Labour	12000	12060	12120	12181	48361	15000	15150	15302	15455	60906
11	Energy	9600	9792	9988	10188	39567	10000	10050	10100	10151	40301
12	Depreciation	2000	2020	2040	2061	8121	2500	2519	2538	2557	10113
13	Total Direct Costs	119600	120832	122078	123338	485848	207500	207719	207939	208162	831320
14											
15	Gross Profit	280400	289228	298295	307607	1175530	596500	596281	596061	595838	2384680
16	Overheads	20000	20300	20605	20914	81818	22000	22220	22442	22667	89329
17											
18	Net Profit	260400	268928	277691	286694	1093712	574500	574061	573618	573171	2295351

This colour coding can then be carried over to summary reports, and other reports pertaining to the different parts of the plan.

From a design point of view it is preferable to place different reports associated with a plan on separate worksheets. The next report has been placed on a separate sheet called *Summary* and is created by referencing the cells from the yearly totals in the main plan.

	A	B	C	D	E	F	G
1	Five Year Summary Profit Projection for Widget Division for 1998						
2	Written by P.A. Jones 31 July 1997						
3							
4		Y1 Total	Y2 Total	Y3 Total	Y4 Total	Y5 Total	5 yr Total
5	Sales Volume	32483	48000	60452	72542	90675	304152
6	Average Annual Price	51.14	67.00	70.97	71.06	71.06	
7	Revenue	1661378	3216000	4290334	5154924	6444709	20767344
8							
9	Raw Materials	389798	720000	1027676	1233211	1813508	5184192
10	Labour	48361	60906	64966	68000	70067	312301
11	Energy	39567	40301	40301	48361	113750	282281
12	Depreciation	8121	10113	10113	12090	12945	53382
13	Total Direct Costs	485848	831320	1143056	1361662	2010270	5832156
14							
15	Gross Profit	1175530	2384680	3147278	3793262	4434439	14935189
16	Overheads	81818	89329	89329	89329	97816	447621
17							
18	Net Profit	1093712	2295351	3057949	3703933	4336623	14487568

13 The use of spreadsheets by management accountants

There are a number of different ways in which the management accountant can use a spreadsheet in his or her work. In the first place, spreadsheets are especially useful in the performance of calculations. In addition to the basic mathematical operators discussed such as addition, subtraction, division, multiplication, etc., there are many other functions which will be of direct use. These include NPV, IRR, PV to mention only three. There are in fact more than 350 built-in functions in Excel. When it comes to repetitive calculation the management accountant can set up templates that can be used again and again.

In addition to the calculation side of the spreadsheet, the management accountant will find useful the ease with which graphs and charts can quickly be created in Excel.

Advantages of using spreadsheets

- Large enough to include a large volume of information.
- Formulae and look up tables can be used so that if any figure is amended, all the figures will be immediately recalculated. This is very useful for carrying out sensitivity analysis.
- The results can be printed out or distributed to other users electronically quickly and easily.
- Most programs can also represent the results graphically e.g. balances can be shown in a bar chart:

Disadvantages of spreadsheets:

- Spreadsheets for a particular budgeting application will take time to develop. The benefit of the spreadsheet must be greater than the cost of developing and maintaining it.
- Data can be accidentally changed (or deleted) without the user being aware of this occurring.
- Errors in design, particularly in the use of formulae, can produce invalid output. Due to the complexity of the model, these design errors may be difficult to locate.
- A combination of errors of design, together with flawed data, may mean that decisions are made that are subsequently found out to be wrong and cost the firm money. This is known as "spreadsheet risk" and is a serious problem. For example, a "cut and paste error" cost TransAlta $24 million when it underbid on an electricity supply contract.
- Data used will be subject to a high degree of uncertainty. This may be forgotten and the data used to produce, what is considered to be, an "accurate" report.
- Security issues, such as the risk of unauthorised access (e.g. hacking) or a loss of data (e.g. due to fire or theft).

The rest of this chapter looks at examples of how some of the analysis carried out throughout this text could be done using excel.

There are many different aspects to the way that Excel can be used for planning and those who are interested in more detail should consult the Elsevier CIMA Publication, Financial Planning Using Excel – Forecasting, Planning and Budgeting Techniques, by Sue Nugus, 2005.

14 Creating formulae in spreadsheets

Within Excel there are times when you will want to take advantage of pre-programmed functions (see the expandable texts below for examples of these) and other times when you will want to set up your own functions and formulae.

Suppose you want to calculate the NPV for the following project:

- Invest 10,000 at t=0
- Get returns of 4000 at t=1, 5000 at t=2 and 4500 at t=3
- Discount rate 10%

You could set up a spreadsheet as follows:

	A	B	C	D	E	F	G
1	**NPV calculation**						
2							
3	Discount rate		10.00%				
4							
5	Year		0	1	2	3	
6	Cash flow		-10,000	4,000	5,000	4,500	
7	Discount factor						
8	Present value						
9	NPV						

To input the discount factors we could do a formula for each.

For example, cell F7 we want a 3 year discount factor, so could type in

=1/(1.1)^3

Note: All formula start with an "=" sign.

The trouble with the above is that we will have to type in a new formula for each discount factor. A quicker approach is to design a generic formula for year 0 to start with. Cell C7 could thus have

=1/(1.10)^C5

You should get a 1 in cell C7 as that is the correct discount factor for t=0. Notice that there is a small black square at the bottom RHS of cell C7

	A	B	C	D	E	F	G
1	**NPV calculation**						
2							
3	Discount rate		10.00%				
4							
5	Year		0	1	2	3	
6	Cash flow		-10,000	4,000	5,000	4,500	
7	Discount factor		1				
8	Present value						
9	NPV						

If you now drag the square to the right up to cell F7 then Excel will automatically give you the formulae for the other discount factors. Your spreadsheet will now show the following

	A	B	C	D	E	F	G
1	**NPV calculation**						
2							
3	Discount rate		10.00%				
4							
5	Year		0	1	2	3	
6	Cash flow		-10,000	4,000	5,000	4,500	
7	Discount factor		1	0.909091	0.826446	0.751315	
8	Present value						
9	NPV						

Next we want to calculate the present values. In cell C8 we want

= C6*C7

Again, this can be dragged to the right to fill in cells D8, E8 and F8, giving

	A	B	C	D	E	F	G
1	**NPV calculation**						
2							
3	Discount rate		10.00%				
4							
5	Year		0	1	2	3	
6	Cash flow		-10,000	4,000	5,000	4,500	
7	Discount factor		1	0.909091	0.826446	0.751315	
8	Present value		-10000	3636.364	4132.231	3380.917	
9	NPV						

Finally to get the NPV we want to sum cells C8 to F8. This is easy in Excel. For example in cell C9 we could enter

= SUM(C8:F8)

This gives

	A	B	C	D	E	F	G
1	**NPV calculation**						
2							
3	Discount rate		10.00%				
4							
5	Year		0	1	2	3	
6	Cash flow		-10,000	4,000	5,000	4,500	
7	Discount factor		1	0.909091	0.826446	0.751315	
8	Present value		-10000	3636.364	4132.231	3380.917	
9	NPV		1149.512				

Supplementary reading – Doing mathematical operations in Excel

Simple mathematical operations in Excel

When performing calculations in Excel the same mathematical rules that have been discussed in Chapter 1 apply. The following examples show how formulae in Excel would be created to calculate the following:

(a) $5 + 6 \times 8$

(b) $(3 + 1) \times 2$

(c) $9 - 7 \div 2$

(d) $(4 + 5) /10$

(e) $5 + 7 \times 8 - 2$

(f) $(9 - 1) \times (6 + 4)$

.

	A	B	C	D	E
1					
2					
3					
4		5	6	8	=B4+C4*D4
5		3	1	2	=(B5+C5)*2
6		9	7	2	=B6-C6/2
7		4	5	10	=(B7+C7)/D7
8		5	7	8	=B8+C8*D8-2
9		9	6		=(B9-1)*(C9+4)
10					
11					
12					
13					
14		9	7	-2	=B14-C14*D14
15		5	8	-6	=(B15-C15)*-6
16		12	8	-4	=B16-8/-4
17		4	16	-2	=(B17-C17)/-2
18		17	8		=(B18-6)*(C18-3)
19		7	20	6	=B19-(2-C19)/(D19-4
20					

Exponential numbers

In Excel a number is raised to a power by using the symbol referred to as a carat (^). Some practitioners refer to this symbol as being the exponential operator.

Thus, for example, to cube 4 the formula required would be = 4^3. To find the square of 4, the formula required is = 4^ 2. The carat can also be used to find the square root. In this case the formula would be = 4^(1/2), or to find the cube root the formula would be = 4^(1/3). The method is used to find the 4th root, 5th root and so on.

Some examples are demonstrated below

	A	B	C	D	E
1					
2		3 squared	9	9	
3		3 cubed	27	27	
4		3 to the power of 4	81	81	
5		4 to the power of 4	256	256	
6					
7		Square root of 4	2		
8		Cubed root of 64	4		
9					

	A	B	C	D
1				
2		3 squared	=3*3	=3^2
3		3 cubed	=3*3*3	=3^3
4		3 to the power of 4	=3*3*3*3	=3^4
5		4 to the power of 4	=4*4*4*4	=4^4
6				
7		Square root of 4	=4^(1/2)	
8		Cubed root of 64	=64^(1/3)	
9				
10				

Supplementary reading – Producing graphs in excel

Using Excel to produce graphs of Linear and Quadratic Equations

Excel can be used to produce graphs of linear and quadratic equations. The first step is to produce a single linear equation, from which a graph can be drawn.

Producing a single linear equation in Excel

The form of the equation that will be used is

$$y = mx + c$$

This equation will be drawn for a given value of c (in this example we will use 20) and a range of 10 values of x (from 1 to 10), calculating corresponding values of y. Thus in this example the formula will be represented as $y = 3x + 20$.

The following graph shows the data for x and the results of entering the formula in the adjacent column.

Single linear equation		
	values for x	y = 3x + 20
	1	23
	2	26
	3	29
	4	32
	5	35
	6	38
	7	41
	8	44
	9	47
	10	50

To show these results graphically in Excel, select the two columns and click on the Chart icon on the Standard Toolbar. This will produce a choice of graph types. Select xy and then choose the joined up line option. Click Finish to complete the chart:

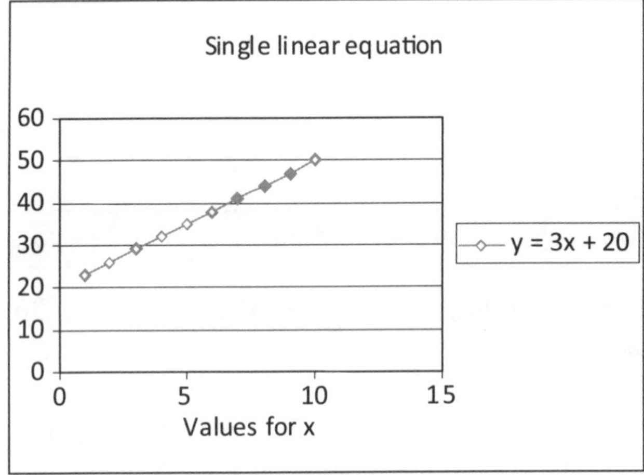

Drawing multiple equations on a single graph

It is possible to produce multiple equations and plot the results onto a single graph, which can be useful for comparison purposes. The next sheet uses the same set of data for x and the results of two different equations are shown in the adjacent two columns.

values for x	y = 3x + 20	y = 6x + 1
1	23	7
2	26	13
3	29	19
4	32	25
5	35	31
6	38	37
7	41	43
8	44	49
9	47	55
10	50	61

The graph is produced in the same way as the first example, by selecting the three columns and clicking on the Chart icon. The results of plotting these two lines onto an *xy* line graph can be seen as follows

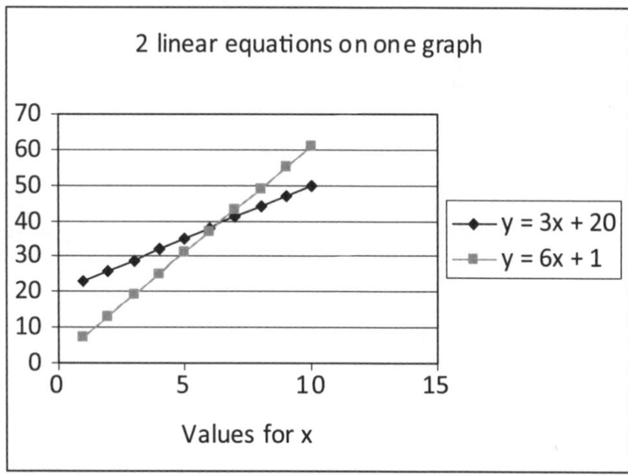

Single quadratic equation

The form of the equation that will be used is

$$y = ax^2 + bx + c$$

This equation will be drawn for a given value of a, b and c, where in this example we will use a = 1, b = 5 and c = 10 and a range of 10 values of x (from –25 to 20), calculating corresponding values of *y*.

Thus in this example the formula will be represented as $y = x^2 + 5x + 10$.

values for x	x^2 + 5x + 10
–25	510
–20	310
–15	160
–10	60
–5	10
0	10
5	60
10	160
15	310
20	510

Using the same method as before a graph can be drawn to show these results.

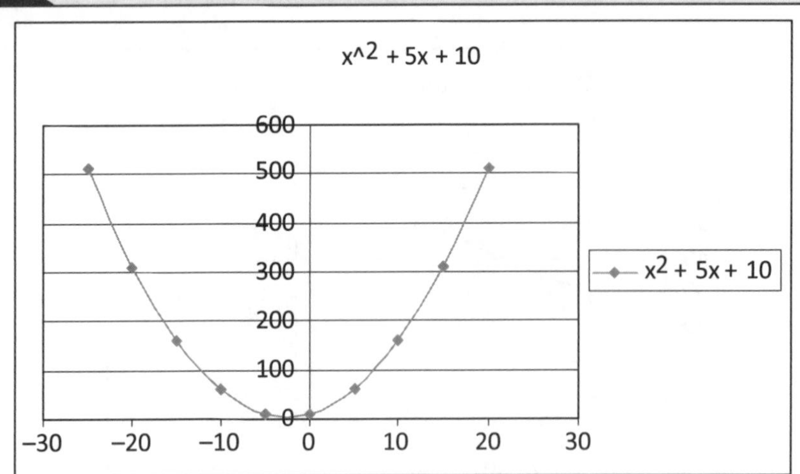

Two quadratic equations on one graph

It is possible to produce multiple quadratic equations and plot the results onto a single graph, which can be useful for comparison purposes. The next table uses the same set of data for x and the results of two different equations are shown in the adjacent two columns.

values for X	x^2 + 5x + 10	−2x^2 −x + 100
−25	510	−1125
−20	310	−680
−15	160	−335
−10	60	−90
−5	10	55
0	10	100
5	60	45
10	160	−110
15	310	−365
20	510	−720

The graph is produced in the same way as the previous example, by selecting the three columns and clicking on the Chart icon. The results of plotting these two lines onto an xy line graph can be seen as

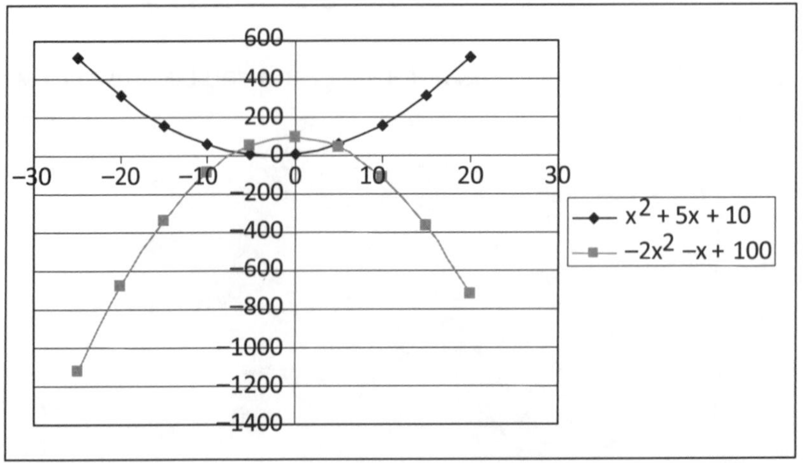

Supplementary reading – Scatter diagrams in Excel

Data can easily be plotted onto a scatter diagram in Excel.

To do this the data must first be entered into the spreadsheet. To create the chart select the range A3:B7 and click on the chart icon. Select X-Y scatter and choose the first chart option.

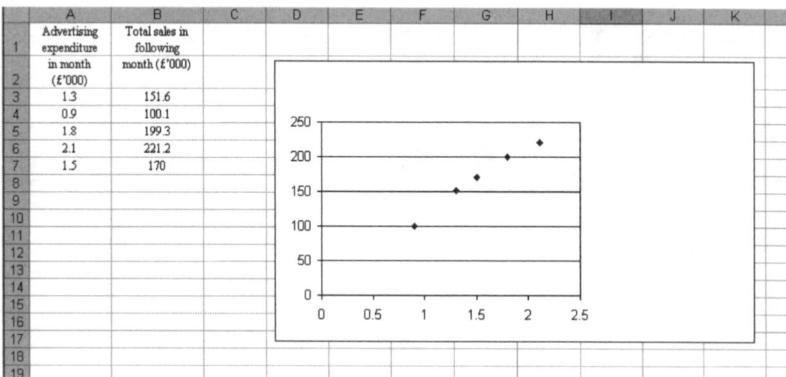

	A	B
1	Advertising expenditure in month	Total sales in following month (£'000)
2	(£'000)	
3	1.3	151.6
4	0.9	100.1
5	1.8	199.3
6	2.1	221.2
7	1.5	170

Supplementary reading – Least square regression in Excel

Least-squares line in Excel

There is a built-in formula in Excel for the calculation of the least-squares line. Having entered the data into the spreadsheet the first step is to draw a scatter diagram described in the previous example.

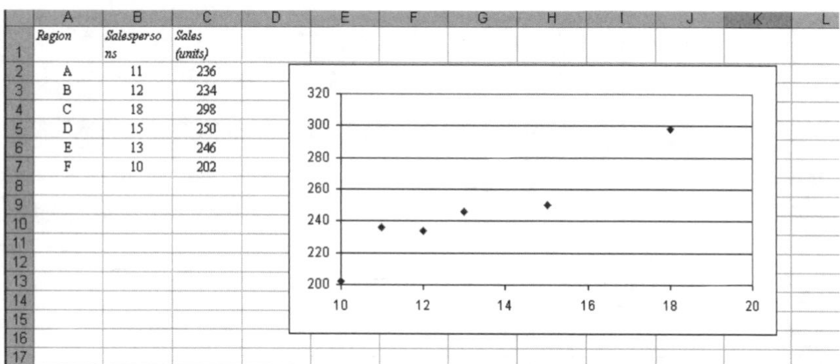

	A	B	C
1	Region	Salespersons	Sales (units)
2	A	11	236
3	B	12	234
4	C	18	298
5	D	15	250
6	E	13	246
7	F	10	202

The Excel FORECAST function can be used to calculate the least-square line. The following needs to be entered into cell D2:

= FORECAST(B2,$C$2:$C$7,$B$2;$B$7)

The formula can then be copied through to cell D7. The range D2:D7 can then be selected, click the copy icon and then click on the chart to make it active before finally clicking the paste icon to plot the forecast data onto the chart. This will initially appear as symbols only, in the same way as the original scatter diagram was produced. However if you right click on one of the new data symbols and select FORMAT DATA SERIES, line can be set to automatic and marker can be set to none. The resulting chart and the FORECAST function formula can be seen as:

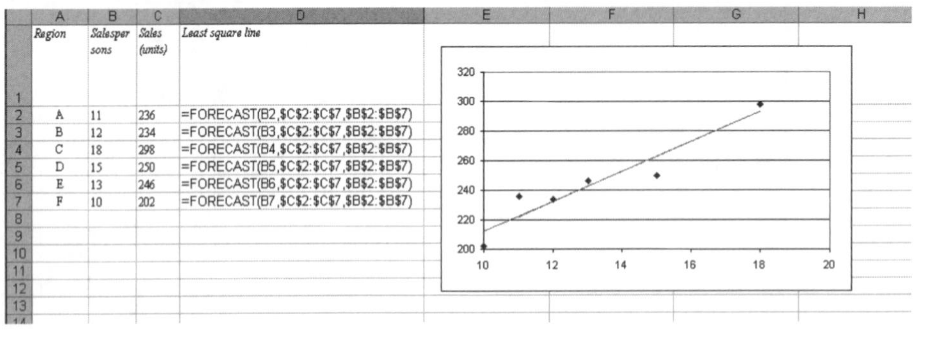

Supplementary reading – Creating bar charts in excel

Creating Bar charts using Excel

There are a wide range of different bar charts that can be created in Excel.

Basic bar chart

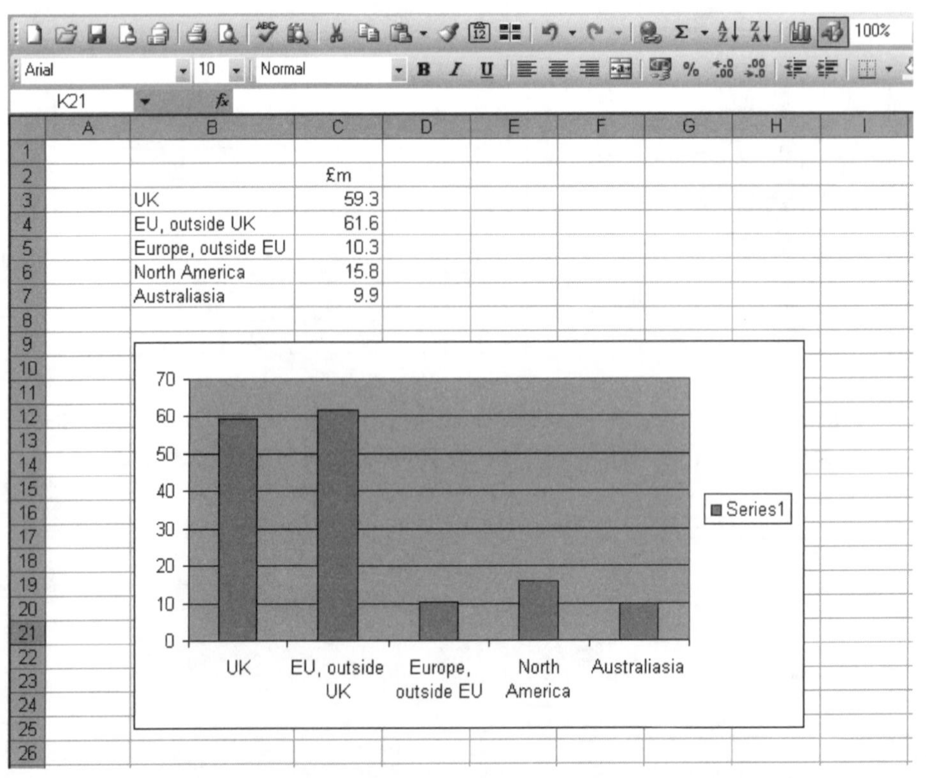

This chart is created by selecting the range B3:C7 clicking on the chart button on the toolbar and selecting the first sub-type option. This chart is representing a single set of data.

Side by side

In the case of the side-by-side bar chart the turnover for both companies for each country can easily be compared.

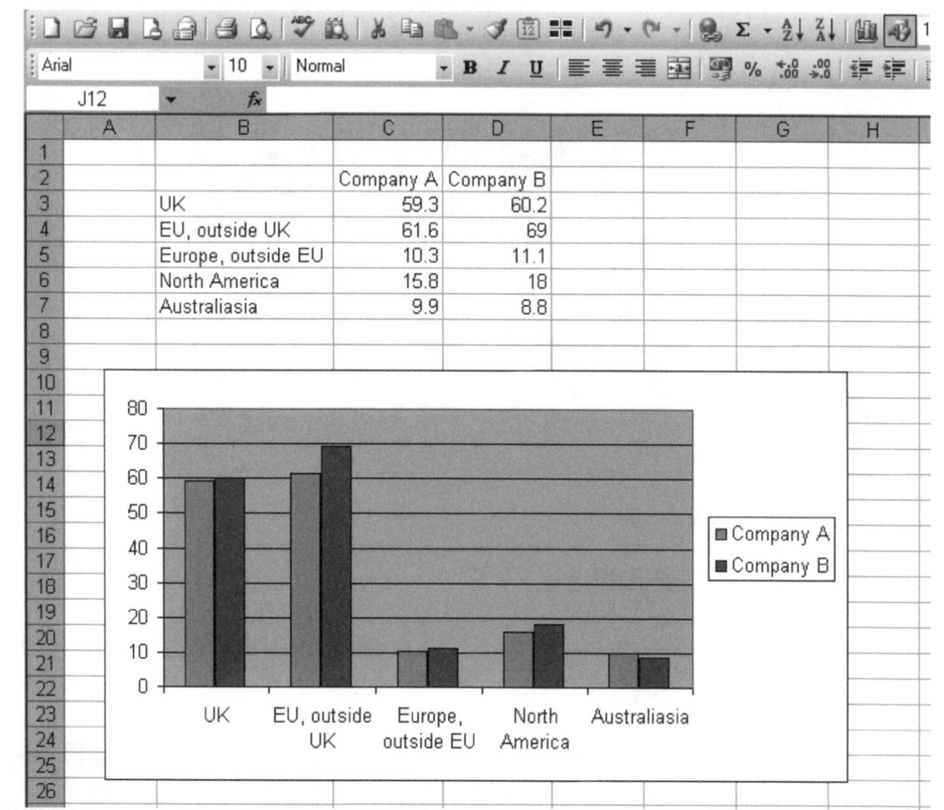

Stacked bar chart

	Company A	Company B
UK	59.3	60.2
EU, outside UK	61.6	69
Europe, outside EU	10.3	11.1
North America	15.8	18
Australiasia	9.9	8.8

140
120
100
80
60
40
20
0
UK
EU, outside UK
Europe, outside EU
North America
Australiasia
Company B
Company A

100 per cent stacked bar chart.

This compares the percentage each company contributes to the total across each country.

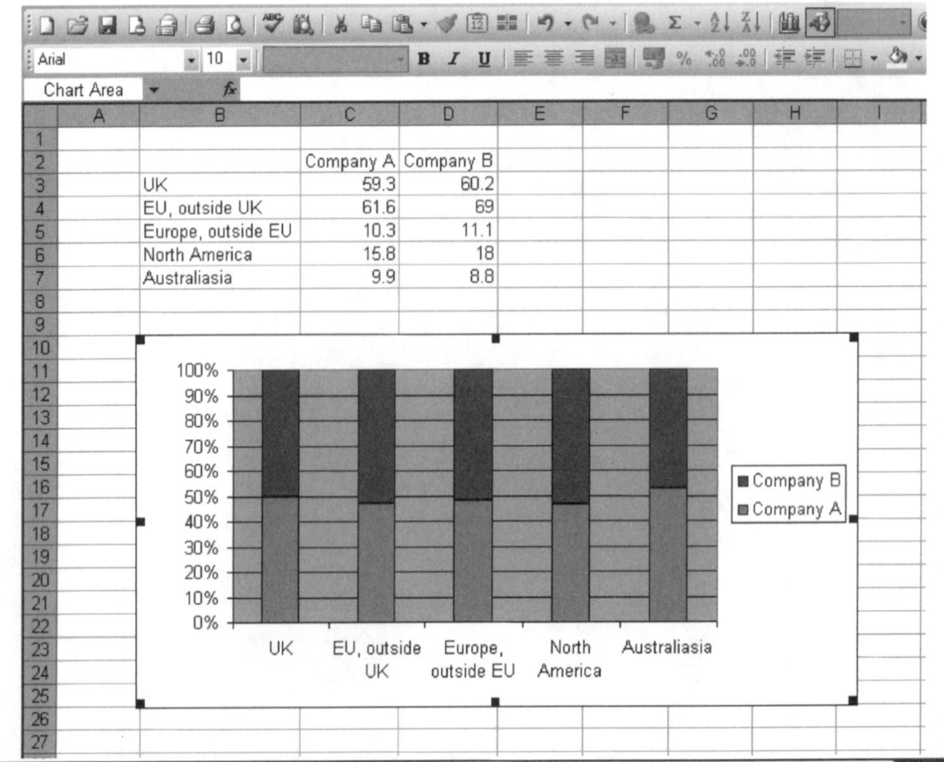

Other shapes

Excel offers a variety of options when plotting data onto charts. Bar charts do not have to be represented by upright bars, but can be pyramids, cones or cylinders. However, you should in each case, consider the most appropriate way is which to display data – often, the simpler methods of display are the most effective.

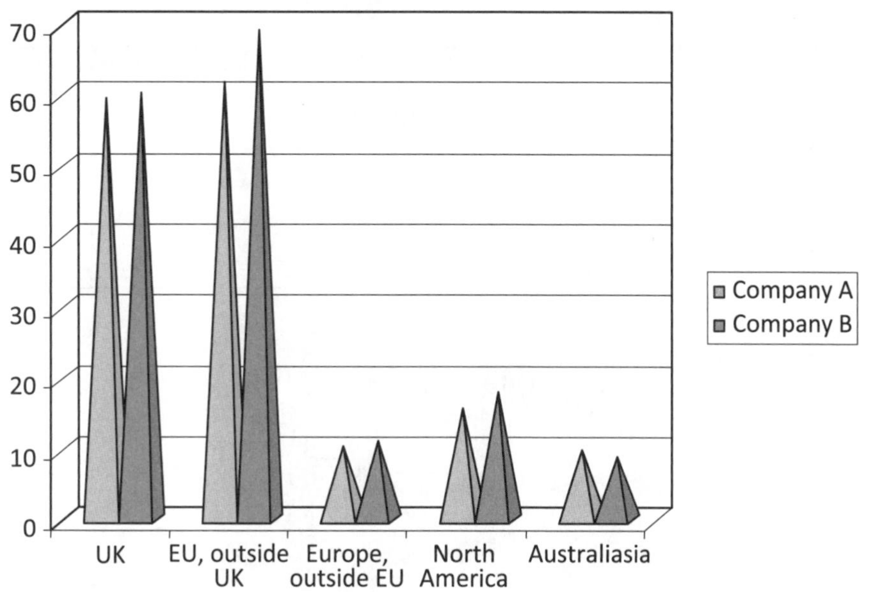

Furthermore bars can be positioned horizontally as opposed to vertically:

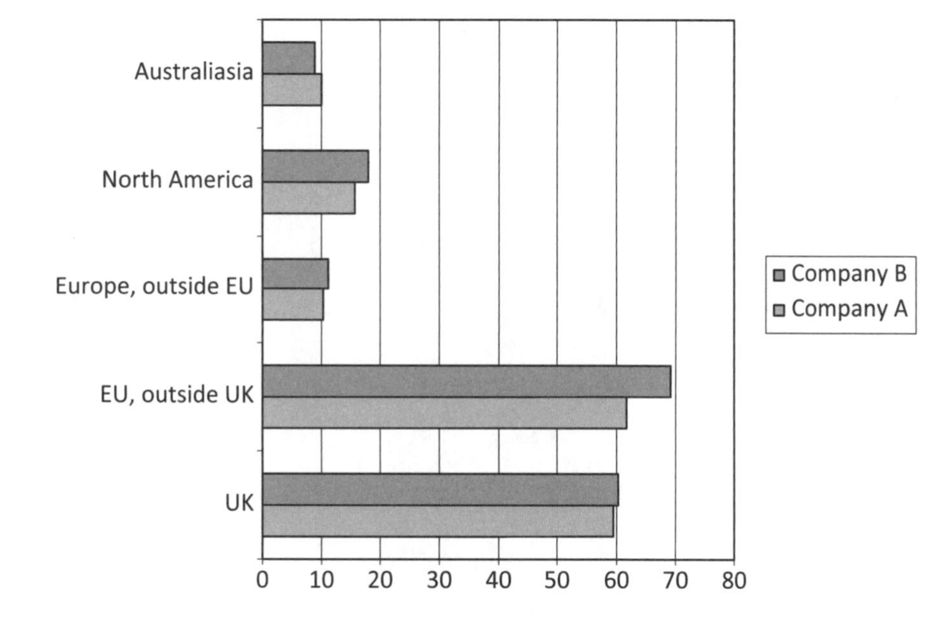

Another way of looking at this data is to chart the turnover of the two companies showing the contribution from each country (as shown previously). This is achieved in Excel by selecting the data as before and selecting the stacked-bar chart option from the chart sub-options.

However after clicking next, change the series setting to by rows instead of by columns.

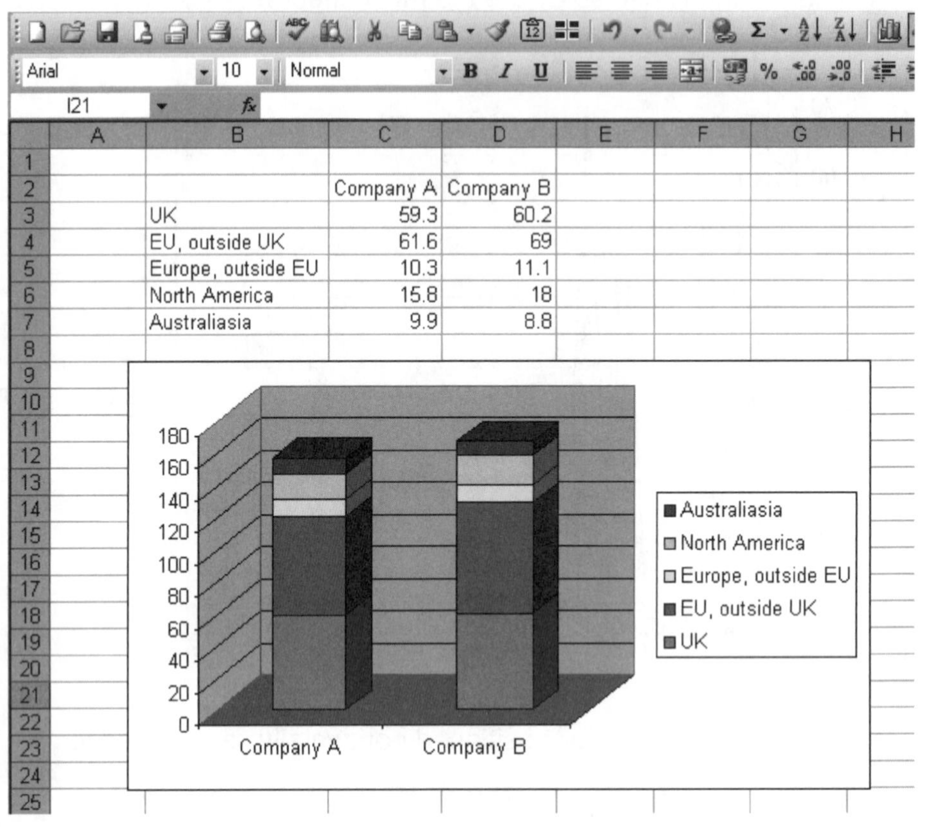

Chapter Summary

This chapter has considered some of the principal design elements that should be considered when embarking on the creation of any business model or plan, be it a financial statement, a budgetary control system, a marketing model or a forecast. A small plan has been used for demonstration purposes, and many of the techniques illustrated become essential when working with larger plans. Taking time to consider the layout and design of a system before embarking on its development has been proven by many users to pay considerable dividends in the long-term. In addition, it is worth talking with colleagues who might find a plan useful before starting development to see whether some additional lines need to be incorporated, as it is always more difficult to add to a spreadsheet later. As the use of information and communications technology has spread, being competent in the use of a spreadsheet has become a pre-requisite for being an efficient and effective management accountant.

Test Your Understanding 1

Which of the following is a major advantage of the use of computer spreadsheets in management accounting?

A Formulas are consistent in that they usually appear as numbers

B They can be printed and hard copies filed

C They can be used to record the cost coding structure

D What-if analysis can be carried out easily and quickly

Test Your Understanding 2

What is the effect of using brackets in a spreadsheet formula?

A Divisions and multiplications are calculated before additions and subtractions

B Additions and subtractions are calculated before divisions and multiplications

C The contents of the brackets are calculated first

D The contents of the brackets are calculated last

Test Your Understanding 3

Which of the following are reasons for formatting data in a spreadsheet?

- (1) To get data into the correct order for analysis
- (2) To make labels visually interesting
- (3) To make numbers more descriptive of what they represent
- (4) To make the data appear as plain text

A 1 and 3 only

B 2 and 3 only

C 2 and 4 only

D 1, 2 and 3

Test Your Understanding 4

Which of the following statements concerning spreadsheet cells are correct?

(1) A formula in a particular cell may determine numbers for several cells

(2) Clicking on a particular cell, and then entering a number or text, will enter data into that single cell

(3) Each cell can contain a number, a label or a formula

(4) Press Shift and Enter to select the cell below in the same column

A 1, 2 and 4

B 1, 3 and 4

C 2 and 3 only

D 3 and 4 only

Test your understanding answers

Test Your Understanding 1

D

Test Your Understanding 2

C

Note: when using functions in Excel, brackets are also used to contain the range of cells and/or argument.

Test Your Understanding 3

B

Test Your Understanding 4

C

chapter

10

Preparing for the Assessment

Chapter learning objectives

This chapter is intended for use when you are ready to start revising for your assessment. It contains:

- a summary of useful revision techniques
- details of the format of the assessment;
- a bank of examination-standard revision questions and suggested solutions.

1 Revision technique

Planning

The first thing to say about revision is that it is an addition to your initial studies, not a substitute for them. In other words, do not coast along early in your course in the hope of catching up during the revision phase. On the contrary, you should be studying and revising concurrently from the outset. At the end of each week, and at the end of each month, get into the habit of summarising the material you have covered to refresh your memory of it.

As with your initial studies, planning is important to maximise the value of your revision work. You need to balance the demands for study, professional work, family life and other commitments. To make this work, you will need to think carefully about how to make best use of your time.

Begin as before by comparing the estimated hours you will need to devote to revision with the hours available to you in the weeks leading up to the assessment. Prepare a written schedule setting out the areas you intend to cover during particular weeks, and break that down further into topics for each day's revision. To help focus on the key areas, try to establish which areas you are weakest on, so that you can concentrate on the topics where effort is particularly needed.

Do not forget the need for relaxation, and for family commitments. Sustained intellectual effort is only possible for limited periods, and must be broken up at intervals by lighter activities. And do not continue your revision timetable right up to the moment when you enter the exam hall: you should aim to stop work a day or even two days before the assessment. Beyond this point, the most you should attempt is an occasional brief look at your notes to refresh your memory.

Getting down to work

By the time you begin your revision you should already have settled into a fixed work pattern: a regular time of day for doing the work, a particular place where you sit, particular equipment that you assemble before you begin and so on. If this is not already a matter of routine for you, think carefully about it now in the last vital weeks before the assessment.

You should have notes summarising the main points of each topic you have covered. Begin each session by reading through the relevant notes and trying to commit the important points to memory.

Usually this will be just your starting point. Unless the area is one where you already feel very confident, you will need to track back from your notes to the relevant chapter(s) in the Study Text. This will refresh your memory on points not covered by your notes and fill in the detail that inevitably gets lost in the process of summarisation.

When you think you have understood and memorised the main principles and techniques, attempt an exam-standard question. At this stage of your studies you should normally be expecting to complete such questions in something close to the actual time allocation allowed in the assessment. After completing your effort, check the solution provided and add to your notes any extra points it reveals.

Tips for the final revision phase

As the assessment comes closer, consider the following list of techniques and make use of those that work for you:

- Summarise your notes into more concise form, perhaps on index cards that you can carry with you for revision on the way into work.
- Go through your notes with a highlighter pen, marking key concepts and definitions.
- Summarise the main points in a key area by producing a wordlist, mind map or other mnemonic device.
- On areas that you find difficult, rework questions that you have already attempted, and compare your answers in detail with those provided in the Study Text.
- Rework questions you attempted earlier in your studies with a view to completing them within the time limits.

2 Format of the assessment

Structures of the paper

The assessment for *Business Mathematics* is a two hours computer-based assessment comprising approximately 45 questions, with one or more parts. Single part questions are generally worth 2 marks each, but two and three part questions may be worth 4 or 6 marks. There will be no choice and all questions should be attempted if time permits. CIMA are continuously developing the question styles within the CBA system and you are advised to try the on-line website demo, to both gain familiarity with the assessment software and examine the latest style of questions being used.

Weighting of subjects

The current weightings for the syllabus sections are:

- Basic mathematics – 15%
- Probability – 15%
- Summarising and analysing data – 15%
- Inter-relationships between variables – 15%

- Forecasting – 15%
- Financial mathematics – 15%
- Spreadsheets – 10%.

In broad terms, the entire syllabus will be covered in each assessment. Please note that the weightings of the syllabus and of the assessment are not exactly reflected by the space allocated to the various topics in the book. Some subjects involve tables, graphs and charts that take up a lot of space but do not require specially large amounts of time or effort to study. In revision and in the assessment, the relative importance of the various topic areas is given by the percentages shown above and not by the space they occupy in this book.

Test Your Understanding 1

An item sells for $3.99 when it includes value added tax (VAT) at 17.5 per cent. Were VAT to be reduced to 15 per cent, what would the new selling price be, correct to the nearest penny?

A $3.79

B $4.08

C $3.91

D $3.40

Test Your Understanding 2

The number 2,490.742 is to be rounded. In each case write the correct answer in the space provided, to the accuracy specified.

A to two d.p.

B to one d.p.

C to the nearest whole number

D to the nearest 1,000

E to three s.f.

F to four s.f.

Test Your Understanding 3

The equation 20/(40 – Y) = 85/Y is to be solved to find Y correct to two decimal places. A solution comprises the following five lines, (A) – (E). In each case, identify whether the line follows correctly from the line immediately preceding it (regardless of whether or not you believe the preceding line to be correct).

A 20Y = 85(40 – Y)

B 20Y = 3,400 –Y

C 19Y = 3,400

D Y = 3,400/19

E Y = 178.94 (two d.p.).

Test Your Understanding 4

A chartered management accountant has established the cost of materials for a particular component as $20.00 to the nearest $1.

A Calculate the maximum absolute error in the cost.

B Calculate the maximum percentage error in the cost.

Test Your Understanding 5

A company has recently set up a mail-order operation to sell direct to the public. As an experiment, two different prices have been tried for a particular product, each for one week, with the following results:

Price per unit	$7	$9
Units sold per week	1050	950

Assuming that the relationship between price (P) and demand (D) is of the form $P = aD + b$, find the values of a and b.

Test Your Understanding 6

If price = 30 – 0.03*D* where D is demand, find an expression for revenue as a function of demand.

Test Your Understanding 7

If Revenue = $25D - 0.01D^2$ and Costs = $1500 + 4D + 0.03D^2$ find an expression for profit as a function of demand (D).

Test Your Understanding 8

Find the two levels of demand at which breakeven occurs, if

profit = $-2000 + 24D - 0.04D^2$.

Test Your Understanding 9

If Price = $30 - 0.03D$ and if breakeven occurs when D is 200 and 400, find the two prices at which breakeven occurs.

Presentation of data

Test Your Understanding 10

A quadratic function has a negative x-squared term, its graph cuts the x-axis at –1 and +3 and the y-axis at 30. Answer the following:

A Does it have a maximum or a minimum value?

B For what value of x does its maximum or minimum value occur?

C Substitute the correct numbers into the following calculation of the quadratic equation:

$y = k\,(? - x)\,(? + x)$
$y = k\,(? + ?x - x^2)$

When x = 0, y = ?k, so k must = ?

Test Your Understanding 11

If the following data is to be illustrated by means of a histogram and if the standard interval is taken to be 5 kg, complete the column showing heights of the bars of the histogram (to the nearest whole number):

Weight	*Frequency*	*Height of bar*
0–5	83	?
5–10	105	?
10–20	160	?
20–40	96	?
40–100	108	?

Test Your Understanding 12

The following data is to be illustrated by means of a pie chart. Complete the table showing the angles that correspond to each category (to the nearest whole number):

Categories	*%*	*Angle*
A	8	?
B	43	?
C	37	?
D	12	?

Test Your Understanding 13

A mail-order company has kept records of the value of orders received over a period. These are given in the following table:

Value of orders $	*Number of orders*
5 and under 15	36
15 and under 20	48
20 and under 25	53
25 and under 30	84
30 and under 35	126
35 and under 40	171
40 and under 45	155
45 and under 50	112
50 and under 55	70
55 and under 65	60
65 and under 85	54
	969

Complete the table, showing frequency densities with a standard interval width of 5 units, by filling in the appropriate numerical values in the spaces indicated by the letters.

Value of orders	*Frequency density*
5–15	A
15–20	B
20–25	...
25–30	...
30–35	...
35–40	...
40–45	...
45–50	...
50–55	...
55–65	C
65–85	D

Test Your Understanding 14

What information is provided by frequency densities?

A The points which must be plotted for an ogive.

B The heights of the bars in a histogram.

C The areas of the bars in a histogram.

D The area under a frequency polygon.

Scenario common to Questions 15–17

The data used for the charts in Questions 15-17 are UK trade balances in $ hundred millions spanning the years 1990–99 and broken down to show visible oil, visible non-oil and invisibles separately.

Balance of payments, 1990

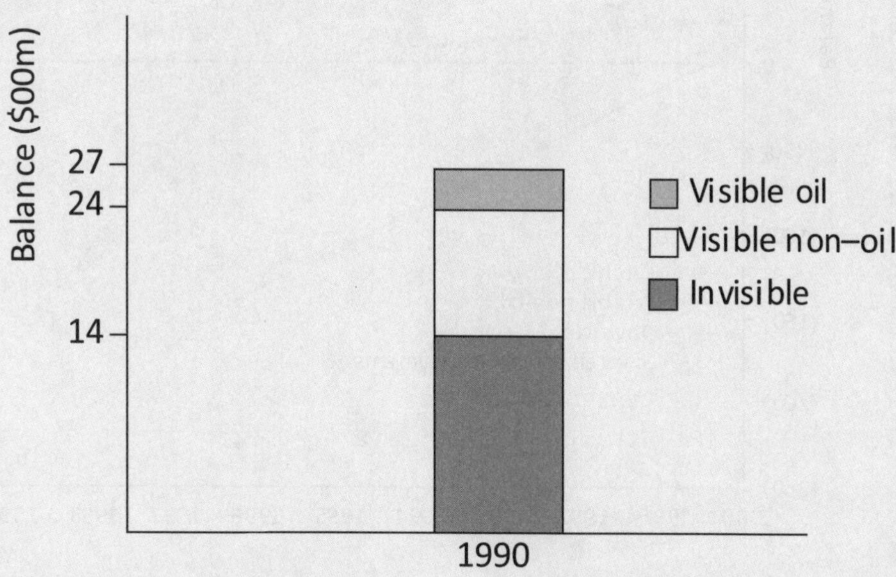

Test Your Understanding 15

What type of chart is shown in the scenario?

A Multiple bar chart

B Simple bar chart

C Component bar chart

D Pictogram.

Test Your Understanding 16

UK trade balances 1990-99

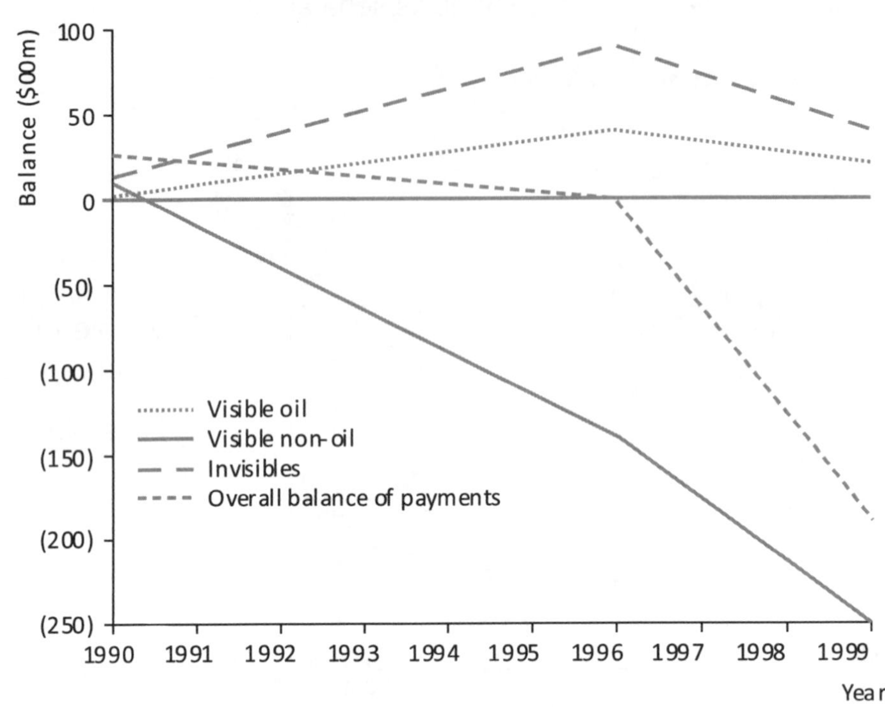

Which of the following statements can be correctly deduced from the above chart showing UK trade balances 1990–99?

A From 1990 onwards the overall balance of payments declined.

B Since 1990 the invisible balance has climbed steadily.

C By 1999 the balance on visible oil was greater than that on invisibles.

D By 1999 the deficit on visible non-oil was so great as to more than offset the two positive balances.

Descriptive statistics

Test Your Understanding 17

A group of people have the following weekly rents ($): 60, 130, 250, 200, 85, 75, 125, 225. Calculate the following, giving your answers correct to two d.p.:

A The mean

B The median.

Test Your Understanding 18

A distribution has $\Sigma f = 100$, $\Sigma fx = 550$ and $\Sigma fx^2 = 12{,}050$. Calculate the standard deviation, giving your answer to one d.p.

Test Your Understanding 19

The director of a medium-sized company has decided to analyse the salaries that are paid to staff. The frequency distribution of salaries that are currently being paid is as follows. Calculate the cumulative frequencies.

Salary $'000	*Number of staff*	*Cumulative frequency*
Under 10	16	–
10–under 20	28	–
20–under 30	36	–
30–under 40	20	–
40–under 50	12	–
50–under 70	4	–
70 and over	4	–

Test Your Understanding 20

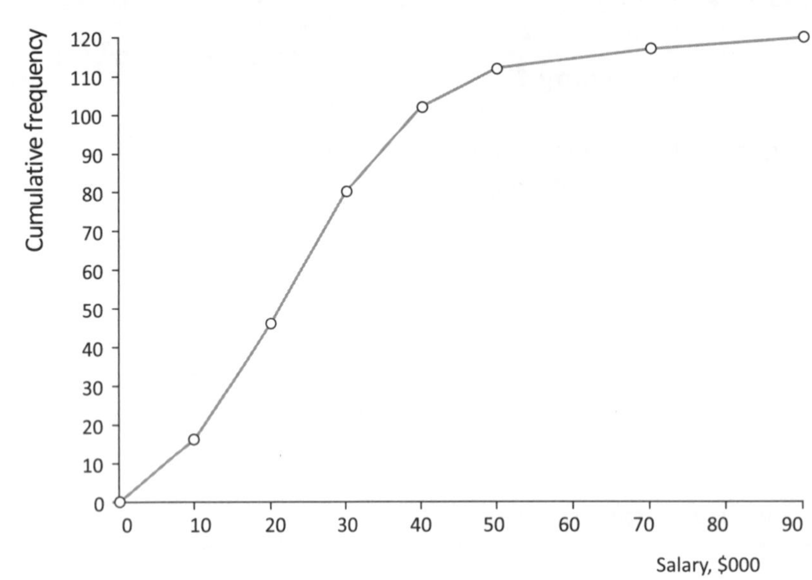

The ogive shows the salary distribution for 120 staff. From the ogive, calculate the median, giving your answer to the nearest $5,000.

Test Your Understanding 21

Given that $\Sigma f = 120$, $\Sigma fx = 3{,}140$ and $\Sigma fx^2 = 112{,}800$, calculate the following:

A the mean (to the nearest $)

B the standard deviation (to the nearest $100).

Test Your Understanding 22

If the mean and standard deviation salaries now and 5 years ago are as follows

	5 years ago	*Now*
Mean	$18,950	$25,000
Standard deviation	$10,600	$15,000

Which of the following statements is/are correct?

A The standard deviations show that salaries are now more variable than 5 years ago.

B The standard deviations show that the average salary has increased.

C The means show that the average salary has increased.

D The means show that variability in salaries has increased.

Test Your Understanding 23

The number of telephone support calls given each day during the last 64-day quarter, which is representative, is shown below in the table and the chart

Telephone support calls

Number of calls:	0-9	10-19	20-29	30-39	40-49	50-59	60-69	70+	Total
Frequency:	Nil	5	10	20	15	20	4	Nil	64

Number of telephone calls

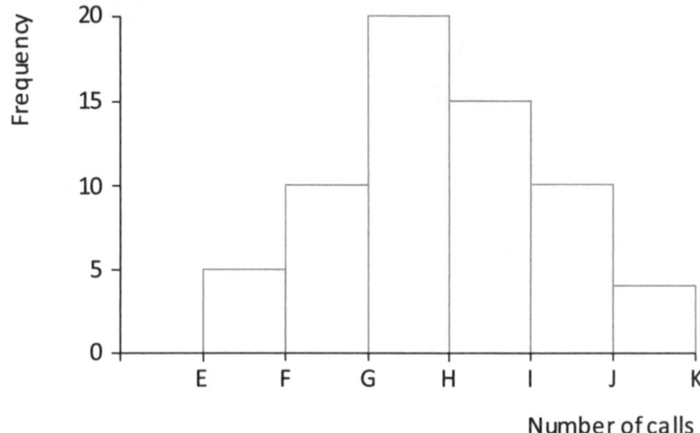

A What type of chart is being used?

(A) Bar chart
(B) Ogive
(C) Multiple bar chart
(D) Histogram

B What are the values represented by the letters E–K?

Test Your Understanding 24

If $\Sigma fx = 2{,}478$, $\Sigma f = 64$ and $\Sigma fx^2 = 106{,}906$, calculate the following:

A the mean (to two d.p.).

B the standard deviation (to one d.p.).

C the average daily cost of calls, to the nearest $, if the average call costs $20.

Index numbers

Test Your Understanding 25

In 2000, a retail price index was 178 with 1990 = 100. Convert a weekly wage of $400 back to 1990 constant prices, giving your answer correct to the nearest penny.

Test Your Understanding 26

Complete the following table which shows two index number series being spliced together to give a single series based in 1997. Give your answers correct to one d.p.

Year	*Price index (1991 = 100)*	*Price index (1997 = 100)*
1994	138	?
1995	142	?
1996	147	?
1997	150	100
	(1997 = 100)	
1998	109	109
1999	113	113
2000	119	119

Test Your Understanding 27

Complete the following table in which a chain-base index is being converted to one with fixed base 1997. Give your answers correct to one decimal place.

Year	*1997*	*1998*	*1999*	*2000*
Chain index	105.4	104.8	103.9	104.2
1997 = 100	100	?	?	?

Test Your Understanding 28

If a price index is 104, which of the following statements is/are correct about average prices?

A Prices have risen by 104 per cent.

B Prices are now 1.04 times their base year value.

C Prices have risen by 4 per cent.

D Prices have risen by 96 per cent.

Test Your Understanding 29

The following table shows data for gross domestic product (GDP), gross earnings and retail prices for the United Kingdom, 1980-89:

	GDP (market prices, $bn)	Ave. gross earnings (1985 = 100)	Retail prices (1985 = 100)
1980	231	65	71
1981	255	73	79
1982	278	80	86
1983	303	87	90
1984	323	92	94
1985	354	100	100
1986	379	108	103
1987	414	116	108
1988	430	126	113
1989	436	136	122

[Source: British Business, 1 Sept. 1989 and Economic Trends (various)]

A Complete the table expressing the GDP series as index numbers with 1985 = 100, by filling in the appropriate numerical values in the spaces indicated by the letters.
Answers should be rounded to one d.p.

Year	GDP 1985 = 100
80	A
81	...
82	...
83	...
84	...
85	100
86	...
87	...
89	B

B Calculate the index for average earnings at constant 1985 prices. Complete the table by filling in the appropriate numerical values in the spaces indicated by the letters.
Answers should be rounded to one d.p.:

Year	*Index at constant 1985 prices* *Average gross earnings*
80	C
81	...
82	...
83	...
84	...
85	100
86	...
87	D
89	...

Test Your Understanding 30

If an index of average gross earnings with base year 1995 and at constant 1995 prices is calculated to be 107 by 2000, which of the following is/are correct about changes in average gross earnings over this 5-year period?

A A total of 1.07 per cent more goods & services can be bought by average earnings.

B A total of 7 per cent more goods & services can be bought by average earnings.

C Earnings have risen by 1.07 per cent.

D The average price of goods & services has risen by 7 per cent.

Test Your Understanding 31

A manufacturer of domestic freezers has produced the following sales figures for the last six months:

	Last quarter 1997		*First quarter 1998*	
	Units sold	Sales value $000	*Units sold*	*Sales value* $000
Small	800	80	1,100	110
Medium	500	70	700	105
Large	200	40	300	60

[*Source*: Statlab Research, internal data]

A Calculate the index of total sales revenue for the first quarter of 1998, with base the last quarter of 1997. Give your answer to one d.p.

B It is possible that what the manufacturer wants is an index showing the quantity of freezers sold. Calculate an unweighted index of the number of units sold.

Test Your Understanding 32

The following table is to be used to calculate a relative index of quantity sold with base revenues as weights.

Items	Q_0	R_0	Q_1	R_0Q_1/Q_0
Small	800	80	1,100	110
Medium	500	70	700	98
Large	200	40	300	60
Totals	1,500	190	2,100	268

Calculate the relative index of quantity sold with base revenues as weights to one d.p.

Financial mathematics

Test Your Understanding 33

A building society adds interest monthly to accounts even though interest rates are expressed in annual terms. The current rate is stated as 4.8 per cent per annum. If an investor deposits $2,500 on 1 January, calculate the value of the account on 31 August, giving your answer correct to the nearest penny.

Test Your Understanding 34

A bond increases from $3,500 to $4,000 over 3 years. Complete the following calculation of the effective annual rate of interest:

- Three-year ratio = ?
- Annual ratio = ?
- Effective annual rate = ? per cent (giving your answer to one d.p.).

Test Your Understanding 35

Complete the following calculation of net present value (NPV) at a 5 per cent discount rate (working to the nearest whole number):

Time	*Cash flow*	*Discount factor*	*Present value*
	$	5%	$
0	(10,000)	1.000	?
1	4,000	?	?
2	5,000	?	?
3	4,000	?	?
			–
NPV			?
			–

Test Your Understanding 36

All answers should be given correct to two d.p.

An amount of $500 was invested at the start of each of 60 consecutive months. Compound interest at a nominal annual rate of 12 per cent is payable.

A If interest is compounded annually, what will be the value of the first year's $6,000 by the end of the 5-year period?

B If interest is compounded annually, what total sum will have accumulated after five complete years?

C If interest is compounded monthly, what total sum will have accumulated after five complete years?

Test Your Understanding 37

A 25-year mortgage of $50,000 is to be repaid by 100 equal quarterly payments in arrears. Interest at a nominal annual rate of 16 per cent is charged each quarter on the outstanding part of the debt.

Note: The discount factor for annuities of $1 over t years interest rate, r, is:

$$\frac{1}{r} - \frac{1}{r\,(1 + r)^t}$$

A Viewing the repayments as an annuity of $A running for 100 quarters at 4 per cent per quarter, use the formula for the present value of an annuity to calculate the present value of the repayments as a function of $A.

B How much are the quarterly repayments?

C What is the effective annual rate of interest?

Test Your Understanding 38

The building services department of a hospital has estimated that the maintenance costs over the next 8 years (payable at the beginning of each year) for an existing air conditioner will be as follows:

Year	*Estimated cost* $	*Year*	*Estimated cost* $
1	3,000	5	4,000
2	3,500	6	4,500
3	4,000	7	5,000
4	12,000	8	13,000

A Given that the discount factor is 6 per cent, complete the following table by filling in the appropriate numerical values in the spaces indicated by the letters.

Beginning of year	*Discount factor*	*cash flow*	*Discounted cash flow*
1	...	3,000	B
2	A	3,500	...
3	...	4,000	C
4	...	12,000	...
5	...	4,000	...
6	...	4,500	...
7	...	5,000	...
8	...	13,000	...
Total			

Test Your Understanding 39

A company will carry out its own maintenance of a new boiler with a life of 7 years estimated at $10,000 per annum now, rising at 5 per cent per annum with a major overhaul at the end of year 4 costing an additional $25,000.

The discount rate is 10 per cent, and all payments are assumed to be made at year ends.

Complete the following table (showing the annual maintenance costs and corresponding present values) by filling in the appropriate numerical values in the spaces indicated by the letters A–E. Throughout this question you should work to the nearest $.

Year	*Annual cost*	*Discount factor*	*Present*
1	A	...	
2	...	C	
3	...	...	D
4	25,000 + B	...	
5	...	...	E
6	...	...	
7	...	...	

Test Your Understanding 40

A boiler supplier offers a 7-year contract with an annual charge of \$13,000 at each year end. If the discount rate is 10 per cent, calculate the present value of the contract, giving your answer to the nearest \$.

Test Your Understanding 41

Given two projects of which you know the net present values and ignoring all other factors, which project would you select?

A The one with the larger net present value.

B The one with the smaller net present value.

C Present value is not relevant to such a decision.

Test Your Understanding 42

In exactly 3 years from now, a company will have to replace capital equipment that will then cost \$0.5 m. The managers have decided to set up a reserve fund into which twelve equal sums will be put at quarterly intervals, with the first being made now. The rate of compound interest is 2 per cent per quarter.

A If the quarterly sum invested is \$A, find an expression for the final value of the fund as a function of A. Do not attempt to simplify it.

B Use the formula for the sum of a geometric progression to evaluate the expression $1.035 + 1.035^2 + 1.035^3 + \ldots + 1.035^{10}$. You should work to four d.p

Test Your Understanding 43

A fixed-interest, 10-year \$100,000 mortgage is to be repaid by 40 equal quarterly payments in arrears. Interest is charged at 3 per cent per quarter on the outstanding part of the debt.

A Viewing the mortgage as an annuity, use the PV of an annuity formula to calculate its present value as a function of the quarterly repayment \$B. You should work to four d.p.

B If the present value calculated in (a) was 24B, calculate the value of B to two d.p.

Test Your Understanding 44

Find the effective annual rate of interest to two d.p. if interest is charged at 3 per cent per quarter.

Test Your Understanding 45

A company is considering the purchase of one of two machines, A or B, for $180,000. The terms of payment for each machine are $90,000 on delivery and $90,000 a year later. The machines are expected to produce year-end net cash flows as follows:

Net cash flows ($000)	*End of year*				
	1	2	3	4	5
Machine A	60	50	40	30	20
Machine B	40	40	40	40	40

At the end of year 5, either machine would be sold for $20,000. The annual cost of capital is 9 per cent for each year.

(a) Complete the following table, to obtain the net present value for machine A, by filling in the appropriate numerical values in the spaces indicated by the letters. Give present values to two d.p.

Year	*Net cash inflow ($000)*	*Discount factor*	*Present value ($000)*
0	C	F	...
1	D	...	...
2	...	...	G
3	...	...	...
4	...	...	...
5	E	...	...
NPV			2.71

(b) Complete the following table, to obtain the net present value for machine B, by filling in the appropriate numerical values in the spaces indicated by the letters. Give present values to two d.p.

Year	*Net cash inflow* *($000)*	*Discount factor*	*Present value* *($000)*
0	...	...	...
1	H	...	...
2	...	...	J
3	...	...	...
4	...	...	...
5	I	...	...
NPV			3.97

(c) Which machine should be purchased?

Correlation and regression

Test Your Understanding 46

You are working with a marketing colleague, trying to establish the relationship, if any, between expenditure on local newspaper advertising and sales revenue of restaurants. The annual data for a random sample of ten restaurants are as follows:

Restaurant code	*Expenditure ($000) on advertising, A*	*Sales, S ($000)*
B	1.0	55
C	1.5	55
D	1.0	45
E	2.0	50
F	2.0	65
G	2.5	60
H	2.5	55
I	3.0	70
J	3.5	65
K	4.0	80
	$\Sigma(A) = 23$	$\Sigma(S) = 600$
$\Sigma(AS) = 1457.5$	$\Sigma(A^2) = 62$	$\Sigma(S^2) = 36,950$

A Calculate the regression coefficient 'b' for the regression line of sales on advertising, giving your answer to three d.p.

B If the value of 'b' was 8.691, calculate the regression coefficient 'a' for the regression line of sales on advertising, giving your answer to two d.p.

C Calculate the correlation coefficient (r) between sales and advertising, giving your-answer correct to two d.p.

Test Your Understanding 47

If data comprising 10 pairs of corresponding ranks has $d^2 = 304.5$ where d represents the difference between corresponding ranks, calculate Spearman's rank correlation coefficient, giving your answer correct to three d.p.

Test Your Understanding 48

If the rank correlation coefficient between variables X and Y is 0.85, which of the following comments is/are correct?

A Values of Y increase as values of X increase

B Y decreases by 0.15 for every increase of 1 in X

C Y increases by 0.85 for every increase of 1 in X

D The link between X and Y values is very strong

E The link between X and Y values is linear

F Increases in X causes corresponding increases in Y.

Test Your Understanding 49

Over a period of 10 months a factory's monthly production costs [Y, $000] range from 5 to 16 whilst output [X, units] ranges from 50 to 500. If the regression equation is
Y = 5.0913 + 0.2119X.

A Which of the following statements is/are correct?

(A) When X increases by 1, Y increases by 0.2119
(B) Fixed costs are $5.0913
(C) When X = 0, Y = 5.11249
(D) Fixed costs are $5,091.3
(E) Fixed costs are $211.9
(F) Variable cost is $0.2119 per unit
(G) Variable cost is $5.0913 per unit

B If the planned output for the next month is 300 units, estimate production costs, giving your answer to the nearest $.

Test Your Understanding 50

If the coefficient of determination between output and production costs over a number of months is 89 per cent, which of the following comments is/are correct?

A Eighty-nine per cent of the variation in production costs from one month to the next can be explained by corresponding variation in output.

B Costs increase as output increases.

C The linear relationship between output and costs is very strong.

D An increase of 100 per cent in output is associated with an increase of 89 per cent in costs.

Test Your Understanding 51

A standard regression equation Y = a + *b*X is to be used for making estimates. Which of the following is/are correct?

A Y can be estimated if X is known.

B X can be estimated if Y is known.

Test Your Understanding 52

If the correlation coefficient is 0.95, what is the coefficient of determination?

A –0.95

B 0.475

C 0.9025

D 0.9747

Test Your Understanding 53

If n = 10, $\Sigma x = 8$, $\Sigma y = 650$, $\Sigma xy = 525$, $\Sigma x^2 = 18$ and $\Sigma y^2 = 43{,}000$, calculate the product moment correlation coefficient, giving your answer correct to three d.p

Test Your Understanding 54

The regression equation Y = 45 + 3.6X has been obtained from 25 pairs of X- and Y-values, with the X-values ranging from 50 to 150. Which of the following is/are correct?

A When X = 0, Y is estimated to be 12.5.

B Y increases by 45 whenever X increases by 1.

C The equation cannot produce reliable estimates of Y if X is less than 50.

D The product moment correlation coefficient is 3.6.

Time series

Test Your Understanding 55

The actual value at a certain point is 1,500 and the seasonal factor is 1.17. Using the multiplicative model, the seasonally adjusted figure (to the nearest whole number) is:

A 1,501

B 1,755

C 1,282

D 1,499

Test Your Understanding 56

In the multiplicative model A = T × S × R, which of the following is/are correct?

A S is estimated by averaging A – T values for the particular season.

B T may be estimated by a moving average.

C T may be estimated from an appropriate regression equation.

D R is estimated from A/T.

E The seasonally adjusted value is given by A – S.

Test Your Understanding 57

If the trend is estimated to be 2,308 for a quarter with a seasonal component of 1.06, estimate the actual value using the multiplicative model and giving your answer correct to four significant figures.

Test Your Understanding 58

The managers of a company are preparing revenue plans for the last quarter of 1993–94, and for the first three quarters of 1994–95.

A The table below is being used for part of the calculations to obtain a centred four-point moving average trend.

Year	*Qtr*	*Actual revenue*	*Sum of 4 qtrs*	*Sum of 8 qtrs*	*Trend*	*Actual/Trend*
90/91	1	49				
	2	37				
			A			
	3	58		C	D	
			B			
	4	67			53.125	E
91/92	1	50				
	2	38				
	3	59				
	4	68				

Calculate the values in the spaces denoted by the letters, giving your answers correct to three d.p. where appropriate.

Test Your Understanding 59

In a time series showing sales in $000, the quarterly values of actual sales divided by trend in sales are as follows:

Year	*Quarter*	*Actual/trend*
2000	1	0.937
	2	0.709
	3	1.095
	4	1.253
2001	1	0.934
	2	0.727
	3	1.088
	4	1.267

Calculate the average seasonal ratios correct to four d.p. using the multiplicative method. Do not adjust the ratios to make them total four.

Test Your Understanding 60

Adjust the following average seasonal ratios so that they total 4.

1st quarter	0.8
2nd quarter	0.6
3rd quarter	1.0
4th quarter	1.2

Test Your Understanding 61

Annual sales of Brand Y over an 11-year period were as follows:

Unit sales, Brand Y: 1983-93 ('000)

1983	1984	1985	1986	1987	1988	1989	1990	1991	1992	1993
50	59	46	54	65	51	60	70	56	66	76

Complete the following table by filling in appropriate numerical values in the spaces indicated by letters in order to find the 3-year moving average trend in sales. Each answer should be correct to one d.p.

Year	*Sales ('000)*	*Three-year moving total*	*Trend*
1983	50		
1984	59	A	...
1985	46	...	C
1986	54	...	...
1987	65	...	...
1988	51	...	B
1989	60	...	
1990	70	...	...
1991	56	...	...
1992	66		...
1993	76		

Test Your Understanding 62

Suppose the actual minus trend values in a time series analysis with a 3-year cycle are as follows:

1990	1991	1992	1993	1994	1995	1996	1997	1998
7.3	–7	–1	8.3	–7.7	–0.3	8	–8	0

Designating 1990 as year 1 of a cycle, calculate the cyclical components for the 3 years of the cycle, using an additive model and giving your answers correct to the nearest whole number.

Test Your Understanding 63

In data with a 4-year cycle, the cyclical components using the additive model are given to be:

Year 1	Year 2	Year 3	Year 4
10	15	25	220

If 2000 is year 1 of a cycle and if the trend for 2004 is predicted to be 70, predict the actual value for 2004.

Test Your Understanding 64

What is the formula for seasonally adjusted data in a multiplicative model? Use the symbols A for actual value, T for trend, S for seasonal component and R for residual.

Test Your Understanding 65

Which of the following correctly describes the purpose of seasonal adjustment?

A It adjusts the trend to give an estimate of the actual value.

B It adjusts the seasonal components to add to zero in an additive model.

C It adjusts the actual value to give an estimate of the trend.

Test Your Understanding 66

The quarterly sales of Brand X for a 2-year period are given below:

	Q1	Q2	Q3	Q4
1997	45	66	79	40
1998	64	99	105	60
1999	90			

Past experience has shown that the average seasonal variations for this product field are as follows:

Q1	Q2	Q3	Q4
–10%	+20%	+30%	–40%

A multiplicative model is assumed to apply: Sales = Trend × Seasonal × Residual.

A Seasonally adjust the sales of brand X for the four quarters of 1997, giving your answers to one d.p.

B Which of the following correctly describes the seasonal variation shown above for the 3rd quarter?

- A Actual sales are 30 per cent above the trend.
- B The trend is 30 per cent above the actual sales.
- C Actual sales are 30 per cent more than the annual average.
- D The trend is 30 per cent more than that of the previous quarter.

Probability

Test Your Understanding 67

A sales representative calls on three unrelated customers. There is an 80 per cent chance of making a sale at any one of them. The probability of making exactly two sales is:

- A 0.128
- B 0.64
- C 1.92
- D 0.384

Test Your Understanding 68

A project may result in the following profits with the probabilities stated.

Profit	*Probability*
$40,000	0.32
$35,000	0.54
($12,000)	0.14

Calculate the expected profit.

Test Your Understanding 69

A variable X is normally distributed with mean 45 kg and standard deviation 5 kg. Find the following probabilities:

A P(X > 50)

B P(X < 58)

C P(38 < X < 54)

Test Your Understanding 70

A porcelain manufacturer has three assembly lines (X, Y and Z) producing decorative plates. An inspector samples finished plates from the assembly lines in the ratio 1:2:3 respectively. During a shift the inspector examines 240 plates. Calculate how many plates the inspector examines per shift from each assembly line.

Test Your Understanding 71

During a shift an inspector examines 50, 100 and 150 items from three production lines X, Y and Z respectively. Analysis of past inspection records suggests that the defective rates from the assembly lines are:

X	*Y*	*Z*
8%	10%	30%

Complete the following table by filling in the appropriate numerical values in the spaces indicated by the letters:

	X	*Y*	*Z*	*Total*
Good	...	...	...	C
Defective	A	B	...	...
Total	50	100	150	300

Test Your Understanding 72

In a typical shift, the numbers of good or defective items examined from three production lines (X, Y and Z) are as follows:

	X	*Y*	*Z*	*Totals*
Good	45	70	120	235
Defective	5	25	45	75
Totals	50	95	165	310

A Calculate the probability that a plate sampled is defective, giving your answer to three d.p.

B Calculate the probability that a plate sampled comes from Assembly line Z, given that it is defective, giving your answer to three d.p.

Test Your Understanding 73

A travel agent keeps a stock of holiday brochures. Currently there is a total of 500 brochures in stock, as follows: 285 for European holidays, 90 for American holidays, 110 for Asian holidays and 15 for African holidays. A brochure is selected at random. Calculate the following probabilities (to two d.p.):

A that a European brochure is selected

B that an African brochure is not selected

C that neither an American nor an Asian brochure is selected

D that either a European or an Asian brochure is selected.

Test Your Understanding 74

What is meant by 'mutually exclusive events'?

A Events which can only occur together

B Events for which the occurrence of one has no effect on the probability of the occurrence of the other

C Events which cannot occur together

D Events for which the occurrence of one makes the probability of the occurrence of the other equal zero.

Test Your Understanding 75

A die is rolled twice and first shows a 3 and then a 5. Are these two events

A Independent

B Mutually exclusive

C Neither?

Test Your Understanding 76

A travel agent decides to use expected profits as an aid to deciding which holidays to offer. Which of the following statements about the use of expected profits is/are correct?

A Options are selected on the basis of how high their expected profits are

B An advantage of the method is that it takes no account of subjective factors such as attitude to risk

C A disadvantage of the method is that it fails to take account of the probabilities of various outcomes

D A disadvantage of the method is that it requires substantial prediction of profits and probabilities.

Test Your Understanding 77

In a forthcoming sales promotion each box of chocolates is to contain a leaflet with eight 'scratch-off square patches, randomly arranged. The purchaser will scratch off one patch to reveal the value of a small prize. The value of the eight patches on the leaflet is to be as follows:

Value of prize	*$0.20*	*$0.50*	*$1*
Number of patches	5	2	1

A The company has to decide on the number of packs in which to put leaflets, given a budget of $75,000. Calculate the average value of prizes per leaflet, giving your answer to three d.p.

B If the mean cost per leaflet were 40 cents, calculate the number of leaflets that would on average be appropriate to a budget of $75,000.

Test Your Understanding 78

In a local town lottery, a scratchcard pictures a roulette wheel with thirty-seven numbers, seven of which are randomly arranged winning numbers. The purchaser is allowed to scratch off seven of the thirty-seven numbers in the hope of winning a prize. It is therefore possible to select 0, 1, 2, 3, 4, 5, 6 or 7 winning numbers on each leaflet.

A What is the probability, to three d.p., that the first number scratched does not win a prize?

B What is the probability, to four d.p., that all seven numbers scratched do not win prizes?

C If there are one million purchases during the promotion and if the probability that all seven numbers do not win a prize were 0.2, what is the expected number of purchasers who will win no prizes at all?

Test Your Understanding 79

The specification for the length of an engine part is a minimum of 99 mm and a maximum of 104.4 mm. A batch of parts is produced that is normally distributed with a mean of 102 mm and a standard deviation of 2 mm.

A Calculate the percentage of undersized parts.

B Calculate the percentage of oversized parts.

Test Your Understanding 80

If 7 per cent of parts are defective, calculate the average number of parts that must be produced in order to obtain 1,000 usable parts, giving your answer to the nearest whole number.

Test Your Understanding 81

A golf club has to decide how many programmes to produce for a charity golf tournament. The best quotation from a local printer is $2,000 plus 10p per copy. Advertising revenue totals $1,500. Programmes are sold for 60p each. Unsold programmes are worthless. Throughout this question, work to the nearest $

A Complete the table showing the cost of producing various numbers of leaflets by filling in appropriate numerical values in the spaces indicated by letters:

Number produced	*Cost ($)*
1,000	A
2,000	B
3,000	...
4,000	...
5,000	C

B Complete the table showing the revenue from selling various numbers of leaflets by filling in appropriate numerical values in the spaces indicated by letters:

Number sold	*Revenue ($)*
1,000	...
2,000	...
3,000	D
4,000	E
5,000	F

Test Your Understanding 82

Suppose the profit table at various production and sales levels and the probabilities of the various levels of demand were as follows:

Profit table ($)

Demand (probability)	*Production levels*				
	1,000	2,000	3,000	4,000	5,000
1,000 (p = 0.1)	0	(100)	(200)	(300)	(400)
2,000 (p = 0.4)	0	500	400	300	200
3,000 (p = 0.2)	0	500	1,000	900	800
4,000 (p = 0.2)	0	500	1,000	1,500	1,400
5,000 (p = 0.1)	0	500	1,000	1,500	2,000

Calculate the expected profit resulting from each production level.

Test Your Understanding 83

A company manufactures automatic vending machines. One of the simplest machines is operated by a $1 coin. Inside the machine, a photoelectric cell is used to assess whether a coin is genuine or counterfeit by measuring the time (t) it takes to roll a fixed distance down a slope. Since coins and machines vary a little in size and wear, there is some small variation in time t.

From extensive testing it has been found that the time t taken by genuine $1 coins follows a normal distribution with a mean of 300 units of time and a standard deviation of 20.

For commonly used counterfeit coins the tests revealed a normally distributed time with a mean of 150 units of time and a standard deviation of 50.

The manufacturer sets the limits of acceptability at a minimum of 260 units of time.

A Calculate the percentage of counterfeit coins that take more than 260 units of time.

B Calculate the percentage of genuine coins taking less than 260 time units.

C Find the value N such that the probability $P(z < N) = 0.01$, where z is the standard normal variable. Give your answer to two d.p.

Test Your Understanding 84

A Solve for y where
$8x + 4y \geq 100$

B Solve for y where
$-10x + 20y \leq -80$.

Test Your Understanding 85

The probability that a student speaks French fluently is 0.20. The probability that a student speaks Greek is 0.10. The probability that a student speaks neither languages is 0.75.

Using Venn Diagrams calculate the probability that a student speaks both.

Spreadsheet skills using Excel

Test Your Understanding 86

Write down the formula required to perform the following calculations.

A A group of 8 people share the cost of a birthday celebration for 34 friends. The price of the meal per person is $25 plus $6 for wine and $4 for coffee. Calculate the amount each of the 8 will need to pay – enter all the variables into your calculation and use only one Excel cell.

B The cost per head of new football shirt and shorts for the village team is $25 plus $6 for socks, and $10 for the goalkeeper's gloves. How much will it cost to kit out the full team of 11 players? Enter all the variables into your calculation and use only one Excel cell.

C Perform these calculations to the specified number of decimal places
= 34/5 × 6.37(to 2 d.p)
= 1126 × 14.2^2 (to nearest whole number)
= (199 + 45) × 1.177 + 78.43 (to 1 d.p).

Test Your Understanding 87

A Given the following spreadsheet give the formula that would be required in cell B4 through B8 to calculate the compound interest rate.

	A	B	C	D	E
1	Investment amount	2000			
2	Interest rate	10%			
3					
4	Year no.	1			
5		2			
6		3			
7		4			
8		5			
9					
10					

B Given that the cost of buying boxes of your favourite breakfast cereal from a supermarket website is $3.45 per box for 1 to 10 units and that there is a discount if 7.5 per cent for purchases of more than 10 units calculate the cost of 15 units. There is also a delivery charge of $5.99. Enter the Excel formula for calculating the cost of 15 boxes.

Test Your Understanding 88

Given the data in the spreadsheet below, show the linear regression formula required in cell C2 to forecast the sale of drinks at a given temperature.

	A	B	C	D
1	Temperature	Litre of cold drinks sold		
2	15	120		
3	17	125		
4	19	125		
5	15	120		
6	21	130		
7	25	130		
8	22	125		
9	19	125		
10	18	100		
11	20	115		
12				
13				

Test Your Understanding 89

State three important principles of spreadsheet design.

Test your understanding answers

Test Your Understanding 1

C

The selling price without VAT would be \$3.99 × 100/117.5 = 3.395745. Hence the price with 15 per cent VAT would be 3.395745 × 1.15 = \$3.91.

(A) is incorrect because the price has been reduced by 17.5 per cent prior to increasing by 15 per cent. (B) cannot be correct because it shows an increase – it results from getting the 17.5 per cent and 15 per cent interchanged. (D) is the price with no VAT at all.

Test Your Understanding 2

A	To two d.p.	2,490.74
B	To one d.p.	2,490.7
C	To the nearest whole number	2,491
D	To the nearest 1,000	2,000
E	To three s.f.	2,490
F	To four s.f.	2,491

Test Your Understanding 3

A	20Y = 85(40 – Y)	Correct.
B	20Y = 3,400 – Y	Incorrect: the Y should also have been multiplied by 85.
C	19Y = 3,400	Incorrect: the –Y should become +Y when taken across to the other side of the equation.
D	Y = 3,400/19	Correct.
E	Y = 178.94 (two d.p.)	Incorrect: 178.947 rounds to 178.95.

Test Your Understanding 4

A Working to the nearest \$, the maximum possible difference between the true figure and the rounded figure is 50 cents.

B The maximum absolute error as a percentage of the rounded figure $= 100 \times 0.5/20 = 2.5$ per cent.

Test Your Understanding 5

a = –0.02; b = 28

If $P = aD + b$

where $P = 7$, $D = 1{,}050$ so $7 = 1{,}050a + b$ (1)

where $P = 9$, $D = 950$ so $9 = 950a + b$ (2)

(2) minus (1) gives $2 = -100a$, so $a = -0.02$

substituting into (1) gives $7 = -0.02 \times 1{,}050 + b$, so $b = 7 + 21 = 28$

hence $P = 28 - 0.02D$

Test Your Understanding 6

Revenue = Price × Demand

$= (30 - 0.03D)D$

$= 30D - 0.03D^2$

Test Your Understanding 7

Profit = Revenue-Costs

$= (25D - 0.01D^2) - (1{,}500 + 4D + 0.03D^2)$

$= -1{,}500 + 21D - 0.04D^2$

Test Your Understanding 8

Breakeven occurs where profit = 0

The solution is given by

$$D = \frac{-b \pm \sqrt{b^2 \pm 4ac}}{2a}$$

where a = –0.04, b = 24, c = –2000

$$D = \frac{-24 \pm \sqrt{576 - 320}}{-0.08} = \frac{-24 \pm 16}{-0.08}$$
$$= 500 \text{ or } 100$$

Test Your Understanding 9

The corresponding prices are

$P = 30 - 0.03 \times 200 = \$24$
or $P = 30 - 0.03 \times 400 = \$18$

Test Your Understanding 10

A Maximum

B Given the quadratic is symmetrical, the maximum or minimum will be half way between the two points where the graph cuts the x-axis.
$x = (1 + 3)/2 = 2$

C $y = k(3 - x)(1 + x)$
$y = k(3 + 2x - x^2)$
When x = 0, y = 3k = 30, so k = 10

Test Your Understanding 11

Weight	*Frequency*	*Height of bar*
0–5	83	83
5–10	105	105
10–20	160	80
20–40	96	24
40–100	108	9

Test Your Understanding 12

Categories	*%*	*Angle*
A	8	29
B	43	155
C	37	133
D	12	43

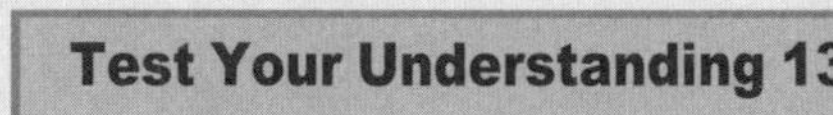

Test Your Understanding 13

Value of orders $	*Frequency*	*Interval width*	*Freq. density*
5–15	36	10	18
15–20	48	5	48
20–25	53	5	53
25–30	84	5	84
30–35	126	5	126
35–40	171	5	171
40–45	155	5	155
45–50	112	5	112
50–55	70	5	70
55–65	60	10	30
65–85	54	20	13.5

Test Your Understanding 14

B

The heights of the bars in a histogram.

Test Your Understanding 15

C

Component bar chart.

Test Your Understanding 16

A and D

The invisible balance peaked in 1996 and then fell, so it has not climbed steadily. Also by 1999 the balance on visible oil was not greater than that on invisibles. The other statements are correct

Test Your Understanding 17

A The mean = 1,150/8 = 143.75
Putting the data into order of magnitude: 60, 75, 85, 125, 130, 200, 225, 250

B The median = (125 + 130)/2 = 127.5

Test Your Understanding 18

Standard deviation = 9.5

$$\text{as } s = \sqrt{\frac{\Sigma fx^2}{\Sigma f} - \left(\frac{\Sigma fx}{\Sigma f}\right)^2}$$

$$= \sqrt{\frac{12{,}050}{100} - \left(\frac{550}{100}\right)^2}$$

$$= 9.5$$

Test Your Understanding 19

Salary ($000)	*Frequency*	*Cumulative frequency*
Under 10	16	16
10–under 20	28	44
20–under 30	36	80
30–under 40	20	100
40–under 50	12	112
50–under 70	4	116
70 and over	4	120

Test Your Understanding 20

Ogive of salaries

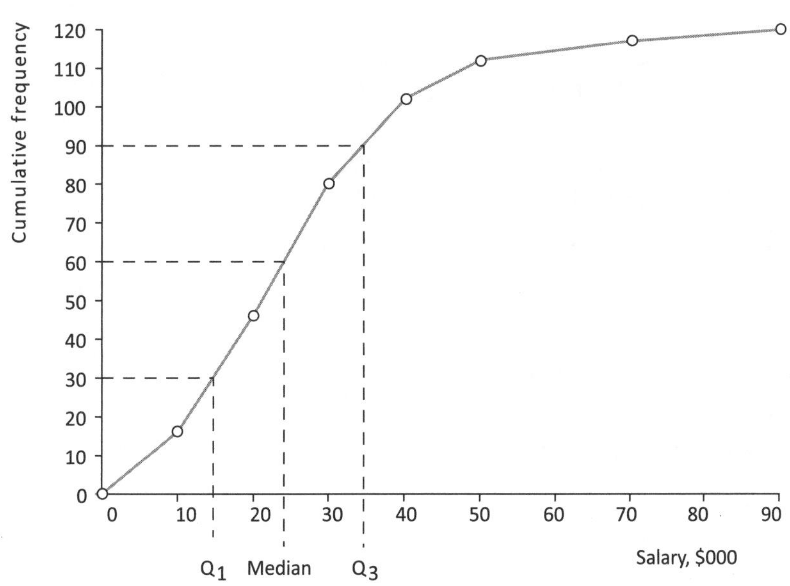

Cumulative frequency of median = $\dfrac{120}{2} = 60$

From ogive, median = $24,000

Test Your Understanding 21

$$\bar{x} = \frac{3,140}{120} = 26,167$$

The mean salary is \$26,167

$$s = \sqrt{\frac{112,800}{120} - \left(\frac{3,140}{120}\right)^2} = 15,978$$

The standard deviation of salary is \$15,978

Answers:
A \$26,167
B \$16,000

Test Your Understanding 22

Both the mean and the standard deviation have increased. The mean measures the average level whilst the standard deviation measures variability so statements (A) and (C) are correct.

Test Your Understanding 23

Number of telephone calls

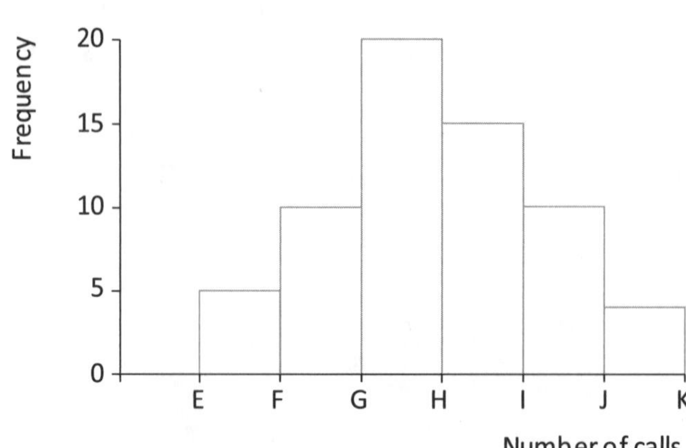

A The chart is a histogram
Answer: (D)

B (E) 9.5
(F) 19.5
(G) 29.5
(H) 39.5
(I) 49.5
(J) 59.5
(K) 69.5

Test Your Understanding 24

The mean number of calls is:

$$\frac{\sum fx}{\sum f} = \frac{2,478}{64} = 38.72 \text{ calls}$$

The standard deviation, s, is given by:

$$s^2 = \frac{\sum fx^2}{\sum f} - \overline{x}^2 = \frac{106,906}{64} - 38.72^2 = 171.17$$

hence, s = 13.08 calls = 13.1 calls (to one d.p.).
Average daily cost is \$20 × 38.72 = 774.4.

Answers:

A 38.72

B 13.1

C 774

Test Your Understanding 25

400 × 100/178 = \$224.72

Test Your Understanding 26

Year	Price index (1991 = 100)	Price index (1997 = 100)
1994	138	92
1995	142	94.7
1996	147	98
1997	150	100
	(1997 = 100)	
1998	109	109
1999	113	113
2000	119	119

Test Your Understanding 27

Year	1997	1998	1999	2000
Chain index	105.4	104.8	103.9	104.2
1997 = 100	100.0	104.8	108.9	113.5

Test Your Understanding 28

B and C

An index of 104 means that prices have risen by 4 per cent, which in turn means that current values are 1.04 times their values in the base year, on average.

Test Your Understanding 29

C = 91.5, D = 108.3

A GDP index (1985 = 100)

1980 $\frac{231}{354} \times 100 = 65.3 = A$

1989 $\frac{436}{354} \times 100 = 123.2 = B$

B C = 65 × 100/71 = 91.5
D = 106/108 = 107.4

Test Your Understanding 30

B

If an index of average gross earnings with base year 1995 and at constant 1995 prices is calculated to be 107 by 2000, it means that 7 per cent more goods and services can be bought by average earnings over a 5 year period.

Test Your Understanding 31

A Index comparing total revenues

$= 100 \times \Sigma R_1 / \Sigma R_0$
$= 100 \times 275/190$
$= 144.7$

B Unweighted index of numbers sold = 100 × 2,100/1,500 = 140

Test Your Understanding 32

Relative index of quantity sold with base revenues as weights

$= 100 \times (\Sigma R_0 Q_1/Q_2) \div \Sigma R_0$
$= 100 \times 268/190$
$= 141.1$

Test Your Understanding 33

$2,500 \times 1.004^8 = 2,581.13$

Test Your Understanding 34

- Three-year ratio = 4,000/3,500 = 1.142857
- Annual ratio = 1.0455
- Effective annual rate = 4.6 per cent

Test Your Understanding 35

Time	*Cash flow* $	*Discount factor* 5%	*Present value* $
0	(10,000)	1.000	(10,000)
1	4,000	0.952	3,808
2	5,000	0.907	4,535
3	4,000	0.864	3,456
NPV			(1,799)

Test Your Understanding 36

A If interest is compounded annually with $6,000 being invested per year, the first year's $6,000 will be invested for four years and will grow to $6,000 \times 1.12^4$.

Answer: 9,441.12

B The second year's $6,000 will grow to 6,000 × 1.123 and so on to the fifth year's $6,000, which will not have grown at all.

$$Total = 6,000(1.12^4 + 1.12^3 + 1.12^2 + 1.12 + 1) = \$38,117.08$$

C If interest is compounded monthly, the first of the 60 payments will be invested for 60 months and will grow to 500×1.01^{60}; the second will grow to 500×1.01^{59} and so on. The final payment will be invested for just one month and so will grow to 500 × 1.01.

$$\text{Total} = 500(1.01^{60} + 1.01^{59} + \cdots + 1.01)$$
$$= 500 \text{ x } \frac{1.01(1.01^{60} - 1)}{0.01} = \$41,243.18$$

Test Your Understanding 37

A The mortgage can be viewed as an annuity of $A running for 100 quarters at a rate of 4 per cent. We can equate the present value of the annuity to the initial cost of $50,000 using the formula for the PV of an annuity:

$$50,000 = A \text{ x} \left(\frac{1}{0.04} - \frac{1}{0.04 \text{ x } 1.04^{100}} \right) = 24.505\,A$$

B 50,000 = 24.505A

A = 50,000/24,505 = $2,040.40 payment per quarter

C The annual ratio is $1.04^4 = 1.16986$, so the effective annual rate is 16.99 per cent (to two d.p.).

Test Your Understanding 38

A

Beginning of year	Discount factor	Cash flow	Discounted cash flow
		$	$
1	1.000	3,000	3,000
2	0.943	3,500	3,300.5
3	0.890	4,000	3,560
4	0.840	12,000	10,080
5	0.792	4,000	3,168
6	0.747	4,500	3,361.5
7	0.705	5,000	3,525
8	0.665	13,000	8,645
			38,640

Test Your Understanding 39

A ***10,500***

B ***12,155***

C ***0.826***

D ***8,694***

E ***7,926***

Present value

	Cash flow	*Discount factor*	*Present value*
	$	10%	$
Year 1	10,500	0.909	9,545
Year 2	11,025	0.826	9,107
Year 3	11,576	0.751	8,694
Year 4	25,000 + 12,155	0.683	25,377
Year 5	12,763	0.621	7,926
Year 6	13,401	0.564	7,558
Year 7	14,071	0.513	7,218

Test Your Understanding 40

The supplier's maintenance contract is a year-end annuity of $13,000 per year. Discounting at 10 per cent and using the cumulative discount factor table gives a present value of 13,000 × 4.868 = 63,284.

Test Your Understanding 41

A

All things being equal, the project with the larger net present value would be selected.

Test Your Understanding 42

A The first payment \$A is invested for 12 quarters at 2 per cent and achieves a value of $A \times 1.02^{12}$. The second achieves a value of $A \times 1.02^{11}$ and so on until the twelfth payment achieves a value of 1.02A. Hence the final value of the fund is $A[1.02^{12} + 1.02^{11} + \ldots + 1.02]$.

B The expression is a GP with first term 1.035, common ratio 1.035 and n = 10. Sum = $1.035(1.035^{10} - 1)/0.035 = 12.1420$

Test Your Understanding 43

A It is easiest to consider a mortgage as an annuity with, in this case, n 5 40, r 5 0.03 and quarterly repayment B. Hence:

$$100{,}000 = B\left(\frac{1}{0.03} - \frac{1}{0.03 \times 1.03^{40}}\right) = 23.1148B$$

B 24B = 100,000
B = 100,000/24 = \$4,166.67

Test Your Understanding 44

Annual ratio =quarterly ratio^4 = $1.03^4 = 1.1255$

Hence the effective annual rate is 12.55 per cent.

Test Your Understanding 45

Year	Net cash inflow ($000)	Discount factor	Present value($000)
0	(90)	1.000	(90)
1	(30)	0.917	(27.51)
2	50	0.842	42.10
3	40	0.772	30.88
4	30	0.708	21.24
5	40	0.650	26.00
			NPV = 2.71

Year	Net cash inflow ($000)	Discount factor	Present value ($000)
0	(90)	1.000	(90)
1	(50)	0.917	(45.85)
2	40	0.842	33.68
3	40	0.772	30.88
4	40	0.708	28.32
5	60	0.650	39.00
			NPV = (3.97)

(c) Answer: Machine A.

Test Your Understanding 46

A Denoting sales by y and advertising expenditure by x,

$$b = \frac{n\Sigma xy - \Sigma x \Sigma y}{n\Sigma x^2 - (\Sigma x)^2}$$

$$= \frac{10 \times 1{,}457.5 - 23 \times 600}{10 \times 62 - (23)^2}$$

B $a = 60 - (8.516 \times 2.3) = 40.41$

C The correlation coefficient is given by:

$$r = \frac{n\Sigma xy - \Sigma x \Sigma y}{\sqrt{(n\Sigma x^2 - (\Sigma x)^2)(n\Sigma y^2 - (\Sigma y)^2)}} = \frac{10 \times 1{,}457.5 - 23 \times 600}{\sqrt{(10 \times 62 - 23^2)(10 \times 363{,}950 - 600^2)}}$$

$= 0.83$

Test Your Understanding 47

$$R = 1 - \frac{6 \times 304.5}{10 \times 99} = 1 - 1.8455 = -0.845 \text{ (to 3dp)}$$

Test Your Understanding 48

A and D

The rank correlation is positive and hence values of Y increase as values of X increase. Numerically its value is close to 1 and hence the link between X and Y values is very strong. We can never deduce cause and effect from any correlation coefficient, however large, so (F) is incorrect as are the numerical comments in (B) and (C). (E) is incorrect because a linear relationship between ranks of values does not necessarily imply one between the values themselves.

Test Your Understanding 49

A, D and F

A Y = 5.0913 + 0.2119X

When X increases by 1, Y increases by 0.2119 and since Y is measured in $000 this means that variable cost is $21.19 per unit. When X = 0, Y = 5.0913 which means that fixed costs are $5,091.3

B Y = 5.0913 + 0.2119 × 300 = 68.661 ($'000)

Test Your Understanding 50

A and C

A coefficient of determination between output and production costs, tells us that 89 per cent of the variation in production costs from one month to the next can be explained by corresponding variation in output. It also tells us that the linear relationship between output and costs is very strong. Only a positive correlation can tell us that costs increase as output increases and we cannot assume this from the coefficient of determination.

Test Your Understanding 51

A

A standard regression equation $Y = a + bX$ can only be used to estimate Y for a known X. It cannot be used to estimate X if Y is known.

Test Your Understanding 52

C

The coefficient of determination is given by squaring the correlation coefficient.

Test Your Understanding 53

0.054

Test Your Understanding 54

A False: Y = 45 when X = 0.

B False: Y increases by 3.6 whenever X increases by 1.

C True.

D False: it is not possible to deduce the correlation coefficient from the regression equation.

Test Your Understanding 55

C

The seasonally adjusted figure is given by A/S = 1,500/1.17

Test Your Understanding 56

A False: S is estimated by averaging A/T, not A – T.

B True.

C True.

D False: R is estimated from A/(T × S).

E False: the seasonally adjusted value is given by A/S.

Test Your Understanding 57

Estimate = 2,446

Test Your Understanding 58

The value of A is given by 49 + 37 + 58 + 67; B is the four quarters starting with 37 and reading downwards and C + A + B = 211 + 212 and the trend D + 423/8 = 52.875.

Year	*Qtr*	*Actual revenue*	*Sum of 4 qtrs*	*Sum of 8 qtrs*	*Trend*	*Actual trend*
90/91	1	49				
	2	37				
			211			
	3	58		423	52.875	
			212			
	4	67		425	53.125	1.261
			213			
91/92	1	50				
	2	38				
	3	59				
	4	68				

Test Your Understanding 59

	Quarter			
	1	2	3	4
	0.937	0.709	1.095	1.253
	0.934	0.727	1.088	1.267
Total	1.871	1.436	2.183	2.52
Average	0.9355	0.718	1.0915	1.26

Test Your Understanding 60

1st quarter	0.8 + 0.1 = 0.9
2nd quarter	0.6 + 0.1 0.7
3rd quarter	1.0 + 0.1 = 1.1
4th quarter	1.2 + 0.1 = 1.3
Total	3.6 + 0.4 = 4

Test Your Understanding 61

Year	*Sales ('000)*	*Three-year moving total*	*Trend*
1983	50		
1984	59	155	51.7
1985	46	159	53
1986	54	165	55
1987	65	170	56.7
1988	51	176	58.7
1989	60	181	60.3
1990	70	186	62
1991	56	192	64
1992	66	198	66
1993	76		

Test Your Understanding 62

A – T values	*Year one*	*Year two*	*Year three*
	7.3	–7	–1
	8.3	–7.7	–0.3
	8	–8	0
Average	7.87	–7.57	–0.43

Rounding to nearest whole number gives cyclical components that total to zero:

Year one	Year two	Year three
8	–8	0

Test Your Understanding 63

The year 2004 will be year 1 of a cycle, with cyclical component = 110
Predicted value = predicted trend + seasonal component = 70 + 10 = 80

Test Your Understanding 64

A/S

The formula for multiplicative model is A = T × S × R. Seasonal adjustment gives an instant estimate of the trend and hence its formula is T = A/S. Note that R is not involved because it can only be calculated when all of the other variables are known. In the multiplicative model we have to assume R = 1 for the purposes of seasonal adjustment.

Test Your Understanding 65

C

Seasonal adjustment adjusts the actual value to give an estimate of the trend

Test Your Understanding 66

A

A The actual seasonal factors are 0.9, 1.2, 1.3 and 0.6, respectively. The seasonally adjusted values are therefore 45/0.9, 66/1.2, 79/1.3 and 40/0.6.

Answers:

1st quarter	50
2nd quarter	55
3rd quarter	60.8
4th quarter	66.7

B If the seasonal variation is given as 130% it means that actual sales are 30% above the trend

Test Your Understanding 67

D

The probability is $3 \times 0.2 \times 0.8^2$.

Test Your Understanding 68

Expected profit = $30,020. This is given by 40 × 0.32 + 35 × 0.54 – 12 × 0.14 ($000).

Test Your Understanding 69

A $P(X > 50) = P(Z > (50 - 45)/5) = P(Z > 1) = 0.5 - 0.3413 = 0.1587$

B $P(X < 58) = P(Z < (58 - 45)/5) = P(Z < 2.6) = 0.5 + 0.4953 + 0.9953$

C $P(38 < X < 54) = P(38 - 45)/5 < Z (54 - 45)/5)$

$= P(-1.4 < Z < 1.8)$
$= 0.4192 + 0.4641 = 0.8833$

Test Your Understanding 70

The ratio to apply is 1:2:3 = a total of 6. Therefore, the number of plates examined from each production line 5

X	240/6 × 1	40
Y	240/6 × 2	80
Z	240/6 × 3	120
		240

Test Your Understanding 71

Good/defective table

	X	Y	Z	Total
Good	46	90	105	241
Defective	4	10	45	59
	50	100	150	300

Test Your Understanding 72

A The probability of a plate sampled being defective is therefore 75/310 = 0.242

B From the table there are 75 defective items and of these 45 come from Z. The probability is therefore 45/75 = 0.6

Test Your Understanding 73

Probability that a European brochure is selected:

285/500 = 0.57

Probability that an African brochure is not selected:

485/500 = 0.97

Probability that neither an American nor an Asian brochure is selected:

300/500 = 0.60

Probability that either a European or an Asian brochure is selected:

395/500 = 0.79

Test Your Understanding 74

C and D

Mutually exclusive events are those which cannot occur together. Another way of saying this is that the occurrence of one makes the probability of the occurrence of the other equal zero.

Test Your Understanding 75

A

The result of the second roll of a die should not be affected in any way by the result of the first roll. So the events are independent.

Test Your Understanding 76

A and D

The method requires the expected profit to be calculated for each decision and then decisions are selected on the basis of how high their expected profits are.

Using expected values in decision-making introduces an objective tool to counter any personal bias of the decision-maker. Expected value analysis can be very useful where decisions have to be made on a repeated basis (e.g. how much stock to produce each day) since, in the long run, the outcomes will tend to average out in accordance with the probabilities set. One-off decisions do not have this attribute and therefore are less predictable.

Expected value analysis, however, restricts the benefits of one choice over another to purely financial considerations and cannot account for factors not directly related to short-term financial gain. For example, decision (A) may have a higher expected value than decision (B), but decision (B) may be preferred for strategic or marketing reasons.

Also, expected value theory does not account for the decision-maker's attitude towards risk. Decision (A) may be more profitable than (B) under expected value rules, but it may involve much more risk of a loss than decision (B). (B) may therefore be chosen on the basis that it will at least return a profit, even though this may not be as high as that possible or probable under decision (A).

Expected values are only as reliable as the data on which they are based. Much of this data may only be obtainable in a subjective way, for examples estimates of probabilities and potential cash flows.

Test Your Understanding 77

A The mean value of the prize paid can be found:

Value of prize, x($)	*Number of patches (f)*	*xf*
0.20	5	1.00
0.50	2	1.00
1.00	1	1.00
	8	3.00

The mean

$$= \frac{\Sigma fx}{\Sigma x} = \$0.375 \text{ per leaflet}$$

B To attain a total budgeted payout of $75,000 at an average payout of $0.40 per leaflet, the number of leaflets should be:

$$\frac{75{,}000}{0.4} = 187{,}500$$

Test Your Understanding 78

A The probability of the first number scratched not winning a prize is 30/37.
Answer: 0.811.

B Once the first number is not a prize winner, there are twenty-nine non-prize-winning numbers left of the thirty-six on the card. The probability of the second number not winning a prize is thus 29/36. Continuing this process, the probability of all seven numbers not winning is:

(30/37) × (29/36) × (28/35) × (27/34) × (26/33) × (25/32) × (24/31) = 0.1977

C The expected number is 1,000,000 × 0.2 = 200,000 purchasers

Test Your Understanding 79

A P (length < 99)

= $P(z < (99 - 102)/2 = -1.5)$
= tail-end area associated with 1.5
= 0.5 – table entry for 1.5
= 0.5 – 0.4332
= 0.0668, that is 6.68%

B P (length > 104.4)

= $P(z > (104.4 - 102)/2 = 1.2)$
= tail-end area associated with 1.2
= 0.5 – table entry for 1.2
= 0.5 – 0.3849
= 0.1151, that is 11.51%

Test Your Understanding 80

In order to end up with 1,000 usable parts we need to produce N parts, of which 0.07N will be too small and will be scrapped. Hence:

$N(1 - 0.07) = 1{,}000$
$N = 1{,}000/0.93 = 1{,}075$

Test Your Understanding 81

A

Number produced	*Cost ($)*
1,000	2,100
2,000	2,200
3,000	2,300
4,000	2,400
5,000	2,500

B

Number sold	*Revenue ($)*
1,000	2,100
2,000	2,700
3,000	3,300
4,000	3,900
5,000	4,500

Test Your Understanding 82

For each decision (i.e. production level), the expected profit is given by multiplying profits by the their probabilities and totalling. For example, the expected profit if 5,000 items were produced is given by $-400 \times 0.1 + 200 \times 0.4 + 800 \times 0.2 + 1,400 \times 0.2 + 2,000 \times 0.1$.

Answers:
Production of 1,000, expected profit = 0
Production of 2,000, expected profit = 440
Production of 3,000, expected profit = 640
Production of 4,000, expected profit = 720
Production of 5,000, expected profit = 680

Test Your Understanding 83

A For counterfeit coins:

P(*t* > 260)
= P(z > (260 – 150)/50 = 2.2)
= tail-end area associated with 2.2
= 0.5 – table entry for 2.2
= 0.5 – 0.4861
= 0.0139 or 1.39%

B For genuine coins:

P(*t*< 260)
= P(z < (260 – 300)/50 = 2)
= tail-end area associated with 2
= 0.5 – table entry for 2
= 0.5 – 0.4772
= 0.0228 or 2.28%

C We want a tail-end probability of 0.01 but CIMA tables give the probability between the mean and the z-value. The tail-end value 0.01 therefore corresponds to a table probability of 0.5 – 0.01 = 0.49 and this in turn corresponds to a z-value of 2.33. Hence P(z > 2.33) = 0.01 = P(z < –2.33).

Test Your Understanding 84

A $8x + 4y \geq 100$
$4y \geq 100 - 8x$
$y \geq 25 - 2x$

B $-10x + 20y \leq -80$
$20y \leq -80 + 10x$
$y \leq 4 + 0.5x$

Test Your Understanding 85

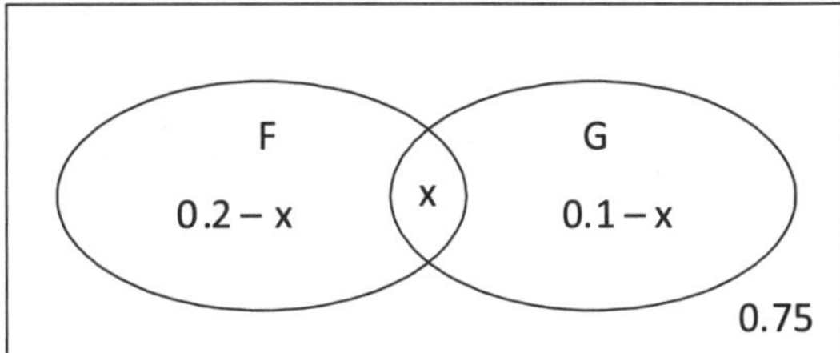

Using a Venn diagram we can easily see that

$0.2 - x + x + 0.1 - x + 0.75 = 1$

$1.05 - x = 1$

$-X = -0.05$

$X = 0.05$

Test Your Understanding 86

A = (34 × (4 + 6 + 25))/8

The answer is 148.75

B = 11 × 25 + 11 × 6 + 10 or = (25 + 6) × 11 + 10

The answer is 351

C = ROUND(34/5 × 6.37,2)

The answer is 43.32

= ROUND(112.6 × 14.2^2,0)

The answer is 22,705

= ROUND((199 + 45) × 1.177 + 78.43,1)

The answer is 365.6

Test Your Understanding 87

$53.86

	A	B	C	D	E
1	Investment amount	2000			
2	Interest rate	0.1			
3					
4	Year no.	1	=$B$1*(1+$B$2)^B4		
5		2	=$B$1*(1+$B$2)^B5		
6		3	=$B$1*(1+$B$2)^B6		
7		4	=$B$1*(1+$B$2)^B7		
8		5	=$B$1*(1+$B$2)^B8		
9					
10					

The answers are 2200.00, 2420.00, 2662.00, 2928.20 and 3221.02

	A	B	C
1	price per box	3.45	
2	no of boxes	15	
3	discount	0.075	
4	delivery	5.99	
5	total	=((B1*B 2)*(1-B 3)+B4	
6			
7			
8			

Test Your Understanding 88

	A	B	C	D
1	Temparature	Litre of cold drinks sold	Formula	Answer
2	15	120	=FORECAST(A2,$B$2:$B$11,$A$2:$A$11)	116.85
3	17	125	=FORECAST(A3,$B$2:$B$11,$A$2:$A$11)	119.12
4	19	125	=FORECAST(A4,$B$2:$B$11,$A$2:$A$11)	121.39
5	15	120	=FORECAST(A5,$B$2:$B$11,$A$2:$A$11)	116.85
6	21	130	=FORECAST(A6,$B$2:$B$11,$A$2:$A$11)	123.65
7	25	130	=FORECAST(A7,$B$2:$B$11,$A$2:$A$11)	128.19
8	22	125	=FORECAST(A8,$B$2:$B$11,$A$2:$A$11)	124.79
9	19	125	=FORECAST(A9,$B$2:$B$11,$A$2:$A$11)	121.39
10	18	100	=FORECAST(A10,$B$2:$B$11,$A$2:$A$11)	120.26
11	20	115	=FORECAST(A11,$B$2:$B$11,$A$2:$A$11)	122.52
12				
13				
14				

Test Your Understanding 89

There are many principles of good spreadsheet design, but perhaps five of the most important are:

(1) Take time to collect all the information you can about the issue to be planned or analysed before entering anything into the spreadsheet.

(2) Do produce monster-sized spreadsheets. Modularise a system into multiple spreadsheets and multiple files where appropriate.

(3) Minimise the use of absolute values (numbers) in formulae and use cell references wherever possible. Remember to use absolute values where appropriate.

(4) Be consistent with formatting and do not over-use different fonts.

(5) Build in cross-checks to validate data/calculations.

chapter

11

Mock Assessment 1

Certificate Level
Fundamentals of Business Mathematics

Instructions to students

You have 2 hours in which to complete this assessment.

You may attempt all questions. Mathematical tables and formulae are available.

Do not turn the page until you are ready to attempt the assessment under timed conditions.

Test Your Understanding 1

Use the following data about the production of faulty or acceptable items in three departments to answer the probability questions. All items referred to in the questions are randomly selected from this sample of 250. Give all answers correct to four d.p.

	Department			
	P	*Q*	*R*	*Total*
Faulty	7	10	15	32
Acceptable	46	78	94	218
Total	53	88	109	250

A What is the probability that an item is faulty?

Answer ☐

B What is the probability that an item from department P is faulty?

Answer ☐

C What is the probability that an item found to be faulty comes from department P?

Answer ☐ **(6 marks)**

Test Your Understanding 2

In an additive model, the seasonal variations given by averaging Y – T values are 25, 18, –5 and –30. They have to be adjusted so that their total is 0. What is the value after adjustment of the average currently valued at –30?

Answer ☐ **(2 marks)**

Test Your Understanding 3

Which of the following examples would constitute a multiple bar chart?

A Three adjacent bars then a gap then another three bars.

B Six separate bars.

C Two bars with a gap between them, each divided into three sections.

D Any bar chart which displays more than one variable.

Answer ☐ **(2 marks)**

Test Your Understanding 4

If $\Sigma x = 500$, $\Sigma y = 200$, $\Sigma x^2 = 35{,}000$, $\Sigma y^2 = 9{,}000$, $\Sigma xy = 12{,}000$ and $n = 10$, calculate the product moment correlation coefficient to three d.p.

Answer ☐ **(2 marks)**

Test Your Understanding 5

Which of the following statements about standard deviation is incorrect?

A It measures variability.

B It uses all the data.

C It is not distorted by skewed data.

D Its formula lends itself to mathematical manipulation.

Answer ☐ **(2 marks)**

Test Your Understanding 6

An investment rises in value from $12,000 to $250,000 over 15 years. Calculate the percentage increase per year, to one d.p.

Answer ☐ **(2 marks)**

Test Your Understanding 7

Events P and Q are said to be independent. What does this mean?

A If P occurs, Q cannot occur

B If P occurs the probability of Q occurring is unchanged

C If P occurs the probability of Q occurring is 0

D If P occurs the probability of Q occurring is 1.

Answer ☐ **(2 marks)**

Test Your Understanding 8

Sales figures are given as 547,000 but after seasonal adjustment using a multiplicative model they are only 495,000. Calculate the seasonal component for the particular season, to 3 d.p.

Answer ☐ **(2 marks)**

Test Your Understanding 9

If a sum of $15,000 is invested at 4.6 per cent per annum, compound interest, find its value after 5 years, to the nearest $.

Answer ☐ **(2 marks)**

Test Your Understanding 10

A Express the following average weekly wages as index numbers with base 1998, to 1 d.p.

Year	*97*	*98*	*99*	*2000*	*2001*	*2002*
RPI	166	172	178	184	190	197
Wages	414	426	440	450	468	480
Index	...	...	...	...	...	...

B If the index for 2003 were to be 116 and the RPI 204, express the index for 2003 at constant 1998 prices.

C If the average wages index for 2003 at constant 1998 prices were to be 96, which of the following comments would be correct?
(A) Average wages in 2003 could buy 4 per cent less than in 1998
(B) Average wages in 2003 could buy 4 per cent more than in 1998
(C) Average wages in 2003 were 4 per cent more than in 1998
(D) Average prices in 2003 were 4 per cent less than in 1998

Answer ☐ **(6 marks)**

Test Your Understanding 11

The expression $(x^3)^2/x^4$ equals

A $1/x$

B 1

C x

D x^2

Answer ☐ **(2 marks)**

Test Your Understanding 12

The pass rate for a particular exam is 48 per cent. In a randomly selected group of three students, find the probabilities (to 4 d.p.) that

A No one passes

Answer ☐ **(2 marks)**

B All three pass

Answer ☐ **(4 marks)**

Test Your Understanding 13

A company has to choose between borrowing $100,000 at 3 per cent a quarter in order to modernise now or saving at 2 per cent a quarter in order to modernise in 4 years time, at an estimated cost of $117,000. Throughout this question, use tables whenever possible.

A Find the cumulative discount factor appropriate to quarter end payments of $1 per quarter at 3 per cent per quarter over 5 years.

Answer ☐

B Calculate the amount $X which must be paid per quarter if the company borrows $100,000 now repayable at the end of each quarter over 4 years. Give your answer correct to the nearest $.

Answer ☐

C Calculate the amount $Y which must be saved at the end of each quarter if the company wishes to cover the cost of modernisation in 4 years time. Give your answer to the nearest $.

Answer ☐ **(6 marks)**

Test Your Understanding 14

Eight samples of wine have been listed in order of taste (with the best taste being ranked number one) and their prices are also listed.

Sample taste	1	2	3	4	5	6	7	8
Price ($)	6.99	4.95	5.99	5.99	4.99	3.99	2.99	2.99
Rank of price	..	..	..	..	..	..	..	..

A Rank the prices of the wines with the lowest price being ranked number one.

B If the differences in corresponding ranks are denoted by 'd' and if $\sum d^2 = 150$, calculate Spearman's rank correlation coefficient to 3 d.p.

Answer ☐

If the rank correlation coefficient was –0.9, which of the following statements would be correct?

C There is a strong link between price and taste.

D There is a strong linear relationship between price and taste.

E Taste rank increases as price gets higher.

F Ninety per cent of the differences in price from one sample to the next can be explained by corresponding differences in taste.

Answer ☐ **(2 marks)**

Test Your Understanding 15

Calculate the present value of an annuity of $2,800 per annum, payable at the end of each year for 10 years at a discount rate of 4 per cent. Use tables and give your answer to the nearest $.

Answer(s) ☐ **(2 marks)**

Test Your Understanding 16

An asset originally worth $80,000 depreciates at 28 per cent per annum. Find its value to the nearest $ at the end of 3 years.

Answer(s) ☐ **(2 marks)**

Test Your Understanding 17

If the following data are to be illustrated by means of a histogram and if the standard interval is taken to be 5 seconds, calculate the heights of the bars of the histogram (to the nearest whole number).

Time taken (seconds)	*Frequency*	*Height of bar*
0-5	47	
5-10	62	
10-20	104	
20-40	96	

(4 marks)

Test Your Understanding 18

In an additive time series model, at a certain point of time, the actual value is 32,000 while the trend is 26,000 and the seasonal component is 6,200. If there is no cyclical variation, calculate the residual variation.

Answer ☐ **(2 marks)**

Test Your Understanding 19

Solve the equation $2x^2 - 5x - 7 = 0$ giving your answers correct to 1 d.p.

Answer ☐ **(2 marks)**

Test Your Understanding 20

A project may result in the following profits with the probabilities stated.

Profit	*Probability*
$40,000	0.2
$25,000	0.4
($12,000)	0.4

Calculate the expected profit to the nearest £.

Answer ☐ **(2 marks)**

Test Your Understanding 21

If weights are normally distributed with mean 43 kg and standard deviation 6 kg, what is the probability of a weight being less than 50 kg?

Answer ☐ **(2 marks)**

Test Your Understanding 22

A sum of $30,000 is invested at a nominal rate of 12 per cent per annum. Find its value after 3 years if interest is compounded every month. Give your answer to the nearest $.

Answer ☐ **(2 marks)**

Test Your Understanding 23

If $\Sigma x = 400$, $\Sigma y = 300$, $\Sigma x^2 = 18{,}000$, $\Sigma y^2 = 10{,}000$, $\Sigma xy = 13{,}000$ and $n = 10$,

A Calculate the value of '*b*' in the regression equation, to 1 d.p.

B If the value of '*b*' were 0.9, calculate the value of '*a*' in the regression equation to 1 d.p.

Answer

A ☐

B ☐

(4 marks)

Test Your Understanding 24

In a time series analysis, the trend Y is given by the regression equation $Y = 462 + 0.34t$ where *t* denotes the quarters of years with 1st quarter of 2010 as t = 1.

A Predict the trend for the first quarter of 2014 to one d.p.

Answer ☐

B If the average seasonal variations are as follow

Quarter	*Q1*	*Q2*	*Q3*	*Q4*
Variation	–20%	0	–20%	+40%

Use the multiplicative model to predict the actual value for a 3rd quarter in which the trend prediction is 500.

Answer ☐ **(4 marks)**

Test Your Understanding 25

A sales representative calls on three separate, unrelated customers and the chance of making a sale at any one of them is 0.7. Find the probability that a sale is made on the third call only, to 3 d.p.

Answer ☐ **(2 marks)**

Test Your Understanding 26

Rearrange the formula $V = P \times (1 + r)^n$ to make r the subject

Answer ☐ **(2 marks)**

Test Your Understanding 27

In November, unemployment in a region is 238,500. If the seasonal component using an additive time series model is –82,000, find the seasonally adjusted level of unemployment to the nearest whole number.

Answer ☐ **(2 marks)**

Test Your Understanding 28

A company is planning capital investment for which the following year end cash flows have been estimated.

Year end	*Net cash flow*
Now	(10,000)
1	5,000
2	5,000
3	3,000

A Use tables to calculate the net present value (NPV) of the project using tables if the company has a cost of capital of 15 per cent.

Answer ☐

B If the NPV is $928 when the discount rate is 10 per cent and –$628 when it is 20 per cent, calculate the internal rate of return to two d.p.

Answer ☐ **(4 marks)**

Test Your Understanding 29

If the regression equation (in $'000) linking sales (Y) to advertising expenditure (X) is given by $Y = 4{,}000 + 12X$, forecast the sales when $150,000 is spent on advertising, to the nearest $.

Answer [ ] **(2 marks)**

Test Your Understanding 30

An item sells for $4.39 including value added tax at 17.5 per cent. If tax were reduced to 16 per cent, the new selling price to the nearest penny will be

A $4.33

B $4.01

C $4.32

D $5.09

Answer [ ] **(2 marks)**

Test Your Understanding 31

If $\Sigma f = 50$, $\Sigma fx = 120$ and $\Sigma fx^2 = 400$, calculate

A The mean (to 1 d.p.)

Answer [ ]

B The standard deviation (to 1 d.p.)

Answer [ ] **(4 marks)**

Test Your Understanding 32

The Economic Order Quantity (EOQ) for a particular stock item is given by the expression:

$$EOQ = \sqrt{\frac{2C_oD}{C_h}}$$

(A) If C_o = \$2 per order, D = 1,000 items and C_h = \$0.25 per item, then EOQ (rounded to the nearest whole number) will be

A 400

B 320

C 160

D 126

Answer [ ]

(B) If, for a different stock item, EOQ = 200 items, C_o = \$4 per order and D = 1,000 items, then C_h (in \$ per item) will be

A 0.05

B 0.10

C 0.15

D 0.20

Answer [ ] **(4 marks)**

Test Your Understanding 33

A graphical presentation of classified data in which the number of items in each class is represented by the area of the bar is called

A an ogive.

B a histogram.

C a bar chart.

D a compound bar chart.

Answer [ ] **(2 marks)**

Test Your Understanding 3434

The following table shows the index of prices (2000 = 100) for a certain commodity over the period 2000-2005:

2000	2001	2002	2003	2004	2005
100	105	115	127	140	152

A The percentage increase in the price between 2002 and 2004 is nearest to
(A) 25.0
(B) 22.3
(C) 21.7
(D) none of these.

Answer ☐

B It has been decided to rebase the index so that 2003 = 100. The index for 2005 will now be nearest to
(A) 193.1
(B) 139.4
(C) 125.0
(D) 119.7

Answer ☐ **(4 marks)**

Test Your Understanding 35

The cost of an office desk is $263 plus value added tax of 17.5 per cent. Using the numbers given what Excel formula is required to calculate the total price to 2 d.p.

Answer ☐ **(2 marks)**

Test Your Understanding 36

	A	B	C	D	E
1	**IT Investment - Cash Out**		250000		
2	**Net IT Benefits**	Year 1		66000	
3		Year 2		87000	
4		Year 3		98000	
5		Year 4		120000	
6		Year 5		110000	
7					
8	**Fixed Cost of Capital or Interest Rate**			24%	
9					
10	**ROI**				
11	**NPV**				
12					

Given the scenario in the spreadsheet above, what Excel formula is required in Cell D10 to calculate the ROI, given as ROI = average profit / capital employed?

Answer [ ] **(1 mark)**

Test Your Understanding 37

	A	B	C	D	E
1	INTEREST RATES AND CASH DEPOSITS				
2					
3	Interest rate	Deposit		Forecast	
4	10.00%	11550			
5	10.25%	11900			
6	10.50%	12500			
7	10.50%	11990			
8	10.75%	12900			
9	11.00%	13000			
10	11.25%	14000			
11	11.25%	13020			
12	11.25%	14000			
13	11.25%	14100			
14	11.50%	13380			
15	11.50%	14200			
16	11.75%	13500			
17	11.75%	14050			
18	12.00%	14500			
19	12.00%	14100			
20	12.25%	14500			
21	12.25%	14600			
22					

Given the scenario above, what Excel formula is required in cell D4 to calculate the forecast (using a least squared line approach). Write your answer so that the formula can be copied into cells D5 through D21.

Answer [ ] **(1 mark)**

Test Your Understanding 38

	A	B	C	D	E	F	G
1			Average weight of pallets				
2	73	62	66	75	70	71	
3	83	69	74	79	78	82	
4	65	72	66	79	82	77	
5	69	61	63	80	82	66	
6	82	82	65	75	71	80	
7	74	84	72	78	67	84	
8							
9	Weight in kg.						
10	60						
11	65						
12	70						
13	75						
14	80						
15	85						
16							

Given the scenario above, what Excel formula is required in the range B10:B15 to calculate the frequency distribution of the pallet weights.

Answer ☐ **(1 mark)**

Test Your Understanding 39

	A	B	C	D	E
1	Average daily temperature in degrees centigrade				
2	29	25	22	29	
3	24	26	25	28	
4	28	27	20	22	
5	21	20	24	24	
6	21	22	27	26	
7	23	26	21	24	
8	25	25	24	25	
9					
10	Median				
11	Mode				
12	Mean				
13					

Given the scenario above, what Excel formulae are required to calculate:

A The median (to 1 d.p.)

Answer ☐

B The mode (to 0 d.p.)

Answer ☐

C The mean (to 2 d.p.)

Answer ☐ **(3 marks)**

Test Your Understanding 40

Solve for y in the following inequalities.

A $-5x + 10y + 120 \geq 25x + 5y + 320$

Answer [ ]

B $240 + 8x \leq 12x + 10y + 140$

Answer [ ] **(2 marks)**

Test Your Understanding 41

A Describe the shaded area in the following Venn diagram.

(A) Even numbers which begin with 3

(B) Numbers that are even but do not have a 3 in them

(C) The numbers 6, 12, 24, 30, 36

(D) None of the above

Answer [ ]

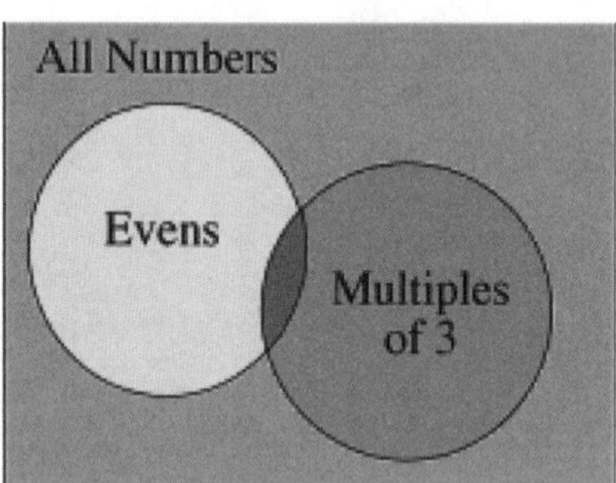

B If 50 people were asked whether they liked apples or oranges or both, 38 liked apples and 32 liked oranges. Use a Venn diagram to help you calculate how many people liked both?

(A) 10

(B) 15

(C) 20

(D) 25

(2 marks)

Test Your Understanding 42

Which of the following is **not** an advantage of spreadsheet software over manual approaches:

A Security

B Speed

C Accuracy

D Legibility

(1 mark)

Test Your Understanding 43

An ogive is:

A another name for a histogram.

B a chart showing any linear relationship.

C a chart showing a non-linear relationship.

D a graph of a cumulative frequency distribution.

(1 mark)

Test Your Understanding 44

A normal distribution has a mean of 150, and a standard deviation of 20. 80% of the distribution is (approximately) below:

A 158

B 167

C 161

D 170

(2 marks)

Test Your Understanding 45

The expression $(x^4)^3/x^6$ equals:

A 0

B 1

C x

D x^6.

(1 mark)

Test your understanding answers

Test Your Understanding 1

A 32 out of 250 items are faulty
Answer = 32/250 = 0.12

B 7 of the 53 items from P are faulty
Answer = 7/53 = 0.1321 (4 d.p.).

C 7 out of the 32 faulty items come from P
Answer = 7/32 = 0.2188 (4 d.p.).

Test Your Understanding 2

–30 – 2 = – 32

Total = 25 + 18 – 5 – 30 = 8
If we subtract 2 from each of the four averages they will add up to zero.

Test Your Understanding 3

A

(B) describes a simple bar chart and (C) describes a compound or component bar chart. (D) is incorrect because a compound bar also shows several variables.

Test Your Understanding 4

0.283

$r = [n\Sigma xy - \Sigma x \Sigma y]/\sqrt{\{[n\Sigma x^2 - (\Sigma x)^2] \times [n\Sigma y^2 - (\Sigma y)^2]\}}$

$= [10 \times 12{,}000 - 500 \times 200]/\sqrt{\{[10 \times 35{,}000 - 500^2][10 \times 9{,}000 - 200^2]\}}$

$= 20{,}000/\sqrt{\{100{,}000 \times 50{,}000\}} = 0.283$(3 d.p.)

Test Your Understanding 5

C

Standard deviation uses all the data in a mathematically exact formula as a means of measuring variability. However, its one big disadvantage is that is greatly exaggerates the dispersion of skewed data so (C) is incorrect.

Test Your Understanding 6

22.4

15 year ratio = 250/12 = 20.83333
1 year ratio = $20.83333^{1/15}$ = 1.2244

Annual % increase = 22.4%

Test Your Understanding 7

B

Events are independent if the occurrence of one does not alter the probability of the other, so (B) is correct. (A) and (C) are both definitions of mutually exclusive events.

Test Your Understanding 8

1.105

Seasonally adjusted value = actual value/seasonal component. So seasonal component = actual value divided by seasonally adjusted value = 547/495 = 1.105

Test Your Understanding 9

18,782

Value = 15,000 × 1.046^5 = $18,782

Test Your Understanding 10

A Wages are indexed with base 98 by dividing each year's wages figure by the '98 figure. (i.e. by 426) and multiplying by 100.

97	*98*	*99*	*00*	*01*	*02*
97.2	100	103.3	105.6	109.9	112.7

B Value at '98 prices = 116 × 98 RPI/'03 RPI = 116 × 172/204 = 97.8

Answer: 97.8

C An index of 96 means a drop of 4 per cent and, in this case, the drop is in the quantity of goods and services which the average wage buys. So the answer is (A).

Answer: (A)

Test Your Understanding 11

D

$(x^3)^2/x^4 = x^6/x^4 = x^{(6-4)} = x^2$

Test Your Understanding 12

A Probability of failing is 1 – 0.48 = 0.52

Probability of all three failing = 0.52^3 = 0.1406

Answer: 0.1406

B Probability of all three passing = 0.48^3 = 0.1106

Answer: 0.1106

Test Your Understanding 13

A There are 20 quarterly payments in 5 years, so the discount factor required is that corresponding to 3 per cent and 20 periods.
Answer: 14.878

B The method is to equate the present value of the repayments with the 100,000 borrowed. The cumulative discount factor at 3 per cent for 16 periods is 12.561 so
100,000 = 12.561X
X = 100,000/12.561 = $7,961 (to the nearest $)
Answer: 7,961

C The present value of the saving scheme must be equated to that of $117,000 discounted at 2 per cent for 16 periods. The cumulative discount factor is 13.578 whilst the single discount factor is 0.728.
Hence 13.578Y = 117,000 × 0.728 and
Y = $6,273 (to nearest $).
Answer: 6,273

Test Your Understanding 14

A Answer: 8 4 6.5 6.5 5 3 1.5 1.5

B $R = 1 - 6\sum d^2/n(n^2 - 1) = 1 - 6 \times 150/(8 \times 63) = -0.786$ (to 3 d.p.)

Answer: –0.786

C The value 0.9 means that there is a strong link between taste and price but it need not be linear. Because of the strange way in which taste is ranked, with the lowest rank being the best taste, rank of taste actually declines as price increases.

Answer: (D)

Test Your Understanding 15

22,711

The cumulative discount factor for 10 years at 4 per cent is 8.111, so the present value is 2,800 × 8.111 = $22,711 (to the nearest $)

Test Your Understanding 16

29,860

If something declines at 28% per year, its value at the end of each year is only 72 per cent of its value at the start, so year-end value is start value times 0.72.

Value after 3 years = 80,000 × 0.72^3 = $29,860 (to the nearest $)

Test Your Understanding 17

47, 62, 52, 24

If the width of an interval is n times the standard width, then the height of its bar is frequency/n. Heights are 47, 62, 104/2 = 52 and 96/4 = 24.

Test Your Understanding 18

–200

The formula for an additive time series is A = T + S + R and hence residual = A – T – S = 32,000 – 26,000 – 6,200 = –200

Test Your Understanding 19

–1, 3.5

Using the formula for the roots of a quadratic, a = 2, b = –5 and c= –7. Alternately, factorisation gives (2x – 7)(x + 1) = 0 and hence x = –1 or 3.5

Test Your Understanding 20

13,200

Expected profit ($'000) = 40 × 0.2 + 25 × 0.4 – 12 × 0.4 = 13.2

Test Your Understanding 21

0.8790

$P(W < 50) = P(z < [50 - 43]/6)\ P(z < 1.17)$
$= 0.5 + \text{Normal table entry for } 1.17 = 0.5 + 0.3790$
$= 0.8790$

Test Your Understanding 22

42,923

A nominal 12 per cent per annum means 1 per cent per month and in 3 years there are 36 months. Value = 30,000 × 1.01^{36} = $42,923 (to the nearest $).

Test Your Understanding 23

A **0.5**

$b = [n\Sigma xy - \Sigma x \Sigma y]/[n\Sigma x^2 - (\Sigma x)^2]$
$= [10 \times 13{,}000 - 400 \times 300]/[10 \times 18{,}000 - 400^2] = 10{,}000/20{,}000$
$= 0.5$

B **–6**

$a = \Sigma y/n - b \times \Sigma x/n = [300 - 0.9 \times 400]/10 = -60/10 = -6$

Test Your Understanding 24

A For the 1st quarter of 2014, t = 17 and trend Y = 462 + 0.34 × 17 = 467.8 (to 1 d.p.)

Answer: 467.8

B Prediction = trend prediction reduced by 20% = 500 × 0.8

Answer: 400

Test Your Understanding 25

0.063

P(not making a sale) = 1 – P(making a sale) = 1 – 0.7 = 0.3
P(sale at 3rd call only) = P(not at 1st) × P(not at 2nd) × P(sale at 3rd) = 0.3 × 0.3 × 0.7
= 0.063

Test Your Understanding 26

$(V/P)^{(1/n)} - 1$

$(1 + r)^n = V/P$ so $1 + r = (V/P)^{(1/n)}$ and $r = (V/P)^{(1/n)} - 1$

Test Your Understanding 27

The additive model is A = T + S and seasonal adjustment provides an estimate of T = A – S = 238,500 – (–82,000) = 238,500 + 82,000 = 320,500

Test Your Understanding 28

A

Year	Cash flow	Discount factor	Present value
0	(10,000)	1	(10,000)
1	5,000	0.87	4,350
2	5,000	0.756	3,780
3	3,000	0.658	1,974
			NPV = 104

Answer: 104

B The IRR is the rate at which NPV is zero. NPV drops by $928 – (–$628) = $1,556 as the percentage rises from 10 per cent to 20 per cent that is by 10 per cent points. The drop per point is therefore 1,556/10 = $155.6. Since it starts at $928, the NPV will reach zero after an increase in the rate of 928/155.6 = 5.96% points. This occurs when the rate = 10 + 5.96 = 15.96% (to 2 d.p.)

Answer: 15.96

Test Your Understanding 29

$5,800,000

When $150,000 is spent on advertising, X = 150 and Y = 4,000 + 12 × 150 = 5,800. Forecast sales = 5,800 ($'000).

Test Your Understanding 30

A

Price with VAT at 17.5% = 1.175 × Price without VAT

So price without VAT = 4.39/1.175

Price with VAT at 16% = 1.16 × Price without VAT = 1.16 × 4.39/1.175 = $4.33

Test Your Understanding 31

A **2.4**

Mean = ∑fx/∑f =120/50 = 2.4

B **1.5**

Standard deviation $= \sqrt{[\Sigma fx^2/\Sigma f - (\Sigma fx/\Sigma f)^2]} = \sqrt{[400/50-(120/50)^2]}$

$= \sqrt{2.24} = 1.5$ (to 1 d.p.)

Test Your Understanding 32

A **D**

$$EOQ = \sqrt{\frac{2C_oD}{C_h}}$$

$C_o = 2$, D = 1,000, $C_h = 0.25$

$$EOQ = \sqrt{\frac{2 \times 2 \times 1{,}000}{0.25}} = \sqrt{\frac{4{,}000}{0.25}} = \sqrt{16{,}000}$$

EOQ = 126.49 = 126 (to the nearest whole number)

B **D**

EOQ = 200 $C_o = 4$, D = 1,000

$$200 = \sqrt{\frac{2 \times 4 \times 1{,}000}{C_h}} = \sqrt{\frac{8{,}000}{C_h}}$$

$$200^2 = \frac{8{,}000}{C_h}$$

$$C_h = \frac{8{,}000}{40{,}000} = 0.20$$

Test Your Understanding 33

B

An ogive doesn't have bars. A bar chart looks similar to a histogram but in a bar chart the height of the bar represents the frequency. In a histogram this is only the case if the classes are of equal width. In general the area of the bar in a histogram represents class frequency.

Test Your Understanding 3434

A **C**

% increase between 2002 and 2004:

$$\frac{140-115}{115} \times 100 = \frac{25}{115} \times 100 = 21.74$$

B **D**

Rebased price

$$\frac{152}{127} \times 100 = 119.69$$

Test Your Understanding 35

= ROUND(263 × 1.175,2)

Test Your Understanding 36

= AVERAGE(D2:D6)/C1

Test Your Understanding 37

FORECAST(A4,$B$4:$B$21,$A$4:$A$21)

Test Your Understanding 38

= frequency(A2:F7,A10:A15)

Test Your Understanding 39

A = ROUND(MEDIAN(A2:D8),1)

B = ROUND(MODE(A2:D8),0)

C = ROUND(AVERAGE(A2:D8),2)

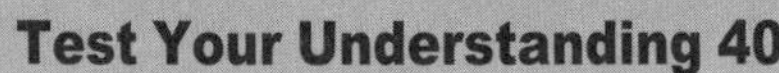

Test Your Understanding 40

A $10y - 5y \geq 25x + 5x + 200$
$5y \geq 30x + 200$
$y \geq 6x + 40$

B $-10y \leq 12x - 8x + 140 - 240$
$-10y \leq 4x - 100$
$-y \leq 0.4x - 10$
$y \geq -0.4x + 10$

Test Your Understanding 41

D and C

Test Your Understanding 42

A

A computer–based approach exposes the firm to threats from viruses, hackers and general system failure.

Test Your Understanding 43

D

Test Your Understanding 44

B

80% = 50% + 30%

From the tables, Z = 0.84

$x = 150 + 0.84 \times 20 = 167$

Test Your Understanding 45

D

$$\frac{(X^4)^3}{X^6} = \frac{X^{12}}{X^6} = X^6$$

based on rules $X^m \div X^n = X^{m-n}$

chapter

12

Mock Assessment 2

Test Your Understanding 1

When a = 4 and x = 3, $(3a^3x)^2$ is equal to:

A 1,728

B 82,944

C 331,776

D 5,184

Answer ______

Test Your Understanding 2

Which of the following is the best explaination of coefficient of detemination:

A the percentage of variation in the variables that cannot be explained by regression analysis;

B the strength of the correlation between the variables;

C the percentage of the variation in the dependent variable that can be explained by regression analysis;

D the proximity of the observations to a straight line.

Answer______ **(1 mark)**

Test Your Understanding 3

In a histogram, one class interval is twice the width of the others. For that class, the height to be plotted in relation to the frequency is

A × 2

B × 0.5

C × 1

D × 0.25

Answer______ **(1 mark)**

Test Your Understanding 4

A market research project has identified that for a particular product, a price of = $12 will sell 2,500 units/month and a price of $10 will sell 3,300 units/month.

If the relationship between price (P) and demand (D) is given by P = aD + b, what are the values of a and b?

A a =18.25	b = 20.0025
B a = 0.0025	b = 218.25
C a = 20.0025	b = 18.25
D a = 218.25	b = 0.0025

Answer______ **(2 marks)**

Test Your Understanding 5

Which of the following are advantages of the median

(i) It is not affected by extreme values.

(ii) It can be used in mathematical tables.

(iii) Data can be taken in any order which speeds calculation.

(iv) It is unaffected by unequal class intervals.

A (i) and (iii)

B (i), (ii), (iii) and (iv)

C (ii) and (iii)

D (i) and (iv)

Answer______ **(2 marks)**

Test Your Understanding 6

At what two levels of demand will X Ltd breakeven if their profitability can be represented by the equation: Profit = –2,400 + 30D – $0.06D^2$

A 67 units and 567 units

B 100 units and 400 units

C 10 units and 40 units

D 167 units and 467 units.

Answer______ **(2 marks)**

Test Your Understanding 7

A company has calculated the least squares regression line for the relationship between staff numbers and unit sales in its national branches, where y = sales units and x = number of staff on duty. The equation is $y = 156.98 + 14.38x$

From this equation it can be stated that:

A 156.98 is the maximum number of units that can be sold;

B unit sales fall by 14.38 for each additional member of staff employed;

C an additional 14.38 staff members are needed to sell one more unit;

D unit sales rise by 14.38 for each additional member of staff employed.

Answer______ **(1 mark)**

Test Your Understanding 8

A product sells for $4.36 inclusive of VAT at 17.5%. What would be the new price (rounded to the nearest penny) if the rate of VAT were reduced to 10.5%?

A $3.71

B $4.09

C $4.10

D $4.64

Answer______ **(2 marks)**

Test Your Understanding 9

A credit card company is charging an annual percentage rate of 26.8%. What three monthly rate is it equivalent to?

A 6.70%

B 8.93%

C 6.10%

D 8.24%

Answer______ **(1 mark)**

Test Your Understanding 10

When using Excel, a macro is:

A the name given to a group of named cells;

B the name for a group of worksheets;

C a series of keystrokes or mouse clicks;

D a cross check designed to validate calculations.

Answer______ **(1 mark)**

Test Your Understanding 11

Factorising the following expression:

$9a^3b^2 - 15ab^3 + 6a^2b$

gives the following

A $3ab(3a^2b - 5b^2 + 2a)$

B $3a^2b(3ab - 5ab^2 + 2a)$

C $3ab^2(3a^2b - 5b + 2ab)$

D $3ab(3ab - 5b^2 + 2ab)$

Answer______ **(1 mark)**

Test Your Understanding 12

A company has calculated the Net Present Value of four mutually exclusive projects and the associated probabilities as follows:

Project A		**Project B**		**Project C**		**Project D**	
NPV £	Probability	NPV £	Probability	NPV £	Probability	NPV £	Probability
10,000	0.6	20,000	0.2	8,000	0.9	7,000	0.5
5,000	0.4	2,000	0.8	3,000	0.1	6,000	0.5

If the projects were ranked in terms of expected values, with the highest first, the order would be:

A B, A, C, D

B A, C, D, B

C D, A and C equal, B

D C, A, D, B

Answer______ **(1 mark)**

Test Your Understanding 13

A number of animals were tested for immunity to a virus

Type of animal	Number tested	Number immune
Dog	1,500	1,200
Cat	750	450

If an animal is selected at random what is the probability of selecting a cat that is immune to the virus?

A 1 in 2

B 1 in 8

C 1 in 3

D 1 in 5

Answer______ **(2 marks)**

Test Your Understanding 14

A down-turn in the size of the population is an example of:

A long-term trend

B cyclical variation

C seasonal variation

D random variation.

Answer______ **(1 mark)**

Test Your Understanding 15

A bag contains nine balls, four are red, three are yellow and two are green. If three balls are selected and not replaced, what is the probability that one ball of each colour will have been selected?

A 0.26

B 0.29

C 0.16

D 0.33

Answer______ **(2 marks)**

Test Your Understanding 16

An investor has the following four investment options available but has the cash only to take up one. Which one would maximise her wealth assuming an interest rate of 10%?

Project	**Initial outlay**	**Return**
A	$7,000	$3,000 each year, payable in arrears, for five years
B	$4,500	$1,000 at the end of the first year, $2,500 at the end of the next two years and $1,500 for the last two years
C	$5,500	$2,000 payable every year in advance for five years
D	$11,000	$1,500 in perpetuity

A Project A

B Project B

C Project C

D Project D

Answer______ **(2 marks)**

Test Your Understanding 17

Solve 7,467 – 356.1/(44.846 – 2) to 3 significant figures (s.f):

A 7,461.023

B 7,460

C 7,458.689

D 7,459

Answer______ **(1 mark)**

Test Your Understanding 18

A $50,000 mortgage is taken out on a property at a rate of 6% over 20 years. What will be the gross monthly repayment?

A $208.33

B $363.25

C $220.83

D $414.67

Answer______ **(1 mark)**

Test Your Understanding 19

A property worth $750,000 is insured against fire. The probability of a fire occurring on the premises has been assessed at 1.5 in 1,000. If the insurance company is paid a premium of $1,500 per year, what is the expected value of the insurance policy to the insurance company?

A $1,500

B $9,750

C $375

D $1,125

Answer______ **(2 marks)**

Test Your Understanding 20

Which of the following statements are true?

(i) In the equation y = mx + c, y is the independent variable.

(ii) A quadratic equation plotted on a graph will have a maximum and a minimum point.

(iii) If $b^2 - 4ac$ is zero in a quadratic equation, there are no real solutions.

(iv) Multiple quadratic equations can be plotted on one graph.

A (i), (ii) and (iii)

B (iv) only

C (i) and (ii) only

D (i) and (iii) only.

Answer______ **(2 marks)**

Test Your Understanding 21

A baker knows that the demand for white rolls follows the following probability distribution:

Demand	**Probability**
500	0.1
600	0.2
700	0.3
800	0.4

Rolls are baked first thing in the morning before demand for the day is known. The cost of a roll is 10p, the selling price is 50p and all unsold rolls are scrapped at the end of the day. To maximise her expected value, how many rolls should the baker bake each morning?

A 500

B 600

C 700

D 800

Answer______ **(2 marks)**

Test Your Understanding 22

The figures below relate to the number of customers buying a particular product in a week, aggregated by quarter:

	Quarter 1	Quarter 2	Quarter 3	Quarter 4
2003	–	–	–	72
2004	79	84	90	45
2005	52	63	66	36
2006	47	51	88	–

The first figure to go in the 4th quarter total is:

A 325

B 298

C 312

D 64

Answer______ **(2 marks)**

Test Your Understanding 23

A company is investigating the effect of outdoor temperature on their sales of heating products. The recorded data has been plotted on a scatter diagram.

Based on analysis of the diagram, which of the following conclusions may be drawn?

(i) The relationship between sales and outdoor temperature appears to be correlated.

(ii) The relationship between sales and outdoor temperature appears to be non-linear.

(iii) The relationship between sales and outdoor temperature appears to be positively correlated.

(iv) Sales would be considered the independent variable.

A (i) only

B (i) and (iii)

C (i), (iii) and (iv)

D (i), (ii) and (iii).

Answer______ **(2 marks)**

Test Your Understanding 24

The Net Present Value of a planned investment project has been calculated at interest rates of 12% and 8%. The NPVs are $1,090 and –$960 respectively. What is the Internal Rate of Return of the project to one decimal place?

A 10.1%

B 11.7%

C 10.8%

D 11.5%

Answer______ **(1 mark)**

Test Your Understanding 25

Four products have the same mean weight of 550 grams but different standard deviations as shown below:

Product WW	34 grams
Product XX	21 grams
Product YY	18 grams
Product ZZ	28 grams

Which has the highest co-efficient of variation?

A Product WW

B Product XX

C Product YY

D Product ZZ

Answer______ **(1 mark)**

Test Your Understanding 26

A factory regularly tests its product X for defects. Two types of defects may be found, either F1 or F2. Past data shows that 2% of production shows defect F1 whilst 3% has defect F2. Having one defect has no impact on whether or not the product has the other. What is the probability that a selected unit has precisely one defect?

A 0.9506

B 0.9512

C 0.0488

D 0.0494

Answer______ **(2 marks)**

Test Your Understanding 27

A frequency distribution of a sample of weekly takings is as follows:

$	Frequency
4,500 and less than 8,500	7
8,500 and less than 10,500	16
10,500 and less than 12,500	28
12,500 and less than 13,500	21
13,500 and less than 14,500	8
	80

If the area between $8,500 and less than $10,500 has a height of 4 cm, what is the height of the rectangle $10,500 and less than $12,500?

A 28 cm

B 8 cm

C 14 cm

D 7 cm

Answer______ **(2 marks)**

Test Your Understanding 28

In a distribution $\sum f = 150$, $\sum fx = 4,200$ and $\sum fx^2 = 156,300$. What is the standard deviation?

A 258

B 18.5

C 16.1

D 342.25

Answer______ **(2 marks)**

Test Your Understanding 29

You have been supplied with the following data regarding the grades of candidates in an interview presentation and their written exam scores:

Candidate	Grade awarded	Exam score
Mr A	A	70
Ms B	B	76
Mrs C	A	58
Mr D	C	88
Mr E	D	81

What is the Spearman's rank correlation co-efficient?

A 0.825

B –0.825

C 0.548

D –0.548

Answer______ **(2 marks)**

Test Your Understanding 30

The regression line of y on x is calculated using the following data: It will be equal to:

n=14, $\Sigma x = 590$, $\Sigma y = 84$, $\Sigma xy = 15{,}390$, $\Sigma x^2 = 87{,}400$

A 20.189 + 1.96x

B 1.96 + 0.189x

C 0.189 + 1.96x

D 21.96 + 0.189x

Answer______ **(2 marks)**

Test Your Understanding 31

In a time series analysis, the trend equation for a particular product is given by:

$$\text{Trend} = (0.0021 \times \text{YEAR}^2) + (0.5 \times \text{YEAR}) + 42.8$$

Owing to the cyclical factor, the forecast for 2008 is estimated at 1.78 times the trend.

In whole units, what is the forecast for 2008?

A 9,514

B 5,345

C 2,856

D 16,935

Answer______ **(1 mark)**

Test Your Understanding 32

A firm is considering a new project and has estimated the following:

- In the first year there is a 60% probability that sales will be 12,000 units and a 40% probability that sales will be 8,000 units
- If sales are high in the first year, then in the second year there is a 70% chance of sales of 10,000 units and a 30% chance of sales of 8,000 units
- If sales are low in the first year, then in the second year there is a 50% chance of sales of 8,000 units and a 50% chance of sales of 7,000 units

Calculate the probability that sales will be 8,000 units in the second year

(2 marks)

Test Your Understanding 33

The figures for December's sales in an additive model for the trend in monthly sales figures has the following values:

T = $25,000

S = $2,300

C = –$500

R = $207

The predicted value of sales in December is given by:

A 27,007

B 27,593

C 27,300

D 25,000

Answer______ **(1 mark)**

Test Your Understanding 34

In a forecasting model based on y = a + bx, the intercept is $467. If the value of y is $875 and x = 35, then b is equal to

A 38.34

B 8.58

C 11.66

D 22.98

Answer______ **(2 marks)**

Test Your Understanding 35

Based on 20 quarters, the underlying trend equation for forecasting is y = 42.81 + 8.7x. Quarter 21 has a seasonal factor of 2.21. Using the multiplicative model, what would be the forecast for the quarter in whole units?

A 226

B 102

C 498

D 62

Answer______ **(2 marks)**

Test Your Understanding 36

A pie chart is to be used to display the following data:

Percentage of passengers flying from airport A	25
Percentage of passengers flying from airport B	36
Percentage of passengers flying from airport C	16
Percentage of passengers flying from airport D	23

What angle in degrees on the pie chart will represent airport C's share of the passengers?

A 16.0

B 57.6

C 16.8

D 4.44

Answer______ **(1 mark)**

Test Your Understanding 37

What is the value of Pearson's correlation co-efficient based on the following data:

$n=5$, $\Sigma x = 7.2$, $\Sigma y = 877$, $\Sigma xy = 1{,}360$, $\Sigma x^2 = 11.7$ and $\Sigma y^2 = 164{,}766.42$

A 0.64

B 0.80

C 0.13

D 0.17

Answer______ **(1 mark)**

Test Your Understanding 38

An inflation index and a sales index of a company's sales for the last year are as follows:

Quarter	1	2	3	4
Sales index	108	113	119	125
Inflation index	100	105	110	116

What is the real value of sales for quarter 4?

A 119

B 116

C 99

D 108

Answer______ **(2 marks)**

Test Your Understanding 39

An investor wishes to have a pension of $6,000 per annum in perpetuity, with the first payment in one year's time. How much would need to be invested now if interest rates are 3.5%?

A $171,429

B $17,143

C $210,000

D $21,000

Answer______ **(1 mark)**

Test Your Understanding 40

Prices of land have been rising by 18% per annum. What does that equate to as a rise over 9 months?

A 13.50%

B 1.13%

C 13.22%

D 24.69%

Answer______ **(2 marks)**

Test Your Understanding 41

A product is found to have a mean weight of 10 kg and a standard deviation of 5 kg.What percentage of items will have a weight of above 6 kg but below 10kg?

A 28.81%

B 0.07%

C 49.93%

D 21.19%

Answer______ **(2 marks)**

Test Your Understanding 42

A cell in an Excel spreadsheet has been formatted to three decimal places. The impact of this is to:

A Change the display to show 3 decimal places but leave the data held unrounded.

B Display data in the cell to 3 decimal places and round the data held.

C Display the data in the cell to 2 decimal places as usual, but round the data held to 3 decimal places.

D Cells cannot be formatted to 3 decimal places.

(1 mark)

Test Your Understanding 43

An annuity pays $15,000 per year every year for 15 years starting in one year's time. The rate of interest is 4.5%. What is the present value of the annuity?

A $50,000

B $29,029

C $161,093

D $100,739

Answer______ **(2 marks)**

Test Your Understanding 44

The figures for December's sales in an additive model for the trend in monthly sales figures has the following values:

T = \$25,000

S = \$2,300

C = –\$500

R = \$207

Which of the following comments explain the values given:

A There is an economic boom increasing sales levels throughout the industry.

B Sales are often higher in December.

C Sales are entirely dependent on the time of year and the economic cycle of the business.

D Sales are usually lower around year end.

(1 mark)

Test Your Understanding 45

How much should be invested now (to the nearest \$) to receive \$20,000 per annum in perpetuity if the annual rate of interest is 20%?

A \$4,000

B \$24,000

C \$93,500

D \$100,000

(1 mark)

Test your understanding answers

Test Your Understanding 1

C

$(3a^3 x^2) = (3 \times 4^3 \times 3)^2 = (3 \times 64 \times 3)^2 = 331,776$

Test Your Understanding 2

C

If the coefficient of determination is 0.899 for example, this tells us that 89.9% of the variations between the observations would be predicted by the regression analysis. The remaining 1.01% is caused by other factors.

Test Your Understanding 3

If one side is multiplied by 2 then the other must be divided by 2 which is × 0.5.

Test Your Understanding 4

C

if P = aD + b

Where P = 12, D = 2,500 so 12 = 2,500a + b (1)

Where P = 10, D = 3,300 so 10 = 3,300a + b (2)

(1) minus (2) gives:

2 = –800 a
so a = –0.0025

substituting into (1) gives:

12 = 2,500 x (–0.025) + b
so b = 6.25 + 12 = 18.25
hence P = 18.25 = 0.0025D

Therefore a = –0.0025 and b = 18.25

Test Your Understanding 5

D

II is not true as it is not suitable for use in mathematical tables.

III is not true as data must be arranged in order of size which can be time consuming.

Test Your Understanding 6

Breakeven occurs where profit = 0
(i.e.) where $-2{,}400 + 30D - 0.06D^2 = 0$

The Solution is given by

$$D = \frac{-b \pm \sqrt{b^2 - 4ac}}{2a}$$

Where a = –0.06, b= 30 and c = –2,400

$$D = \frac{-30 \pm \sqrt{30^2 - (4 \times -0.06 \times -2{,}400)}}{2 \times -0.06}$$

$$D = \frac{-30 \pm \sqrt{900 - 576}}{-0.12}$$

$$D = \frac{-30 \pm 18}{-0.12}$$

D = 100 or 400 units

Test Your Understanding 7

D

156.98 units is the number that would be sold if no sales staff are employed. The correlation is positive so sales units are increased as more staff are employed.

Test Your Understanding 8

C

The price excluding VAT is currently:

$$\frac{4.36}{1.175} = 3.71$$

If VAT were 10.5%, the price would become \$3.71 × 1.105 = \$4.10 to the nearest penny.

Test Your Understanding 9

C

Three months is a quarter of a year.

There are four quarters in a year so $(1 + r)^4 = 1.268$

$$(1 + r) = \sqrt[4]{1.268}$$

$$r = \sqrt[4]{1.268} - 1 = 0.061$$

Test Your Understanding 10

C

A group of worksheets is called a workbook.

A named group of cells does not have a specific name although is often referred to as a range.

Test Your Understanding 11

A

3ab is common to all three of the terms. Dividing each term by 3ab gives the figures inside the brackets.

Test Your Understanding 12

Project A = [0.6 × 10,000] + [0.4 × 5,000] = 8,000

Project B = [0.2 × 20,000] + [0.8 × 2,000] = 5,600

Project C = [0.9 × 8,000] + [0.1 × 3,000] = 7,500

Project D = [0.5 × 7,000] + [0.5 × 6,000] = 6,500

Therefore project A is best, followed by C, then D then B. Answers: (B).

Test Your Understanding 13

D

Probability of selecting a cat: 750/(750 + 1,500)

Probability of the cat selected being immune: 450/750

Probability of selecting an immune cat:750/(750 + 1,500) × 450/750 = 0.2 = 1 in 5

Test Your Understanding 14

A

Cyclical variation is caused by business cycles resulting from changes in the economy. Seasonal variations account for the regular variations that occur at certain times of year. Random variation is caused by unpredictable factors.

Test Your Understanding 15

B

A ball of each colour can be selected in one of six different ways:

Ball 1	**Ball 2**	**Ball 3**
Red p(4/9)	Yellow p(3/8)	Green p(2/7)
Red p(4/9)	Green p(2/8)	Yellow p(3/7)
Green p(2/9)	Red p(4/8)	Yellow p(3/7)
Green p(2/9)	Yellow p(3/8)	Red p(4/7)
Yellow p(3/9)	Red p(4/8)	Green(2/7)
Yellow p(3/9)	Green p(2/8)	Red p(4/7)

The probability of each selection occurring is (4 × 3 × 2)/(9 × 8 × 7) = 24/504 = 0.048

So the probability of selecting one of each colour is 6 × 0.048 = 0.29

Test Your Understanding 16

A

Project A has the highest Net Present Value

	PV	**Return**
A	= –\$7,000 + (\$3,000 × 3.791) = 4,373	\$3,000 each year, payable in arrears, for five years
B	= –\$4,500 + [(\$1,000 × 0.909) + (\$2,500 × 0.826)	\$1,000 at the end of the first year,
	+ (\$2,500 × 0.751) + (\$1,500 × 0.683)	\$2,500 at the end of the next two years
	+ (\$1,500 × 0.621)] = \$2307.5	and \$1,500 for the last two years
C	–\$5,500 + [\$2,000 × (1 + 3.17)] = \$2,840	\$2,000 payable every year in advance for five years
D	–\$11,000 + (1500/0.1) = \$4,000	\$1,500 in perpetuity

Test Your Understanding 17

B

7467 – 356.1/(44.846 – 2)

=7,467 – 356.1/42.846

=7,467 – 8.311

=7,458.689

=7,460 to 3 s.f.

Test Your Understanding 18

B

\$50,000 = Repayment × 20 yr factor

$$AF = \frac{1}{r}\left(1 - \frac{1}{(1+r)^n}\right) \quad \text{or} \quad \frac{1-(1+r)^{-n}}{r}$$

$$AF = \frac{1}{0.06}\left(1 - \frac{1}{(1.06)^{20}}\right) \quad \text{or} \quad \frac{1-(1+0.06)^{-20}}{0.06}$$

AF = 11.4699

\$50,000 = Repayment × 11.4699

Repayment = 50,000/11.4699 = \$4,359 per annum to the nearest \$

Gross monthly payment = \$4,359/12 = \$363.25.

Test Your Understanding 19

C

The insurer receives	\$1,500
Less: 0.0015 × 750,000	\$1,125
Value of the policy	\$375

Test Your Understanding 20

B

(i) False – y is the dependent variable

(ii) False – Quadratic equations have one turning point – either a minimum or a maximum depending on the equation

(iii) False – If $b^2 - 4ac$ is zero there is one (repeated) solution

(iv) True – any number of equations can be plotted on the same graph

Test Your Understanding 21

D

					Expected value
Probability	0.1	0.2	0.4	0.3	
Demand	500	600	700	800	
Bake					
500	500 × 0.4 = 200	200	200	200	0.1 × 200 + 0.2 × 200 + 0.4 × 200 + 0.3 × 200 = 200
600	500 × 0.5 – 600 × 0.1 = 190	600 × 0.4 = 240	240	240	0.1 × 190 + 0.2 × 240 + 0.4 × 240 + 0.3 × 240 = 235
700	500 × 0.5 – 700 × 0.1 = 180	600 × 0.5 – 700 × 0.1 = 230	700 × 0.4 = 280	280	0.1 × 180 + 0.2 × 230 + 0.4 × 280 + 0.3 × 280 = 260
800	500 × 0.5 – 800 × 0.1 = 170	600 × 0.5 – 800 × 0.1 = 220	700 × 0.5 – 800 × 0.1 = 270	800 × 0.4 = 320	0.1 × 170 + 0.2 × 220 + 0.4 × 270 + 0.3 × 320 = 265

Test Your Understanding 22

A

72 +79 + 84 + 90 = 325

Test Your Understanding 23

A

The correlation is approximately linear as the data roughly follows a straight line, but the correlation is negative as the line is downward sloping. Since sales depend on the temperature, sales would be considered to be the dependent variable.

Test Your Understanding 24

A

$$IRR = A + \frac{NA}{NA-NB} \times (B-A)$$

$$IRR = 8 + \frac{1{,}090}{1{,}090-(-960)} \times (12-8)$$

$$IRR = 8 + \frac{1{,}090}{2{,}050}(4)$$

IRR = 10.13%

Test Your Understanding 25

A

Co-efficient of variation = σ/X

Product WW	34/550 = 6.18%
Product XX	21/550 = 3.82%
Product YY	18/550 = 3.27%
Product ZZ	28/550 = 5.09%

So product WW has the highest co-efficient of variation.

Test Your Understanding 26

C

P(one defect only) = P(F1 but not F2) + P(F2 but not F1)

= [0.02 × 0.97] + [0.03 × 0.98] = 0.0488

$P(F_1)$ = 0.02
$P(\text{not } F_1)$ = 1 – 0.02 = 0.98
$P(F_2)$ = 0.03
$P(\text{not } F_2)$ = 1 – 0.03 = 097

Test Your Understanding 27

D

The scale is 1 cm = 4 frequencies, so 28 should have a height of 7 cm

Test Your Understanding 28

C

The standard deviation is calculated as follows:

$$\sigma = \sqrt{\frac{\sum fx^2}{\sum f} - \left(\frac{\sum fx}{\sum f}\right)^2}$$

$$\sigma = \sqrt{\frac{156{,}300}{150} - \left(\frac{4{,}200}{150}\right)^2}$$

$$\sigma = \sqrt{1{,}042 - 28^2}$$

$$\sigma = \sqrt{1{,}042 - 784} = \sqrt{258} = 16.1$$

Test Your Understanding 29

B

Candidate	Rank of grade	Rank of exam score	D (difference)	d2
Mr A	1.5*	4	–2.5	6.25
Ms B	3	3	0	0.00
MrsC	1.5*	5	–3.5	12.25
MrD	4	1	3	9.00
Mr E	5	2	3	9.00
				36.5

* Since Mr A and Mrs C share the 1st position, ranks 1 and 2 are split to give them 1.5 each

$$R = 1 - \frac{6\,\Sigma\,d^2}{n(n^2-1)} = 1 - \frac{6 \times 36.5}{5\,(25-1)} = -0.825$$

Test Your Understanding 30

D

The equation of the line is y = a + bx

$$\text{where } b = \frac{n\Sigma xy - (\Sigma x)(\Sigma y)}{n\,\Sigma x^2 - (\Sigma x)^2}$$

$$b = \frac{(14 \times 15{,}390) - (590 \times 84)}{14 \times 87{,}400 - 590^2}$$

$$b = \frac{165{,}900}{875{,}500}$$

$$b = 0.189$$

$a = \bar{y} - b\bar{x}$ ($\bar{y}$, $\bar{x}$: means of y and x, respectively)

Therefore

a= 84/14 – 0.189 × 590/14 = – 1.965

Regression line is therefore:

Y = – 1.96 + 0.189x

Test Your Understanding 31

D

Trend = $0.0021 \times 2008^2 + 0.5 \times 2008 + 42.8 = 9{,}514.13$

Forecast = 1.78 × Trend = 16,935 to nearest whole number.

Test Your Understanding 32

P(8,000 in year 2) = P(high sales in year 1) × P(8,000 in year 2 | high sales in year 1) + P(low sales in year 1) × P(8,000 in year 2 | low sales in year 1) = 0.6 × 0.3 + 0.4 × 0.5 = 0.38

Test Your Understanding 33

A

Where T = trend,

S = seasonal component,

C = cyclical component and

R = random component

Test Your Understanding 34

C

875 = 467 + 35b

b= (875 – 467)/35 = 11.66

Test Your Understanding 35

C

Trend forecast = 42.81 + 8.7 × 21 = 225.51

Forecast = trend × seasonal factor
= 225.51 × 2.21 = 498.38 = 498

to the nearest whole number

Test Your Understanding 36

B

Since the data is given in percentages already, the angle is simply 16% × 360°.

Test Your Understanding 37

B

$$r = \frac{n\Sigma xy - \Sigma x \Sigma y}{\sqrt{(n\Sigma x^2 - (\Sigma x)^2)(n\Sigma y^2 - (\Sigma y)^2)}}$$

$$= \frac{5 \times 1360 - 7.2 \times 877}{\sqrt{(5 \times 11.7 - 7.2^2)(5 \times 164{,}766.42 - 877^2)}}$$

$$= \frac{6800 - 6314.4}{\sqrt{6.66 \times 54{,}703.1}}$$

$$= \frac{485.6}{603.59}$$

$$= 0.8$$

Test Your Understanding 38

D

(125/116) × 100 = 108

Test Your Understanding 39

A

present value = Annual payment/r

$6,000/0.035 = $171,429

Test Your Understanding 40

C

Nine month ratio = $1.18^{9/12} = 1.1322$

The nine month rate is therefore 13.22%.

Test Your Understanding 41

A

$$z = \frac{x - \mu}{\sigma}$$

$$z = \frac{6-10}{5} = 0.8$$

From the tables, the shaded area is p = 0.2881

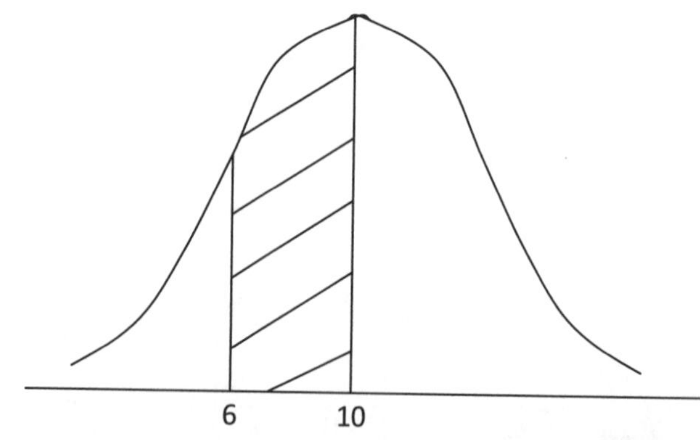

Test Your Understanding 42

A

Formatting only changes the display, the full number is still the one used for any further calculations. To round the actual data, the = ROUND function must be used.

Test Your Understanding 43

C

$$AF = \frac{1}{r}\left(1 - \frac{1}{(1+r)^n}\right) \quad \text{or} \quad \frac{1-(1+r)^{-n}}{r}$$

$$AF = \frac{1}{0.045}\left(1 - \frac{1}{(1.045)^{15}}\right) \quad \text{or} \quad \frac{1-(1+0.045)^{-15}}{0.045}$$

AF = 10.7395

PV = 15,000 x 10.7395 = 161,093

Test Your Understanding 44

B

The cycle factor is negative suggesting less than normal sales activity. The existence of a random factor shows that sales are dependent on more than just the season and the cycle. Since the seasonal factor is positive, sales usually rise at this time of year.

Test Your Understanding 45

D

PV = $20,000/0.20 = $100,000

Index

80:20 Rule, 73

A

Accuracy and approximation, 7
ACCURATE, 52
Addition rule of probability, 359
Additive model for time series, 233
Annuities, 297, 3036
Arithmetic mean, 98

B

Bar charts, 64,
  Component, 65
  Compound, 65
  Multiple, 65
BEDMAS, 2
Brackets, 2

C

Cells, 428
Charts
  Bar charts, 64
  Excel 438, 450
  Histograms, 66
  Ogives, 67
  Pie charts, 61
  Scatter diagrams, 185
Coefficient of determination, 190
Coefficient of variation, 116
Compound bar chart, 65
Compound interest, 281
Conditional events, 366
Continuous variables, 58, 382
Correlation, 184
  Coefficient of determination, 190
  Pearson's correlation coefficient, 188
  Rank correlation, 193
  Spurious, 191
Coefficient of variation 116
Cost of capital, 291
Cumulative frequency distribution, 59

D

Data, 50
  Continuous, 58, 360
  Discrete, 58, 355, 381
Decimal places, 5
Depreciation, 285
Discrete variables, 58, 355
Discounting, 292
  Annuities, 297,306
  Discount factors, 294, 297, 301
  Discount rate, 291
  Equivalent annuities, 305
  IRR, 302
  NPV, 294
  Perpetuities, 301
  Sinking funds, 287

E

Equations, 12
  Factorising, 20
  Linear, 17
  Quadratic, 18
  Rearranging, 14
  Simultaneous, 22
Equivalent rates of interest, 283
Errors, 7
Expected values, 376, 380
Exponents, 2, 7, 444

F

Factorising equations, 20
Forecasting, 231,241
Formulae, 12, 419
Functions, 13

G

Geometric progressions, 289
Graphs
  Excel, 445
  Linear equations, 17
  Quadratic equations, 18
  Simultaneous equations, 23
Gross margin, 10
Grouped distributions, 56

H

Histograms, 66

I

Independent events, 365
Index numbers, 141
  Chain-base, 148
  Change of base year, 145
  Combining series, 147
  Composite, 150
  Quantity indices, 154
  Relative price indices, 151
Inequalities, 23
Inflation, 155
Information 50
  Qualities of good information, 52
Interest
  Compound, 281
  Equivalent rates, 283
  Simple, 280
Internal rate of return (IRR), 302
Investment appraisal, 290

L

Least squares regression, 196, 199 449
Linear equations, 17
Linear regression, 196, 235

Index

M

Mark-up, 10
Mean, 98,110
Median, 104,110
Mode, 108, 110
Mortgages, 305
Moving averages, 244
Multiplication rule of probabilities, 365
Multiplicative model of time series, 233
Mutually exclusive events, 360

N

Negative numbers, 4
Net present value (NPV), 294
Normal distributions, 381
Numbers
- Decimals, 3
- Fractions, 3
- Integers, 3
- Negative, 4

O

Ogives, 67
Order of mathematical operations, 2

P

Pareto analysis, 73
Payoff tables, 378
Pearson's correlation coefficient, 188
Percentages, 9
Perpetuities, 301
Pie charts, 61
Powers, 7
Present values, 292
Probabilities, 351
- Addition rule, 359
- Conditional, 366
- Discrete, 355
- Definition, 352
- Expected values, 376, 380
- Independent events, 365
- Multiplication rule, 365
- Mutually exclusive events 360
- Normal distributions, 360
- Rules, 359
- Simple, 353
- Tables, 357, 363, 371, 378
- Venn diagrams, 373

Q

Quadratic equations, 18
Quantity indices, 154

R

Range, 111
Rank correlation, 193
Ratios, 11
Real cash flows 155
Regression, 184, 196
Relative price indices, 151
Rounding, 5
Risk, 376
Roots, 7
Rules of probability, 360

S

Sales tax, 10
Scatter diagrams, 185
Seasonal adjustments, 243
Seasonal component of time series, 232, 238
Significant figures, 5
Simple interest, 280
Simultaneous equations, 22
Sinking funds, 287, 308
Spearman's rank correlation, 193
Spread, 111, 117
- Coefficient of variation 116
- Range 111
- Standard deviation 112
- Variance 112

Spreadsheet risk, 441
Spreadsheets, 427
- Advantages and disadvantages, 440
- Good design, 431

Spurious correlation, 191
Standard deviation, 112

T

Tabulating data, 54
Tallying, 54, 58
Terminal values, 286
Time series analysis, 232
- Trend, 232, 235
- Moving average, 244

Time value of money, 291

U

Uncertainty, 376
Unequal class sizes, 69

V

Variables 13
- Continuous 58, 382
- Dependent, 196
- Discrete 58, 381
- Independent, 196

Variance, 112
VAT, 10
Venn diagrams, 373

W

Weights for index numbers, 152
Workbooks and worksheets, 428